NEW

WORLD

DRAMA

NEW AMERICANISTS

A SERIES EDITED BY

DONALD E. PEASE

Elizabeth Maddock DILLON

NEW WORLD DRAMA

THE PERFORMATIVE COMMONS IN THE ATLANTIC WORLD

1649–1849

DUKE UNIVERSITY PRESS

DURHAM & LONDON

2014

Printed in the United States of America
on acid-free paper ∞
Cover designed by Natalie Smith. Text designed
by Amy Ruth Buchanan. Typeset in Adobe
Caslon Pro by Graphic Composition, Inc.

Library of Congress
Cataloging-in-Publication Data
Dillon, Elizabeth Maddock.
New World drama : the performative commons
in the Atlantic world, 1649–1849 / Elizabeth
Maddock Dillon.
pages cm—(New Americanists)
Includes bibliographical references and index.
ISBN 978-0-8223-5324-9 (cloth : alk. paper)
ISBN 978-0-8223-5341-6 (pbk. : alk. paper)
1. Theater—Political aspects—Atlantic Ocean
Region—History—17th century. 2. Theater—
Political aspects—Atlantic Ocean Region—
History—18th century. 3. Theater—Political
aspects—Atlantic Ocean Region—History—
19th century. I. Title. II. Series: New Americanists.
PN2049.D55 2014
792.09171'241—dc23
2014000764

Cover art: Koo, Koo or Actor-Boy, by Isaac
Belisario (Kingston, 1838). Courtesy of Yale
Center for British Art, Paul Mellon Collection.

FOR CHARLOTTE

AND SOPHIE

CONTENTS

ILLUSTRATIONS

ACKNOWLEDGMENTS

The writing of this book has been supported by a community of friends, colleagues, students, mentors, archivists, and family members who have made the process of engaging in the world of ideas, archives, and aesthetics all seem valuable and worthwhile.

I am particularly grateful for financial support from the National Endowment for the Humanities, which supported a year of study at the American Antiquarian Society. A grant from the John Carter Brown Library allowed me to complete research there. And Northeastern University has generously supported me with funds to travel to archives in England and the Caribbean. Librarians at the many collections and archives consulted were invaluable in their assistance: special thanks to the hard-working and helpful archivists at the American Antiquarian Society, the John Carter Brown Library, the National Library of Jamaica, and the Charleston Library Society.

Conversations, commentary, collegiality, engagement, and support from many people have helped the project along. A warm thanks to Nicole Aljoe, Nancy Armstrong, Paula Backscheider, David Baruchoff, Ralph Bauer, Nancy Bentley, Lauren Berlant, Kristina Bross, Kimberly Juanita Brown, Nick Butler, Chris Castiglia, Amanda Claybaugh, Lara Cohen, Kathleen Donegan, Michael Drexler, Paul Erickson, Duncan Faherty, Molly Farrell, Lisa Freeman, Philip Gould, Laura Green, Jack Hitt, Amy Hungerford, Matthew Jacobson, Julie Kim, Jill Lane, Edward Larkin, Marina Leslie, Robert Levine, Pericles Lewis, Sonia de Loreto, Meredith McGill, John McKay, Michael Meranze, Monica Miller, Jocelyn Moody, Dennis Moore, José Esteban Muñoz, Hania Musiol, Andrew Parker, Susan Scott Parrish, Diana Paulin, Lloyd Pratt, Peter Reed, Michelle Reid, Mark Rifkin, Nancy Ruttenburg, Lisa Sanders, Jason Shaffer, Ivy Schweitzer, Jonathan Senchyne, David Shields, Cristobal Silva,

Danielle Skeehan, Jordan Stein, Taylor Stoermer, Leonard Tennenhouse, Mac Test, Elliott Visconsi, Leonard Von Morzé, Candace Ward, Bryan Waterman, Laura Wexler, and Kathleen Wilson.

The group of fellows who shared the pleasures of a year's residence in Worcester at the American Antiquarian Society with me provided important and valuable feedback on the manuscript: my thanks to Sean Harvey, Daniel Rood, Kyle Volk, and Lisa Wilson for their wisdom and friendship. Jason Sharples generously shared his archival research with me; Caleb Smith read much of the manuscript and encouraged and provoked in equal measure; and reader's reports from Donald Pease and Dana Nelson illuminated the shape of the book to me in new and profoundly helpful ways. Kate Simpkins assisted valuably and valiantly in the final moments of bringing it all together.

The Dartmouth Futures of American Studies Institute has been an important space for me in working through the ideas at the core of this book. I am particularly grateful for the intellectual examples of and formative conversations with Donald Pease, Cindi Katz, Anthony Bogues, Eric Lott, Hamilton Carroll, Colleen Boggs, Soyica Diggs Colbert, and Donatella Izzo. Many more of the speakers and participants at the Institute have shaped my thoughts in important ways and provided valuable feedback: my thanks to those who are too numerous to name here.

Portions of chapter 4 have appeared in a different form in the collection *Transatlantic Traffic and (Mis)Translations*, edited by Robin Peel and Daniel Maudlin (Hanover, NH: University Press of New England, 2013). I also draw on portions of another previously published essay, "John Marrant Blows the French Horn: Print, Performance, and Publics in Early African American Literature," which appeared in *Early African American Print Culture in Theory and Practice*, edited by Lara Langer Cohen and Jordan Stein (Philadelphia: University of Pennsylvania Press, 2012). I am also grateful to my editor at Duke University Press, Ken Wissoker, for his patience with and commitment to this project, as well as to Kathleen Kageff for her careful work in copyediting the manuscript and to Susan Albury for shepherding it through production.

Special debts are owed to a few friends with formidable minds and hearts. This work would not be possible without the foundational scholarship in Atlantic studies and performance of Joseph Roach; his mentorship, friendship, and generosity have enabled this project in equally important ways, and I am deeply grateful to him. Jonathan Elmer has been a crucial interlocutor on matters literary, philosophical, and otherwise over the years during which this book was written: I could not have gone far down this road without the pleasure and provocation of his conversation and friendship. And Serene Jones helps keep my soul alive and my mind in motion, for which I feel blessed.

I remain grateful to my parents, Margot and Steve Maddock, for helping me to chart routes bookish and otherwise. And I am grateful to John Dillon, without whom very little of the writing, thinking, eating, performing, or playing that goes on in our household would be possible; his love and labor are sustaining. This book is dedicated to my daughters, Charlotte and Sophie; while I was writing this book they ceased to be children and became extraordinary individuals, headed full tilt into their own writings, performances, and communities, at which I am occasionally invited to be present. Nothing could give me more pleasure than to see them so.

INTRODUCTION

The Performative Commons

AND THE

Aesthetic Atlantic

> We live in a world in which
> the traces of the colonial modern
> are not just haunting shadows
> but are part of the everyday
> technologies of rule.
> —Anthony Bogues,
> *Empire of Liberty*

> The production of commons
> requires first a profound trans-
> formation in our everyday life, in
> order to recombine what the social
> division of labor in capitalism
> has separated. . . . No common is
> possible unless we refuse to base
> our life and our reproduction on
> the suffering of others, unless
> we refuse to see ourselves as
> separate from them.
> —Silvia Federici, "Feminism and
> the Politics of the Commons"

This book begins and ends with scenes of violent execution: it opens with the
beheading of King Charles I in Whitehall in 1649 and closes at the moment
when twenty-two protestors and bystanders were gunned down by police in
the streets of New York City at the Astor Place Riot in 1849. What do these

scenes of violence have to do with theatre? With the Atlantic world? Both, I argue, stand as turning points in the history of popular sovereignty and theatrical performance in the Atlantic world. Specifically, I draw on these two scenes to serve as bookends of an account of the development of a performative commons in theatrical spaces that emerges with the advent of popular sovereignty and Atlantic modernity.

On the day of the public execution of King Charles I, on January 30, 1649, the House of Commons officially declared "that the People are, under God, the Original of all just Power; And do also declare, That the *Commons of England*, in Parliament assembled, being chosen by and representing the People, have the supreme Power in this Nation."[1] This declaration announced the power of the commons, investing state sovereignty in the people of England. The English Civil War, with the beheading of Charles I, thus commenced a revolution that dislodged power from above (in the king), in the name of locating it below (in the people). The history of the shift from monarchical to popular sovereignty enacted in a series of revolutions around the Atlantic world—from the English Civil War and the Glorious Revolution, to the American Revolution, the French Revolution, and the Haitian Revolution—is a long story, and the moment of regicide cited here is one among many episodes in this broader history. But at this decisively theatrical moment in the history of popular sovereignty we see the significance of the *commons* as the new location of political authority.

Ironically, just at the moment when the commons as a body of people gained new meaning as the source of political power, a second form of the commons dramatically diminished in scope. This commons—namely, the land held in common use for time immemorial in England including forests, pastures, and manorial "wastes"—was increasingly subject to privatization. Across the seventeenth and eighteenth centuries, common lands were wrested from the collective use of community members, who subsisted in part by hunting, herding, and farming on such land; this property was placed in the hands of private owners, who then held exclusive rights of use to the land. The enclosure of the commons accelerated dramatically in the eighteenth century, coinciding with new property ownership regimes and the development of capitalism. As Karl Marx writes,

> The forcible usurpation of [common property] generally accompanied by the turning of arable into pasture land, begins at the end of the fifteenth century and extends into the sixteenth. . . . The advance made by the eighteenth century shows itself in this, that the law itself now becomes the

instrument by which the people's land is stolen. . . . The Parliamentary form of the robbery is that of "Bills for Inclosure of Commons," in other words decrees by which landowners grant themselves the people's land as private property, decrees of expropriation of the people.[2]

According to historians, the English Parliament passed no fewer than 2,208 separate acts of enclosure, privatizing specific portions of the English commons from 1710 to 1801.[3] From 1649 forward, then, Parliament simultaneously declared the political power of the common people and fenced off the common land used by those very people to survive.

Locating the rise of popular sovereignty and the enclosure of the commons in rough historical proximity reveals a political story that moves in one direction—toward the rising power of the commons—coupled with an economic story that moves in the opposite direction—toward the eradication of the commons. These two narratives are arguably distinct, circling around two different definitions of the commons: the first concerns a common body of people—a *demos*, the people of a democracy or a republic who wield the power of sovereignty; the second concerns a common body of land, a shared resource, a material entity possessed and/or used by a multitude of people. In this book, however, I argue for and explore the mutual constitution of the commons as a people and as a material resource, the shared terrain of which is the complex and entwined nature of embodiment and representational force.

Tracing a movement from the loss of the commons as shared use rights in property, toward the rise of the commons as a political force, reveals what I describe as a "virtualization" of the commons: the collectivity of the commons that was once embedded in material and economic practices is increasingly understood as an abstraction—as a virtual body that appears less in material than figurative terms. And indeed, the question as to how to represent the virtual body of the people, and most particularly, the political will of the people, is a central one in the history of the rise of popular sovereignty in the Atlantic world.[4] Yet it is a mistake to imagine that the physical, embodied dimensions of the people disappear and/or cease to matter as their abstract prestige rises. The virtualization of the commons is, precisely, a practice—one that occurs at the intersection of the material and the representational, at the crossroads of the ontic and the mimetic. A dimension of political rights, I argue, is inextricably bound to the materiality of embodiment *and* the figurative nature of the representation of the commons: moreover, the entwined material and figurative nature of the "people" appears forcefully in the space of the theatre in the eighteenth-century Atlantic world.

The theatre proper may seem like an odd place to turn to examine the political force of the "people": a site of leisure and entertainment, the theatre might appear to be of marginal importance to the tectonic shifts in political life that occurred in the revolutionary Atlantic eighteenth century. However, the theatre was a singular space at this time—a space at which large numbers of common (and elite) people gathered with regularity and, thus, a space at which the body of the people was, literally, materialized. Moreover, the people not only gathered at the theatre, but also performed themselves as a people in the space of the theatre. Attention to the mutually informing practices of embodiment and representation found at the theatre ultimately reveals that the dichotomy that apparently separates the two commons—the materiality of the commons as land and the abstraction of the common people as a sovereign political force—is itself false. The common lands that were enclosed in the eighteenth century were never simply material in nature, any more than the common people who wield popular sovereignty are simply virtual. As Lewis Hyde suggests, the commons, understood as commonly used property, structure a social and political relation: "The commons are not simply the land but the land plus the rights, customs, and institutions that organize and preserve its communal uses. The physical commons—the fields and woods and so forth—are like a theater within which the life of the community is enacted and made evident."[5] Hyde's language is particularly evocative for my purposes given that he describes the physical commons as a theatre: in this book, I argue that the "theatre" of the physical commons was, in some sense, replaced by the theatre itself in the eighteenth century—the location at which a new performative commons appeared. What such an argument proposes is an understanding of the commons as a relation rather than an object: the property that was held in common use for time immemorial created and sustained a set of social relations—an "assemblage" to use Bruno Latour's term—in which both land and persons were actors in a shared network of relations.[6] In the space of the theatre, in turn, audience and actors together form an assemblage that both embodies and represents the collectivity of the people.

As the chapters that follow demonstrate, eighteenth-century audience members attended the theatre as much to represent themselves as to watch a play unfold before them on the stage. Thus in 1804, a writer to Boston's *Columbian Centinel* complained about the lack of *audience* lighting in the theatre: "We think the Manager deserves well of the public; and would more, were he not quite so *economical* of the candles by which the house is, or rather ought to be illuminated. . . . We are satisfied, the Manager has not yet to learn, that *all* the visitors of a theatre do not attend *solely* to witness the stage exhibi-

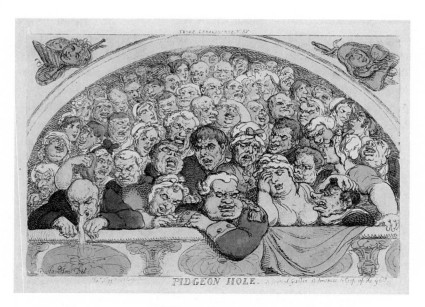

FIGURE I.I. The active audience in Covent Garden, London. Etching by Thomas Row-
landson. Courtesy of the Lewis Walpole Library, Yale University.

tions."[7] As this complaint indicates, audience members did not attend the
theatre to sit in the dark and silently watch what occurred on stage: rather,
they sought to display and represent themselves *in* public and represent themselves *as* a public. In a configuration far different from that which obtains in
today's theatre, audience members assumed an extraordinarily active status in
eighteenth-century theatres around the Atlantic world.[8] Voluble and volatile,
audiences might, for instance, demand that a given song within a play be
performed multiple times in succession should it particularly please them;
or pelt the stage and one another with apples, nuts, and epithets; or join the
actors on stage in moments of heightened excitement; or, indeed, mount a full-
blown riot to express their displeasure with a manager's misbegotten casting
of a given actor in a given role. Consider, for example, the following scene:
in the closing sword fight of *Richard III* as performed at the Bowery Theatre in New York City in 1832, more than three hundred audience members
joined the actors on stage to assist in the successful slaying of the tyrannical
king.[9] And while the size of the crowd enjoying the "freedom of the scenes"
in this instance was unusual, the participatory vigor of the audience was
anything but in the two centuries of performance explored in this book (see
figure I.I).[10]

The particular scene of regicide within *Richard III* that drew New Yorkers onto the stage arguably enacts a transition from monarchical to popular sovereignty and, as such, echoes and cites the regicide of Charles I at the hands of the commons.[11] In 1832, then, the crowd of audience members on the Bowery stage is both literally and figuratively enacting its collective sovereignty by performing the killing of the king. The action of the audience thus reveals a key structural aspect of the theatre: the meaning of what occurs at the theatre, between spectators and performers and at the complicated intersection and crossover of the two, unfolds in both symbolic and material terms. What is particularly intriguing about the theatre, then, is the oscillation that occurs there between physical embodiment and representation. To enact a relation—an assemblage of the commons—is both to occupy space in some significant way and to *stage* the occupation of space or to foreground a relation of bodies to one another. If the older, physical commons was largely understood as material in nature, and the new political commons of the people is largely construed in terms of representation and abstraction, theatricality and the specific space of the theatre foreground the inextricable nature of these two dimensions of the commons.

The physical geography of the theatre is germane to this process as well. With seats arrayed in hierarchical order, the seating sections (each with a different ticket price) segmented the audience in terms that roughly spoke of class distinctions in an arrangement maintained around the Atlantic world. As Peter Buckley argues, the audience of the eighteenth-century theatre was construed as "the town"—that is, the audience served as a corporate body that was representative of existing social relations within the polity. The historically stratified hierarchy of seating arrangements mirrored widely accepted social stratification and enabled a "transparency of roles and actions" that permitted a "ritual of mutuality" among audience members.[12] In short, audience members understood themselves as a collective that represented the town as a whole. Dispute among audience sectors and active participation of the audience in the stage performance was possible because of the mutual understanding of all players (including those in the audience) about the nature and limits of their roles: in this way, Buckley contends, "the nature of the game made the town a self-policing arrangement."[13]

The not infrequent scenes of riot and riotous participation that occurred in theatres around the Atlantic in the eighteenth century thus partook of an oxymoronic status: that of the well-regulated riot. The theatre was a space where relations structuring social belonging were performed and legitimately contested as well. At once out of control and within bounds, theatre riots bore some resemblance to riots over food prices that E. P. Thompson describes in an earlier era in England. Such riots, protesting soaring prices of bread or other food stuffs in small towns across England, were not merely chaotic scenes of self-interested violence: according to Thompson, they typically had at their core a notion of collective norms and economic justice for the community as a whole. As such, writes Thompson, these riots enacted a "moral economy"—a notion that the economic realities of a community (such as the price of bread) should reflect a morality that protected the whole of the town. Thompson writes that price riots "operated within a popular consensus as to what were legitimate and what were illegitimate practices in marketing, milling, baking . . . grounded upon a consistent traditional view of social norms and obligations, of the proper economic functions of several parties within the community."[14] The "moral economy of the crowd" that Thompson, and numerous historians since him, have traced in the direct action of riots is thus, like the theatre riot, both within and without bounds: it is a riot that has at its center a view of collective order. Understood as performance, the price riot described by Thompson might, further, be viewed not as simply citing traditional social norms but as *creating* them through the act of performative citation. The price riot convokes, in its performance, a concept of the commons and the common good, announcing a set of relations and obligations among the members of a community aimed at the sustenance of the whole. Similarly, the theatre riot is what we might call a commoning practice—one that generates a performative commons by articulating relations of mutual belonging in a collective whole.

My thinking concerning the political force of the theatrical crowd draws on and intersects with a range of work on commoning and collective practice, including the recent work of Michael Hardt and Antonio Negri, which foregrounds the biopolitical power of the multitude over and against the "republic of property" embodied in state authority. Hardt and Negri argue that the radical democratic possibilities of the republican revolutions of the eighteenth century were curtailed by an imbrication with capitalism, one that ultimately took the form of protecting the rights of property over those of people:

> In the course of the great bourgeois revolutions of the seventeenth and eighteenth centuries, the concept of the multitude is wiped out from the political and legal vocabulary, and by means of this erasure the conception of republic . . . comes to be narrowly defined as an instrument to affirm and safeguard property. Property is the key that defines not only the republic

but also the people, both of which are posed as universal concepts but in reality exclude the multitude of the poor.[15]

According to Hardt and Negri, then, "the establishment of the constitutional order and the rule of law served to defend and legitimate private property," and as a result the people were fundamentally not represented: rather, "'a people of property' faced off against 'a multitude of the poor.'"[16] In Hardt and Negri's republic of property we can see the way in which a capitalist logic of absolute ownership and enclosure forms an unholy alliance with the political logic of popular sovereignty such that a severely curtailed system of popular sovereignty results—one in which unpropertied persons are written out of political representation as well as, on a biopolitical level, deprived of the resources to sustain themselves as social, living beings.

Hardt and Negri's account of the role of law and capitalism in the erasure and exploitation of the "multitude" is compelling, and I share an interest in turning attention to practices of commoning that are foreclosed from cultural visibility by the centrality of property ownership within modern political dispensations: nonetheless, I take issue with both the history of Hardt and Negri's multitude and its future in this book. Central to my account of the performative commons in the Atlantic world is a deeper history than that addressed by Hardt and Negri; specifically, the history of what I call the "colonial relation"—a geopolitical relation that underpins capitalist modernity and that enables settler colonialism racialization to serve as the bedrock of an expropriative biopolitics from the late seventeenth century forward to today.[17] In this book, I argue that colonialism subtends and structures new dispensations of political freedom insofar as they depend on a shadow economy of dispossession, specifically, the dispossession of property (from Native Americans) and labor (from New World Africans) that fuels the property ownership regimes of metropolitan and creole Europeans. The colonial relation (discussed at greater length in the first chapter of this book) names a geopolitics that simultaneously fosters capital accumulation among the propertied—in the European metropole, initially—and renders the scene of expropriative violence in the colony "invisible" (distant, dismissable, nonpertinent) to those who reap its economic and political benefits. Further, as settler colonialism transforms the colonies of North America into the white-identified nation of the United States, a theatrics of erasure becomes increasingly significant in rendering scenes of racialized oppression politically unintelligible and thus "distant" while they remain materially present within the early national United States. The "multitude" of the Atlantic world thus comes into being as a condition of colonialism, capitalism, and the republic of property: the geographical and racial dimensions of this history must be central to any account of commoning that follows.

With respect to the future of the multitude, I place far more value on the possibilities of representation than do Hardt and Negri. According to Hardt and Negri, the move from the "multitude" to the "people" who are represented as enfranchised citizen-subjects is necessarily imbued with violence: "representation" is, for Hardt and Negri, premised on a logic of erasure insofar as models of political contract constitutively fail to represent the multitude when the multitude is reduced to the sovereign "people." With respect to Hobbes's and Rousseau's accounts of social contract, for example, Hardt and Negri conclude, "The contract of association is intrinsic to and inseparable from the contract of subjugation."[18] While I do not disagree with the broad terms of this analysis—it is indeed the case that the multitude and the sovereign people are not identical—I nonetheless am not ready to abandon representation as a key aspect of political power: rather, I would contend that representation must be rethought in far broader and more complex terms than it often is within contemporary understandings of the political.

Representation (and political power attached to representation) should not be understood solely in terms of the right to vote: to limit representation to suffrage alone is to foreclose arenas of cultural contestation and meaning making that have political force and value. At the theatre, for instance, no one aims to cast a ballot, but the public that stages and debates its own representation there nonetheless wields cultural and political authority that has effects in the lives of the multitude. In this sense, my understanding of the political force of theatrical publics is related to the account of the political articulated by Jacques Rancière. In contrast to the move toward abandoning representation proposed by Hardt and Negri, Rancière effectively drills down within representation itself to locate the political. Specifically, Rancière suggests that the struggle over what constitutes representation is the core of the political, and thus representation is a signal location of political action.

According to Rancière, politics is located in the shifting site of the division between two modes of sensory apprehension, namely, *phonê* and *logos*— sound (mere noise) as distinct from language. What constitutes noise (the "babble," say, of a foreign tongue) and what constitutes language (meaning shared among a group of people), is determined by the contingent line drawn between the two at any given time and place by those collected there: the "distribution of the sensible" (*partage du sensible*—we could even say, "division of sense") that divides those who accede to the power of meaning making from those who do not is both a political and an aesthetic divide. Indeed, for Rancière, the disruption and rearticulation of this divide is the precise location of the political: "The essence of equality is not so much to unify as to declassify, to undo the supposed naturalness of orders and replace it with controversial figures of division. Equality is the power of inconsistent, disintegrative and ever-replayed division."[19] On this account, representation does not effect the exclusion of the multitude but describes a constant form of engagement by the multitude in the debate over new articulations of the people and equality.

The significance of Rancière's account is threefold with respect to the core ideas explored in this book. First, much of Rancière's conceptualization of how political commons are created relies on theatrical metaphors: his work thus underscores the particular force of theatricality itself in understanding the commons. Second, his understanding of politics is centrally concerned with the relation between the "part of no part" (whom he also calls, simply, the "poor") and the demos or the "people" who have access to representation. Thus, he offers a fluid account of the way in which commoning is a political practice that unfolds in contestations over the representation of the people: this account has particular purchase for understanding the way in which Atlantic world publics coalesce and assume authority insofar as such publics rely heavily on strategies of representation *and* erasure. Atlantic publics do not comprise individuals who are fully formed subjects in advance of assuming political status; rather, Atlantic publics are generated out of ongoing contestations over who accedes to the status of meaning-making subject in a territory defined by the colonial relation—a relation that imposes an uneven distribution of humanness across racialized bodies. And third, Rancière's account of the political gives a prominent role to the aesthetic: in doing so, it locates an understanding of the political constitution of publics in the field of culture, and not simply in the traditional domain of official citizenship and suffrage rights in which contestations over the *sensible* have been largely constrained in advance.

What is the specific force of theatrical metaphor in Rancière's work, and what relation does this metaphor bear to the reality of theatrical performance in the eighteenth-century Atlantic world? "Politics is always about creating a stage," writes Rancière. "Politics always needs to establish those little worlds in which . . . forms of subjectivation can take shape and stage or enact [*mettre en scène*] a conflict, a dispute, an opposition between worlds. . . . Politics is about the establishment of a theatrical and artificial sphere."[20] In contrast to a Habermasian subject, who enters the public sphere fully formed as a rational speaker, the subject-citizen does not preexist the stage on Rancière's account; rather, we could say that the stage itself opens the occasion for a performance that brings a people—and the contest over the limits of that people—into view.[21] Significantly, Rancière defines this stage as "artificial" rather than natural. And indeed, this artificiality is key to the political possibility opened up by theatricality insofar as the theatre is a location at which, as discussed above, the relation between embodied (ontic) persons and represented (mimetic) subjects is definitionally in play. In other words, it is not the ontically present multitude that manifests itself on stage; rather the stage opens a space in which a visible mediation transpires between materiality and mimesis—one that is made possible by the artificiality of the stage. Any representation that emerges is thus clearly staged, not given in advance by nature. As such, any representation of the people is also historically contingent, which is to say, political.

For an example of this contingency as it plays out in the eighteenth-century Atlantic world, we might turn to Charleston, South Carolina, the subject of the fourth chapter of this book. In eighteenth- and early nineteenth-century Charleston, the theatre saw the largest regular gathering of physical bodies that occurred in the city: the theatre, built in 1793, housed fourteen hundred seats during a time when the population of the city was roughly twelve thousand persons (of all races).[22] Laws on the books prohibited blacks, including free blacks, from attending the theatre: as a result, historians have assumed that blacks were not a significant part of the Charleston audience and thus of its theatrical public. However, archival evidence indicates that blacks regularly attended the theatre in substantial numbers occasioning decades-long debates over their presence there in the pages of Charleston newspapers. Moreover, evidence indicates that blacks were participatory members of the "town" at the Charleston theatre, able to make use of the freedom of the scenes to appear on stage despite being legally forbidden from even being present. What one 1793 theatre-goer in Charleston condemned, in a beautifully telling phrase, as the "promiscuous multitude" that gathered at the theatre thus opened up the possibility for staging a version of the "people" that was far more inclusive and subject to open debate than that countenanced by the juridical system of the state.

Riots over who could and should have access to the theatre as audience members as well as who and/or what ought to appear on stage (which occurred with regularity in the eighteenth and nineteenth centuries in diverse Atlantic locations including London, Boston, New York, Charleston, Philadelphia, and Kingston, Jamaica) might thus be understood as stagings of "the part of no part," or of what Rancière defines as "dissensus"—namely a contestation over what constitutes the "common" of common sense, a contestation over the shape of the commons. And indeed, the "part of no part"—that is, the part of the multitude that is excluded from representations of the sovereign people—takes concrete shape in both England and early America in the form of what is known as "the people out of doors." The phrase was often used in the late eighteenth century to describe the public that was literally outside the doors behind which elected officials deliberated. Newspaper reports at the time regularly describe and debate, for instance, the mechanisms by which information from the Continental Congress, state assemblies, and other representative bodies is conveyed to the "people out of doors" in late eighteenth-century North America. Thus, in one case, the *New-York Daily Gazette* reports in 1790 on the deliberations of the first U.S. House of Representatives, at which James Jackson (of Georgia) argues in favor of printing bills under review in committee such that they can be distributed to the "people out of doors" for further discussion: "[Jackson stated that he] thought that printing reports and bills was generally advantageous; it gave the members an opportunity of obtaining an opinion of the *people out of doors* and he was ever inclined to pursue measures the best calculated for acquiring full and complete information on every subject that came before them, whether it arose within or without the walls of the house."[23] Given that the franchise was extremely limited prior to the mid-nineteenth century, even among white men, the "people out of doors"—or those with no legal voice in the workings of the state—were a considerable portion of the population. And as this newspaper account indicates, they were not entirely absent from political conversations, although the nature of their political "voice" was by no means formalized or guaranteed.

Indeed, the expression of the people out of doors was precisely not that of electoral representation, but that of the "part of no part." Thus, as Benjamin Irvin explains,

> The people out of doors articulated their political will through the vernacular of folk ritual. They hanged and burned effigies and buried them in mock funerals; they assaulted houses and public buildings; they carted offenders about town to the discordant rhythms of "rough music"; and they paraded mock heroes, often persons of low social standing, in saturnine parody of their "betters." . . . When not acting collectively, in a theatrical or violent fashion, the people out of doors found other ways to participate in the making of, or in the critique of, revolutionary civic tradition.[24]

Irvin here describes persons who were not represented by the Continental Congress at the close of the eighteenth century in North America, but we might apply this description more broadly, as well, to a range of historical performances around the Atlantic world—theatrical, visual, and sonic—among members of the multitude, including slaves, free blacks, women of all classes and colors, Native Americans, and the unpropertied. Notably, the modes of representation adopted by the people out of doors as described here (folk ritual, performance, music, riot), constitute something of a contest over voice itself: that is, these modes of collective action challenge the distinction between what counts as noise and what counts as sensibly apprehensible, and politically legible, shared forms of meaning. The very term "rough music"— one that describes the sound of a crowd beating on pots and pans—has an oxymoronic edge that speaks precisely of the uncertain line between noise and music, between chaos and collectivity. Significantly, as well, performance is a key category through which the part of no part—the people out of doors—achieves visibility and provokes dissensus within existing regimes of representation.

However, unlike the street performances richly described by Irvin and other historians, the theatrical performances that are the subject of this book occur within doors, not outside them. The theatres that are built in urban enclaves around the Atlantic world in the eighteenth century create stages that are enclosed by walls and doors. As such, these are not spaces in which the multitude, or the people out of doors, finds an unfettered or unstructured space of gathering or representation. Nonetheless, the theatre is a space where contestations over the right of access to enter the doors and the right to occupy various spaces within those doors are actively played out. While the theatre proper is largely associated today with cultural elitism, historically the opposite has been the case. Associated with crowds and public festival, eighteenth-century theatre attracted broad swaths of the population—so much so that state authorities often sought to limit the ability of theatres to gather "promiscuous multitudes" in which persons commingled across lines of class, race, and gender. The London Licensing Act of 1737 (discussed at length in the third chapter of this book) attests to official anxiety about crowds that gathered at theatrical performances. Further, as Peter Reed argues, the theatre had an ongoing association with an Atlantic underclass in the eighteenth century—a "lumpen proletariat" of shape-shifting rogues and tricksters who appeared on stage as well as within a mobile Atlantic population consisting, in part, of slaves, servants, sailors, soldiers, pirates, planters, players, prostitutes, and projectors—all of whom were (con)scripted into the performance of colonial modernity.[25] The rabble as well as the elite had seats (or standing room) marked out for them inside the theatre: in this way, the theatrical public was of a distinctly different shape than the white, male, property-owning electorate on either side of the ocean *and* distinct, as well, from a literate print public.

The distinction between embodied, theatrical publics and the print public is important, in part because the field of early American literature has, in recent decades, been largely dominated by the model of the print public sphere—a model articulated at the intersection of the work of Jürgen Habermas and that of Benedict Anderson, and taken up in relation to the early national United States in the work of Michael Warner, as well as myself and critics from Joanna Brooks to Trish Loughran.[26] *New World Drama* began, in part, as an effort to understand what an Atlantic (rather than American) public sphere might look like, as well as an effort to understand the role of the early American theatre in the public sphere. What emerged from my work with this material is a change of frameworks: rather than "public sphere" I have moved to the framework of a "performative commons" to understand the relation between the politics of popular sovereignty and cultural production both in print and in person in an Atlantic geography.

There are two key issues that necessitate this shift: first, the print public sphere is decisively limited by literacy in such a way that often renders this limitation largely outside the field of political and cultural vision and analysis. Individuals who do not read and write in English in the eighteenth-century Anglo-Atlantic world tend to disappear from view in accounts of the print public sphere; more significantly, the a-literate are erased from the scene of cultural analysis as if access to literacy were a preexisting, structural constraint rather than a contingent, political division among diverse peoples.[27] Attention to the colonial relation—to the geopolitics of the uneven distribution of humanness in the colonial Atlantic world—reveals the deeply political nature of literacy and access to the print public sphere. Unpropertied whites and many propertied women had little access to education. More significantly, however, the enslaved African diasporic population of the Americas was not simply denied access to education but was also subject to corporal punishment for seeking access to any form of literacy; colonial laws made it a crime to teach slaves to read or write; Africans who shared languages were separated from one another by slave-holders to prevent any common language other than English from generating communities of sense among the enslaved. Forced a-literacy is thus a key political dimension of the colonial relation, but it is one that fades from view in accounts of Atlantic world culture that center on the print public sphere.[28]

Second, the model of the print public sphere in the work of both Habermas and Anderson is implicitly (if not always explicitly) national; as such, it is difficult to account for Atlantic publics with this model. Habermas's model of the public sphere centers on the concept of persons joining together in acts of communicative reason to offer a critique of the state in the name of the people of the nation. The nation-state is thus the preexisting and determining frame of the Habermasian public sphere. For Anderson, in turn, the technology of print (in the form of newspapers and novels, most particularly) enables a fantasy of nationalism—a shared, language-based, national identity—among readers (defined as "print nationalism") that emerges out of the geography of empire. The eighteenth-century Atlantic world, however, is a field imaginary that is not organized by the nation-state.

At the forefront of the field of Atlantic studies, historians have traced, in particular, the colonization of the Americas, the competition for imperial wealth and influence among European powers, and the development of the slave trade between Africa and the Americas: this is a history, then, of the circulation of goods and bodies embedded within a network of relations that traverse the oceanic basin of the Atlantic and its littoral.[29] It has been more difficult to talk about an Atlantic public sphere than an Atlantic history, however, because the Atlantic is not a unified political or communicative field and cannot be imagined as one by recourse to the fictional unity of the nation-state, as is the case with a nationalized public sphere. How, then, might we describe Atlantic publics that do not correspond to national frameworks? What is the defining field imaginary of the Atlantic world? The latter question is difficult to answer, in part because there is not a single "imaginary" that defines the field: the Atlantic world is geographically framed by the Atlantic ocean, economically framed as the site of the advent and growth of the capitalist world system, and politically framed as the "first" scene of European colonial expansion and empire. Aníbal Quijano and Immanuel Wallerstein use the term "Americanity" to describe the sense in which the European colonization of the Americas constituted a new world system, rather than just a larger geographical sprawl of European power: "The creation of this geosocial entity, the Americas, was the constitutive act of the modern world-system. The Americas were not incorporated into an already existing capitalist world-economy. There could not have been a capitalist world-economy without the Americas."[30] The Atlantic field imaginary conjures the network of political, economic, religious, and cultural relations that constituted a new world system—one in which colonialism and capitalism structured new relations of belonging and nonbelonging across disparate and distal sites around the Atlantic.

This model of developing capitalist and colonial relays, or "nodes and networks," presents an uneven spatial field; or rather, it describes a field that is spatially distended and contracted in various ways so as to form anything but a unified territory.[31] Thus, for instance, historian Lauren Benton evocatively describes the "the peculiar and enduring lumpiness of imperial legal space"—space that places colonial subjects both far from home, and on new ground that they seek to configure as home in relation to communities comprising indigenous peoples, New World Africans, and Europeans of a variety of stripes. As Benton points out, one of the effects of the uneven spatiality of this world was a resultant uneven or bifurcated construction of subjecthood in relation to the dual poles of metropole and colony: the "politics of subjecthood in early European settlements" involved "a process that blended preoccupation with imperial claims and anxieties about membership in colonial political communities."[32]

In related terms, I have come to think of the communities of the Atlantic world as structured by ties of "intimate distance." As I argue in the first chapter of this book, maintaining relations of intimacy across great distances was crucial to the structure of empire: thus, for instance, colonials sought to maintain close connections with metropolitan culture as well as with individuals—friends, family members, employers—and social and political knowledge networks in the metropole despite inhabiting opposite shores of the Atlantic. Conversely, European colonials sought to assert that vast cultural (if not biological) distance separated them from the individuals with whom they shared the intimacies of daily life and physical habitation in the colony, including New World Africans and Native Americans. Uneven structures of intimate distance thus required creating a sense of presence in the face of physical absence, and generating a sense of absence or erasure in the face of physical presence. This configuration is fundamentally structured by the colonial relation—namely, an ideology according to which race and geography subtend understandings of humanness, cultural intelligibility, and political belonging.

Furthermore, territorial sovereignty in the Atlantic world was often highly negotiated, and negotiated from below rather than above, as Benton suggests. Geopolitical models that rely on a post-Westphalian map of discrete territorial nations fail to catch at the on-the-groundness of negotiated and contingent sovereignty that held sway in the eighteenth-century Atlantic world. A shift to an Atlantic geopolitical frame (away from that of the nation-state) makes it clear that shared space (held in common, politically or culturally) must be assembled and created; moreover, such shared spaces of collectivity in the eighteenth-century Atlantic world are repeatedly disputed, redrawn, and recreated. The framework of the Atlantic performative commons, in contrast to that of a national print public sphere, thus gives us a sense of the spatial unevenness of collectivities formed in an eighteenth-century Atlantic world as well as their provisional and contested natures. At the site of the theatre, the framework of the performative commons brings into view the extent to which collectivities were generated from the ground up. But insofar as scripts, actors, and languages at the center of theatrical performance traveled the routes of empire and diaspora, the performative commons simultaneously speaks of (indeed, performs) claims to larger associations and collectivities that structure the Atlantic world. Enacting relations of intimate distance, the performative commons links the material nature of the multitude and the figurative nature of the people insofar as it generates a public with both ontic and mimetic dimensions.

Importantly, clearing and creating the space of a performative commons and forming a public therein is as much a matter of erasure as it is one of appearance. And it is for this reason that I turn to aesthetics to describe the uneven spatiality of Atlantic publics, rather than to the political model of a sphere that has been invoked and elaborated by theorists from Hannah Arendt to Habermas. The various spatial terms I use here—unevenness, distension and contraction, nodes and networks, provisional clearings, assemblages and reassemblages—all aim to unsettle the dominance of the metaphor of the sphere for understanding the framework of culture in this period. If the Atlantic is fundamentally disjunctive in spatial terms, then the image of a spatially homogenous and extensible sphere fails to capture key aspects of cultural production, dissemination, and meaning making. Briefly put, the "sphere" model implies that a boundary delimits the space of the sphere, but the precise nature of that limit is often not addressed by those who envision the public as a sphere: what, for instance, lies beyond the edges of the sphere? Can the persons engaged in scenes of imperial encounter, violence, settlement, and unsettlement be accounted for by simply expanding the sphere? I would posit that they cannot, although this is often the implicit suggestion of accounts of the public sphere.

The imagined community of the nation—and the public sphere associated with it—writes out of its purview the indigenous peoples and diasporic Africans who inhabit the Americas side by side with creole European functionaries, while nonetheless relying on the land and labor of these peoples to generate the economic wealth that sustains the rise of the European bourgeoisie who find their political voice in the public sphere. Enslaved Africans in Jamaica or Virginia, for instance, had no voice in matters of state in England, whereas their white owners insisted on their rights in this regard: while crucial to the story of the creation of British imperial wealth, diasporic Africans and Native Americans are largely absent from accounts of English national identity and of the emergence of the public sphere in England. The account of aesthetic commoning I explore in this book—one that involves generating a *sensus communis* (to use Immanuel Kant's term for the aesthetic)—presupposes debate over epistemic belonging (and erasure) as determinative at the site of the representation of the people.

It is significant, then, that the two most powerful existing accounts of Atlantic culture—those articulated, respectively, by Paul Gilroy and Joseph Roach—both give considerable scope to the power of erasure, evasion, and substitution: as Roach and Gilroy persuasively demonstrate, to speak of representation in the Atlantic world is to speak as much of what disappears as of what appears or, in somewhat more complex terms, to speak of the way in which appearance and disappearance, speech and silence, are entwined with one another in Atlantic culture and history. Indeed, Gilroy advances a model of diasporic African-Atlantic culture—a "counter-culture of modernity"— which is antithetical to norms of Habermasian communicative reason and print publicity. Instances of the African-Atlantic counterculture Gilroy describes include music and memory—aesthetic forms that are, pointedly, "not reducible to the cognitive."

Specifically, Gilroy argues that "the extreme patterns of communication defined by the institution of plantation slavery dictate that we recognise the anti-discursive and extra-linguistic ramifications of power at work in shaping communicative acts."[33] Gilroy thus suggests that because slaves within an Atlantic plantation culture were forbidden from self-expressive, rational communication, an alternative counterculture of expression developed, characterized by its resistance to the form and content of procedural rationality. Indeed, the knowledge regime that enforced a system of racial oppression was precisely what slaves sought to evade. In this way, then, meaning might profitably be lodged, for the enslaved, in the locations where an imperial, plantocratic public sphere ended—in sites and sensations that were precisely not self-evident to the master class. As Édouard Glissant writes, "Since speech was forbidden, slaves camouflaged the word under the provocative intensity of the scream. No one could translate the meaning of what seemed to be nothing but a shout. . . . This is how the dispossessed man organized his speech by weaving it into the apparently meaningless texture of extreme noise. There developed from that point a specialized system of significant insignificance."[34] And indeed, I would argue that the nonparticipation of New World African voices in a plantocratic public sphere might be understood as more than a matter of self-camouflage or protective secrecy: the very fact of race slavery contradicted the premises of the liberal equality and popular sovereignty allegedly embedded (proceduralized) in a public sphere of rational critical debate. Slaves occupied a position that gave the lie to the epistemology of the public sphere and its logic. From the point of view of the enslaved, communicative norms based on such a logic could only be understood as epistemologically unsound—namely, illogical.

In Joseph Roach's influential account of circum-Atlantic performance culture, the presence of absence is equally decisive. Performance, as Roach points out, operates by way of substitution—substitution that both stands in for (represents) and takes the place of (erases) that which is absent. In the specific context of the Atlantic world, the violent effort to erase indigenous peoples and the enslavement of Africans are foundational acts whose unspeakable terrors have been elided from dominant European accounts of the westward progress of empire. However, as Roach argues, "the unspeakable cannot be rendered forever inexpressible." In acts of performance, the play of memory and forgetting, of substitution and surrogation, both creates new worlds and revives unspoken pasts: "the scope of the circum-Atlantic interculture may be discerned most vividly by means of . . . performance traditions . . . because performances so often carry within them the memory of otherwise forgotten substitutions—those that were rejected and, even more invisibly, those that have succeeded."[35] For Roach, then, the phenomenology of performance has a specific ability to address the violent and contested history of the multiple peoples who inhabit the Atlantic world.

Both Roach and Gilroy thus reach beyond protocols of reason, rational debate, and print nationalism in order to account for the varied and uneven field of Atlantic culture. Drawing on these meditations on the politics of Atlantic world representation, I would suggest that accounts of the Habermasian public sphere, insofar as they focus primarily on print, risk reinscribing the technologies of "social death" associated with race slavery (such as forced a-literacy) rather than attending to the rematerializations and resignifications of enslaved and indigenous peoples that take place through performance. The term "social death" is derived from Orlando Patterson's account of the workings of race slavery. As I argue in the chapters that follow (most particularly chapters 4 and 5), although slavery sought to impose forms of social death on slaves through diverse technologies—technologies operating by way of law, language, and corporal violence—the plantocracy ultimately did not and could not effect the social death of slaves; however, the social life that emerged in the shadow of such technologies was marked by the structural violence visited on New World Africans by slavery.[36] Further, I argue that scenes of performance often transform the absences produced by technologies of social death into the substance of creole culture. The performative commons of an Atlantic public that I explore in this book is thus above all aesthetic: at stake is creating a sensus communis on the ground—perhaps in the form of a scream or a curse that voices "significant insignificance," perhaps in the death of Richard III at the hands of the audience or his revival in a Jonkonnu dance—that extends in relations of intimacy to immediate and distant sites of empire.

Reframing the study of theatre in Atlantic rather than national terms also throws into relief the vitality of theatre as a cultural form in the colonial Americas and the early national United States. Such a framing recasts a familiar narrative of cultural nationalism that has been largely used as the lens through which to view the history of the theatre in the United States—a narrative in which the fledgling nation of the United States had no drama of its own while still in cultural leading-strings to its British parent following the American Revolution. Only the nineteenth century saw the first signs of an independent national drama as Americans sought to cast off British models and express their own ideas in theatrical form. According to this narrative, the nineteenth century served as a boisterous, albeit unattractive, adolescence for U.S. drama: homegrown performances included the raging successes of blackface minstrelsy and popular melodrama with U.S. themes, such as *Metamora*, *Nick of the Woods*, and *Uncle Tom's Cabin*—all forms of drama authored in the United States; yet not until the coming of Eugene O'Neill in the twentieth century would the United States have a recognized, canonical dramatic author of its own.

In the shadow of this narrative, early American theatre has received scant attention from literary critics or historians, in large part because of the way in which the field of literary studies privileges a national frame for the understanding of culture, and determines the national character of a performance on the basis of a play's authorship rather than on the basis of the location at which a performance is staged or the composition of the audiences and actors involved in the performance. The vast majority of plays performed in North America prior to 1820 were of British authorship; often the actors performing on stage were British as well. For this reason, studies of early American drama have tended to focus on a narrow range of scripts—Royal Tyler's *The Contrast* and William Dunlap's *André*, for example—that represent the merest fraction of theatrical performances viewed by the throngs of audience members who regularly attended the theatre in the eighteenth and early nineteenth centuries. Scholarship on pre-Jacksonian U.S. theatre has thus often consisted in what Jeffrey Richards describes as a "search for national needles in the (British) theatrical haystack."[37] Further, a focus on the written script or "work" over "performance" in the field of literary studies has contributed, as Loren Kruger has observed, to critical neglect of American drama: "dramatic texts look insufficiently literary or only impurely and illegitimately autonomous."[38]

However, the "impurity" of the dramatic work—the promiscuous circulation of scripts and the improvisational local revisions of these scripts—in sites around the Anglo-Atlantic world is precisely what generates the significance of the theatre as a cultural site at which the dynamics of political belonging, modern sovereignty, and aesthetics are coarticulated. The innovation of an Atlantic, performative commons that I explore in this book disappears from sight when literature is viewed through the conceptual lens of authorial ownership (including its attendant discourses of privatization such as copyright) and that of the author function as it has shaped the discipline of literary studies. Thus, viewed through an authorial optic familiar to the field of literary studies, it might be possible to imagine that scripts first written and performed in England somehow lose their force as they migrate from metropole to colony—that such a movement entails a derogation of cultural and aesthetic value as the original performance is imitated in a fashion that is increasingly derivative and distant. However, viewed through the optic of the performative commons, the opposite is the case with respect to New World drama, as tracking the movement of plays that galvanized audiences around the colonial Atlantic littoral demonstrates. The performance of the colonial relation did not lose force as it circulated to locations distant from the metropole; rather, the contradiction inherent in the colonial relation achieved hyperbolic proportions when geographic distance disappeared as a means of ameliorating the paradoxical interrelation of British liberty, colonialism, and race slavery. The pressing questions of sovereignty that convoked and animated the embodied public in England achieved new force in the space of the colony where the contradictions of the colonial relation were posed in a more condensed and insistent form: out of these performances emerged stagings of what we know as modern sovereignty in its racialized forms.[39]

Central to the whole of the book, moreover, is a chapter on theatre and the performative commons in eighteenth-century Jamaica. Eighteenth-century Jamaica has had little place in cultural and/or theatrical histories of England, the United States, or even Jamaica, despite the fact that a thriving theatre existed in the colony for much of the eighteenth century; indeed, the American Company—the most prominent touring company in North America in the eighteenth century—decamped to Jamaica for the duration of the Revolutionary War after Continental Congress outlawed theatre (together with cockfighting and expensive funerals) as, in effect, a British luxury good, the consumption of which was presumably antithetical to U.S. independence.[40] The fact that Kingston was a regular stop on the theatrical circuit of such a touring company (together with cities such as Boston, New York, and Charleston) gives one a sense of the extent to which Jamaica was very much on the cultural map of the Anglo-Atlantic world. However, Kingston, Jamaica was not only one node in the eighteenth-century Anglo-Atlantic economy—it was, perhaps, the *key* node. Far more than Boston, for instance, Kingston was at the center of the production of wealth for the British economy, and theatres most often appeared in wealthy urban enclaves around the Atlantic.

Indeed, Richardson Wright's 1935 history of the theatre in colonial Jamaica proposes, "Anyone looking up the family tree of the American theatre soon finds . . . that one side of its lineage stems from Jamaica."[41] I am not interested in advancing a genealogical argument about the relation of colonial Jamaican theatre and a U.S. national tradition of theatre; however, I would suggest that it is significant that colonial Jamaican theatre was of a piece with colonial North American and early national U.S. theatre. Placing colonial Jamaican theatre back on the map with that of colonial Charleston and early national/ Jacksonian-era New York City, as I do in this book, reveals the Atlantic/colonial nature of the theatrical commons in the eighteenth century as well as the extent to which that very coloniality was later the subject of both active erasure and citation in Jacksonian-era theatre in the United States. Located at the center of the Anglo-Atlantic performative commons, rather than assimilated to British imperial, U.S., or even African traditions, Jamaican theatricality stages the colonial relation in its most unmitigated, contradictory form and thereby reveals the force of the aesthetic in its capacity to open a performative commons.

In order to define and explore the Atlantic performative commons of the long eighteenth century, this book begins with a chapter on what I call the colonial relation. The colonial relation names the sustaining structure of economic dependence by the metropole on the colony at the core of capitalist modernity and the bourgeois ascendency in Europe. But I use the term, as well, to foreground a relation that is often rendered invisible in nationally framed accounts of history and culture: specifically, the circumscription of full human identity in relation to race. The racialization of Native Americans assisted in the systemic disappropriation of lands inhabited by indigenous people by European settler colonialism in the Americas and the racialization of Africans enabled a system of forced labor at the same time that theories of universal human rights gained political ground on both sides of the Atlantic. The story of the rise of freedom in the Atlantic world—the newfound authority of the commons within a politics of popular sovereignty—cannot be separated from its hidden dependence on the colonial relation.[42] Much of this first chapter addresses, then, the complex articulation of "English liberty" in the Atlantic eighteenth century as a simultaneous naming of the authority of the commons and as a site of colonial racialization. I consider, as well, the structures of intimate distance that assisted in sustaining the contradictions of the colonial relation in the Atlantic world. Further, I argue that performance in the space of the theatre, where presence and absence appear in tandem, affords a particular lens onto the colonial relation and its connections to the commons and popular sovereignty that is not found in print.

The second chapter, "London," opens a geographical and historical narrative of the Atlantic performative commons that unfolds across the whole of the book: this narrative begins (in chapter 2) in 1649 in London with the regicide of Charles I and ends (in chapter 6) in 1849 in New York City with the Astor Place Riot. As indicated at the outset of this introduction, I take the regicide of Charles I to be a decisive moment in the history of the commons— a moment at which new authority was lodged in the common people. But it was also a decisive moment in the history of theatre, precisely because the physical gathering of the multitude as a common body acquired new meaning and political significance at this time. The second chapter thus focuses on the creation of an English "people" in the space of the theatre in London, with specific attention to the changing shape of theatre at this time, from the performance of monarchical authority in the court masque before the regicide to the shifting optics and political dispensations on display at the patent theatres of the Restoration. At the historical core of this transition, I locate the centrality of the performance of imperial scenes—dramas concerning the New World, and most particularly, William D'Avenant's *Cruelty of the Spaniards in Peru* in relation to Oliver Cromwell's "Western Design" and the figure of the tortured Native American king—as they directly shape concepts of the people in England. In short, this chapter suggests, New World drama reveals the workings of empire that subtend the creation of a domestic English people.

I use the term "New World drama" to speak, narrowly, about theatre in the Atlantic world that directly performed and engaged scenes of American-ness: scenes concerning Native Americans, European colonialism and wealth extraction in America, race slavery, and forced or coerced "transportation" across the Atlantic. I use the term "New World drama," as well, to speak more broadly of the drama of Americanity—a drama concerning the newness of a modern world system that took shape in the Atlantic world in the long eighteenth century. I am keenly aware that the term "New World" has a history of imperialism and settler colonialism embedded within it: the notion that America was "new" was so only from the point of view of non-indigenous peoples, and thus the term carries with it a freight of assumptions about the erasability of indigenous peoples and the inevitability of imperial conquest. However, it is precisely the history of imperialism and the performances of erasure embedded therein that I seek to trace and make visible in this chapter and others: moreover, the "newness" of Americanity, as I argue throughout, was one that redounded in all directions, such that, for instance, new forms of popular sovereignty in England were in significant part performed and instantiated (as I argue in chapter 2) in relation to the figure of the tortured Native American king and such that the ascendancy of Whig property regimes in England (as I argue in chapter 3) was fueled by the stolen labor of enslaved Africans in the Americas. To the extent that it is possible, then, my analysis throughout aims to dislodge the term "New World" from a geographical and ideological binary opposition with an "Old World"—a Europe construed as temporally and spatially prior, static, and given in advance of America—in favor of analyzing an Atlantic conjuncture of modernity that exceeds the national borders that have typically framed scholarly analyses of eighteenth-century culture.

While the second chapter attends to the emergent politics of popular sovereignty in London and the relation between English liberty and imperialism, the third chapter, "Transportation," turns to the developing economic picture of the Atlantic world and most particularly to the segmentation of the commons in relationship to the need to conscript labor for imperial projects in the New World. English settler colonialism required the production and reproduction of bodies that could people the colonies in the name of England *and* bodies that would perform forced labor to extract value from the colonies to enrich the English metropole and fuel the development of capitalism. Initially, forced labor in the colonies was performed by transported English convicts, paupers, and political enemies of the crown. By the close of the seventeenth century, however, racialization had become the central mechanism for segmenting the labor force in the English Atlantic world, and Charles II had created (and profited mightily from) the Royal African Company, which transported kidnapped Africans from their homes to slavery in the New World. In this chapter, then, we see the foundational terms of racialization embedded in the colonial relation materialize in an Atlantic context.

In theatrical terms, the chapter explores the appearance of the colonial rela-tion on stage in plays such as William D'Avenant's *The Enchanted Island*—a play that adapts Shakespeare's *Tempest* to address the peopling of the New World with English bodies—and in Thomas Southerne's representation of the geographically bifurcated identity of the title character in *Oroonoko* as both African king and New World (laboring) slave. The chapter tracks, as well, efforts to enclose the physical commons in England and to segment the body of the commons as a people to suit the labor and capital needs of the new Whig-controlled economy in the eighteenth century. In a reading of John Gay's *Beggar's Opera* (1727), I suggest that the widely popular ballad opera helped to generate the new performative commons that took shape in response to enclosure legislation, including the reviled Black Act of 1723, which prescribed a punishment of transportation for convicted members of the bands of poachers who donned blackface to transgress laws prohibiting hunting and foresting on newly privatized common lands. Then prime minister Robert Walpole responded to the popularity of the *Beggar's Opera* with the Licensing Act of 1737—an act that sought to curtail the gathering of large mixed-class crowds (multitudes, we might say) at the theatre by banning popular forms of entertainment such as pantomime from patent theatres and implementing state censorship of all scripts performed at the patent theatres. Ironically, one direct effect of the Licensing Act was the creation of the American Com-pany of Comedians by William and Lewis Hallam: after William's theatre in London was shut down by the Licensing Act, he and his brother created the first major touring company to assay the Anglophone Atlantic. This company would, in the coming decades, transport plays such as *The Enchanted Island* and *The Beggar's Opera* to audiences in Williamsburg, Virginia; New York City; Philadelphia; Kingston, Jamaica; and Charleston, South Carolina.

The fourth chapter, "Charleston," turns to late eighteenth-century South Carolina to explore the creation of a creole performative commons in colonial America and the early national United States. In Charleston, the contradiction embedded within the colonial relation was intensified: a politics of "freedom" (popular sovereignty) was embraced in a society that was founded on the appro-priation of Native lands and peoples together with the forced labor of enslaved Africans. Political claims to popular sovereignty thus stood in direct contradic-tion to the economics of race slavery, particularly in a location where the major-ity of the population was black. The geographical distance between colony and metropole that enabled slave labor to seem unrelated to English popular sover-eignty in London was collapsed into scenes of daily intimacy between enslaved blacks and free whites in Charleston. The chapter thus explores the tension between a political imperative to erase from view the black majority and an economic demand to enumerate and increase the black population. Here, then, the dual structure of intimate distance comes to the fore as white colonials work to both distance themselves (through legal codes, biologism, civic performance) and benefit from the black-white intimacies at the core of everyday life in the colony. This chapter traces the ontic and mimetic presence of a genealogy of theatrical figures of the enslaved laborer as it assumes aesthetic form, from Caliban to Friday, looking forward to Jim Crow. Despite the more than occasional degradation associated with such theatrical figures, a second scene of colonialism arises, I contend, in relation to the theatrical presence of such figures—one in which the relation of the ontic and the mimetic enables an aesthetic commoning (a dissensus) that contests and revises the boundaries of the people.

In Charleston, the racial status of the creole commons was a matter of extreme contestation. However, the *existence* of a creole commons was not, in itself, a matter of controversy: the political break between England and the United States at the close of the eighteenth century underwrote the legitimacy of the increasingly non-British (creole) shape of this commons. During the same period of time in Jamaica, however, no such political break occurred: as such, the white plantocracy in Jamaica sought to disavow not only the presence of a black majority on the island, but also the creole nature of life in the colony. Slave labor was a central aspect of life in Jamaica; moreover, the brutality of the conditions of enslavement, together with the sustained violence required to maintain the enslavement of such a large population of slaves, resulted in an implicit (and oftentimes explicit) state of ongoing war between the enslaved population and the white plantocracy. In such a situation, colonial whites in Jamaica insisted more strongly than ever on their British identity, precisely because only the claim to "English liberty" justified their own standing within a starkly bifurcated society, and because a break with England was unfathomable given the need for British military support to keep a majority slave population from revolting against plantocratic rule.

The deeply contradictory imperatives that informed white creole life in Jamaica were ones that required the performance of erasure in the face of a set of lived, material realities—realities that placed political and economic narratives in direct conflict with one another. For black creole and African enslaved peoples in Jamaica, the contradictory, non-sense of life in the public square was even more pronounced, and in particularly vicious terms. New World Africans in Jamaica lived at the crossroads of two theatricalizations: one a theatre of terror, in which brutalized black bodies were spectacularly displayed as a means of enforcing a life of what I describe as "bare labor"—a life stripped of official access to forms of social life, identity, and belonging.[43] The theatre of terror that sought to reduce slaves to "bare labor" was coupled with a theatre of erasure: one in which the meaning-making capacities and social lives of New World Africans—whose lives were unavoidably *not* bare, but necessarily imbued with social and collective meaning and identity, albeit meaning produced in the shadow of technologies of social death—were performatively screened from imperial sight lines and imperial knowledge.

In the fifth chapter of the book, "Kingston," I thus describe Jamaica as the site of what we might call an impossible commons. The colonial Caribbean was, within the emergent system of capitalist modernity, understood as the site of *production* (of sugar, of coffee), geographically distant from the metropolitan scene of *social reproduction* where juridically recognizable human subjects were christened, educated, coupled, and endowed with Englishness. This division between sites of production and social reproduction is one of fundamental un-commoning: it is not only a form of enclosure that privatizes property needed for communal survival, but also one that seeks to enforce social death by separating a community of persons from the resources (cultural, legal, social) through which they might live as social beings. Social reproduction for both whites and blacks, and particularly among a creole community comprised of both whites and blacks, can appear, in such a site, only as *hors-scène*—as off-scene and obscene with respect to imperial and capitalist structures and sensibilities. But it is precisely in the space of this impossible commons, I argue, that we see the emergence of the full force of the aesthetic as a materialization of dissensus. The Jamaican performative commons thus encapsulates the core possibility of the aesthetic Atlantic—a poesis of the people arising from the very grounds of enclosure, erasure, and social death. The haunted and haunting nature of this poesis is pronounced: this is not a narrative of triumph, but it is one that speaks to the political possibility of the aesthetic insofar as it reveals the aesthetic origins of the "people" and, as such, points to modes of aesthetic mobilization in the face of the systemic violence embedded in capitalist modernity and the colonial relation.

The final chapter of the book, "New York City," locates the structuring presence of the colonial relation at the heart of Jacksonian-era performances of a national white "people" in the nineteenth-century United States. At such a nationalizing political moment, one might conjure a narrative describing the emergence of a "new" people—a tale, for instance, of the way in which a new American people articulates itself as distinct from its colonial British "parent." And indeed, this is precisely the narrative that has solidified around the iconic Astor Place Riot that took place in New York City in 1849, a riot in which more than two dozen people were gunned down in the streets following controversy over the performances of two competing actors—the "native" American actor Edwin Forrest, known for his muscular embodiment of roles such as the Indian King, Metamora, and the British actor, William Charles Macready, accused by his foes of exemplifying an effete aristocratic acting style. The riot has been viewed as emblematic of a desire for a nationalized American culture—a desire for white Americans to cut their ties to British cultural domination. Taking the Astor Place Riot as endpoint rather than origin, however, I explore the Atlantic history of the nationalizing U.S. performative commons in relation to a series of theatre riots that took place *before* the Forrest/Macready feud erupted in 1849 into violence—riots in which both Native Americans and African Americans figure prominently.

Stylings of Native American kingship by black actors at the African Theatre and by white actors at the Bowery Theatre suggest competing efforts to engage in strategies of performative commoning that rely on indigenization and "playing Indian." The performances of the African Theatre were violently shut down—both by the physical destruction of the theatre and, perhaps more significantly, by the development of blackface minstrel performance, a "native" U.S. theatrical tradition that emerged at precisely this historical moment (with specific ties to efforts to destroy and denigrate the African Theatre) and found astounding and enduring commercial success. An analysis of riots preceding the Astor Place event thus suggests that creating a white, national performative commons in the United States requires embodying both New World African figures and Native American ones: in other words, the shift from a creole commons to the performance of a white-national "people" in the Jacksonian era involved a theatrics of indigenization performed by way of invoking, erasing, and rewriting a history of settler colonialism and the racial politics of the Atlantic world's colonial relation.

I take the Astor Place Riot as the endpoint of both the sixth chapter of the book concerning New York City and the narrative of the Atlantic performative commons that the book as a whole relates. The riot marks the closing of an Atlantic performative commons insofar as it is indicative of a shift in the public nature of theatre itself. Following the Astor Place Riot, as Lawrence Levine and Peter Buckley have argued, a new segmentation of theatrical audiences in the United States takes place along class lines; as Levine contends, "highbrow" culture was increasingly performed in venues distinct from "lowbrow" ones in the second half of the nineteenth century. Norms of audience participation (audience "sovereignty") were curtailed, particularly in highbrow venues, and the understanding of the audience as an embodiment of the "town" or the collectivity of the people receded from public view. Accordingly, I suggest, the mid-nineteenth century saw the enclosure of the theatrical commons as the audience itself was subject to segmentation and privatization; significantly, theatrical scripts were privatized as well under new copyright law that enforced exclusionary models of ownership of cultural texts. In this regard, the privatizing force of capitalism triumphs rather decisively over the democratizing possibilities contained with a politics of popular sovereignty. However, as I suggest throughout this book, the aesthetic force of the performative commons works to open and give scope to the material *and* representational nature of the multitude, even as capitalism and racialized forms of nationalism circumscribe the radical possibilities of popular sovereignty. The performative commons emerges at the site of the nonidentity of capitalist enclosure and popular sovereignty: while it is certainly possible (if not normative) for capitalist privatization to conscript popular sovereignty toward its own ends, the performative commons emerges as a condition of the dissonance between capitalist privatization and popular/democratic collectivization. In such a world, sites at which an unpropertied public can appear and achieve representational force become deeply important and potentially revolutionary. More importantly, the performative commons introduces the aesthetic as a key modality needed to augment our understanding of the relation between economics and politics: the sensate, aesthetic nature of the performative commons enables us to attend to a world mediated by the relation between materiality and figurality, and to the deeply political nature of this mediation.

The regicide of Charles I marked the beginning of popular sovereignty—a political dispensation in which the crowd—now the "commons"—had new meaning. The Astor Place Riot, in tandem with copyright law, marked a decisive privatization of the commons, a closing of the theatre as an institutional site at which a collective—a commons—might legitimately seek to perform itself as the embodiment of the town. The Atlantic performative commons I trace in this books remains, however, a rich archive of figures, costumes, sounds, dance steps, and scenarios with which to perform the material relations of common sustainability (moral economy) and the embodiment of the "promiscuous multitude" that capitalist enclosure eradicates.[44] The local and embodied nature of the performative commons renders it fragile in its material evanescence; however, the simultaneously virtual and mimetic nature of the performative commons lends it enduring force in its historical repertoire of commoning possibilities—possibilities that can be mobilized at the site of the ontic and mimetic intersection of the embodied public, possibilities that can be (and still are) mobilized in scenes of dissensus and epistemic disruption. If the theatre no longer offers a fixed site for the emergence of the Atlantic performative commons, this does not mean that such a commons cannot still find itself present in the theatre from time to time, or convene elsewhere, whether within or without doors.

CHAPTER 1

THE COLONIAL
RELATION

NEW WORLD DRAMA AND THE COLONIAL RELATION

In the simplest terms, the "colonial relation" refers to the connection between the colony and the metropole in the Anglo-Atlantic world of the eighteenth century. It concerns, then, the way in which far-flung territories become entwined with the central site of English political and economic power—namely, London. In more complex terms, however, the colonial relation names the centrality of colonialism to metropolitan modernity and denominates the representational strategies that simultaneously conveyed and masked this fact. Coloniality is not external and ephemeral with regard to the advent of metropolitan modernity (defined here specifically in relation to forms of popular political sovereignty and the economy of capitalism) but internal and constitutive *as well as* inimical to dearly held propositions concerning English liberty and the political authority of the British commons.[1] More specifically, the colonial relation takes shape as a racialized segmentation of labor and a differential distribution of humanness across races from the seventeenth century forward: this racialization emerges in relation to the development of an Atlantic world economy shaped by European colonial appropriation of lands, peoples, and resources in Africa and the Americas. Importantly, the colonial relation is not a one-way vector of power (in which the metropole dominates the colony) but an assemblage of connections that shapes peoples and polities around the Atlantic littoral (including the metropole) in the form of colonial modernity.[2]

The enduring and intractable contradiction of the eighteenth-century Anglo-Atlantic world appears in the simultaneity of the growth of doctrines of political liberty and popular sovereignty, together with the advent of systems of enforced labor, enclosure, and violent dehumanization in the form of race slavery.[3] The colonial relation, insofar as it informs both political freedom and race slavery, is at the core of this contradiction: perversely, an account of the colonial relation both is required to narrate the emergence of popular sovereignty and freedom in the Atlantic world, and must be erased in order to articulate this very story. Thus, we might think of the colonial relation as naming the interdependence of two seemingly separate scenes: one of the extraction of land and labor in the colonies and a second concerning the establishment of political liberty and parity among Europeans and, later, among white creoles in the Americas. And it is on the stage itself, and in the dynamics that inhere between and among the bodies and geographies that inhabit and constitute Atlantic world theatre, that the colonial relation appears most fully.

For a concrete illustration of the colonial relation as it appears in performance, we might turn to the theatrical figure of the enslaved African prince, Oroonoko, in Thomas Southerne's play of the same name, or related figures such as Belcour, the title character in Richard Cumberland's enduringly popular play *The West Indian* (1771), and Montezuma, the tortured Aztec king in John Dryden's *The Indian Emperour* (1665). Belcour is, literally, a colonial relation—a white creole born in the West Indies (specifically, the illegitimate son of an English businessman), who arrives in the metropole with a pocketful of money and dubious credentials as an Englishman. By the close of the play, Cumberland has successfully integrated (laundered, one might say) West Indian riches into a promising bourgeois, English marriage uniting the creole Belcour with the lovely English Louisa. The colonial relation, in this instance, underwrites the romance of bourgeois, English marriage in the eighteenth century. Similarly, the royal slave, Oroonoko, stars in a plot that results in his own torture and suicide together with the consummation of two bourgeois, English marriages, each enabled by an infusion of West Indian wealth accumulated from slave labor. The colonial relation—embodied on stage in figures such as Belcour, Oroonoko, and Montezuma—displays the colony in association with the metropole, making visible (often fleetingly) a set of Atlantic connections that are not peripheral to life in the metropole (as traditional accounts would have it), but that underwrite and sustain evolving forms of metropolitan economic, political, and cultural life.[4]

As I argue in this chapter, however, theatrical stagings of the colonial relation are significant as much for the publics they convoke and articulate at sites around the Atlantic world as they are for their performance of events and characters on stage. Any particular staging of the colonial relation is also a staging of relations among the members of the audience gathered to respond to the play they are watching—gathered to respond as a "people" according to the new dispensations of popular sovereignty that emerge in the eighteenth-century Atlantic arena. As such, a theatrical commons develops in the Atlantic world—one that is both interracial and racializing in different ways. Performative practices in specific sites, I argue, both proliferate and secure political identities in *res communis*, opening a space for an aesthetic and political commoning that has porous and contested boundaries in an imperial geography. Civic commons thus emerge and develop at sites of theatrical performance, and these performative commons articulate emergent possibilities and foreclosures of popular sovereignty by means of embodiment and representation, and in the promiscuous interaction between the two.

The model of the colonial relation articulated here recasts two central theoretical narratives of modernity by bringing the abject colonial scene into focus as spatially connected to the European metropole—namely, the narratives of modernity associated, respectively, with Michel Foucault and Karl Marx. According to Foucault, a historical transition takes place as the terrorized and punishable body of the subject of monarchical sovereignty is replaced by the disciplined body of the liberal political subject: at some point during the eighteenth century, Foucault argues, we move from a social and political organization based on punishment to one based on discipline, from sovereign power to what Foucault calls, variously, "governmentality" or "biopower"—namely, a power that does not operate by external force, but that operates by way of constructing (and thus controlling) viable bodies and lives. In contrast to Foucault's temporal narrative, however, I propose a spatial one: the theatre of horror deployed by sovereign power is not supplanted by the disciplined body of governmentality; rather, it is displaced to the colony.[5] Consider, for instance, the statements of four (white) judges in Antigua, in the mid-eighteenth century, as they contemplate their juridical response to a thwarted slave uprising there: "Wee Conceive the former ways of puting the Criminals to Death was too lenative and not Sufficiently Examplary, because the Criminals were not long Enough under their Sufferings which has prevailed upon us to lengthen their Pains in hopes of striking greater Terror into the Slaves that may see their Sufferings."[6] Three months into the proceedings of the trial, sixty-nine slaves had already been "made Examples of on the Wheel[,] the Jibbet[,] and at the Stake" in the English colony of Antigua and "about thirty to forty more" were scheduled for banishment.[7]

By 1736, the "Wheel, the Jibbet, and . . . the Stake" had disappeared from the public squares of London, but they nevertheless appeared in public spaces there—namely, on the stages of Drury Lane and Covent Garden. As I discuss in the next chapter, the torture rack appears on stage in London in 1658, with the opening of the public theatre under Oliver Cromwell's rule in William D'Avenant's drama *The Cruelty of the Spaniards in Peru*. If Londoners were unable to view the sixty-nine slaves who were tortured to death in Antigua in 1736, they were nonetheless able to view Oroonoko tortured and killed on stage at Drury Lane, Covent Garden, and Lincoln's Inn Fields—once "by command of their Royal Highnesses the Prince and Princess of Wales"—during the same year.[8] And too, in 1736 they might have viewed Montezuma tortured on the rack in performances of John Dryden's *Indian Emperor* at Lincoln's Inn Fields and Goodman's Fields.[9] On stage in London, the "wheel" represents the faraway space of the New World; torture thus appears as what has "disappeared" into the colony. As such, then, the theatre of horror is disappeared (embedded, buried) within the theatre of a newly self-governing (politically modern) people.

On Marx's account, the New World is, too, a scene of violence and horror—but one characterized less by an effort to control bodies by means of terror than by an economy of disappropriation; that is, by systems dedicated to enabling the European *extraction* of raw materials, labor, and life from the colony. Specifically, Marx argues that the colonies are a scene of "primitive accumulation" or, to render Marx's German term, *ursprüngliche Akkumulation*, more exactly, "original accumulation." Given that capitalism requires capital for investment, one must ask where that capital or excess money comes from in the first place. According to Marx, that original capital is acquired by theft or violent disappropriation—namely, by ejecting peasants (or, I would add, indigenous peoples) from the land and taking that land and its resources. Much of Marx's work describes this theft in terms of the enclosure of the commons in England; however, in a few instances, he states that primitive accumulation also occurred in the colonial exploitation of the New World:

> The discovery of gold and silver in America, the extirpation, enslavement and entombment in mines of the indigenous population of that continent, the beginnings of the conquest and plunder of India, and the conversion of Africa into a preserve for the commercial hunting of blackskins, are all things which characterize the dawn of the era of capitalist production. These idyllic proceedings are the chief moments of primitive accumulation.[10]

Marx thus places the colony on the map of capitalist production but does so in a way that locates the colony in the distant past—in the "dawn" of capitalism associated with feudalism rather than in the present or even the more recent past.[11] Further, Marx argues that primitive accumulation is associated with proletarianization: when individuals are ousted from the land, they are forced to work for others (rather than themselves) and thus become members of the proletariat.

In contrast to the narrative proposed by Marx, which relegates primitive accumulation in the colony to the distant past, I would suggest that the distance between capitalist production and primitive accumulation should be viewed as spatial rather than temporal.[12] In the eighteenth-century Anglo-Atlantic world, the colony is not the long-ago scene of primitive accumulation but is a contemporary scene of violent disappropriation, institutionalized in the form of slave labor. Further, the labor of the slave cannot be described as proletarian because that labor is extracted by means of technologies of social death—that is, by a system that does not reproduce proletarian workers as a class, but that extracts life itself from the workers, replacing the lifeless bodies of slaves who have been worked to death with "new negroes" from Africa. The slave is, then, a figure of "bare labor"—labor stripped of the resources of social life and the capacity for social reproduction. Thus, for instance, in Southerne's play we see Oroonoko stripped of his ability to parent his child and to husband his wife when he is transformed into bare labor by the system of slavery. Simultaneously, however, Southerne's play narrates the success of two white, English sisters, Charlotte and Lucy Welldon, in finding husbands and entering into relations of social reproduction (marriage) because of the wealth that the English have extracted from the colony of Surinam. Taking full advantage of the spatial (*not* temporal) distance that characterizes the colonial relation, Charlotte and Lucy—who have overstayed their welcome on the marriage market in London—cross the ocean to Surinam and acquire wealthy English husbands in the colony: Charlotte and Lucy thus go directly to the source of wealth that underwrites eighteenth-century English social reproduction—a source that is located in Surinam, not London. The uncomfortable simultaneity of the scenes of English social reproduction (the comedic marriage plot involving Charlotte and Lucy) and African-diasporic social death (the tragic torture-suicide plot involving Imoinda and Oroonoko) is managed on stage by a discourse of sentimentalism, but significantly, the stage is the location where the simultaneity (the spatial colonial relation) of the colony and the metropole does appear.[13]

Both Foucault and Marx contribute, to some extent, to derealizing the colony and the significance of the colonial relation by proposing that structures of violence embodied and enacted in the colony are not germane to modernity; that is, both relegate colonial violence to a temporally distant moment, and as a result, the colony disappears from the map of modernity—a map that is increasingly drawn in terms of discrete nation-states and in terms of citizen-subject relations and identities. This map of discrete territories and the doctrine of territorial sovereignty is associated with the interstate European system formalized in the 1648 Peace of Westphalia—one that, as Carl Schmitt argues, relegates colonial expansion and inter-European warfare occurring in the New World to a location "beyond the line."[14] This geography expunges the colonial scene from the map of European nation formation, relegating New World colonialism to a site utterly distinct from a territorial England where new models of popular sovereignty emerge at precisely this time. Notably, the execution of Charles I and the advent of parliamentarian rule occurs in 1649. The political story of the development of English liberty into a politics of popular sovereignty in England thus seemingly occurs in isolation from the development of race slavery in the colonial Atlantic world, mitigating any sense that a contradiction inheres in the simultaneity of these developments.[15] In terms of simple chronology, it is worth noting, however, that the Company of Royal Adventurers Trading to Africa was granted the first monopoly charter over the English slave trade in 1663 (reorganized as the Royal African Company in 1672); in 1688 the Glorious Revolution assisted in establishing modern parliamentary democracy in England; and in 1713, England's South Sea Company acquired the lucrative *Asiento*, a thirty-year contract to supply an unlimited number of slaves to Spanish colonies in the New World.[16]

If there is increasing consensus among historians that changes in the economy and class structure of England in the eighteenth century were underwritten by returns on investments in an Atlantic economy fueled by slave labor, there remains a wall of sorts separating political and cultural accounts of English liberty and the rise of popular sovereignty—often rehearsed in terms of the development of the public sphere—and Atlantic slavery.[17] While there is a vast historiography on the advent of the public sphere and popular sovereignty, virtually none of this literature entertains any discussion of colonialism. However, popular sovereignty and the growth of the public sphere were entwined with colonialism in England and at sites around the Atlantic world.[18] Indeed, colonialism had a role in both the economic and the political production of popular sovereignty in England; further, the colonial relation is hidden in plain sight in an Atlantic performance public sphere. In the gathering of embodied publics at theatres in London and around the Atlantic world, the coproduction of liberty, colonialization, and slavery is performed, negotiated, and contested: in the performative commons that appear at sites around the Atlantic world, new forms of popular sovereignty take shape that are articulated in relation to colonial, and not simply national, geographies.

Doctrines of British liberty and popular sovereignty suggest that political authority resides in the British people and, as such, presuppose that the identity of a British *people* is stable and verifiable. The colonial relation enacts a strategic racialization to separate British from non-British bodies in the colony; however, the strenuous labor performed by discourses of biologism, Enlightenment civility, and law in performing this racialization demonstrates that Britishness is rendered precarious by its transportation to the New World. And indeed, this uncertainty masks a more fundamental question: in what did Britishness consist in England? Although liberty is repeatedly proclaimed as the birthright of Englishmen, the full measure of English liberty—particularly the right to political representation—was never accorded to a very broad segment of the population of England in the seventeenth or eighteenth centuries: further, debates over the extent of the franchise are coterminous with the advent of the politics of popular sovereignty in England and persist into the present day.[19] If supreme political authority resided in the English people, who then, were the people, and how might they be accurately represented? As seventeenth-century opponents to popular sovereignty rather accurately pointed out, it was difficult to invest authority in a people that had no defined shape or substance: "for the people, to speak truly and properly, is a thing or body in continuall alteration and change, it never continues one minute the same, being composed of a multitude of parts, whereof divers continually decay and perish, and others renew and succeed in their places."[20] How might the chaotic *multitude* described here assume the shape of a representable *people*?

Indeed, as Edmund Morgan argues in tracing the history of popular sovereignty in England, the concept of the English *people* is a political fiction, albeit a highly functional one: "The people to whom [Parliamentarians] attributed supreme power were themselves fictional and could most usefully remain so, a mystical body, existing as a people only in the actions of the Parliament that claimed to act for them." This account suggests that the *people* are a back-formation of the substitutional political logic of representation rather than an entity that preexists representation. As Morgan concludes, "The very existence of a such a thing as *the* people, capable of acting to empower, define, and limit a previously nonexistent government required a suspension of disbelief. History recorded no such action."[21] The status of the people as a political force thus presents a quandary of representation. Historically, the specific contours of the British *people* were never entirely clear—whether in England itself or in colonial locations such as Charleston, Kingston, or New York.

Despite the uncertain nature of the "people," doctrines of English liberty claimed by these people were foundational with respect to new political dispensations in England *and* in British colonial settlements at sites around the Atlantic, including North America and the Caribbean. As Jack P. Greene argues, "From first to last, settler claims to their inherited rights of Englishmen, by which they principally meant the rights to consensual governance and the rule of law, were a critical element in the dispersal of authority throughout the settler empire."[22] In Jamaica, white planters clung fiercely to a sense of their identity as Englishmen with hereditary rights to English liberties, even as they developed a legal apparatus that enforced slavery on the majority of the population of the island: indeed, by the close of the eighteenth century, white planters defended themselves against abolitionists by arguing that it was precisely their British right to self-government that gave them the authority to enforce slave laws that bore no resemblance to legal practice in England.[23] And in the North American colonies, as numerous historians have demonstrated, deeply held notions of British liberty were integral to protests against metropolitan authority and thus foundational with respect to the American Revolution and the creation of an independent U.S. state.[24]

However, when English liberty is reproduced in the Americas—in locations such as Kingston, Jamaica; Charleston, South Carolina; and New York City, all of which are examined in this book—the contradictions between slavery and freedom inherent in the colonial relation assume hyperbolic form because geography is not a resource for writing them off the map. In lieu of geography, however, an intensified discourse of racialization serves to mediate the contradictions of the colonial relation.[25] Spatial distance is thus remapped as racial distance, separating out doctrines of freedom from those of enslavement. And indeed, colonial racial discourses have been rehearsed and naturalized to such an extent that it is possible to lose sight altogether of the contradiction between English liberty and race slavery. Jack Rakove writes, for instance, that "the customary stuff of English liberty provided the most influential values that England's emigrants, whatever their class of origin, carried overseas; it was the item in their cultural baggage that mattered most. That this concern was primarily about their rights alone, and had nothing to do with the excluded peoples that they would dominate, can hardly be surprising."[26] Such an account supposes that the distinction between English emigrants and those whom "they would dominate" in colonial locations is not difficult to discern—that insofar as a bright line separates the two, there is, on the colonial ground, little contradiction between the performance of English liberty and practices of enslavement. But what, precisely, would make the body of a person born in the Americas an *English* body?[27]

As Edward Long reports in his early history of Jamaica, Charles II, in his efforts to encourage English migration there, issued a proclamation in 1661 stating that Englishmen born in Jamaica would be considered "free denizens of England" with all the privileges of "free-born subjects of England." Long comments that such reassurance was a crucial incentive to migration: "Nor could any thing less than this have been sufficient to induce the free subjects of England to quit their country, and settle in a remote climate [in Jamaica]."[28] There is a clear supposition, evident in Long's words, that the *freedom* of English subjects might be jeopardized by inhabiting the colonial space of Jamaica. And indeed, the status of those Englishmen who peopled the colonial isle was in no way clear when Charles II issued this proclamation: Long notes, for instance, that Charles II attempted (unsuccessfully) to take control of the Jamaican colonial assembly by imposing a set of laws resembling those in place in Ireland—laws that, Long states, "would enslave [the] posterity" of the Jamaican planters by curtailing their rights as free Englishmen.[29]

The question of how to maintain the colonial relation in the colony—the free, national identity of Englishmen, and the enslaved, laboring identity of subalterns—thus presents a crisis of sovereignty when regarded close at hand: if, in Ireland, the matter was resolved geographically (those Englishmen inhabiting Ireland lost their rights and became "enslaved" in Long's words, while those in the metropole remained free), in Jamaica, English planters fought for and achieved a different resolution—one that hinged on race.[30] Thus, in contrast to Ireland, racialization became the primary mechanism for adjudicating the problem of colonial sovereignty in the Americas—for constructing two separate codes of law to govern free and unfree peoples who inhabited the same New World territory. However, racialization requires the reproduction and purity of the race—of "freeborn" Englishmen who sustain their rights as a matter of biological rather than geographical prerogative. Charles II's proclamation—which rules, by fiat, that certain denizens of Jamaica are legally "free denizens of England"—transmutes literal territorial habitation into figurative terms in order to enable British imperial conquest: a geographical discourse of Englishness is thereby transformed into a racial one. As Long's gloss of this history indicates, then, the issue of reproducing Englishness in the New World was a prominent concern in the late seventeenth century and a key paradox of the colonial relation.

Producing the individual English body was an issue, then, particularly in colonial climes. However, in England as well as the colonies, and later, the early national United States, the related question of producing the people as a representative body presented an enduring political dilemma. Indeed,

FIGURE I.I. Detail from the frontispiece of Thomas Hobbes's *Leviathan* (1651). The engraving is by Abraham Bosse, with consultation from Hobbes, after a drawing by Wenceslaus Hollar. Courtesy of Beinecke Rare Book and Manuscript Library, Yale University.

the question of how to represent the corporate body of the people arguably lies at the crux of political theories of popular sovereignty, from Thomas Hobbes, to John Locke, to James Madison and Alexander Hamilton. Without rehearsing those theoretical debates, I nonetheless want to point to the pivotal significance of embodied, public masses of people in such a political setting: if the representational authority of the public was newly at stake in the seventeenth-century Anglo-Atlantic world, then the physical body of the public gathered at sites such as the theatre acquired new meaning and political importance. As the famous frontispiece to Hobbes's *Leviathan* (1651) indicates (see figure 1.1), the many bodies of the people now wielded representational force—in this instance, the amassing bodies that comprise the people are organized so as to generate and sustain the representative force of the king.[31]

And as William D'Avenant—theatre manager, playwright, and member of Hobbes's intellectual circle—recognized (as did others), the theatre was a physical site at which the English people were regularly amassed and deeply engaged in questions concerning collective representation. The theatre in the Anglo-Atlantic world of the eighteenth century thus achieved political force

FIGURE I.2. The interior of Drury Lane Theatre during a performance, London. Engraving by Isaac Taylor after Edward Pugh, from *Modern London; Being the History and Present State of the British Metropolis* by Sir Richard Phillips (1805). Courtesy of Yale Center for British Art, Paul Mellon Collection.

not simply or even primarily in terms of the subject matter of plays enacted on stage, but in terms of the force of the bodies that were gathered together in public at the theatre and the representational strategies that were deployed to give meaning to that collection of bodies. An early nineteenth-century image of the audience collected for a performance at Drury Lane in London thus offers an intriguing analogy to the frontispiece to Hobbes's *Leviathan*: here the bodies of people are gathered, as in Hobbes's frontispiece, and they are amassed in a highly structured form (see figure 1.2). As in the frontispiece to Hobbes's *Leviathan*, the image is informed by a tension between the sheer multitude of bodies represented and the formal coherence achieved by the collective body. But in the image of Drury Lane, it is the stage that serves as the central organizing force of the multitude rather than the figure of the king. Notably, the figure of the king often occupied center stage in the Atlantic theatrical world in roles ranging from the eighteenth-century African prince, Oroonoko, to the English king, Richard III, to the Indian king, Metamora, in the early nineteenth-century United States. But this theatrical king's most important function on the stage was to die before the assembled audience: in staging the king's death at the (applauding) hands of the gathered body of the audience, theatrical performances thus enacted the power of popular sovereignty. Theatre was the location at which a new commons—the sovereignty of the people—was performatively articulated.

THEATRICAL EMBODIMENT: OROONOKO DISAPPEARED

In February 1795, the newspapers of Charleston, South Carolina, announced that Thomas Southerne's play *Oroonoko* would be enacted at the Church Street Theatre. Hayden Edgar, the actor slated to star in the title role of the enslaved African prince, Oroonoko, advertised the play as a moving love story, sure to touch the hearts of a right-feeling audience. Further, he trumpeted the proven track record of the play on the London stage: "This piece met with very great success—on its first appearance it was performed upward of thirty nights in its first season, and has ever since continued to give pleasure to every sensible and feeling auditor. The love of *Oroonoko* to *Imoinda* being, perhaps, the tenderest and at the same time the most manly, noble, and unpolluted, that we find in any of our dramatic pieces; his firmness and resolution, alike perfect in action and in suffering, are truly heroic, and perhaps unequalled."[32] Interestingly, Edgar promoted the play as a prior hit, but his advertisement did not mention that the location of the previous success of the play was London, not Charleston.[33] Only one day after advertising the upcoming performance, a second notice appeared: the mayor of Charleston had ordered the performance of *Oroonoko* to be cancelled. The move to quash the performance on the part of the Charleston city government indicates that the "heroic," "manly," and "noble" love of an enslaved African prince for his enslaved wife generated different sentiments among potential viewers in Charleston than in London. Indeed, the "firmness and resolution" that Oroonoko shows in his refusal to live as a slave or to be separated from his wife might be viewed, among slaveholding Charlestonians, as sentiments not suitable for emulation.

There is no record of why, precisely, the performance was cancelled: a second newspaper notice concerning the countermanded performance mentions that the cancellation of *Oroonoko* should be applauded as an act of "vigilance and prudence," and it is certainly easy to conjecture the reasons why a play representing slave rebellion might be suppressed in the name of prudence by the white plantocracy in Charleston in 1795.[34] Just seven months before the proposed date of Edgar's benefit performance of *Oroonoko*, the city of Charleston had enacted a law to prohibit the entry of any free blacks from St. Domingue out of concern that antislavery revolution then under way on the Caribbean island would spread to South Carolina. Edgar himself did not protest the cancellation but rather acceded to the wisdom of it and immediately proposed a substitute play for his benefit night, namely, *The Albion Queens*—a play concerning English, rather than African, nobility. Moreover, in a subsequent newspaper notice, Edgar indicates that geography was decisive in the order to suppress the performance of *Oroonoko*: "The Tragedy of Oroonoko" writes Edgar, "was laid aside in consequence of an official (yet polite and friendly) notification from his honor the Intendant, that *that* play was improper for representation *here*."[35]

Interestingly, this was not the first time Edgar had inadvertently courted controversy with his choice of scripts. Earlier the same month, a letter had appeared in a Charleston newspaper taking Edgar to task for the display of anti-republican sentiment in a performance of *Louis XVI* by William Preston. Unquestionably, Preston's script displays profound sympathy with monarchy (the play's original title—*Democratic Rage; or, Louis the Unfortunate, A Tragedy*—provides ample evidence of Preston's political leanings); however, in a printed response to the critique of the play, Edgar vigorously defends his performance in the name of republicanism. Specifically, he argues that he has sufficiently altered the script to suit the "country" in which it appears, and thus, he concludes, "There is not . . . a single passage . . . which can be offensive to the admirers of that excellent government under which our liberty is so happily protected." Indeed, Edgar states, it is the theatre manager's job to suit the script to the audience, and he has therefore taken it upon himself to excise a number of speeches from the play that might offend republicans because "the manager of every theatre is considered at liberty to erase such matter (where he can preserve the sense of the piece) as he thinks may be offensive to the country he lives in." Further, Edgar concludes, the proof of his politics is in the action of the play: his critic "must be informed that all Tragedies must consist of two parties, and the winding up of the business by the death of Louis the Sixteenth by the guillotine, shews which party it was meant to please."[36]

Edgar's travails are of interest not simply because of his apparent tin ear with regard to the audiences he sought to court, but because of the fact that within the space of two weeks his theatrical choices err in seemingly opposite directions: on the one hand, his selection of *Louis XVI* struck some members of the public as critical of the egalitarian spirit of the French Revolution (and by extension of U.S. republicanism as well); on the other hand, his choice of *Oroonoko* apparently struck the mayor of the city as too welcoming of the egalitarian politics of racial revolt on display in the Haitian Revolution (and by extension, welcoming of racial revolt against slavery in the United States). As Edgar's letter indicates, he clearly understood that he was expected to suit each specific performance and script to the public before which it was performed: in other words, he had a strong sense of the geopolitical specificity of the embodied public sphere and the workings of audience consent as locally determined—a play performed in London was not the same play when it was performed in Charleston, nor did Edgar expect it would be. And yet, his inability to consistently align the performance with the public indicates the intrinsic difficulty of catalyzing the alchemy of popular consent in the late eighteenth-century Atlantic world. Edgar's woes indicate, as well, that the theatre was a site at which audience consent was solicited and, in turn, performed or withheld in conspicuous, public terms.

Edgar's difficulties gauging the public taste begin to point, then, not just toward matters of commercial success, but to the political status of the audience in a location such as Charleston. As indicated by widespread public debate over the subject matter of plays, the casting of actors in specific roles, and the make-up of audiences and the acceptable limits of their behavior, the theatre was viewed as an important site of public debate and collective representation. In short, theatre was not a private affair. Charleston, like other port cities in the Atlantic littoral at this time, was geographically and temporally located between and among four revolutions of the Atlantic world—England's Glorious Revolution, the American Revolution, the French Revolution, and the Haitian Revolution. Each of these revolutions involved the ceding of authority to the populace, but each did so in different political terms and in relation to different populations. In London, a politics of popular sovereignty, emerging from the English Civil War and taking institutional form following the Glorious Revolution, enabled the creation of an embodied public convened in the space of the theatre. The subsequent republican revolutions of the Atlantic world—all of which occurred in the late eighteenth century—had the effect of rendering the embodied public both more important (as a site of political consent and formation of the people) and more volatile (as the uncertainty as to what constituted a public ramified across different populations—metropolitan, colonial, creole, white, black, enslaved, free, postcolonial, and/or indigenous—in the Atlantic world). In the postcolonial United States, in particular, the Atlantic history of revolution rendered the public and its authority politically significant but also unsteady, tumultuous, and, more than occasionally, riotous.

The fragility of audience consent to a staged performance—and thus to a performance of itself as a consenting people—was wholly evident in the theatres of a city such as Charleston in the late eighteenth century.[37] Indeed, audiences generally had no compunction about expressing their consent or dissent with respect to the activities occurring in the theatre, both on and off stage. As theatre historians have demonstrated, the restrained norms of spectatorship familiar to us today were unknown in U.S. theatres prior to the late nineteenth century. Audience members were expected to be active attendees of eighteenth- and nineteenth-century theatre: indeed, their activity was evidence of what Richard Butsch has described as audience "sovereignty" over the stage—a description that accords well with an account of the theatre as the scene of a performative commons at which a people exercised republican prerogatives.[38]

In the 1795 Charleston newspaper in which Edgar's performance of *Louis XVI* is advertised, a letter to the editor gives some flavor of just how vigorously the audience exercised its control of theatrical space. A writer who signs himself "A Friend to the Theatre" describes the public in action at the theatre in Charleston:

> Your correspondent was, on Monday last, at West and Bignall's theatre . . . when the good humour of the audience was much ruffled by a dispute and boxing match between two men in the gallery, which for a time stopped the performance; the delinquent was soon taken from his seat, and introduced on the stage, and there exposed to the contempt of the house. You, mr. printer [*sic*], and the public would naturally suppose that such a punishment was sufficient to prevent, at least for that evening, any further interruption of the performance; but to the astonishment of the audience, a quart bottle was flung, with the utmost violence, from the front gallery into the pit . . . the fully-enraged audience again ascended to the gallery, and by force dragged the culprit on the stage, where he was required, but peremptorily refused, to ask pardon for the unprovoked insult he had offered; he was then turned out of the house, and the actors proceeded to finish the third act.[39]

As the letter indicates, audience members who misbehaved were not simply muzzled and removed from the theatre in order to avoid further interruption of the performance in progress: rather, they were placed on stage in order to solicit audience disapprobation and thus became, in a sense, a part of the performance that unfolded during the evening. The contrapuntal staging of the play and of the vigilante powers of justice exercised by the audience on those who violated the collective standards of conduct suggests that the theatre was a site where the public actively constituted *itself* through policing and performing its own limits.

While applauding this behavior on the part of the audience, in the second half of the same letter, the "Friend to the Theatre" remarks on his own discontent with the exertions of a segment of the audience that he views as excessively and inappropriately active:

> I shall further remark on the misbehaviour of the young gentlemen who frequent those places, by stating what has too frequently met with the disapprobation of the public; I mean the irregularities that take place before the curtain is drawn up and between the acts, by the extreme rudeness of a few youths, who, calling themselves gentlemen, conceive they have a right to enter the theatres with a small bludgeon, politely called a *tippy*, and to continue such a thumping on the seats as to affect the feelings of every person who visits the playhouse as a place of rational amusement; this misbehaviour was particularly noticed on Saturday last, at the Church Street theatre; and on the young gentlemen being requested to be less noisy, they politely answered, that the theatre was like a public tavern, when having paid for his admission, the guests had a right to do as they pleased.[40]

This second passage of the letter offers a somewhat different assessment of the active audience: in this case, the audience is not acting en masse, but rather, dissension is evident within the audience as to what the norms of spectatorship should be. Should pounding with bludgeons for the sake of raising a thunderous din be considered permissible behavior in the theatre or not? The "Friend to the Theatre" invokes norms of polite behavior that are not universally shared by the audience: one portion of the audience, bludgeons in hand, asserts a "right" of assembly and expression that violates at least some portion of the audience's expectation of "rational" and gentlemanly behavior on the part of the theatrical public.

The two opposing assessments of the workings of the theatrical public within the same letter rehearse a debate that appears repeatedly with respect to the theatre in Charleston: on the one hand, the theatre is described as a "rational" entertainment that schools the public in virtuous behavior and knowledge of the world—the theatre in this way educates and organizes the public. Thus, for instance, in 1773, David Douglass, a theatre manager who is seeking permission to open a theatre in Charleston, writes, "a well-regulated Theatre, wherever the Polite Arts have been cherished, has been allowed to be a noble Institution, calculated for the Improvement and Refinement of Human Society—to be the *most rational* Entertainment an enlarged Mind can enjoy—and of the *utmost Utility* to the Common Wealth."[41] On the other hand, critics of the theatre maintain precisely the opposite: the theatre enables an unconstrained public to gather in defiance of existing social regulations. In the latter view, the very gathering of diverse bodies in a single space has the effect of violating social norms that require differential occupations of space by differently categorized bodies (black, white, male, female, upper class, lower class, free, and enslaved). As one critic of the theatre in Charleston, "Sylvanus," opines, theatres "present too great a variety of objects, occasion too much hurry and dissipation of thought, excite too many different passions or emotions, and to too high a pitch to answer the intention of rational amusements." As Sylvanus complains in a beautifully telling phrase, at the theatre one finds collected a "promiscuous multitude."[42]

A sense of the promiscuity Sylvanus refers to is evident in newspaper accounts from the eighteenth century that record the orchestrated chaos that attended the act of gathering large numbers of bodies in the space of the theatre in Charleston. Notices habitually announce that the theatre will open at least an hour before the performance is scheduled to begin, suggesting that an hour of commotion precedes the lifting of the curtain. We have accounts of boys who swarm about the doors to sell stolen tickets: one notice warns that "Gentlemen are particularly requested not to purchase Ticets [*sic*] or Checks of the Boys who crowd about the doors, as such Tickets and Checks are (for the most part) fraudently [*sic*] obtained."[43] Another notice admonishes theatre attendees to strictly manage their horses upon arriving and departing from the playhouse, thus giving a flavor of the chaotic traffic in the streets outside the theatre: "[Ladies and Gentlemen] will be pleased in order to prevent confusion to desire their servants to set down and take up with their horses heads to the northward."[44] And in addition to routine accounts of boisterous audience response to performances, on at least one occasion in 1794, French pirates chase the entire audience into the street.[45] The confusion and general mayhem that seems to regularly attend theatre attendance is more explicable if one considers that white Charlestonians, and probably free Charlestonians of color as well, would typically have sent their slaves to hold their seats prior to their own arrival at the theater, thus multiplying the number of bodies in motion to and from the theatre, in and out of its doors, on the narrow streets of Charleston. A newspaper advertisement suggests that a certain amount of instability attended even the practice of having seats held by slaves: "Ladies and Gentlemen will please to send their servants to keep places as soon as the doors are opened, with positive orders not to quit the box for which they hold tickets on any account; without this is done, the manager cannot possibly prevent a continuance of the disappointments that have lately happened."[46] And in fact, simple numbers are telling: with roughly twelve thousand residents in 1795, and a theatre seating capacity of fourteen hundred or more, a fairly large portion of the city's population might be congregated in one location for an evening that stretched to three or four hours of entertainment and included, on any given night, a full-length tragedy, *entr'actes* of rope dancing, pantomime, and singing, followed by a farce or afterpiece.[47] The sheer number and diversity of bodies in motion are significant here, as are the chaotic and indistinct borders generated by the theatre itself: borders between the inside and outside of a circumscribed yet public space and between licit and illicit entry into and representation within this space—borders tracing the dynamic edge between two competing versions of the performative commons: the "rational" order of a people and the "promiscuous" disorder of a multitude.

The contested and fractious nature of the audience's constitution in Charleston—the status of this theatrical public as a "promiscuous multitude"—attests to the complex nature of political representation at stake in the space of the theatre. Indeed, the term "multitude" returns us to debates concerning the politics of popular sovereignty and the representation of the people as they were taken up by political philosophers in the seventeenth century. Thomas Hobbes, for instance, defines the "multitude" as a collected faction of individuals who have yet to form into the coherent body of a "people" with representative political authority. Hobbes defines a multitude as "not any *one body*, but many men, whereof each one hath his own will and his peculiar judgment concerning all things that may be proposed." In contrast to the multitude, the *people* have assembled into an orderly form—one capable of collective self-representation and thus capable of wielding legitimate political authority. "If the same multitude do contract one with another," writes Hobbes, "that the will of one man, or the agreeing wills of the major part of them, shall be received for the will of all; then it becomes one person. For it is endued with a will, and therefore can do voluntary actions, such as are commanding, making laws, acquiring and transferring of right, and so forth; and it is oftener called the people, than the multitude."[48] Whereas the people have assembled and contracted—consented—to act as one, the multitude remains fractious and "dissolute" (the adjective that most often precedes "multitude" in Hobbes's work), incapable of assuming an orderly, politically meaningful form.[49] The unity of the "people" is thus created from out of the multitude by way of "an operation of representation."[50] This "operation of representation" has been variously construed by political theorists: whereas Hobbes views the exchange of the clamorous noise of the multitude for the representative unanimity of the people as the highest good—as, in fact, marking the transition from the chaos of the state of nature to the order of civil society—others (most recently Antonio Negri and Michael Hardt, drawing largely on Spinoza) celebrate the liberatory possibilities of a multitude that productively "banishes sovereignty from politics," thereby creating "a politics of permanent revolution . . . in which social stability must always be re-created through a constant reorganization of corporeal life, by means of a perpetual mass mobilization."[51]

Rather than define the "promiscuous multitude" of the theatrical public as *either* a (dissolute or revolutionary) multitude *or* an (orderly or exclusionary) people, I would suggest that in the space of the theatre we see the "people" being composed—that is, we see the act of political representation implicit in a politics of popular sovereignty as it is formulated and thus as it *eclipses* as well as *represents* the multitude. The emphasis of this reading lies, then, on the political-aesthetic significance of the "operation of representation" that occurs in the theatre—an operation or political practice that oscillates between moments of embodiment and mimesis, between riotous disorder and collective consent. The sharing of sensibility among a people—or more specifically, the sharing of meaning making—is a fundamentally aesthetic matter that is, in its collective nature, also inherently political. Insofar as a group of people consents to find meaning in a shared set of sense data (an aesthetic decision), they constitute themselves as a political community. Significant, as well, are the limits of meaning making—that is, the kinds of sense information (a royal slave on stage in Charleston, for instance) that are denied or foreclosed from the status of meaningful signifiers and, as such, constitute the *limits* of a political community. This "distribution [*partage*] of the sensible" (in the words of Jacques Rancière) defines both what is included and what (or who) is excluded from the community as well: to change the "distribution" of sense will change the boundaries of the political community.[52]

The communal decision as to what constitutes meaning—as to wherein the sensible lies—is thus not one that is collectively adjudicated by means of rational critical debate. Rather, such a decision involves an *aesthetic* debate—what Rancière calls a "dissensus" or dispute—as to what constitutes the limits of collective meaning.[53] This model of forming a collective or a public—of generating a commons—is notably theatrical: dissensus is the ground from which common sense and the commonality of political belonging arises, and it arises out of scenes of performance in which multiple epistemes occupy a contested space. The theatre, then, is a space where precisely such questions of framing are at stake: the theatrical frame makes visible the possibility of consensus in the making as well as the possibility of rendering such a frame out of joint—of dissolving the collective scene of meaning making into one of noise and riot. As such, New World drama stages the political and aesthetic making of the *people*—a performatively constructed commons—at sites around the Atlantic world, and the unmaking of Atlantic peoples as well.

The significance of theatre with respect to understanding the colonial relation and the Atlantic performative commons is twofold: in addition to serving as a historical locus at which publics debated modes of collective representation, the theatre has a specific phenomenology which figures prominently in my account of the representational force of theatre in the eighteenth-century Atlantic world. Theatre, by its very nature, conveys meaning by operating at the intersection of embodiment and representation—by coupling physical presence and mimetic reference. As Bert O. States contends, "there is a sense in which signs [in the theatre] . . . achieve their vitality . . . not simply by signifying the world but by being of it."[54] In other words, the signifying economy of the theatre operates in two registers: one that is *ontic* (thingly, material, resolutely present) and one that is *mimetic* (referential, immaterial, gesturing toward a scene located elsewhere). In general, one might expect the ontic to become the vehicle for the mimetic: when the body of a particular actor is transformed into a representation of, say, Belcour or Oroonoko, the ontic disappears, to a large extent, behind the mimetic and we thus "see" Belcour or Oroonoko rather than the actors who are performing the characters. But, as States argues, this is not always the case; the power of the sign is not "exhausted . . . by . . . its referential character" in the theatre. In an evocative example, States explains, "In theater, image and object, pretense and pretender, sign-vehicle and content draw unusually close. . . . [On stage] a chair is a chair pretending to be another chair."[55]

In the theatre, then, unlike the pages of a book, the *material* character of the sign retains particular presence and force, precisely because the sign is not solely linguistic in nature (not just the words spoken by an actor, for instance) but is also embedded within the physical movements or presence of a body or object on stage. Indeed, in something of a reversal, the thingly quality of the materiality of the theatrical sign can begin to unwind mimesis—can offer a challenge to the very script that is being performed, or, at the very least, begin to send a script in an entirely new and unexpected direction.[56] It is for this reason that the meaning of any given play will change enormously from one production to the next—namely, because the meaning of the theatrical event resides only partially in the language of the script. And it is for this reason, as well, that the meaning of *Oroonoko* on stage in London might be quite different from the meaning of *Oroonoko* performed in Charleston. In 1795 in Charleston, the physical presence of the staged black body apparently registered in an entirely different manner than it did in Covent Garden or Drury Lane: as we have seen, the mayor of Charleston asserted when prohibiting the performance of *Oroonoko* that "*that* play was improper for representation *here*."

Not only do the actors on stage participate in the double nature of theatrical signification, but so too does the audience: in collecting as a common body with representational force, the eighteenth-century Charleston audience participated in both embodying and representing itself in relation to the figures on stage before it. *Oroonoko* in Charleston thus assumed a different meaning in relation to a different assembly of spectators than those who regarded the play in London, thereby indicating the way in which different Atlantic world publics were geopolitically articulated with respect to the colonial relation. How was the Charleston public distinct, then, from that which gathered to watch *Oroonoko* in London? With respect to the body of potential spectators who were forbidden from watching the performance of *Oroonoko*, we know the following: the majority of the population of South Carolina in 1795 was nonwhite.[57] While the majority (albeit not the entirety) of audience members in Charleston were white, the staging of popular sovereignty achieved in the assemblage of audience and actors at a successful performance would have required the spectacular erasure of quotidian experience: that is, a representation of popular sovereignty in plantocratic Charleston could only be imagined or performed by erasing from view the majority of the population. At the site of the performative commons, then, political representation takes shape not only as a matter of embodiment, but as a process of refracting embodiment through strategies of display and erasure and contests over the terms of these processes.

The routine scenes of riot and debate that erupted at the theatre in eighteenth-century Charleston (and many other Atlantic locations) concerned not only what should and should not appear on stage—a bowdlerized *Louis XVI*, Southerne's sentimental *Oroonoko*—but also, as we have seen, how the public should or should not constitute, conduct, represent, and recognize itself in relation to such performances. Further, the question as to who was allowed to be a member of the theatrical audience was very much at issue in 1795 in Charleston. On the one hand, existing legal ordinances forbade blacks from attending the theatre. On the other hand, evidence indicates that blacks routinely attended the theatre at the time and regularly defied or evaded decades' worth of legal statutes aimed at curtailing the congregation of blacks and the formation of black publics—whether in the street, the church, the bar, the schoolhouse, the racetrack, or the playhouse.[58] What might it have meant, then, for *Oroonoko* to appear before this contested and combustible Charleston public? On the one hand, the lead role of the putatively black royal African, Oroonoko, would have been performed (possibly in blackface) by the white actor Hayden Edgar.[59] On the other hand, black men and women would certainly have been part of the putatively white public at the theatre—both as slaves sent to reserve seats for white masters and as ticket holders in their own right. This strange crisscrossing of imitated and inhabited racial categories underscores the peculiar phenomenology of theatrical performance. As a figure who mobilized both ontic and mimetic meanings, Oroonoko's "black" body on stage in Charleston might conceivably have given representational force and political meaning to black bodies inhabiting the audience: just as Oroonoko was materialized on stage by way of mimesis, so too might black audience members achieve representational force as members of the "people" of Charleston—as representatives of popular sovereignty.

Two sets of meaning thus contend and collaborate within the theatrical sign—one set that operates by way of embodiment and one set that operates by way of imitation. This makes theatre a remarkable resource for mediating between embodied publics and representational ones, and a resource for playing out the contradictions of the colonial relation that structure the Atlantic world and the Atlantic performative commons. More specifically, the theatrical sign has the capacity to display and erase meanings simultaneously—to eclipse embodiment in favor of mimesis or to foreground embodiment in such a way as to challenge mimesis—which enables theatrical performance to express the contradictions of the colonial relation with surprising agility.[60] Theatre is able to say the thing which is not, as well as the thing which is not said.

What, then, of *Oroonoko* on stage in London? Were audiences in eighteenth-century London as provisional, fractious, and political in nature as those in Charleston at the same time? If the contradictions embedded within the colonial relation were particularly hard to ignore in a Charleston theatre peopled with a mixed-race audience, was such an oversight more easily effected in London? Together with *Oroonoko* and *The West Indian*, New World dramas such as George Farquhar's *The Recruiting Officer* (1706) and Isaac Bickerstaff's *The Padlock* (1768) were among the most standard of fare on the eighteenth-century London stage: all four were popular for decades in London, as well as in the English provinces. And notably, all four plays have a significant New World component: Farquhar's *The Recruiting Officer* is a comedy set in the English provinces that concerns the contentious subject of impressment by the British military—a military that was stretched thin and in perpetual need of additional bodies to exercise British colonial order in the Atlantic world.[61] Isaac Bickerstaff's *The Padlock* was a comedy based on Cervantes's "Captive's Tale" but was updated to include one of the first stage New World Africans, the dialect-speaking trickster Mungo.[62] Just as goods such as salt cod, cane sugar, palm oil, linen, and Madeira wine circulated between the Caribbean, North America, Africa, and England, and just as the bodies of enslaved Africans, impressed British provincials, and wealthy creole planters traveled from one Atlantic port to another, so too did these goods and bodies appear on and circulate among the stages of the Atlantic world. Commodities and labor from the Atlantic world became increasingly important in the metropole as they formed the basis of a new economic, cultural, and political order in the eighteenth century. And the transformative power of such commodities and wealth, as they touched the metropole, appeared on stage as well: when Belcour, the colonial relation at the center of *The West Indian*, arrives in London, a servant comments, "He's very rich . . . They say, he has rum and sugar enough belonging to him, to make all the water in the Thames into punch."[63]

To a large extent, however, historians and scholars of England have tended to imagine that colonialism occurred off stage, as it were, with respect to the development of an English public sphere in the eighteenth century. The popularity of *Oroonoko*, *The Recruiting Officer*, *The West Indian*, and *The Padlock* indicates otherwise, as does recent scholarship documenting the centrality of New World colonialism to the repertoire and economy of British theatre in the eighteenth century. Julie A. Carlson reports that plays focusing on African and New World African characters were among the most popular and profitable in London at the close of the eighteenth century: "From the 1770s to the 1830s London patent theatre managers stood a good chance—often, their best chance—of being in the black by staging plays including black characters, topics or settings."[64] Kathleen Wilson argues, furthermore, that imperialism was key to shaping a "sense of the people" in Britain in the eighteenth century. Theatre in particular, Wilson argues, "contributed to public discourse on empire, converging with other branches of the contemporary 'media' to promote language, images and ideologies through which the empire could be comprehended and signified at home."[65] For London to understand itself as the metropolitan center of an expanding empire seemingly required that Atlantic colonial goods and bodies appear within its collective view, inhabiting time and space together with the English audience itself.[66]

However, interest in colonial bodies involved more than a passing enthusiasm for gazing on the cabinet of curiosities collected from the New World. Not just ephemeral entertainment, empire made visible on stage was intrinsic to materializing an English public that gathered in the space of the theatre. As I argue at greater length in the next chapter of this book, a novel geography of public theatre takes shape for the first time in London during the Interregnum (provisionally) and the Restoration (formatively)—a geography that is the scene of the political embodiment of the English public. More specifically, the apparatus of state spectacular authority merges with that of the public theatre to create an embodied public with new political prestige in this period: beginning with the execution of Charles I—itself a spectacular scene of the transformation of sovereign power—popular sovereignty begins to coalesce in varied instantiations and representations, including in the shape of an embodied English public gathered at the theatre.[67] However, as the popularity of New World drama in the eighteenth century indicates, a far more expansive geography is constitutively intertwined with the local geography of the English public—namely the geography of the Atlantic world and British imperialism. The events of the mid-seventeenth century afford two iconic symbols of a new geography of power and representation in Europe that have been touched on already: first, the execution of Charles I in London in 1649 marked the end of the absolutist authority of the sovereign ruler in the British nation; second, the Treaty of Westphalia signed in Europe in 1648 marked the end of overarching religious authority among the states of Europe and the beginning of an interstate system of independent state sovereignty, a territorial sovereignty in which authority was no longer located above (in God or the Roman Catholic Church) but in the people—the state—occupying the land in question. Regicide and territorial sovereignty both thus usher in new geographies of authority and representation, internal to the British state and external to it. In the domestic space of the public theatre in London, then, two stories are being worked out at once: one concerning the power of the people as a new political force in a postabsolutist political system, and one concerning the power of the English state in the new geography of a territorialized world. These two stories are articulated through one another in the spectacular world of the theatre in plays from William D'Avenant's early New World drama *The Cruelty of the Spaniards in Peru* to Southerne's more canonical *Oroonoko*. Atlantic world imperialism was not merely a subject of fleeting interest for metropolian theatre audiences but was constitutive of a new public in England at a historical moment when the English people had newly acquired political and representational authority.

Thomas Southerne's play *Oroonoko* appeared on stage in London every year without exception from its introduction in 1695 until 1829: references to the play often advert to the number of tears that were shed by audience members who wept in the final act as Oroonoko murdered his beloved pregnant wife, Imoinda, and committed suicide in the name of resisting enslavement. In 1707, a London paper described "Mr Southern" as the man "who has so often drawn Tears from the Fairest eyes in England by his Oronoko."[68] In a similar vein, John Whaley's poem "On a Young Lady's Weeping at Oroonooko" (1732) memorialized the tears of one Lucretia, who wept at a performance of Southerne's play; and, in 1749, an African prince, William Unsah Sessarakoo, prince of Annamaboe, who had been recently rescued from slavery, attended a performance of *Oroonoko* at Covent Garden and obligingly shed copious tears as the audience watched intently for his affective response to the scene before him.[69] *Oroonoko* is, however, a tragicomedy: although Oroonoko and Imoinda die at the end of the play, as we have seen, the two English husband-seeking sisters at the center of the play's comic plot succeed in securing wealthy spouses in the colonial setting. The audience thus receives compensation for the tears it sheds over Oroonoko's death in the form of an optimistic vision of the bourgeois possibilities of colonialism for English men and women. In the tragicomedy of *Oroonoko*, a London audience member might discern (and indeed, *feel* in a somatic register) losses in the form of African bodies as well as gains in the form of British imperial acquisition.

The radically different reception and different collective meaning of *Oroonoko* as performed in London and as banned from the stage in Charleston point to the importance of bringing performance into view as foundational with respect to convening a public. As indicated in the introduction, the model of the performative commons I propose here differs sharply from the print-centered account of a Habermasian public sphere. Notably, the public among whom print circulates is decisively limited to those who are literate in the language of the text in question. In Charleston (and indeed, in many cities of the Anglo-Atlantic world), a significant number of theatre-goers were not literate in English, and this group, in itself, comprised diverse populations including unlettered African Americans (enslaved and free); unlettered white creoles; non-English-speaking colonials and Europeans (most particularly French colonial refugees from St. Domingue); and possibly Africans and Native Americans who did not read or write English.[70] The performance public is thus broader than the print public because it includes those who are excluded from English-language print culture. This broader performance public, then, brings dimensions of the public into sight that are not visible within print and, more specifically, brings groups of people (and their roles within the public sphere) into visibility who are occluded when examining print alone. While the theatrical public is one among a number of embodied publics that were actively forming and informing a larger political public in the period, the theatrical public is of particular interest because of its visible wrangling over the construction and representational powers of the public. The print public, in contrast, renders invisible the foundational debate as to who is permitted entry into the public sphere because literacy is construed as a structural constraint not subject to debate and thus not political in nature: in the performative commons, debate over the boundaries framing the people becomes a subject of open contention and innovation.

It is worth noting, however, that extant evidence of the workings of the performative commons in a location such as Charleston at the close of the eighteenth century is available to us primarily through print. Given that most accounts of performances in the period are filtered through print, it is difficult to draw a sharp line of demarcation between the print public sphere and the performative commons as separate arenas of knowledge and information about the period. Indeed, the print public and the performance public were closely related to one another at the time: newspaper notices about the theatre were responsible for alerting the public to performances and thus had a role in generating the theatrical public, and print was also the means of reporting on the activities of the public gathered in theatrical spaces. Accordingly, one might say that print generated the embodied public and vice versa. The entwined nature of print and performance is thus not simply an artifact of our temporal distance from the period but, rather, reflects the workings of public gathering in the period.[71] Moreover, the mutual implication of print and performance in the creation of the multitude and the "people" in locations such as Charleston is particularly relevant in the Atlantic world, where "intimate distance" defines a key aspect of colonial and postcolonial culture.

I use the phrase "intimate distance" to describe the way in which colonial culture in the Atlantic world involved bringing communities together and sustaining them—creating intimacy—across great distances such as that between the colony and the metropole, or that between Africa and the slave quarters of the New World plantation. If it was important to a London public to have a sense of its relation to the New World, it was even more pressing for colonials and/or diasporic subjects to maintain a sense of connection to the metropole/homeland and its culture. In other words, colonials sought to maintain intimacy with cultures on the other side of the Atlantic world, despite the distance separating them from those sites and scenes. One might understand "intimate distance" in terms of communities of absence and communities of presence: whereas communities of absence are defined by spatial distance between points on various sides of the Atlantic, communities of presence are defined by the immediate proximity of bodies in New World spaces. The print public sphere is one conditioned on absence: print stands in for an absent speaker; printed artifacts traverse the routes of the Atlantic world, connecting and forming communities of diaspora, of imperial bureaucracy, of religious diffusion, and of capitalist development. The performative commons of the theatre, by way of contrast, is comprised of bodies that are sweating, applauding, weeping, and occasionally rioting when gathered together in a single location for a brief period of time. In short, the commons gathered at the theatre is a community of presence as opposed to the community of absence of the print public sphere.

And yet the performative commons of the theatre and the disembodied print public sphere are not so much different publics, or opposed publics, as mutually constituting publics. In the space of the Charleston theatre, scripts that had been written and often printed in England were used as the basis of performances that brought together members of a local, New World public. Despite the eventual political break with Britain, the theatre—even following U.S. independence—was the location for the affirmation of the centrality of certain British cultural norms and ideals, and as such, a location for the assertion of the cultured and cosmopolitan nature of the former colony.[72] As both Leonard Tennenhouse and Elisa Tamarkin demonstrate, U.S. citizens in the late eighteenth century sought to maintain a cultural intimacy with the English metropole despite their newly established political distance from Britain.[73] Moreover, cultural Britishness arguably developed with time into cultural whiteness in the United States following the revolution; in other words, cultural Anglophilia (asserting intimacy with Britishness) served as a credentialing form of whiteness in a society in which racial demarcations were increasingly sharply drawn and in which whiteness was becoming a form of cultural and economic capital.

The simultaneous emphasis that I place here on the scale of the local (Charleston) and that of the global (Atlantic) significantly revises existing understandings of the early national U.S. public sphere because the *national* framework is largely absent. As Trish Loughran points out, scholars have equated the eighteenth-century advent of the print public sphere with U.S. nationalism and, further, have ascribed to print a decisive role in generating that national framework. Yet as Loughran's work demonstrates, there "was no 'nationalized' print public sphere in the years just before and just after the Revolution, but rather a proliferating variety of local and regional reading publics scattered across a vast and diverse geographical space."[74] In other words, according to Loughran, print communities were persistently local, in part because print materials did not and could not circulate to a national audience because the circuits of transportation that existed were not designed to link the disparate states of the nation to one another. Building on Loughran's argument, I would suggest that communities of print were local *and* Atlantic, but *not* national: the circuits of transportation that were in full-fledged operation in the eighteenth century were those developed and fine-tuned by the economic systems that sustained the colonial Atlantic world, linking Charleston, for instance, to London, the Caribbean, and Africa. Both print materials, such as newspapers, journals, scripts, and novels, and the performance publics animated around these texts testify to the conceptual proximity (intimacy) of Paris, London, Kingston, and Le Cap Français to the local Charleston public and, by way of omission, a lack of conceptual proximity to, say, Philadelphia, Hartford, or Portsmouth—centers of population in the United States at the time.

The bifurcated nature of Charleston and other cities in the colonial Atlantic, shaped as both communities of absence and communities of presence—as both local, intimate publics and as nodes in a larger Atlantic/imperial network—reveals a key dimension of the way in which the print public and the performance public were mutually informing: print bridged great distances without shifting a letter of the words embedded on the page, that is, with great stability. But the reception of print—its meaning, legibility, and performance in a given location—shifted enormously in space and time in the Atlantic world, as did the public that was formed in relation to print and its performance: nowhere is this more evident than in the stage career of *Oroonoko*. And indeed, I would argue that this is a general, albeit underexamined, condition of print in the Atlantic world—namely, its differential local, site-specific reception—but it is a condition that is thrown into quite spectacular relief at the site of the theatre in the cities of the colonial Anglo-Atlantic littoral where the *performance* of print (of an English script) before a local, New World public takes center stage.

While the local performance of print—the performance of Britishness across great distance—may serve to generate a sense of intimacy with those on opposite shores of the Atlantic, the term "intimate distance" also names an opposing Atlantic colonial mode of performance, namely, that used to generate distance between and among bodies that are exceedingly intimate on colonial ground. The colonial relation, as I argue above, names the often occluded interdependence of two scenes—that of British liberty and that of racialized, enslaved labor and violent dehumanization. On the London stage, the blackened figure of Oroonoko represents a distant colonial body, the death of which enables London audiences to cement their sensate habitation of British liberty. On the Charleston stage, the blackened figure of Oroonoko cannot appear precisely because it is not distant—the presence of the royal slave on stage brings to the fore the intimacy of black and white bodies in the audience of the theatre, an intimacy at the heart of the "people" of Charleston: as such, Oroonoko embodied on stage brings to the fore the contradictions within the colonial relation. The strategies of erasure performed at the theatre—eclipsing the representational force of black persons on stage and in the audience—thus impose, in the face of physical intimacy, a figurative distance separating black from white.

Christina Elizabeth Sharpe refers to foundational New World intimacies between blacks and whites as "monstrous" insofar as such intimacy names the quotidian violence, often of a sexual nature, used to sustain plantocratic power and systems of racialization. "Monstrous intimacy" names, for Sharpe, "a set of known and unknown performances and inhabited horrors, desires and positions produced, reproduced, circulated, and transmitted, that are breathed in like air and often unacknowledged to be monstrous."[75] The simultaneously commonplace and unspeakable nature of such physical, embodied proximities, imbued with desire and violence, is a central aspect of the colonial relation—one whose optics of appearance and disavowal are managed through discourses of intimate distance. The nature of the theatrical sign—both ontic and mimetic, as we have seen—is such that presence and reference compete for authority and legibility: at the theatre, then, intimate distance achieves particular force insofar as both disavowed presence (ontic intimacy) and presence in the face of absence (mimetic intimacy) are articulated and debated as aspects of the performative commons.

Discourses of intimate distance thus serve to mediate the contradictions of the colonial relation insofar as they manage the spatial unevenness of the colonial Atlantic. Intimate distance names a dual strategy of asserting intimacy across great distance and that of asserting distance in the face of intimacy. The colonial relation enabled the economic intimacy and interdependence of distant sites around the Atlantic central to the foundation of the developing capitalist world system in the eighteenth century. In political terms, the colonial relation enabled the production of British liberty in England and in colonial sites by positing an unbridgeable distance between white and nonwhite persons, despite the quotidian proximities of these bodies and the necessity of this "monstrous intimacy" to the colonial relation. At the theatre, intimacy and distance are enacted in performative strategies that enable the emergence of debates over the shape of the "people" to appear. The theatre, as a scene of collective embodiment, makes present the physical proximity of bodies—including the monstrous intimacies of slavery on colonial ground—even while performances on stage cite and erase such intimacies, thereby enacting a debate over the sensus communis of the people that formed the ground of claims to political authority in an age of popular sovereignty.

CHAPTER 2

LONDON

REGICIDE AND THE THEATRICS OF POPULAR SOVEREIGNTY

When the head of King Charles I of England was severed from his neck on January 30, 1649, the nature of theatre changed. Executed in front of the Banqueting House where lavish court masques had been staged for his pleasure, the tables were literally turned as Charles I held center stage in a role that the audience, rather than he, commanded (see figure 2.1). At the moment of his execution, Charles I defended his right to absolute sovereignty, asserting that "a subject and a sovereign are clean different things."[1] Arguably, however, this distinction was never so clean again once Charles I's head left his shoulders: the authority of divine kingship suffered a lethal blow before the gathered audience of thousands at Whitehall that day.[2] On the day of his execution, the House of Commons officially declared "that the People are, under God, the Original of all just Power; And do also declare, That the Commons of *England*, in Parliament assembled, being chosen by and representing the People, have the supreme Power in this Nation."[3] Assertions as to *how* the people might best be represented remained an issue of conflict in the years to come, but the assertion *that* the basis of sovereign authority lay in the people emerged forcibly in this period and did not, thenceforth, disappear. When the axe fell on the bared neck of Charles I, the king's two bodies—physical and political—were both attacked, but at that same moment, the people's body gained new political significance.[4]

Amassed into a single body—applauding, weeping, rioting—the theatrical audience constituted an embodiment of the people that wielded political meaning in an era of emerging popular sovereignty. Moreover, in terms of the history of theatre, the death of Charles I marked not only the new authority of public audiences, but also the historical end point of the genre of the court

FIGURE 2.1. The Execution of Charles I before the Banqueting House (anonymous engraving, 1649/1655). © The Trustees of the British Museum.

masque. The elaborate court masques—spectacles combining poetry, dance, music, and moveable scenery—that Charles I and other monarchs had commanded were rendered extinct together with sacred kingship; under Oliver Cromwell's rule, Parliament closed all public theatres and when Charles II was restored to the throne in 1660, he licensed two *public* royal theatres. Despite Charles II's attempts to imbue his kingship with a theatricalized sacred majesty, he was largely unsuccessful at reclaiming any aura of divinely endowed sovereignty. Indeed, his highly public performance of kingship at the theatre was emblematic, as I argue below, of the new force the consenting public wielded in the staging of his power. The court masque, which enacted the divine status of the king before the court, thus gave way to a public theatre at which the king courted public opinion and at which the commons performed its sovereignty.

But there is an interesting interruption of this chronology that is suggestive of the way in which empire and the colonial relation are at stake in the shift from monarchical to popular sovereignty. In the years before his death, Cromwell did authorize the performance of several public plays and was apparently persuaded to do so by the argument that plays concerning empire would assist in consolidating public sentiment in his favor. In this chapter, I turn, in particular, to the writings and performances of William D'Avenant, the author of an inaugural New World drama—*The Cruelty of the Spaniards in Peru* (1658)—featuring, at its center, a tortured Native American prince as a figure of the colonial relation. D'Avenant's efforts to create a new public theatre following the regicide were thus advanced in relation to images of the New World, most particularly Cromwell's imperial imaginary and the tortured Native American prince who held sway there as an authorizing figure for British imperial aggression.

In tracing the emergence of an embodied English public in the space of the theatre, I argue that making present a new political sovereignty—a sovereignty from below—involves a complex effort of rendering visible and invisible relations among bodies, places, and power that are debated and formalized in the physical space of the theatre. This geography is both exceedingly local—it concerns the intimate space of the theater—and Atlantic in scope: the 1658 staging of *The Cruelty of the Spaniards in Peru* responds to and engages not only the emerging nature of popular sovereignty in England, but recalibrations of territorial sovereignty in Europe and the New World at stake in the 1648 Treaty of Westphalia and Cromwell's "Western Design" for establishing dominance over Spain in the New World. In what follows, I trace the emergence of two intertwined geographies that take shape in London in the second half of the seventeenth century: one concerning the inside of the nation and one concerning the outside. Popular sovereignty within England, and interstate negotiations concerning territorial sovereignty outside of England, conjointly usher in a new geography of political authority and representation that takes visible shape in the spectacular world of the theatre. As the performative commons first assembles in England, then, it does so by means of conjuring a colonial relation in the figure of the tortured Native American prince. As such, the theatricalization of torture, in particular, serves as an index of a new political subjectivity; scenes of torture on stage simultaneously mark the bounds of national belonging and imperial violence while enrolling a sentient audience into the newly sovereign body of a consenting people—allowing them to feel as one, to perform the sensus communis of the people.

FROM COURT MASQUE TO PUBLIC THEATRE

The court masque is a spectacle that materializes the authority of the king: the public theatre, in contrast, materializes the sovereignty of the public. Tracing the engagement, and political opportunism, of William D'Avenant in both forms of spectacle—and across three political regimes (those of Charles I, Cromwell, and Charles II)—we can track the shifting locus of political authority in the transition from the genre of the court masque to that of the public theatre. The court masque is a particular kind of performance that is congruent with the workings of monarchical power in England: both the elaborately painted scenery of the masque and the arrangement of the audience, with the monarch at the perspectival center of the two, materialized and celebrated the ordering of space and time around royal authority such that the masque and the court itself became the shared and undifferentiated ground of a world imbued with the divine right of kings. Stephen Orgel's description of the working of the masque—as performed for an audience of royalty and courtiers—emphasizes the centrality of the moment when imitation (mimesis) gives way to embodiment (ontology) or a collective scripting of the real: "Every masque moved toward the moment when the masquers descended and took partners from the audience, annihilating the barrier between the ideal and the real, and including the court in its miraculous transformations."[5] Notably, the ontological force of the masque does not emerge from language, but from spectacle and performance.

The elaborate moving spectacles or "machines" (such as a sea of waves or clouds descending from above) that appeared in the court masque "are not stage-sets," writes Orgel: "On the contrary, for the most part they are themselves the 'action,' providing the crucial developments and transformations; and it is the dialogue that is clearly ancillary, elucidating or moralizing the spectacle."[6] The function of spectacle here is not illusion, but the generation of ontological consensus: the masque produces and maps the present—the time and space—of the court that the audience and masquers inhabit. In the masque, the force of spectacle rather than dialogue bridges and annihilates the distinction between the ideal and the real: in other words, the ritual force of community formation inheres in spectacle and action, not in argument and reasoned consensus.

The scenic and mechanical innovations of the court masque are well documented: elaborate perspectival backgrounds, changing scenery, and "engines" and "machines" were central to the genre. This form of spectacle was not employed in the public theatre prior to the English Civil War but emerged as an important aspect of Restoration drama following the Interregnum.[7] William D'Avenant is the single person most clearly associated with transferring the theatrical techniques of the court masque to the Restoration public stage; he was one of two individuals granted royal patents by Charles II to open public theatres following the Interregnum, and his innovations in moveable scenery earned him both acclaim and public patronage. Intriguingly, however, the very earliest successes of D'Avenant in bringing the masque form to the public stage occurred not under the reign of Charles II, but under the rule of Cromwell during the Interregnum.

D'Avenant had written masques for the court of Charles I, and during Cromwell's rule he fled to France, where he was part of a royalist circle formed around Queen Henrietta Maria (the widow of Charles I): his intellectual cohort in Paris included the philosopher Thomas Hobbes as well as the writers Margaret Cavendish, Duchess of Newcastle, and her husband, William Cavendish. In one particularly intriguing turn of service to the monarchy in exile, D'Avenant was deputized treasurer of Virginia, and then lieutenant governor of the colony of Maryland: he collected a crew of workers from French prisons to bring to the New World, but his ship was intercepted by Cromwell's forces just off the shores of England. D'Avenant was arrested and placed in prison—first on the Isle of Wight and later in the Tower of London. After being released from prison, with the intercession of individuals who may have included John Milton, D'Avenant went about the work of attempting to open a theatre under Puritan rule—an effort at which he was modestly successful.[8]

D'Avenant premiered four performances, with state permission, under the Protectorate: *The First Days Entertainment at Rutland House* (performed in 1656), *The Siege of Rhodes* (1656), *The Cruelty of the Spaniards in Peru* (1658), and *The History of Sir Francis Drake* (1659). The first of these performances, *First Days Entertainment*, was something of a staged dialogue, the topic of which was the legitimacy of theatre. The subsequent three performances were all of a much more elaborate nature, taking the form of modified masques and including extensive scenery, singing, dancing, and limited dramatic narrative. The generic nature of these performances is somewhat vexed: D'Avenant was evidently not eager to identify these performances as masques, given the political undesirability of associating the (new) theatre with monarchy and the culture of the court; however, the masque-like elements of the productions remain pronounced despite D'Avenant's concern to reframe the productions as generically novel.[9]

If the form of the productions remained similar to that of the masque, however, their political force was decisively reoriented away from the celebration of monarchical authority. D'Avenant's efforts to reformulate the political meaning of theatre during the republic are in full view in two documents that he prepared in an effort to convince Cromwell's council of state to allow public theatre in England. The first of these documents, titled *A Proposition for Advancement of Moralitie, By a New Way of Entertainment of the People*, was published anonymously in 1653 and argues in favor of opening a public theatre aimed at the moral instruction of the public. What distinguishes the republican theatre proposed by D'Avenant from the masques he had written for kings and courtiers is, most obviously, the audience the performance aims to reach: whereas the masque took the monarch as the central addressee, republican theatre addresses the people as a whole. But the shift in audience address speaks of a more fundamental shift in the understanding of the political aims of theatre itself: no longer the scene of making immanent the authority of the king, the theatre is now the location of mobilizing a public.

The first paragraph of D'Avenant's 1653 *Proposition* makes this aim clear:

> As 'tis the principal Art of Military Chiefs to make their Armies civil, so is it of Statesmen to civilize the people; by which Governours procure much ease to themselves, and benefit to those that are govern'd: For the civilizing of a Nation makes them not effeminate, or too soft for such discipline of war as enables them to affront their Enemies, but takes off that rudeness by which they grow injurious to one another and impudent towards Authority. And subjects should receive good education from the State, as from vertuous Philosophers, who did anciently with excellent success correct the peoples manners, not by penall Statutes and Prisons, but by Morall Schooles and Heroick Representations at the public charge; obliging them thus to the Supream Power for their mutual quiet, without which Life is not a benefit, but punishment from God.[10]

In this passage, D'Avenant emphasizes the benefit the theatre offers in teaching the public civility—in *civilizing* the people of the state. In such emphasis, he gives no indication that he is interested in giving the public a voice or a role in political authority. And yet, the question of authority is very much at stake in these few sentences: the danger of an uncivilized public looms large as a threat to state power, and accordingly, we hear an implicit claim that the public may, in fact, wield a great deal of power. Indeed, the operations of power in this passage resemble quite strikingly Foucault's well-known thesis concerning the historical shift from the power of sovereignty embodied in the king—a power of force and spectacle—to the power of governmentality, a "capillary" power that operates at the level of subject formation. D'Avenant, like Foucault, argues that shows of external force will not control the public; rather, the operation of subtle corrective power in the form of "schooles" and "representations" will generate self-control and garner obedience among the people. For D'Avenant, then, the education of the public at the theatre is clearly aimed at gaining the people's assent to state authority—at pacifying rather than energizing the public. But it is worth underscoring that the assent of the people now seems to be worth soliciting—indeed, it stands as the organizing principle of the theatre. In the Foucauldian vocabulary that D'Avenant himself seems to grasp after, the management of bodies and sensations is newly of concern in a world that has seen the dramatic waning of absolutist authority: power is no longer punitive ("penal") but gently persuasive ("civilizing").[11]

As a number of critics point out, D'Avenant's 1653 *Proposition*, in its concern with unifying and pacifying the public, is deeply indebted to the political theory of Thomas Hobbes's *Leviathan*.[12] James Jacob and Timothy Raylor, in particular, not only detail the close interaction of Hobbes and D'Avenant in Paris during D'Avenant's exile as well as in the 1650s in London, but they also demonstrate the extent to which the circle of writers with whom Hobbes and D'Avenant consorted was acutely concerned with the question of public order, given the recent history of the English Civil War: both Hobbes's *Leviathan* and D'Avenant's *Proposition* directly address the question of how to control and pacify a potentially unruly public.[13] However, an even more fundamental similarity connects Hobbes's and D'Avenant's politics in these two texts: namely, both propose that legitimate state authority originates in the consent of the people and not in the divine right of the king. In other words, both presuppose that authority operates—in its original form—from below. For Hobbes, an avowed monarchist, the authority of the king is derived from the consent of the people: out of fear of war and death, the people allow the head of state (the Leviathan/monarch) to represent them.[14] Once the people have consented to transfer their authority to the king, however, they do not have the right to dissent from monarchical rule. Hobbes is thus something of a contradictory political figure: according to debates among political theorists, he is both the founding father of liberalism (grounding his account of state sovereignty on the free consent of the people) and an anti-liberal thinker (disputing the people's right to throw off the yoke of tyrannical authority and supporting absolutist monarchy).

D'Avenant's *Proposition* embraces remarkably similar politics: the power of the state should be obeyed, D'Avenant contends, yet that power requires the assent (however garnered) of the people. As Christopher Pye argues, Hobbes's *Leviathan* articulates a new theory of politics and representation in which the will of the people assumes central status: "[In *Leviathan*] the legal and philosophical belief that the sovereign's person 'embodies' the collective in a hypostasized and quasi-mystical form is decisively supplanted by a contractual theory in which the monarch—even the absolute monarch—is conceived as the designated representative of the subjects' will."[15] Pye's formulation is useful in underscoring the extent to which new representational techniques and forms are at stake in the account of political authority shared by Hobbes and D'Avenant. And indeed, his language seems particularly germane to D'Avenant's new, republican theatre: the "quasi-mystical form" of the court masque, one might argue, is replaced in D'Avenant's *Proposition* by a performance concerning the "representa[tion] of the subjects' will." Thus, D'Avenant's *Proposition* can be seen as centrally concerned with key questions Hobbes's theory poses: How might one represent, in a controlled fashion, the newly important will of the people? How might one represent the consent of the people to the Leviathan? These questions return to a central dilemma of popular sovereignty that emerges in Hobbesian theory (as we saw in the last chapter): what is the relation between the collected body of the people—the *multitude*—and the sovereign authority of that body as a *people* capable of self-representation?

If the politics of the court masque are no longer relevant in answering this question, D'Avenant nonetheless argues that the techniques of spectacle developed in the court masque remain valuable in doing so. D'Avenant's *Proposition* repeatedly mentions the extent to which enticing the senses of the people with the techniques of masquing—scenery, music, motion, and lights—will assist in "enamour[ing] [the people] with consideration of the conveniences and protections of Government."[16] Significantly, then, it is at the level of the sensorium that a new sensus communis takes shape. Further, D'Avenant suggests that heroic military activity and torture should form the subject of the new drama. In a letter summarizing the *Proposition*, D'Avenant explains that he proposes the creation of a state-supported theatre,

> in which shall be presented severall ingenious Arts, as Motion and transposition of Lights; to make a more naturall resemblance of the great and vertuous actions of such as are eminent in Story; . . . representing the Generalls and other meritorious Leaders, in their Dangers Successes and Triumphs; and our Enemies in such acts of Cruelty (like that in Amboyna) as shall breed in the Spectators courage and animosity against them; diverting the people from Vices and Mischiefe; and instructing them (as in a Schoole of Morality) to Vertu, and to a quiet and cheerefull behaviour towards the present Government.[17]

Here we see not only an account of the transporting effects of scenic innovation, but also a prescription for the correct subject matter of republican theatre. In the absence of a representation of monarchical authority, the subject of the drama, according to D'Avenant, should be military leaders, and, intriguingly, *scenes of torture* performed by enemies of the English state. The focus on military heroics seems a fairly self-evident choice as a topic of republican theatre—heroes of the court are replaced by heroes of the republican state. But the turn to scenes of torture is less obvious as a republican strategy of representation, and worth further attention, particularly given that the scene of torture appears repeatedly in D'Avenant's account of the new theatre during the Interregnum. In the 1653 *Proposition* cited above, as well as in his second argument in favor of the theatre, a letter written to Secretary of State John Thurloe in 1656, and once again in the first masque D'Avenant wrote to be performed during the Interregnum, *The Cruelty of the Spaniards in Peru*, torture and the colonial relation associated therewith are the central theatrical subjects of the new republican theatre.

TORTURE AND NEW WORLD SOVEREIGNTY

The so-called Amboyna Massacre mentioned in D'Avenant's 1653 *Proposition* occurred in 1623 but was infused with new life under Cromwell's rule. Amboyna, an island located in the Moluccas (currently Indonesia) was the site of sustained trade disputes between the British East India Company and the Dutch East India Company in the seventeenth century; in 1623, ten agents of the British East India Company were allegedly tortured and beheaded by the Dutch on charges of treasonous violation of Anglo-Dutch trade agreements. Almost thirty years later, an anonymously authored pamphlet concerning the event, *A Memento for Holland*, was published with engravings depicting the torture of the Englishmen (see figure 2.2). The inflammatory pamphlet helped garner support for the First Anglo-Dutch War, launched by Cromwell in an effort to secure British access to portions of the East and West Indian trade dominated by the Dutch, and, as Steven C. A. Pincus convincingly argues, to prevent the threat of "universal monarchy" by the Dutch.[18] That war, begun in 1652, was the occasion for D'Avenant's mention of the desirability of staging the torture of English merchants by the Dutch (twenty-nine years earlier) as an ideal subject for the theatre of moral instruction he proposed to Cromwell's Council of State. On the one hand, then, D'Avenant seems to be appealing to a political issue of the day merely in order to make the case for theatre, and yet on the other hand, torture proves to be more than incidental to D'Avenant's account of the new theatre: in his subsequent defense of the theatre, submitted to Cromwell's government in 1656, torture again is foregrounded as an ideal subject for dramatic staging, albeit in this second case, the torture of Native Americans by the Spanish rather than the torture of English merchants by the

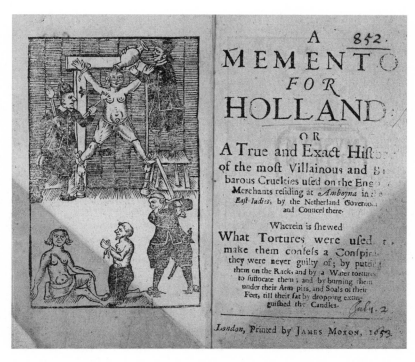

FIGURE 2.2. Frontispiece and title page of *A Memento for Holland* (1653), with woodcuts showing the torture of English merchants at the hands of the Dutch in Amboyna thirty years earlier. © The British Library Board.

Dutch. Moreover, it is the second document that seems to succeed in garnering state support for the theatre: shortly after the submission of this letter to Thurloe, D'Avenant moves forward with the staging of the first sanctioned public dramatic performance under Cromwell's rule. Why the centrality of torture to the creation of a theatre of popular sovereignty? The torture of an alien—a colonial relation—assisted in generating a new collective, namely, a national people united (from below) in affective and sensate terms.

In the 1656 letter to Thurloe, written three years after the *Proposition*, D'Avenant claims that the subject of theatre should, ideally, be torture in colonial contexts: "If morall representations may be allow'd," writes D'Avenant, "the first arguments may consist of the Spaniards' barbarous conquests in the West Indies and of their severall cruelties there exercis'd upon the subjects of this nation: of which some use may be made."[19] Again, D'Avenant is undoubtedly capitalizing on current political concerns of the Protectorate: in 1654, Cromwell launched a British attack on the Spanish empire in the Caribbean;

his imperial initiative—the Western Design—aimed to capture the wealth of the New World and cripple Spanish economic and religious dominance. But as much as D'Avenant may be citing the Western Design to further his own cause, his letter also participates in a fairly complex recalibration of imperial ideology and a novel articulation of English public identity that emerges in the wake of the collapse of the Western Design. By 1656, when D'Avenant wrote to Thurloe, news had reached England that the expedition at the center of Cromwell's Western Design had failed: English forces had been rebuffed by the Spanish in their efforts to take the island of Hispaniola (currently Haiti and the Dominican Republic); Admirals William Penn and Robert Venables had succeeded in taking from the Spanish the island of Jamaica, which, although it would later become a source of great wealth for England, was not seen as valuable at the time. Indeed, in March 1655, Cromwell called for a national day of fasting and humiliation to contemplate the failure of his providential "design" to wrest power from the Spanish in the New World.[20]

Some historians have taken this pronounced sense of defeat as evidence of the end of Cromwell's imperial plans; however, Cromwell's attacks against the Spanish continued in force: following the defeat of the Western Design, Cromwell officially declared war on Spain, publishing a manifesto justifying his attack on Spain in terms of the "Black Legend" of the cruelty of the Spanish to Native Americans in the New World.[21] Cromwell subsequently used naval force to interrupt the Spanish treasure fleet's supply of gold and silver to the Spanish crown from the New World and, in 1658, successfully attacked Spanish holdings in the Netherlands. A series of publications appears after the defeat of the Western Design, written by Cromwell and his allies, which rearticulates the nature of English hostilities against the Spanish away from the providential language used to justify the Western Design: the focus of these publications remains the New World, but rather than suggesting that it is God's desire that the English take the New World from Spain, these publications elaborate the so-called Black Legend—the claim that Spanish cruelty to native peoples in the New World justifies English rather than Spanish colonial rule there. The shift from imperial aggression justified by divine will (providence) to one justified by sentiment (a response to torture and cruelty) is enormously significant: it marks a revision of the terms of English nationhood, from one constituted from above to one constituted from below.

Historians have by and large seen the providential argument and the Black Legend argument as of a piece, but I would suggest that they belong to quite separate logical and political arguments concerning New World sovereignty. Cromwell's 1655 *A Declaration . . . against Spain* lays out a case for war against

Spain that indicates that he was not pursuing a solely or even primarily religious vision of New World sovereignty after the Western Design failed. Rather, as Steven Pincus argues, the first Anglo-Dutch War (and the lack of unity it demonstrated between two Protestant nations) brought a recognition, on Cromwell's part, that it was not Protestantism that would guide English imperialism, but Englishness.[22] While providentialism did not wholly disappear from Cromwell's language, the foreign policy he pursued after the failure of the Western Design was no longer that of Protestant against Catholic, but that of England against any threat of universal monarchy, be that Dutch (Protestant) or Spanish (Catholic). Indeed, because the war against Spain was not primarily religious, new moving forces—cruelty, sympathy, nationalism—gained rhetorical ground in the argument for imperialism, and it is this rhetoric that appears on the stage in performances such as D'Avenant's masque, *The Cruelty of the Spaniards in Peru*. It is this argument, moreover, that D'Avenant takes up in his second proposal to open the theatre under Cromwell's rule, and it is this argument that successfully unlocks the doors of the public theatre in England.

As I have argued, a people comprised from below can be effectively fashioned and staged in a theatrical setting, and thus it is possible to trace the striking parallels between Cromwell's new imperial policies and D'Avenant's theatrical innovations, both of which grant a central place to the torture of the Indian prince. In October 1655, Cromwell issued the clearest articulation of the "cruelty" argument in *A Declaration of His Highness, by the Advice of His Council: Setting Forth, on the Behalf of This Commonwealth, the Justice of Their Cause against Spain*. This document was translated into Latin by Cromwell's foreign secretary, John Milton, and in 1738 was reissued in English, under the title *A Manifesto of the Lord Protector . . . Wherein Is Shewn the Reasonableness of the Cause of This Republic against the Depredations of the Spaniards*, the title page of which asserts that the document was "Written in Latin by Jon Milton, and first printed in 1655, now translated into English." Given this attribution, it is possible that the declaration issued in Cromwell's name bears the marks of Milton's authorship.[23] The original publication of this document coincides with that of another key document elaborating the Black Legend, namely John Phillips's new English translation of Bartolomé de las Casas's *Brevísima relación de la destrucción*, tendentiously retitled *Tears of the Indians: Being An Historical and true Account of the Cruel Massacres and Slaughters of above Twenty Millions of Innocent People* (January 1656). Phillips is Milton's nephew, and as Elizabeth Sauer suggests, "The appearance of Phillips's translation of *Brevíssima relación* very shortly after Milton's translation of Cromwell's *Declaration* cannot be coincidental. *Tears of the Indians*, moreover, is dedicated to Cromwell and 'To all true English-men.'"[24] In the *Declaration*, Cromwell asserts that the Western Design was not an unwarranted act of aggression against the Spaniards but rather an appropriate response to the ongoing war that the Spanish had waged against the English in the New World and the unjust claims of the Spanish to sovereignty there.

Cromwell's declaration of war against the Spanish relies heavily on the rhetorical force of scenes of torture: Cromwell indicts the Spanish "for having treated us with so much Cruelty and Barbarity in the West Indies, for having inslav'd, hang'd, drown'd, tortur'd and put to death our Countrymen, robb'ed them of their Ships and Goods, and demolish'd our Colonies even in the time of profound Peace" (*Declaration*, 26). But his account of torture and cruelty also, importantly, extends to the Spanish treatment of Native Americans: the English should be engaged in "avenging the Blood of the *English*, as well as that of the poor *Indian*, which in those places has been so unjustly, so cruelly, and so often shed by the Hands of the *Spaniards*: since God has made of one Blood all Nations of Men for to dwell on all the Face of the Earth, having determined the times before appointed, and the Bounds of their Habitation" (*Declaration*, 6).

The unexpected claim, on Cromwell's part, that the English and the Indians of the New World are of one blood is best understood not as an argument concerning race or racial equality, but in terms of the final clause of the sentence cited above—namely, Cromwell's concern to deny that the Spanish have any just claim to territorial control of the New World, and hence no just defense of their aggression against the English in these territories. And indeed, in the next paragraph, Cromwell partially withdraws his argument concerning "one Blood," noting that "in order to justify our Conduct, there is no need of having recourse to the common Relation that Men have to one another, which is no other than that of Brethren . . . since [the Spaniards] having so often robb'd and murder'd our own Countrymen was cause sufficient of itself" (*Declaration*, 6). Cromwell hedges here about the need for including tortured Indians in his account of English imperial authority in the New World, and it is worth attending to the precise logic that seems to make the tortured Indian both rhetorically necessary and logically unnecessary for Cromwell's new imperial vision.

⌐Central to the emergent imperial ideology Cromwell announces in the *Declaration* is a new account of territorial sovereignty—one that is no longer authorized by God (from above), but one that is legitimated on the basis of territorial occupation and popular consent (from below).[25] As Carl Schmitt argues, a new spatial order emerged in Europe following the European discovery of the New World, and this spatial order was defined, above all, by the disappearance of overarching politico-religious authority (Catholicism) and dynastic alliance in favor of territorial state sovereignty. Schmitt defines this new order as a "nomos of the earth"—"earth" being an important term here insofar as it refers to physical soil and territory and thus gestures toward the concept of geopolitical empire founded on a cartographic, spatial episteme which emerged after 1492.[26] According to Schmitt, a spatial and territorial state sovereignty, known as "Westphalian sovereignty," took definitive political shape in Europe following the 1648 Treaty of Westphalia, which ended the Thirty Years War in Europe and, in effect, institutionalized the right of European states to control religion within their own borders, thus enacting a post-Reformation state sovereignty that dislodged the political power of the Roman Catholic Church.[27]

Schmitt's account of sovereignty is useful in connecting the Westphalian interstate European order and the notion of territorial sovereignty articulated therein through the new spatial order that emerged with the European encounter with and colonization of the New World.[28] In his *Declaration*, Cromwell, too, links the Reformation to the "discovery" of the New World, defining both as key events forming the basis of the new, territorial sovereignty he seeks to assert. Cromwell begins his *Declaration* by dismissing the legitimacy of a papal mandate granting Spanish ownership of the New World—which he refers to as the "ridiculous Gift of the Pope"—and he similarly critiques the cozy, familial deals and feuds between Spanish and English crowned heads which were of a "private," rather than national nature and thus do not form the basis of legitimate state sovereignty. Cromwell writes, "Thus far the foresaid Princes were not wanting to their Subjects when they made War in those places privately for their own Interest, tho' by reason of the Power of the above mention'd *Spanish* Faction they would not espouse their Cause publickly, in the way they ought to have done, and in a manner suitable to the ancient Glory of the *English* Nation" (*Declaration*, 5–6). Cromwell's rejection of the international relations negotiated between crowned heads as essentially private rather than national agreements demonstrates the way in which republicanism (domestically) involved an entirely new set of foreign relations for England. As David Armitage explains, "The turn to a non-dynastic foreign policy, which could repudiate past alliances and be propelled by economic or religious motives, left the commonwealth and Protectorate open to take an aggressive attitude towards the dominions of competing powers."[29] In short, a Westphalian, post-dynastic notion of national sovereignty laid the groundwork for an entirely new order of empire.

In order to discount the authority of the pope with respect to New World sovereignty, then, Cromwell invokes the Reformation and its contemporaneity with the European discovery of the New World: to understand sovereignty in the New World correctly, writes Cromwell,

> We must cast our eyes back a little upon things that are past, and strictly examine all the Transactions betwixt the *English* and the *Spaniards*, consider what has been the State of Affairs on both sides, so far as may respect the mutual relation of the two Kingdoms, both since the first Discovery of *America*, and since the Reformation: Which two great Events, as they happened much about the same time, so they produced every where vast Changes and Revolutions, especially amongst the English and the Spaniards, who since that time have conducted and managed their Affairs in a very different, if not quite contrary way to what they did formerly. (*Declaration*, 7)

Cromwell's invocation of the Reformation as an event that has correlative meaning with the "Discovery of America" is particularly significant insofar as he seeks to define a new spatial and geographical order of the world that corresponds to a new religio-political order of the world. The Reformation, Cromwell indicates, decisively changed the relation of Spain to England, severing the religious link between the two and necessitating a new logic for the legitimation of sovereignty. In the statement cited above, Cromwell, then, rewrites history ("casts back in time") in order to assert that the Reformation opened an epistemological gap between England and Spain (one in which no shared ground of religious authority existed), which then was given full scope to be enacted in struggle over the territory of the New World: the lack of shared ground, in politico-religious terms, becomes literalized in the uncertain title to the new ground of America. In effect, Cromwell proposes a new history of Europe that dates to the Reformation and the discovery of America as simultaneous events that rewrite the meaning of sovereignty.

Cromwell introduces two principles on which to justify the English right to colonial possession in the Americas: that of settlement (occupation) and that of the consent of the people. Cromwell thus discounts the nominal act of "discovery" as well as the nominal act of papal pronouncement in favor of an embodied, territorial logic of sovereignty:

> Nor is the other [Spanish] Title [of Discovery] of any greater weight, as if the Spaniards in consequence of their having first discovered some few parts of America, and given names to some Islands, Rivers and Promonto-

ries, has for this Reason lawfully acquir'd the Government and Dominion of that New World. But such an imaginary Title founded on such a silly Pretence, without being in Possession, can't possibly create any true and lawful Right. The best Right of Possession in America, is that which is founded on one's having planted Colonies there, and settled in such Places as had either no Inhabitants, or by the Consent of the Inhabitants, if there were any.... If this be true, as the Spaniards will be found to hold their Possessions there very unjustly, having purchased all of them against the Will of the Inhabitants. (*Declaration*, 24–25)

Cromwell's claim in this case is a familiar one for the English; he suggests that without having settled the land, the Spanish have not truly taken possession of it.[30] In this claim, Cromwell invokes a particularly territorial account of sovereignty: the literal occupation of the land—the settling of the land—is necessary in order to claim control over it. But the second aspect of his claim is perhaps more surprising, because here Cromwell invokes the "Will of the Inhabitants" as an important aspect of sovereignty—that is, he suggests that land in the New World can be occupied justly only with the consent of native peoples.

Cromwell's argument is somewhat difficult to press on behalf of the English, given that scant evidence of the "will" of Native Americans, requesting English domination of their land, was extant. Here, accordingly, the body of the tortured Indian becomes particularly important: Cromwell argues that because the Spanish have tortured the Indians, and because the English have witnessed this torture, the English can safely impute to the (dead and silent) Indians a desire for English rule. It is to make this point that Las Casas's text is republished at this moment under the title *Tears of the Indians*. Published with woodcuts (not present in earlier original Spanish editions) depicting the physical torture of Native Americans by the Spanish, the book enables the English public to visually witness acts of torture and the genocidal violence of the Spanish (see figure 2.3). The invocation of a sympathetic relation to the scene of torture—registered in the "tears" of the new title of the book—suggests a new, affective relation between the reader and Indian victim not present in Las Casas's text—a text that, despite arguing forcefully against genocide, is nonetheless remarkably unsentimental in tone regarding the slaughter of Native American peoples.

In the *Declaration*, Cromwell not only invokes the cruelty experienced by Native Americans at the hands of the Spanish but also constructs a somewhat labyrinthine counterfactual scenario by which the murdered and absent Indian

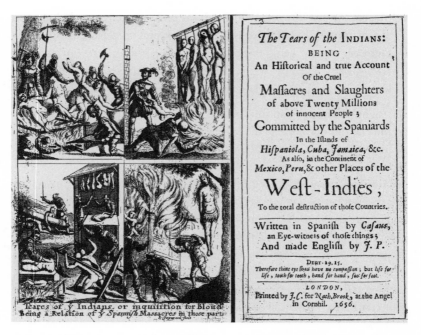

FIGURE 2.3. Frontispiece and title page of *The Tears of the Indians* (1656) with woodcuts of scenes of the torture of Indians that propagate the "Black Legend," concerning the cruel behavior of the Spaniards in the New World. This item is reproduced by permission of the Huntington Library, San Marino, California.

body becomes the sign of the native peoples' "consent" to English sovereignty in the New World. Specifically, Cromwell states that lands occupied by the English in the New World were empty when the English took possession of them because the Spaniards had already killed the Indians who had once lived there; however, Cromwell indicates, *if* the Indians had been living there, they would have welcomed English rule because it did not involve torture and cruelty, as did Spanish rule:

> Granting we had beat the *Spaniards* out of those places where we have planted our Colonies, out of which they had at first expell'd the Inhabitants, we should have possess'd them with better Right, as the Avengers of the Murder of that People, and of the Injuries sustain'd by them, than the *Spaniards*, their Oppressors and Murderers. But since we have settled our Colonies in such places as were neither possess'd by the Native nor the *Spaniards*, they having left behind them neither Houses nor Cattle, nor

any other thing that could by any means keep up the Right of Possession, the Justness of our Title to these Places was so much the more evident. (*Declaration*, 26)

Cromwell's lengthy, and seemingly unnecessary, conjectural aside in this passage—the English "should have possess'd [the land and people] with better Right" than the Spanish *if* Native Americans had been living there, but in the end did not because the land was uninhabited in any case—suggests, again, something of a tension around the figure of the tortured Indian who both needs to be present rhetorically (as we have seen, murdered Indians are invoked repeatedly in the *Declaration*) and yet, factually and logically, is not called for. The tortured Indian is conjured for the sake of counterfactual argument (to elaborate the implied "if" of Cromwell's sentence), but in the repetition and centrality of the tortured Indian body in political discourse, it is nonetheless evident that staging this tortured body is quite important to the new imperial logic of English sovereignty.

Something crucial inheres, then, in the triadic structure of encounter that Cromwell sets forth in the *Declaration*—that of cruel Spaniard, mute and mutilated Indian, and justly sovereign Englishman. This triadic structure and its political force are in full view both in D'Avenant's letter to Thurloe and in *The Cruelty of the Spaniards in Peru*. Indeed, D'Avenant's masque might be understood as, in essence, a full-scale elaboration of the fantasmatic trio Cromwell convokes in the *Declaration* of Spaniard, Englishman, and tortured New World Indian.[31] The conjunction of a defense of the theatre for the education of a newly empowered public and the articulation of a novel logic of imperial sovereignty in the New World that appears so forcefully in D'Avenant's work at this point indicates a relation between a politics of the inside and a politics of the outside—a connection between the radically new internal politics of English sovereignty in the absence of absolutist monarchy and the external politics of imperialism and colonialism in the war with Spain over sovereignty in the Americas. In other words, D'Avenant's insistent conjunction of the politics of republican theatre and representations of the New World points to a relation that is not simply incidental but rather structural in nature: a theatre that generates public consent for state authority and the politics of a new imperialism each help to elaborate, instantiate, and give meaning to the other. The novel account of imperial sovereignty on view in *The Cruelty of the Spaniards in Peru* is one that organizes a new public *within* England while authorizing the pursuit of colonialism *outside* of England.[32] The shift from a religious and dynastic imperial policy to one based on nationalism requires an articulation of Englishness that relies, as we will see at further length below, on sentient and affective modes of representation: *cruelty* thus becomes a key term for articulating a humanity that is associated with sentient nationalism. The tortured Indian prince—the colonial relation—at the center of D'Avenant's masque *The Cruelty of the Spaniards in Peru* is thus not only at the center of a new imperial policy, but at the center of the concept of public embodiment and public consent that the theatre enacts in relation to English republicanism. It is perhaps not overreaching to propose, then, that the tortured Indian—seemingly unnecessary, gratuitous, in excess of the logic of sovereignty—is the condensed sign of political modernity.

THE DESIGN OF *CRUELTY*

The innovation of D'Avenant's public masque *The Cruelty of the Spaniards in Peru* is twofold: first, D'Avenant's masque performs the creation of a people—an English people, who are themselves the audience for the performance of the torture of Indians. Second, the creation of this English people—of a performative commons—is achieved not by words but by way of scenic movement, the effects of which can be charted in sensate and surprisingly physical, even geographical, terms. The people take shape, then, in relation to a shared sensorium. *The Cruelty of the Spaniards in Peru* was performed at the Cockpit Theatre in Drury Lane in London in 1658 for a public audience who likely held printed copies of the libretto in hand when they entered the theatre.[33] The libretto helpfully contained not just the words to songs, but the explicit "argument" of each scene presented in the masque. The performance itself was a generically hybrid combination of masque and opera, consisting of six scenes depicting the Inca of Peru, who are represented as a chorus of dancers, singers, and acrobats surrounding the central figure of the Sun Priest. Over the course of the performance, the peaceful kingdom of the Inca is disrupted by internal strife and the arrival of the Spanish, who are initially welcomed as gods, but are subsequently revealed to be cruel and inhuman. In the second half of the performance, English troops arrive and drive away the Spanish; the Inca then welcome the English as their rulers and peace is restored. Notably, there are no individual characters in the masque other than the Inca Sun Priest; the Sun Priest narrates the action of the masque in declamatory speeches in each scene, but the central activity of each scene involves the singing of the chorus (who are Inca), the depiction of the actions of the English and the Spaniards, and a certain amount of ludic activity in the form of dancing apes and somersaulting attendants to the Sun Priest. Accordingly, narrative is not a pronounced element of the performance, nor is dialogue or speech a major component of the masque.

Rather than inhering in dialogue and narrative development, then, much of the meaning of the masque is located in the unfolding of the scenery itself. D'Avenant debuted the use of perspectival scenery (translated from the court masque) in the public theatre in his production of the *Siege of Rhodes*, presented both at Rutland House (D'Avenant's home) and at the Cockpit Theatre in 1656.[34] The production of *The Cruelty of the Spaniards in Peru* used similar scenery and thus participated in the novelty of D'Avenant's theatrical techniques—techniques that were later given more enduring institutional form during the Restoration with the opening of D'Avenant's royal patent theatre at Lincoln's Inn Fields. As the libretto of *The Cruelty of the Spaniards of Peru* makes clear, the "argument" of each scene can be discerned in the scenery and the argument of the masque as a whole is visible in the procession of scenes rather than the specific action within the scenes. Indeed, the title of the libretto—*The Cruelty of the Spaniards in Peru: Expressed by Instrumental and Vocal Music, and by Art of Perspectives in Scenes, &c.*—underscores the centrality of the new scenery to the masque as a whole.[35]

The first page of the libretto introduces another innovation—namely, a nomenclature that, borrowing from the court masque, refers to the portions of the performance as a series of "entries" rather than "scenes." Specifically, on the first page of the libretto, D'Avenant gives a summary account of the "Argument of the Whole Design, Consisting of Six Entries," which explains that the masque unfolds as a series of "discoveries": initially the "happy condition of the people of Peru anciently" is represented; subsequently, dissension within their kingdom is "discovered"; the conquest of the Inca by the Spaniards and the cruelty of the Spaniards are "discovered"; and finally the arrival of the English is "inferred," after which the Inca are "freed from the yoke of the Spanish" (*Cruelty*, 243). The presentation of the masque as a series of "entries" rather than static "scenes" introduces a rhetoric of movement into the performance. And the language of "discovery" reinforces a sense of movement and mobility that is significant with respect both to the new theatre D'Avenant creates (given the centrality of moveable scenery and discovery scenes therein) as well as to the debate over imperial sovereignty in the New World (as is evident in Cromwell's *Declaration*). Indeed, the "Whole Design" of the masque ultimately presents a redemptive imperial logic that rewrites the failure of Cromwell's Western Design as a success.

As Julie Stone Peters points out, the effect of perspectival scenery is to locate the audience in a spatial (albeit virtual) fashion: "Unified perspective entailed, ideally, perfect control of the gaze of the spectator. The perspective scene was to amaze, to enrapture, to conquer. . . . Rather than the spectator creating the scene (focusing on one house or another), the scene created the position of the 'astonished and entranced' spectator."[36] The mirroring spatial and geographical effects of the performance are thus complex and intriguing: as the English troops on stage justly conquer the New World and its peoples, rightfully setting them free from Spanish cruelty, so too is the audience "conquered" or controlled as it is led from one scene to the next, in a processional fashion, toward the moment of being set "free" at the close of the masque. This moment of freedom entails consent to the performance, a consent that accepts the constructed nature of the drama as the truth of discovery—as the experiential knowledge of the sovereign subject. As D'Avenant would later write to Charles II, describing the effects of moveable scenery in his dramatic productions, the audience's expectations become "entangled" in the procession of scenes, "But not so long, as never to *get free*."[37] At the close of the masque, the English audience sitting in the Cockpit Theatre has gotten "free" in its clear knowledge of the righteousness of humane, sympathetic Englishness, and so too have the New World and its people gotten "free" (on stage) in their consent to English rule.

A closer look at the procession of the scenes indicates exactly how this embodied, territorial argument unfolds on stage and for the audience. The first "entry" is framed, according to the libretto, by a ceremonial arch, crowned with the shield of Peru, but bordered on either side by the competing shields of the Spanish and the Inca. The pastoral contentment of the Inca is conveyed in the scene by the declamations of the Sun Priest, a "rustic air," and the pas de deux of two apes, dancing and leaping around a rope that has descended from the clouds. In the second through fourth entries, the Spanish arrive, exploit tensions within the Inca empire, and conquer the Inca. Although the arrival of the Spanish is portrayed as a sorrowful interruption of the previously peaceful idyll, the Spanish are initially accorded a martial aura that subdues the Inca; in the fifth entry, however, the tone shifts significantly when the Spanish are revealed to be cruel and inhuman rather than awe inspiring in their might. This entry begins with the scenic "discovery" of the Spanish cruelty and constitutes the fulcrum of the masque's argument.

The libretto's description of the scenery for the entry states:

> A doleful pavane is played to prepare the change of scene, which represents a dark prison at great distance; and farther to the view are discerned racks and other engines of torment, with which the Spaniards are tormenting the natives and English mariners, which may be supposed to be lately landed there to discover the coast. Two Spaniards are likewise discovered, sitting in

their cloaks and appearing more solemn in ruffs, with rapiers and daggers by their sides; the one turning a spit, whilst the other is basting an Indian prince, which is roasted at an artificial fire. (*Cruelty*, 255)

D'Avenant's staging here follows closely the lines of Cromwell's argument in the *Declaration*—like Cromwell, D'Avenant initially introduces the specter of Spaniards torturing Englishmen, but subsequently represents, with far more substance and flourish, the Spanish torture of Native Americans. While English mariners are tortured in the background of this scene, the sight of two Spaniards roasting an Indian prince on a spit assumes center stage. Like Cromwell, then, D'Avenant relies on the tortured body of the Indian to indicate the justness of the English presence in the New World: only the act of witnessing Spanish cruelty generates the identity of the Englishman as rightful occupant of the New World. *compared 2*

Significantly, the word "discover" appears twice in this brief account of the scene: first, the reader is told that the English have landed to discover the coast, and in the next sentence, two Spaniards are "likewise" discovered in the act of torturing an Indian. The similarity imputed to the two discoveries with the term "likewise" elides the fact that these discoveries are of utterly different orders: the discovery of the New World is a legal act, according to the Spanish, but in D'Avenant's passage, this (putatively) legal discovery is displaced by the revelation or *discovery* of Spanish inhuman cruelty. The second discovery is not of a legal nature but constitutes experiential, affective knowledge, a point that is reinforced later in the masque when the Sun Priest addresses an apostrophe to the personified figure "Experience," in which he praises the knowledge of Spanish perfidy that Experience has revealed: "Experience now (by whose true eyes, though slow,/We find at last, what oft too late we know)/Has all [the Spaniards'] cozening miracles discerned:/'Tis she that makes unlettered mankind learned" (*Cruelty*, 258). And indeed, here again we see the spinning out of a Cromwellian logic of territorial sovereignty: it is not the discovery of the New World by the Spanish that is the basis for authority, but their inhumane behavior; and it is the contrastingly humane behavior of the English that legitimates their own possession of the land. The Spanish destroy the "people"; the English generate a "people" in the New World. Once the cruelty of the Spanish to the natives is "discovered," the Spanish "discovery" of the New World becomes nugatory, a "ludicrous title" to territorial sovereignty.

The torture scene, at the center of the masque, thus makes visible the just nature of the English in contrast to the Spaniards' inherent unfitness for rule. The sixth entry, accordingly, reveals the logical conclusion of the previous scenic "arguments": namely, that the English should, by all rights, possess the New World. The sixth entry represents, then, the rout of the Spanish from Peru by English forces. As D'Avenant feels compelled to note, however, this is a counterfactual scenario, given that the English never arrived in Peru while the Spaniards were there. Again, just as Cromwell has done in the *Declaration*, so too does D'Avenant in the masque conjure a fantasmatic encounter of the trio of Spaniard, Indian, and Englishman. But D'Avenant offers an explanatory note in the libretto for the appearance of this counterfactual scenario: "These imaginary [English military] forces may seem improper, because the English had made no discovery of Peru in the time of the Spaniards' first invasion there; but yet in poetical representations of this nature, it may pass as a vision discerned by the Priest of the Sun before the matter was extant, in order to his prophecy" (*Cruelty*, 258). D'Avenant here acknowledges that it may be historically incorrect to represent a scene in which Spanish, English, and Inca simultaneously inhabit Peru, but he defends his license to do so on the grounds that the scenario represents a vision of the future by the Sun Priest. Even given this defense, however, D'Avenant's argument is strange because of the temporality invoked at the close of his sentence: the Sun Priest, D'Avenant states, had the vision of Spaniards, Englishmen, and Inca assembled together "before the matter was extant." This phrasing implies that the "matter" later became extant, when in fact, the future prophesied in the vision has already not come to pass—that is, the English have not routed the Spanish from Peru and have, indeed, already failed to do so.

Like Cromwell (again), D'Avenant is thus not prophesying the future, but rewriting the past in order to authorize a new future. As Cromwell's *Declaration* spelled out: *if* the English had arrived in the New World while the Spanish tortured and killed the Indians, the Indians *would have* invited the English to rule them—and this is precisely the scenario that unfolds in the final scenes of D'Avenant's masque. In the last entry of the masque, the English put the Spanish to flight, and the Peruvians invite the English to join them for a feast, proclaiming that the English "shall sit and rule as our guests" (*Cruelty*, 260). Set free from the Spaniards, the Indians on stage invite English rule, thus enacting the justness of English territorial sovereignty in the New World. Notably, this is not a providential vision of English occupation of the New World: it is not the discovery of God's will that mobilizes bodies and justice in the masque; rather, the discovery of Spanish cruelty and English sympathy in relation to the mutilated Indian body legitimates English sovereignty. Although it is technically a prophecy—the Sun Priest's "vision"—that reveals the scene of the English military defeat of the Spanish in Peru, the masque suggests that it is a natural order that reveals itself (is "discovered") in the New World. The knowledge that is revealed is thus cast as decidedly experiential: imperialism, here, discovers the English people to themselves, and prophecy (divine knowledge) is recast as experiential, embodied, sensate, territorial knowledge. And indeed, this is precisely what the formal aspects of D'Avenant's theatre have enabled for the public audience sitting in the Cockpit Theatre—an embodied knowledge that is the result of territorial transportation, achieved virtually through perspectival, moveable scenery and the technologies of the court masque transposed onto the public stage.

TORTURE AND CONSENT

The specificity of the Englishness that is at issue in the new public theatre is crucial to understanding the stakes of New World drama in London: the public theatre is the site of consent—consent among the spectators to the framing of a shared experiential reality and, in the context of England in the second half of the seventeenth century, political consent to the sovereignty of the state (be that the republic or, following the Restoration, the monarchy). Both D'Avenant, in his Hobbesian arguments for opening the public theatre under republican rule, and later Charles II, in his licensing of public theatre at the outset of the restoration of his (de facto if not de jure) no longer absolute monarchy, understood the theatre as the site where the will of the public—and specifically the *consent* of the public—might be enacted. Thus, one might say that the Englishness at stake in the theatre involves the performance of a consent to state sovereignty. Moreover, D'Avenant's efforts to reconfigure the masque from a monarchical to a republican form, and his persistent emphasis on theatricalizing torture therein, suggest that popular sovereignty bears some relation to empire that is figured through scenes of torture. Theorists have argued that torture is the signal instrument of sovereign power: as Lisa Hajjar explains, torture is in part defined by the fact that "the body of the tortured must be ritually marked and publicly displayed so that it can function as a symbol of the crime and the power of the king to punish."[38] Yet when the locus of sovereignty shifts from the king to the people, torture seemingly becomes an instrument of the past: when the subject is sovereign, the rack, the wheel, and the gibbet fall into desuetude. Or so it would appear if one did not look to the stage in a place such as London.

Why the need for *staged* torture in the theatre of popular sovereignty? According to Paul Kahn, torture may be rendered obsolete within the state when power shifts from the monarch to the people; however, the sovereign power exercised by the people takes the form of the violent inscription of authority exercised against the (non-)subject who is external to the state—namely, the foreigner or alien. Moreover, the specific condition under which such sovereignty is exercised arises in relation to the threat to the nation itself: torture of the alien is justifiable to defend the people of the nation and reciprocally, the national subject must be susceptible to enduring torture in the name of the people. Accordingly, under the conditions of political modernity in the postabsolutist state, writes Kahn, "circumstances are [always] imaginable in which the polity can make a demand on my life and can demand that I take the lives of others. . . . The source of that demand is exactly what we mean by sovereignty. Imagining that moment of action is the founding point of the social imaginary of the political; . . . it connects the individual citizen to the transtemporal, collective subject that is the popular sovereign."[39] The scene of torture—when the citizen is called on to commit violence in the name of the sovereign or to suffer violence in the name of the sovereign—is thus pinpointed here as the "founding point of the social imaginary" of a modern politics of popular sovereignty.

Two aspects of Kahn's account of torture and popular sovereignty are worth underscoring here: first, popular sovereignty does not render torture obsolete so much as displace it from the inside of the polity to the outside. The king no longer marks his sovereignty by way of acts of torture on the body of his subjects; rather, the sovereign (popular) subject performs torture on the body of the alien who threatens the sovereignty of the state with his/her lack of consent to its authority. Torture thus takes place at the limits of national belonging, and specifically, in imperial spaces where contests over territorial sovereignty are played out. Second, the tortured individual—the individual who suffers excessive pain in the name of the sovereign—thereby performs his or her connection to (in Kahn's words) the "collective subject that is the popular sovereign." The tortured Englishman in Amboyna performs the belonging of Englishmen in the East Indies to popular sovereignty; the tortured Indian in Peru performs his potential consent to English popular sovereignty and thus to the English occupation of the New World. As Talal Asad points out, torture is, by definition, the infliction of *cruel* and *inhuman* pain.[40] Understanding the pain inflicted on a body as torture (as excessive and cruel rather than acceptable) involves extending human and sympathetic identification to the tortured body. The tortured body, as it suffers, performs its human status and its belonging to sovereignty. It is this tortured body that appears on stage as a figure of liminal and/or contested English sovereignty: to the extent that the audience identifies with and affectively claims the tortured body before it, popular sovereignty is enacted in the theatre.

Kahn's formulation concerning the relation between the torture of the threatening alien and the founding of the social imaginary of popular sovereignty offers new insight into the publication and circulation of pamphlets concerning Amboyna and the Black Legend in the 1650s as well as the political force of staging torture at the public theatre. In 1652, for instance, an inflammatory pamphlet appeared concerning the Amboyna massacre of 1623 (the full title of which gives a sense of its content and general import): *A Memento for Holland: or A true and exact history of the most villainous and barbarous cruelties used on the English merchants residing at Amboyna in the East-Indies, by the Netherland governor and conncel [sic] there. Wherein is shewed what tortures were used to make them confess a conspiracy they were never guilty of; by putting them on the rack, and by a water torture, to suffocate them; and by burning them under their arm pits, and soals of their feet, till their fat by dropping extinguished the candles* (see figure 2.2). As noted, this inflammatory pamphlet was printed thirty years after the events it describes, and it is this scene of torture that D'Avenant cites in his *Proposition* concerning the need for public theatre in England; as such, a new mobilization of torture is evidently at stake that bears a relation to the new republican and imperial politics forged by Cromwell and spectacularized by D'Avenant.

Featuring woodcuts of tortured Englishmen (see figure 2.2), the pamphlet decried the perfidy and cruelty of the Dutch in the East Indies and specifically compared the Dutch to the Spaniards in the New World: the tortured body of one Englishman is described as "a perfect Embleme of the Spaniards cruelty to the poor Indians; for they used not them with more cruelty, then [sic] the Dutch did our poor English Merchants."[41] Interestingly, then, the pamphlet directly associates empire and torture in the East Indies with empire and torture in the West Indies, both of which serve to justify English imperial aggression against European enemies by way of sympathetic identification with Englishness. This association is given further substance in a second pamphlet published in 1653 titled *The Second Part of the Tragedy of Amboyna: or, A True Relation of a Most Bloody, Treacherous, and Cruel Design of the Dutch in the New-Netherlands in America. For the Total Ruining and Murthering of the English Colonies in New-England.* This pamphlet reports that the Dutch had recently armed Native Americans to attack English settlers in New England, but the English were alerted to the plot by a Native American informant and were able to disarm the Native Americans and extract confessions from them of the Dutch conspiracy. Both pamphlets have recourse to spectacular logic: in the first, woodcuts of torture are used on the title page; and in the second, the title of the pamphlet itself describes the unfolding of events as a theatrical drama—namely, a "tragedy" with two acts—one of which occurred in the East Indies and the second in the West Indies.[42]

The insistent conflation of the Spanish torture of the Indians and the Dutch torture of the English is, at first glance, puzzling (particularly given that the Indians are on the Dutch side in the second instance). Although Spain was, at the time, the longtime Catholic enemy of Protestant England, the Dutch, as Protestants and republicans, were historically allies of the English against the Spanish. Conflating the Dutch and the Spanish in order to attack their right to imperial sovereignty thus requires a shift to a new, nonreligiously oriented logic of sovereignty—a move consistent with a Westphalian territorial order.[43] The scene of torture, spectacularized in pamphlets concerning Amboyna and the New World, thus assists in articulating a new order of sovereignty within and without England. The scene of sovereign violence (and the threat to the English nation that is trumpeted, for instance, in the title of the 1653 pamphlet that describes the Dutch effort to effect "*the Total Ruining and Murthering of the English Colonies*" in New England) in these productions thus displays (to cite Kahn's words) "the founding point of the social imaginary of the political" in such as way as to "connec[t] the individual citizen to the transtemporal, collective subject that is the popular sovereign." In 1653, the pamphlet describing the Amboyna massacre as a tragedy with two acts was printed in London; in the same year, D'Avenant proposed that the display of "acts of Cruelty (like that in Amboyna)" were the ideal subject for dramatic representation at the republican theatre. With regard to popular sovereignty, then, we can see how the scene of torture functions to enroll the audience, as D'Avenant claims in the *Proposition*, in "a quiet and cheerefull behaviour towards the present Governement"—that is, scenes of torture garner consent to the conditions of English sovereignty and imaginatively extend that sovereignty, in a seemingly consensual and compassionate form, to New World climes.[44] The perverse codependence of English popular sovereignty and imperialism—specifically, settler colonialism in America—is thus displayed in the staged figure of the colonial relation: namely, the tortured Indian prince.

THE EMBODIED PUBLIC SPHERE AND THE POLITICS OF SENSATION

If the tortured Indian prince on stage in London enables or calls forth the enactment of audience "consent" to the English state—as I have argued above—then one might ask precisely what kind of consent is at issue. To what extent is the act of sitting in a theatre seat—or even the more substantive act of buying a theatre ticket and then occupying a theatre seat for the duration of a performance—tantamount to actively consenting to a political order? In fact, might not the experience of being "conquered" by the moveable, perspectival scenery of D'Avenant's masque be more accurately described as submitting to coercion than demonstrating consent? Critics Jacob and Raylor argue that D'Avenant's proposal for using the theatre for moral education strays significantly from the educational aims it espouses; rather, they suggest, D'Avenant views the sensory effects of the theatre as particularly effective means of subduing and controlling the public—not of educating them in order that they might make informed decisions. Unlike Hobbes, they argue, who viewed education as useful for the development of rational thought, D'Avenant emphasized the sensory impact of the theatre in terms unrelated to the exercise of reason: "In D'Avenant's sinister combination of Hobbism and humanism," they conclude, "the common people were little more than engines, incapable of choice or rational behaviour, and determined entirely by the impact of sensory experiences."[45]

The comparison with Hobbes, however, is perhaps less decisive than Jacob and Raylor suggest, particularly with respect to the question of consent. In Hobbes's formulation, sovereignty from below is not incompatible with absolute monarchy because once the people have consented to enter into the civil state in order to escape the life-threatening anarchy of the state of nature, they also consent to be ruled by the sovereign who represents them, and they forfeit the right to rebel. How, then, is the crucial consent of the people registered or enacted according to Hobbes? As A. Zaitchik argues, consent in Hobbes's philosophy is of a historical-fictive nature: that is, consent has always occurred at some time in the past, prior to the subject's entry into the state (*before* the law), but this consent remains valid because it can (in the present) be verified as rationally called for by the narrative of man's political development. Zaitchik explains that according to Hobbes,

A person in the state of nature would rationally agree to abide by the laws of nature, whenever so doing would enhance his chances for survival. A sequence of rational undertakings on the part of small groups of such individuals would result in confederations. As the value of such confederations becomes more obvious . . . people will, eventually, decide upon a general, mutual abdication of rights and erect one civil power (or sovereign) vested with absolute power and authority. Thus the civil state could or would, in time, result (in this fictitious story of rational decisions) from the state of nature. Any civil society that meets this condition of "possible, rational genesis"—and indeed, any civil society with a strong sovereign *will* meet this condition according to Hobbes—has a legitimate claim on its subjects' obligation. It does not matter that the sovereign power was not, historically, set up through covenant; the point is that (rationally) it could have been.[46]

Zaitchik's characterization of Hobbes's account of consent as a "fictitious story of rational decisions" seems particularly apt and resonant with respect to the similarities between consent in Hobbes and D'Avenant. Although Hobbes emphasized that reason should be cultivated among the people of the state, he did not do so in order that people could hone their capacity for judgment of the sovereign; rather, as Zaitchik's account makes clear, he did so in order that people could agree that the "fictitious story" of a possible past covenant was a reasonable one. Reason, for Hobbes, is necessary to verify a fiction of prior consent. Both D'Avenant and Hobbes construct consent as the act of agreeing to a fiction of the justness of state sovereignty, not consenting to a given ruler.[47]

A Habermasian account of the postabsolutist public sphere emphasizes that reason is the guiding force of critical debate, and thus the guiding force of the power exercised by the public over and against the state. Rational, critical debate of the sort Habermas describes as occurring in print and at coffeehouses in the eighteenth century did not occur at the theatre. Nonetheless, forms of consensus and dissensus were played out in the performative commons convened at the theatre. A number of theorists and historians have argued that theatre had a role in the emergence of the public sphere in England. Paula Backscheider, for instance, argues that "the drama of the Restoration illustrates the transformation of the people's conception of their duty as citizens from acting with 'public spirit'... to being 'public opinion,' that is, adding responsibility for participating in an evaluative process (a 'civic task' characterized by debate). Thus, in these early [Restoration] performances we can find evidence of the beginning of the conception of Habermas's public sphere."[48] Backscheider thus emphasizes the shift in the meaning of the gathered public—from the passive embodiment of "public spirit" to the more active embodiment of "public opinion." As Peter Lake and Steven Pincus argue, a revaluation of public opinion and the political use of appeals to the people ("popularity") occurred in the 1640s and 1650s such that "public opinion" became a recognized and increasingly legitimate source of political authority, and contenders for authority sought to court and create opinion in their favor.[49] In what sense, however, did debate and deliberation occur at the theatre—a theatre where the activity of the audience was more often described in physical terms (applause, laughter, tears, uproar, riot) related to sensation than in terms related to language and ratiocination? And if public opinion wielded new political power in the period following the English Civil War, in what sense did the theatre enable the people gathered there to express their political views?

As Jeffrey Alexander points out, the way in which theatre functions as a space of civic debate is quite different from the way that print does. Alexander argues that theatre has the capacity to fuse knowledge and power, thus generating a collective sense of consent to the structure of meaning that informs a given understanding of the world.[50] Erving Goffman's reflections on frame analysis and theatre are useful here as well: according to Goffman, the theatergoer is a *participant* in the frame presented by theatrical performance, whereas the reader of a text is an onlooker. Goffman writes, "Each person who is a theatergoer is something else, too. He collaborates in the unreality onstage. He sympathetically and vicariously participates in the unreal world generated by the dramatic interplay of the scripted characters. He gives himself over."[51] Whereas a reader stands outside of the frame of a text passing judgment about the nature of what occurs within that frame, the audience member at the theatre is implicated as a collaborator—his or her response belongs *within* the frame of the theatre. As Alexander points out, however, agreement on a set of background categories that inform a given performance is never quite assured. In the most successful theatrical performance, disagreement over fundamental categories fades out of sight: the successful theatrical performance persuades an audience to participate in a given set of political and cultural assumptions "without thinking about it," thereby "fusing" knowledge and power. In this sense, theatre is the site of consent or ratification, albeit a consent that is implicit rather than explicit: the audience consents to participate in a frame of meaning that enables the performance to make sense. The public that is formed in relation to the theatre, then, is not organized around rationally articulated propositional content, as is the case in the Habermasian public sphere, nor even in relation to an abstract sense of belonging, as is the case with Benedict Anderson's "imagined community" of the nation; rather, the public formed in the theatre is created through its material engagement in a shared frame or horizon of meaning making—in sharing a sensorium and the sensus communis embedded therein.

D'Avenant's account of republican theatre similarly indicates that public knowledge might be articulated in terms that are not primarily rational and propositional—terms that involve not a debate about specific proposals or actions, but a debate about the premises of knowledge, meaning, and public identity that occur in the field of frame alignment. The "consent" described by both D'Avenant and Hobbes thus concerns an alignment of meaning that involves accepting the premise of a fictive political origin rather than, say, enacting a plebiscite on behalf of an individual or a policy. Frame alignment, then, occurs at a level that is embodied and sensory—lived and experienced—rather than argued in a Habermasian sense.

In his proposal for an educational theatre, D'Avenant points to the disjunction between speculative argument and experience: he suggests that the theatre will reform "*Morality*: not *speculative Morality*, but that which is active and brought home to the senses."[52] And indeed, in a lengthier passage from the same document, D'Avenant comments on the extent to which sensory experience—rather than ratiocination—is a defining aspect of the education he imagines that the theatre will impart to the audience:

> And we are to consider, that the generality of mankinde are solely instructed by their senses, and by immediate impressions of particular objects, never vexing their heads with reviews and subtle examinations; and are so much the sooner gain'd, by how much the first representations are either more illustrious or charming; whether this be by the Eye or Eare, wants not its severall effects; it being in the most refin'd and Æthereal Spirits a curiosity and desire of knowledge; in common soules, an abject admiration: For as great *Buildings*, fair *Pictures*, *Statues*, and *Medals*, intice the *Virtuosi*, so *Triumphs*, *Pageants*, *Caualcades*, or any thing new, brings the common people about them. What is hitherto said, infers, that since there hath not been found a perfect meanes to retain the people in quiet (they being naturally passionate and turbulent, and yet reducible) and that Perswasion must be joyn'd to Force, it can be compass'd no other way then by surprisall of their Eyes and Ears. The people will ever be unquiet whilst they are ignorant of themselves, and unacquainted with those Engins that scrue them up, which are their passions, in true characters of the beauties and deformities of vertue and vice.[53]

On the one hand, this passage seems to suggest that a form of sensory propaganda might be the best means of pacifying the lower classes, who are not susceptible to higher forms of argument or knowledge. On the other hand, D'Avenant does insist that this is a form of education rather than simply containment: the theatre, he suggests, gives people genuine knowledge of themselves (knowledge of "those Engins that scrue them up") that assists in creating public order. This second line of argument comes much closer to that of Hobbes: it is knowledge that allows people to consent or to imagine that they would consent or have already consented to government. Importantly, this argument concerning consent is not rational and linguistic, but is a matter of sensory experience, of coming to believe the premises that frame our knowledge, that register experience as knowledge.

From 1649 forward, the collective body of the English people had new political meaning, and the public theatre was a place for this body to take both ontic and mimetic shape—that is, to gather physically and to engage in recursive modes of self-representation and self-understanding.[54] The audience thus stands in a particular relation to the "framing" or supralinguistic argument at the public theatre: when the audience consents to a performance or a framing of meaning, they are, in part, consenting to the construction of an image of themselves as a public. That is, they are consenting to participate in a certain framing of reality, and, in doing so, they are also performing themselves as a public. The "consent" of the audience thus has a performative dimension that is politically significant: the audience is a public whose primary political act at the theatre is to enact its own self-constitution in relation to the framing of meaning that is occurring on the stage. Although critics have viewed the theatre as the place where political debate, or training in political debate, occurred, a key aspect of understanding the functioning of the performative commons in the theatre concerns what we might call the aesthetics of consent: that is, the way in which sensation and embodiment themselves become ways of being in the world, and ways of political being in the world insofar as these bodies form collectivities with boundaries that determine the parceling out of subjectivity-citizenship and its other.

CHARLES II AT THE THEATRE

When Charles II assumed the throne in 1660 following the Interregnum, the British monarchy was restored, and the public theatre was fully reopened following nearly two decades of closure under Puritan rule. The restoration of the monarchy thus inaugurated a new theatrical as well as political era in England; however, given the increased authority of Parliament and twenty years of Cromwellian rule, the monarchy that was reinstalled was not that which had been deposed, nor was the theatre that was restored that which had occupied stages previously. Two notable differences between pre-Interregnum public theatre and Restoration-era public theatre include the introduction of moveable scenery and the introduction of female actors. And it is significant that both of these innovations involve importing techniques from the court masque to the public stage: for this reason, one might argue that the genres of court drama and public stage performance that D'Avenant merged in the waning days of Cromwell's rule took root and came to define the theatre of the Restoration.

Charles II issued two licenses to open public royal theaters when he resumed the throne: one to Thomas Killigrew, who formed the King's Company, and a second to William D'Avenant, who formed the Duke of York's Company. In each of the two theatres, the king retained a royal box located centrally for the display of his person. However, the theatrical audience—despite the presence of the king—at Lincoln's Inn or Drury Lane was decidedly not the court of James I or Charles I, before whom the masques of Ben Jonson and Inigo Jones had appeared. Although the audiences at the patent theatres were relatively elite, the political geography of the theatre was utterly transformed: no longer the scene of the homogenous mapping and display of royal authority, the theatre became a space in which the *argument* for royal authority was waged and in which the public staged itself as a public. As such, Restoration theatre remained an important scene of popular sovereignty, despite the restoration of Charles II to the throne.

Charles II labored mightily to harness spectacle as an element of royal power in the elaborate staging of his own entry into London in 1660 as well as in his two-day coronation ceremony there in 1661: intent on dramatizing his royal status before the public by every means possible, the king rejected the allocated sum of £70,000 as inadequate for his coronation. As Paula Backscheider explains, "Charles II intended public spectacles to perform a number of functions. Above all, he wanted to reinscribe the monarchy on his country."[55] The theatre as well as the street was targeted by Charles II as the site of royal spectacle according to Susan Owen: "The Restoration of the theatre together with the king was to be a symbol of the rejection of the 'puritan' regime of interregnum. Charles saw the drama as a political instrument: from the first he was actively engaged in discussing with the dramatists what they should write, and with the theatre management what should and should not be staged." But, as Owen and others conclude, the theatre ultimately became more a scene of "contradiction" than a display of royal power: "The dramatists address a politically divided audience, and they seek to *persuade*, not just to celebrate a monolithic absolutism."[56]

The reason for this contradiction lay not simply in a politically divided audience, but in the fact that Charles II faced a fundamental antithesis concerning the nature of political authority when he returned to claim the English throne after the rule of Cromwell's republic: on the one hand, Charles II was asserting the return of a dynastic and absolutist order; on the other hand, he was doing so in accordance with the will of the people. In effect, the location of authority—*either* in the will of the people *or* in divine right—was no longer clear, and Charles II sought to assert his authority in the mutually exclusive terrain of both logics. Jonathan Sawday argues that the restored monarch thus faced a "symbolic crisis of representation":

It was now not enough merely to assert a constitutional claim to the throne rooted in the facts of historical succession. Instead, any claim had to be guaranteed via an appeal to that very body of public opinion which, in 1649, had either implicitly or explicitly sanctioned a replacement of the monarch. Needless to say, the king was not to be considered a democratically chosen king, and yet the people had to *appear* to have had some voice in his assumption of royal power.[57]

As Sawday suggests, then, the appearance of the voice of the people suddenly had new political significance: indeed one might say that the will of the people had to simultaneously *appear* in order to sanction the new monarch and to *disappear* as the illegitimate (republican) basis of political authority. The monarchy clearly saw public spectacle and theatre as sites where such a simultaneous appearance and disappearance of public will might felicitously occur: public consent could be staged in a geography of amassed, applauding bodies while that consent was directed toward the newly reerected symbols of royal authority.

The self-conflicted argument about the nature of political authority under the restored monarchy was one that played out, then, in relation to theatrical performance and the physical, embodied geography of theatrical performance and spectacle. The consent of the public that the supporters of the Stuart monarchy sought was not one that could be articulated as anything resembling a plebiscite, but it might be performed as the sort of consent to which Goffman alludes in his account of audience "collaboration" and "consent" to dramatic performance. As such, audience consent would seem to resemble that which was generated by the court masque—a ritual-like participation in a frame of meaning that enabled the divine right of kings to "go without saying." But, unlike the court masque or ritual, in which a shared ontology was the basis for the elaboration of meaning, the performance of royal power with the aim of garnering public support was based on the notion that public support did not, in fact, go without saying and was thus not the basis for a shared ontology. As Nancy Maguire comments, "for the first time, those in power promoted a consciously contrived campaign to build a new monarchy and a new culture."[58]

Charles II clearly imagined that the theatre would serve as a site at which his authority was to be displayed and confirmed before the public audience, but the associative force of the public augured otherwise and opened the possibility a politics of "dissensus"—namely, a politics that interrupts consensus by "putting two worlds in one and the same world."[59] Despite the fact that the content of plays was censored by Charles II's court, the theatre served as a site for the articulation of a new political assemblage. As Odai Johnson argues, the logic of popular sovereignty—a resistance to the authority of divine kingship and the absolutism that Charles II and later James II sought to instantiate before the Glorious Revolution—was often acted out in performative terms, at both the royal theatre (in subdued tones) and in the streets (more overtly) in the form, most prominently, of mock pope-burning festivities: the "assertion of commonwealth rights" over those of divine kingship "is . . . mapped out not just rhetorically in Parliament, but performatively, in the theatres, and more efficaciously, on the streets of a city hostile to a Catholic succession. In this light, the Pope-Burning Processions become both performances of exclusion by dismantling popery and, in a larger context, rehearsals of the popular rebellion that was envisioned to come."[60] This popular mobilization, Johnson argues, effectively staged a revolution before the revolution: crowd performances in the street "rehearsed" the Glorious Revolution such that when it occurred, it was a matter of collective or common sense.

Although Johnson stresses the limited nature of the political content that was permitted to be performed on stage in the Restoration theatre, I would suggest that the "riotous assembly" that collected in the street to ritually torture the effigy of the pope was a version of the public that materialized in the theatre as well. The historian Thomas Macaulay comments, with respect to the "citizens of London [who] assembled by tens of thousands to burn the Pope in effigy," that 1680 was the "year . . . our tongue was enriched with two words, *Mob* and *Sham*, remarkable memorials of a season of tumult and imposture."[61] Both words have resonance with respect to theatricality as much as with respect to street festival and riot. In their 1884 dictionary, John Ogilvie and Charles Annandale describe the etymology and definition of "mob" as follows: "The *mobile vulgus* was first shortened to *the mobile* and then to *the mob*. . . . A crowd, especially a promiscuous multitude of people, rude, tumultuous, and disorderly; a rabble; a riotous assembly."[62] This assembled crowd—a mobile, promiscuous multitude—emerged as a political force and took up habitation in the English language in precisely this period. The status of the audience at the theatre, gathered and addressed as a public, hovered on the cusp between forming a promiscuous multitude and forming a people—between a disorderly and threatening amalgamation of bodies, and an ordered, coherent body of persons who consented to a shared frame of meaning. Historians have documented at some length the rise of public opinion, popular assembly, and crowd mobilization as factors in the run-up to the Glorious Revolution: I would argue that the conceptual and sensate force of public collectivity as an enunciation of popular sovereignty was put into play at the public theatre as well.[63]

Indeed, when Charles II sought to mobilize public opinion in favor of a war with the Netherlands—namely, the Second Anglo-Dutch War—the playwright John Dryden arguably assisted in this effort with the staging of the play *Indian Emperor* (1665), in which a Native American king, Montezuma, is tortured by the evil Spaniard Pizarro. As critics have demonstrated, a key source of Dryden's popular play was D'Avenant's *The Cruelty of Spaniards in Peru*.[64] Just as D'Avenant's scenes of theatrical torture were used to mobilize an English national identity that would underwrite Cromwell's hostilities against the Dutch, so too did Dryden's invocation of torture at the theatre serve to support Charles II as he launched a second war against the Dutch. This pattern of torture on stage in London, timed to correspond with Anglo-Dutch war for imperial power on the seas, was iterated a third time in 1673, when Dryden's new drama, *Amboyna*, appeared in the midst of the Third Anglo-Dutch War. Fueling English outrage at the Dutch, the play had recourse to the familiar scenes of the Dutch torture of the English at Amboyna. As Robert Markley argues with respect to Dryden's *Amboyna*, "it is in and through the spectacle of English merchants' being falsely accused of treason, tortured, and executed that English nationalism emerges."[65] While Dryden's panegyric to Charles II *Annus Mirabilis* praises the monarch, the poem is also known for its striking articulation of "benevolent imperialist fantasy"—one that Laura Brown identifies as laying the groundwork for eighteenth-century English imperial discourse.[66] Thus Dryden, like D'Avenant, uses the stage as a location in which imperialism and nationalism are coarticulated in such a way as to give new force and meaning to the English as a (benevolent, imperial) people.

Should the resonance of the historical link to D'Avenant's support of Cromwell's imperial policy be lost, we might note that Dryden used the same torture rack in *Amboyna* that had appeared on stage in D'Avenant's *Cruelty of the Spaniards in Peru*.[67] Moreover, the same actor, Michael Mahoun, who played the tortured Montezuma in Dryden's *Indian Emperor*, was assigned the lead role as English torture victim in *Amboyna*. Dryden's *Amboyna* clearly participates in a lengthy textual and performative chain of citations, rehearsing, once more, the history of English merchants tortured at the hands of the Dutch. And as Blair Hoxby argues, one effect of Dryden's *Amboyna* is thus "to make the viewers aware of themselves as a community bound by a common knowledge of Dutch perfidy. . . . In that capacity, the audience is expected not only to see but to feel; . . . the play feels like a ritual recreation meant to confirm a communal article of faith."[68] The communal article of faith here concerns the community itself: the feelings evoked here are those of the consent of the people, not those of reverence for divine monarchy. More importantly, a public is brought into being that has the capacity to recognize itself as a public by means of rituals articulated through nationalism and empire—a language that it has learned to speak and feel with the assistance of a long series of Amboyna spectacles and tortured Indian kings, both textual and theatrical. The recitation of this language—that of torture, empire, and English nationalism—was one that assisted in generating the very collectivity that Charles II and the absolutist who followed him, James II, sought unsuccessfully to eradicate. A performative commons—"the Commons of England [with] Supreme Power in [the] Nation"—was both fashioned and staged at the theatre.[69] An English people was shaped, together with new imperial and domestic politics, while gazing on the colonial relation.

CHAPTER 3

TRANSPORTATION

ATLANTIC CROSSINGS

Although there is some uncertainty as to what is historical fact and what is fictionalized biography, the playwright and novelist Aphra Behn evidently traveled to the English colony of Surinam in 1663, when her stepfather was appointed lieutenant governor there; in 1688, during the waning days of James II's rule, she published the novel *Oroonoko*, written on the basis of her experiences two decades earlier in Surinam.[1] In the opening pages of the novel, Behn's narrator describes the exotic flora and fauna of Surinam and asserts that she has brought feathers "whose tinctures are inconceivable" from Surinam back to England to serve as costumes for John Dryden's Indian plays. Accordingly, the feathers worn by the tortured Montezuma on stage in London in Dryden's *Indian Emperor* were quite possibly transported there from Surinam in Aphra Behn's hands.[2] Yet between the moment when Montezuma was strapped to the rack in Dryden's play in 1665 wearing Behn's feathers from Surinam, and the moment when Behn's revised and adapted Oroonoko was stretched out on the ground to be tortured in Thomas Southerne's play in 1695, much had changed with regard to English imperialism in the New World.[3] Like Montezuma, Oroonoko is a royal figure, but unlike Montezuma, he is not a native of America but has been transported there against his will for the purpose of providing slave labor to the English. The tortured Indian king served to politically and affectively perform English territorial sovereignty in the New World, assisting in the usurpation of land and advancing the logic of colonialism in England and America. The tortured African prince on stage in London engages in a different form of cultural work that is not unrelated but is nonetheless distinct. As Oroonoko literally and figuratively takes Montezuma's place on stage in performing as an American victim of torture, we see a substitution that registers a shift from a concern with colonization to one with racialization. Where the staged Indian king performs a political logic in consolidating territorial empire and English nationalism for London viewers, the royal slave performs an economically oriented role: not only a figure of tortured, liminal humanity, the royal slave is also a figure of labor. The slave body on stage thus registers another aspect of English imperialism that was increasingly at issue from the time of Cromwell's imperial Atlantic aggression forward—namely, the need for forced labor to power the growing, entwined systems of capitalism and British Atlantic colonialism. Further, as Oroonoko's racialized body is layered upon the colonial relation of the Indian king, we see an early instance of the "vanishing" of the Indian—an erasure of indigeneity that serves to underwrite the development of settler colonialism.

In this chapter, I turn, then, to a second colonial relation—namely, the enslaved African, transported to the New World and conscripted into an increasingly racialized Atlantic modernity. While the last chapter described the emergent politics of English popular sovereignty together with imperialism, in this chapter I trace the uneven career of British liberty as it crosses the Atlantic in the company of a developing system of race slavery. The need for intensive labor to extract profit from American colonies, and efforts to enforce people to perform that labor, brought into crisis a conflict between English liberty and colonialism—a conflict that was ultimately managed (albeit not erased) through the institution of race slavery. In the years following Charles II's restoration to the throne, then, the colonial relation takes a decisively new form, binding the metropole to the colony in increasingly significant and sustained economic terms and covering the terms of coercion and violence embedded in that relation by means of a racial segmentation of the labor force and humanity itself. If popular sovereignty gives power to the commons, capitalism—particularly on an Atlantic scale—involves privatization and enclosure, including the enclosure and theft of lands belonging to natives of America. In turn, the racial segmentation of humanity that takes shape as race slavery in the eighteenth-century Atlantic world must be considered a form of enclosure insofar as it excludes portions of the population from the real and virtual commons.

Looking to the theatre in the early eighteenth century, particularly during the ascendancy of Whig politician Sir Robert Walpole, it becomes clear that performative commoning has a revolutionary edge to it—one that stands in sustained tension with the privatizing aims of the new Whig economy, capitalism, and enclosure. As I argue in this chapter, the stunning success of John Gay's ballad opera *The Beggar's Opera* demonstrates the extent to which the theatre convened a virtual, performative commons just as the Whigs increasingly privatized the material commons with acts of enclosure. However, I also argue that the commoning force of theatrical performance operated in multiple directions, both displaying and enacting moments and modes of collectivization, and relying on "screen scenes" to stage the segmentation of the commons in racialized terms. In each case, however, the Atlantic dimensions of the commons were increasingly at stake on stage in London, and on the colonial stages to which British theatre was itself transported.

In the seventeenth century, the developing economic machinery of the Anglo-Atlantic world was one that violently impressed bodies—black, white, and Native American—into forms of unfree labor. From the 1640s forward, the English Atlantic suffered from an acute shortage of labor. Although slaves from Africa were a source of labor, in the early years of British colonialism, whites were often bound into servitude in New World locations to supply labor needs. Cromwell addressed the need for colonial labor by encouraging the growth of the slave trade with Africa, but also by forcibly transporting thousands of political enemies, criminals, paupers, and Irish Catholics to the New World as bound laborers. Yet, with labor-intensive crops such as sugar (introduced in Barbados in 1643) newly under cultivation in the Americas, the need for conscripted workers continued to increase.[4] Moreover, Cromwell's tactics drew considerable opprobrium and alarm. For instance, as Carla Gardina Pestana indicates, reports in England of enforced New World labor were so rampant that "soldiers impressed for the Western Design had initially feared that the purported military campaign was a hoax and that they were to be sold ... into slavery. That some may have been sold as laborers after surviving their grueling experiences in Hispaniola and in Jamaica suggests that these fears were based in a New World reality." In the streets of London, the word "barbados" became, at this time, a verb synonymous with kidnap.[5]

Cromwell's massive transportation of unwilling conscripts into forced New World labor brought to the fore the contradiction between English liberty and colonialism. While the English Revolution had been fought in the name of liberty from monarchical tyranny, the freedom of the people did not seem to be guaranteed under parliamentarian rule when Englishmen were subject to slavery in the New World. In a 1659 pamphlet addressed to Parliament, titled *Englands Slavery, or Barbados Merchandize*, two gentlemen reported their experience (and that of many others with them) of being kidnapped from their homes in England and sold into slavery in Barbados. They demanded that Parliament pass an act "to secure the free people of *England*, from this violent spiriting."[6] In the colonies as well as the metropole, management of the contradiction between the politics of English liberty and the demand for forced labor to fuel the development of capitalism in the colonies would ultimately lie in the racialization of slave labor (as black) and of liberty (as white).[7]

Barbados, where colonials became engaged in the enormously lucrative production of sugar, led the way in turning to Africa for slave labor. Before the introduction of sugar cultivation, the labor force in Barbados consisted primarily of white, British indentured servants. But beginning in 1650, this labor force was rapidly replaced with slaves transported from Africa.[8] Barbados passed its first comprehensive slave code in 1661, defining "Negroes" as "an heathenish brutish and an uncertain dangerous pride of people" over whom a new set of laws must be extended. "Surely in anything we may extend the legislative power given us of punishionary Laws for the benefit and good of this plantation," reasoned the preamble to the Barbados act, "not being contradictory to the Laws of England, there being in all the body of that Law no track to guide us where to walk nor any rule set us how to govern such Slaves." The code thus insisted that African slaves could not be governed by English law precisely because they were not English and thus not fully human: certainly they were not governable by the tenets of English law, nor were they rightful claimants to English liberty. The draconian terms of this code would, in turn, serve as the basis and authority for slave laws subsequently enacted in the colonies of Jamaica and South Carolina.[9]

The colonial relation thus changes form in the second half of the seventeenth century and the early eighteenth century as the relation between a domestic politics of liberty and an imperial geography of slavery takes shape. Whereas the seventeenth-century figure of the colonial relation—in the form of the tortured Indian—assisted with imagining Englishness as well as the English right to appropriate land from Native Americans, the eighteenth-century colonial relation—in the form of the royal slave—provided the labor needed to extract value from New World lands. Through a developing discourse of racialization, the colonial relation mediates the contradiction between political liberty and enforced race slavery that structures the politics and economics of colonialism and the emergent capitalist system of the Atlantic world. As Robin Blackburn points out, "in the period 1630–1750 the British Empire witnessed an increasingly clamorous, and even obsessive 'egotistical' revulsion against [political] 'slavery' side by side with an almost uncontested exploitation of African bondage."[10]

The signal contradiction of the colonial relation, moreover, lies not simply in the opposition between English liberty and race slavery, but in the fact that the slave is both required to be present to produce English liberty and required to disappear so as not to contradict the premise of English liberty. In economic terms, slave labor is required to produce the wealth that will fund the rising and politically empowered Whig class; in political terms, the slave must remain a shadowy figure who inhabits a land far away from England and does not threaten accounts of English liberty in the metropole or the colony. The slave is thus not ushered off the English stage altogether but is strategically made present and absent on the stage at once.[11] Like the Indian king, who lends his tortured body to the performance of a logic of territorial sovereignty and then obligingly "vanishes," the royal slave performs enforced labor in the West Indies that generates English wealth, while also assuming the mantle of disappearing, tortured subjectivity in need of sympathetic salvation.

Southerne's *Oroonoko* exemplifies this logic, displaying the triumph of Whig capitalism while lamenting with sorrow the tortured body of the (disappearing) African prince. Whereas Behn's novel serves as an elegy for monarchical sovereignty, Southerne's play rescripts the narrative of the royal slave to serve precisely the purposes of the colonial relation and Whig capitalism. According to Southerne, Behn was unwilling to adapt her novel concerning the royal slave to the stage. Southerne speaks briefly of his work of adaptation in the play's dedication:

> [Behn] had a great Command of the Stage; and I have often wonder'd that she would bury her Favourite Hero [Oroonoko] in a Novel, when she might have reviv'd him in the Scene. She thought either that no Actor could represent him; or she could not bear him represented: And I believe the last when I remember what I have heard from a Friend of hers. That she always told his Story, more feelingly, then she writ it. Whatever happen'd to him at Surinam, he has mended his Condition in England.[12]

In Behn's text, the flesh of Oroonoko is itself the scene of horrific and unwarranted destruction: in the final chapter of the novel, Oroonoko is literally torn limb from limb by the "rude and wild . . . rabble" and the "inhuman . . . justices" who order his execution. Southerne, however, indicates that he has succeeded in putting Oroonoko back together again—in mending the dismembered body that Behn's novel staged for her readers. Oroonoko is tortured on stage in Southerne's play, but this torture does not take the form of dismemberment; rather, Oroonoko is chained to the ground with his arms and legs stretched out in a scene reminiscent of the torture of Montezuma on the rack in Dryden's *Indian Emperour*. Ultimately, moreover, Oroonoko's death occurs at his own hands in Southerne's play (unlike the novel), suggesting a heroic resolution of Oroonoko's fate. The suicide in the final scene of Southerne's play places Oroonoko's fate in his own hands and attenuates the culpability of the colonial judicial system and the white "rabble" who assume villainous proportions in the novel's conclusion.

Emphasizing the injustice of the disparity between Oroonoko's regal bearing and his enslaved state, Behn contrasts the values and ideology of divine monarchy with those of colonialism and nascent capitalism and the (disturbingly, for Behn) de-hierarchizing effects of the latter. In so doing, she offers not a direct critique of slavery so much as a critique of Whig ideology and the "monstrous mercantile middle class" whose ascendancy was directly tied to British colonialism, race slavery, and the extraction of wealth from the New World.[13] Both slavery and mercantilism involve the elevation of values involving commodity exchange—the commodification of people as well as goods—which clearly troubles Behn. In contrast, Southerne celebrates the liberties and possibilities of mercantile capitalism, Whig ideology, and colonial expansion. If monarchical sovereignty has disappeared in the colonial arena (as mourned by Behn), a new sovereignty has emerged in its stead—that of the bourgeois, self-possessed individual (as celebrated by Southerne) and exemplified in the Welldon sisters, who appear in the comic plot that Southerne adds to the play. The English Welldon sisters travel to Surinam and successfully transform themselves from spinsters into wealthy wives; that they do so in relation to the enslavement of Oroonoko is both revealed and obscured within the play insofar as the parallel plots (marriage and enslavement) are presented as geographically linked, but not causally related to one another. What Behn's novel renders asunder—the geography of colonialism, the ideology of colonial commodification, and the body of the Royal Slave—Southerne's play "has mended . . . in London." However, this repair has been effected only by patching on a new plot—one that makes the Welldon sisters marriageable and thus enables their social reproduction at the cost of Oroonoko's social and physical death.[14]

In 1695, Southerne's *Oroonoko* thus reassuringly depicted New World labor as racialized and, for a London audience, represented slavery as a geographically distant phenomenon. However, the formation of racialized labor played out in terms that were more tense and more fraught in colonial spaces than in the metropole—indeed, the fact that *Oroonoko* was cancelled in South Carolina in the eighteenth century (as we saw in chapter 1) and never performed there offers testimony to the ongoing tension around racialization and racial performance in colonial locales. The program of colonial expansion pursued by Charles II (which followed the lead of Cromwell to a large extent, despite the shift in political dispensations signaled by the Restoration), involved increased settlement of New World territory together with an increase in the size of the labor force required to generate profit from newly settled lands.[15] Such an imperial program required the production of both colonial whiteness (more settlers) and colonial blackness (more labor) as well as the ongoing elimination of Native peoples (more "vanishing" of Indians): importantly, neither the whiteness of colonial settlers nor the blackness of forced laborers was given in advance—rather, both needed to be constructed in legal, social, and cultural terms to create a racialized geography that polarized white and black while seeking to erase indigeneity. As we have seen, bound British labor initially provided the greatest number of workers in the British Atlantic; however, shortly after assuming the throne, Charles II implemented a series of policies that assisted in enabling a shift to a racialized geography of labor and freedom in the British colonies. In 1661 (as discussed in chapter 1), Charles II sought to encourage the settlement of Jamaica and issued a proclamation "for the encouraging of our subjects" to plant in Jamaica, offering "thirty acres of improveable lands" to every man, woman, and child over the age of twelve who began a plantation there. Moreover, Charles II proclaimed, "We do further publish and declare, that all children of our natural-born subjects of England, to be born in Jamaica, shall, from their respective births, be reputed to be, and shall be, free denizens of England, and shall have the same privileges to all intents and purposes as our free-born subjects of England."[16] The promise that English settlers would remain English and that their children would be English as well was thus evidently a necessary inducement, together with land, for Englishmen to plant in Jamaica. The decision on Charles II's part to hold on to Jamaica and settle it, in the manner of Barbados, thus required that he reassure English settlers that they would remain English—by law—in the colony. Speaking directly to the anxieties of Brits who did not wish to be "barbadosed," Charles II's policy sought to eradicate the notion that the colonies were associated with forms of white slavery.[17]

Further, Charles II had effectively doubled down on the promise of English liberty in Jamaica by increasing unfree labor in the colonies in the form of African slaves: in 1660 (the very year he assumed the throne) he founded the Company of Royal Adventurers Trading to Africa (later to become the Royal African Company), to which he granted a monopoly on the English slave trade. Charles II himself invested heavily in the company, as did other members of the Stuart family: the company aimed to destroy the Dutch hold over the trade in slaves to the English colonies. With respect to sugar production in the colonies, as Hilary McD. Beckles and Andrew Downes argue, Charles II thus "attempted to integrate vertically the entire production process by breaking into the slave trade and driving the Dutch out" of the market.[18]

While the metropole and the colonies struggled with one another for years over the precise terms of English liberty that would be granted to whites as well as the price of slaves from Africa, the fundamental structure of a racialized geography was established in these years, and the ratio of black to white forced labor in the colonies soared with the importation of slaves from Africa by way of English traders licensed by and directly profiting the crown.[19] Just two years after issuing the Jamaican proclamation, Charles II created a new colony in 1663 by means of proprietary grants: this colony—South Carolina— would flourish on the model established in Barbados, adopting wholesale the system of labor as well as the legal terms of the Barbados slave code. Named after Charles II, Charles Town was its capital.

THE REPRODUCTION OF ENGLISHNESS:
THE ENCHANTED ISLAND

The reproduction of Englishness in colonial space thus required the simultaneous production of free Englishness and of an unfree labor force that was not English. Theatrically, the shifting optics of sovereignty, settlement, liberty, and labor in the colony appear in the form of figures whose status hovers between sovereign, native, and slave, including Oroonoko, as well as an earlier, potent figure—namely, Shakespeare's Caliban—who is also remembered and reanimated on stage in this period. In 1667, a new version of Caliban debuted on stage in John Dryden and William D'Avenant's, *The Tempest, or The Enchanted Island*: this significantly revised version of *The Tempest* would push Shakespeare's original from the stage and hold the boards for the duration of the eighteenth century in both the metropole and the colonies.[20]

In Dryden and D'Avenant's *The Enchanted Island*, dialogue is significantly reduced from Shakespeare's script in favor of a plot that turns on key acts of sight: most specifically, the revised plot takes as its focal point the fact that Miranda is said to have never before seen a man prior to laying eyes on Ferdinand. In order to make the most of this conceit, Dryden and D'Avenant supply Miranda with a sister, Dorinda, who has also never before seen a man and further supplement the cast with the character of Hippolyto, a man (originally cast by Dryden and D'Avenant as a woman in drag) who has never before seen a woman, having been brought to the island as an infant by Prospero, and raised there in isolation. To further underscore the significance of coupling as a primary plot device, both Ariel and Caliban have also been supplied with sexual partners (Milcha and Sycorax—the latter a sister of Caliban named after their mother) who are not present in Shakespeare's original play. The additional characters, together with the emphasis on the visible revelation of sexual difference, change the overall meaning of the play considerably: at its heart, *The Enchanted Island* is a play concerned with sexual reproduction in the New World, or, one might say, the play is concerned with the transportation of Europeans to and regeneration of European society in the New World at the most basic, biological level—that is, at the level of bodily production.

Shakespeare's *Tempest* and Dryden and D'Avenant's version do share one crucial line of dialogue: when Prospero accuses Caliban of having attempted to have sex with Miranda, Caliban replies, "Would't had been done!/Thou didst prevent me, I had peopl'd else/This Isle with Calibans" (1.2.352–54).[21] This line becomes central to the Davenant and Dryden revision insofar as the play takes as its aim the peopling of the Isle, and does so in a way that seeks to render Caliban sterile and Miranda (and Dorinda) fecund. Thus, whereas Shakespeare's *Tempest* might be seen as largely *restorative* with respect to European social order in the New World—all the European characters plan to return to Europe at the close of the play—Dryden and D'Avenant's play might better be described as *generative* with respect to the European population of the New World. In contrast to Shakespeare's *Tempest*, in *The Enchanted Island* the European characters do not plan to leave the island at the close of the play; rather, they plan to go to bed and procreate. In its emphasis on physicality—both in terms of its form and its content—*The Enchanted Island* revises the *Tempest* in a direction that is seemingly more oriented toward the exigencies of settler colonialism— toward the material occupation of the colonial isle that was a central concern of late seventeenth-century and eighteenth-century colonial policy. Further, the continued centrality of Caliban, and his dehumanization and enforced labor within the play, performs a historical layering of colonial relations characteristic of settler colonialism: in this layering, the figure of the native is banished to a distant past in order to foreground the centrality of racialized labor. As Jodi A. Byrd has argued, it is worth remarking that Ariel is the indigenous resident of the island. Ariel is displaced by Prospero's authority as well as by Caliban's (rebuffed) claim to the island; the play (as well as many postcolonial readings of it), according to Byrd, thus enacts a "translocation of indigeneity from the prior Ariel to Caliban and his mother, Sycorax," such that it displays "the machinations of settler discourses that detach indigeneity from the original inhabitants of the Americas and relocate it on settlers and arrivants themselves."[22]

Shakespeare's *Tempest* offers an intriguing pretext for Dryden and D'Avenant insofar as it is presciently attuned to the terms of colonial authority, particularly with respect to reproduction and sovereignty. Unlike *The Enchanted Island*, however, Shakespeare's play engages issues of reproduction and sovereignty as questions of narrative rather than of bodily reproduction and settler colonialism. As such, the force of Shakespeare's play is primarily mimetic and genealogical, whereas that of Dryden and D'Avenant's is tilted toward the physical and the ontic. The opening scenes of Shakespeare's play—following the scene of shipwreck—are largely dominated by lines uttered by Prospero, and specifically by Prospero's efforts to supply origin stories for each of the key characters that he (and the audience) encounter at the outset of the play: Prospero tells Miranda the story of her infancy and their mutual flight to the island after he was deposed from his Dukedom in Milan; Prospero tells Ariel the story of his imprisonment by Sycorax and his release by way of Prospero's magic; and Prospero tells Caliban the story of his enslavement, which, he states, followed on the heels of the sexual attentions Caliban directed at Miranda. Accordingly, one might read Prospero's efforts as highly linguistic and narrative: that is, his central labor in the play is that of assigning separate origin stories and trajectories to each of the characters he seeks to control (Miranda, Ariel, and Caliban), and guaranteeing that the narratives he has constructed unfold properly so as to achieve the results he desires. Prospero, then, exerts his sovereignty in the New World as a capacity to generate and enforce genealogical narratives.

Notably, in *The Tempest*, the passage in which Caliban professes his thwarted wish to people the isle with his offspring is directly followed by the well-known lines in which Miranda recounts her kindness to Caliban in teaching him to speak English. Thus, when Caliban complains that Prospero "didst prevent" him from "people[ing] . . . this isle with Calibans," Miranda spits back, in direct response:

> Abhorred slave,
> Which any print of goodness wilt not take,
> Being capable of all ill! I pitied thee,
> Took pains to make thee speak, taught thee each hour
> One thing or other: when thou didst not, savage,
> Know thine own meaning, but wouldst gabble like
> A thing most brutish, I endow'd thy purposes
> With words that made them known. But thy vile race,
> Though thou didst learn, had that in't which good natures
> Could not abide to be with; therefore wast thou
> Deservedly confined into this rock,
> Who hadst deserved more than a prison. (1.2.354–65)

Miranda's benevolent gesture of extending language and the capacity for meaning making to Caliban has failed, she states, having foundered on Caliban's refusal to adhere to strictures placed on his identity—including his own lack of sexual access to Miranda—associated with the language in question. Caliban's famous response to Miranda's language lessons—"You taught me language; and my profit on't/Is, I know how to curse. The red plague rid you/For learning me your language!" (1.2.366–68)—expresses his rejection of both the language lesson and the narrative of nonreproductivity that Prospero enjoins on him. It seems worth remarking, then, that the scene of language instruction (and its rejection) is embedded within a larger scene of origin-story instruction. These origin stories, in turn, will determine whose offspring will (and will not) populate the island, and whose purposes will (and will not) be endowed with meaning. Thus the question as to who will populate the isle and the question as to whose linguistic acts will have force and meaning are proximate within the play: more broadly, matters of epistemic force (language) and physical occupation (bodily reproduction) are the elements of power that colonial authority must control. And indeed, viewed as a scene in which foundational narratives are constructed and provisionally tacked into place, Prospero's first scene in *The Tempest* is one that exemplifies the carefully constructed nature of colonial authority and the multiple moving parts that are managed within this construction process.

The twofold nature of the colonial relation, as I have argued, relies on dual scenes or stories—one of forced labor and racial oppression in the colonies and a second concerning the establishment of political liberty and parity among Europeans. In effect, Prospero lays the groundwork to bring a version of each of these narratives to fruition in this scene, although his concern is less with English liberty than with maintaining his own sovereign authority in genealogical terms: in the origin story Prospero constructs for him, Caliban is rendered an enslaved colonial laborer—fit only to be confined in a rock, wracked with pains, and relied on for manual labor. Miranda, on the other hand, receives an origin story that indicates her royal status, and thus her suitability for marriage to another royal, namely, Ferdinand. The marriage of Miranda and Ferdinand will, in turn, ultimately serve to secure peace among the warring dukedoms of Europe. Seemingly separate narratives, the two stories nonetheless threaten to become visibly entangled at the moment when Caliban proposes intercourse with Miranda. And indeed, the exhaustive work performed by Prospero to keep the two stories moving forward on separate tracks indicates the extent to which they are not intrinsically separate but are only forcibly divagated by managerial labor. If Caliban's desire to propagate with Miranda points to the physical intimacy of European and non-European bodies in the New World, Prospero's linguistic and narrative labors point to an effort to locate European and non-European bodies in distant epistemic registers despite their physical proximity. The colonial relation that Prospero sets forth in this scene thus relies on the construction of two separate narratives that spring forth from the same set of physical circumstances. Narrative—the language of mimesis—becomes the means by which Caliban is rendered abject (a figure of bare labor) and Miranda is rendered socially reproductive: the daughter whose marriage will inaugurate a new political order among the warring dukes of Europe.

In their revision of Shakespeare's play, D'Avenant and Dryden turn, as I have suggested, toward the realm of physical bodies—toward the ontic—in a way that is distinct from Shakespeare's interest in using language and mimesis to manage the relation of bodies to one another and forms of genealogically based sovereignty and hierarchy. Thus, for instance, D'Avenant and Dryden extend the second act, directly following Prospero's masterful origin stories, by inserting a scene of nonknowledge of origins that focuses on bodies rather than stories: in a brief dialogue between the two sisters, Dorinda and Miranda display an (intentionally) absurd ignorance of sexual difference, sexual reproduction, and familial and genealogical structure—in short, the two sisters demonstrate a complete ignorance of the origins of bodies.

In the dialogue, Miranda tells Dorinda that she has learned that "shortly we may see that thing, Which you have heard my father call a Man." "But what is that?" answers Dorinda. "I know no more than you," responds Miranda. "But I have heard my Father say, we Women were made for him," she continues. Miranda muses that their father is a man, and Dorinda opines that "it would be finer, if we two Had two young Fathers." Miranda replies that two young fathers would be called brothers, rather than fathers, thus raising the specter of a kind of incestuous disorder associated with nonknowledge of sexual difference and familial organization—a specter closely linked to the failure of patriarchy as well: "How did he come to be our Father too?" asks Dorinda. Miranda answers that Prospero must have found the girls "when we both were little, and grew within the ground." Dorinda, augmenting, for comic effect, the absurdity of her ignorance, then asks, "Why could he not find more of us? Pray, Sister, let you and I look up and down one day, to find some little ones for us to play with."[23] The opening act of D'Avenant and Dryden's version of the play thus poses succinct questions: Where do babies come from? How do people reproduce?

Dryden and D'Avenant's adaptation of Shakespeare indicates that the question of bodily reproduction—the reproduction of Englishness on an island far from England—became a significant scene of interest as colonialism became increasingly important to the English economy and the English imaginary in the late seventeenth century. More specifically, in their revision of Shakespeare's play, Dryden and D'Avenant manage bodies in the colony by portraying a version of the colonial relation in which sexual reproduction between white Europeans is wholly natural and that of non-Europeans is unnatural. Thus, for instance, in *The Enchanted Island*, the sight of the young men, Ferdinand and Hippolito, is enough to lead Dorinda and Miranda into overheated, mock-innocent protestations of desire evincing a sort of hypernaturalness that attends their sexual coupling in the play: Dorinda and Miranda clearly want to do it, even when they have no idea what "it" is. And as the play throws up and then disentangles impediments to the future intercourse of the two happy couples, it also disqualifies Caliban for reproduction, placing him in an incestuous relation with his sister, Sycorax: in other words, Caliban's sexual desire is shown as just the opposite of Miranda and Dorinda's—as wholly unnatural.

The play concludes as the couples are sorted into reproductive pairs by Prospero: "For you, *Miranda*, must with *Ferdinand*, And you, *Dorinda*, with *Hippolyto* lie in One Bed hereafter." Dorinda happily concludes that the sisters have now overcome their prior ignorance as to the provenance of children: "we meant like fools/To look'em in the fields, and they, it seems,/Are only found in Beds."[24] While Dorinda and Miranda secure sexual partners, Sycorax (Caliban's sister) loses hers: she has been allied with both Trinculo and Stephano—the low, comedic characters in the play—but Trinculo announces that she is disqualified for union with both of them because he has seen her having sex with Caliban: "I found her an hour ago under an Elder-tree, upon a sweet Bed of Nettles, singing Tory, Rory, and Ranthum, Scanthum, with her own Natural Brother."[25] Dryden and Davenant's play thus seeks to reinvent the social order by means of naturalizing a set of rules for the exchange of women in the space of the colony—rules that will form the basis of a colonial social structure that will people the isle with Europeans and not with Calibans.

Despite its focus on white colonial reproduction, the pantomime-oriented (scenic and aural rather than linguistic) form of the play opened *The Enchanted Island* to a wide community of spectators and thus to a wide possibility of readings and performances. As we saw in the previous chapter, D'Avenant was particularly masterful in his use of the transporting effects of perspectival scenery, music, and dance in generating embodied audience consent—that is, in locating the audience within a frame of meaning generated by the theatre and collectivizing its consent to that epistemological emplacement of itself. While Dryden and D'Avenant's pantomime of sexual reproduction seeks to

rely on the force of plain sight—a man sees a woman, a woman sees a man—
to represent the naturalness of sexual desire, it also unhinges, to some extent,
the force of Prospero's intensive linguistic labor in producing and imposing
origin stories for each of the characters on the island—origin stories that
decisively separate the diverse bodies that inhabit the island. The bodily force
of sexual desire, which is meant to secure English possession of the colony by
reproducing English bodies in Dryden and D'Avenant's play, also contains the
possibility of less well-policed physical relations (the ontic force of theatre)
that evade the control of linguistic stabilization.

Thus while the emphasis on bodies, and on bodily reproduction, might
seem to be enabling of colonialism, the force of bodies, in the absence of
language, also opens up possibilities around the body and its rearticulation—
indeed, the comedic ruse of cross-dressing Hippolito, for instance, would seem
to intentionally open a distance between the mimetic nature of gender and
its ontic instantiation. On the one hand, then, Dryden and D'Avenant's play
emphasizes the natural, physical nature of sexual reproduction, but on the
other hand, it raises the possibility of decoupling that reproduction from the
very social genealogies it seeks to naturalize: thus, as we have seen, Dorinda
and Miranda have difficulty determining which men are desirable sexual
partners and which men are not (Fathers? Brothers? And what is the difference between them in any case?). Ultimately, the play suggests that Dorinda
and Miranda are naturally drawn to suitable male partners, but the play also
raises the dual specters of miscegenation—in the form of Caliban's desire to
couple with Miranda and Sycorax's coupling with Trinculo and Stephano—
and incest—in the form of both Caliban's coupling with his sister Sycorax
and Miranda and Dorinda's uncertainty about their familial relations with
men. In other words, the apparent naturalness of white sexual reproduction
occurs within the context of endogamy (incest) and exogamy (miscegenation),
which are placed on view in the play as well. Moreover, despite the fact that
both endogamy and exogamy are represented as "unnatural" within the play's
script, the ontic nature of the theatrical venue may enable more force (and
pleasure) to be generated around these possibilities—between and among
these bodies—than the scripted dichotomy between natural and unnatural
might seem to allow.

The Enchanted Island was *The Tempest* of choice throughout the late seventeenth and early eighteenth centuries. However, the popularity of the Dryden
and D'Avenant version waned as a result of the generic association of the play
with the "low" form of pantomime—a form that was actively pushed to the
margins of the London theatre world by the Licensing Act of 1737. As John

O'Brien writes, pantomime in particular was associated with the threat of un-disciplined audiences, precisely because of its a-linguistic form: "In its reliance on spectacle, scenic effects, and the kinetic bodies of performers, pantomime awakened traditional ambivalences about the materiality of the stage as it promised—as least to some—a means of bypassing the barriers of linguistic competence or expense that had limited the potential audience for the the-atre."[26] According to Michael Dobson, revivals of Dryden and D'Avenant's play took an increasingly carnivalesque turn in the eighteenth century as the productions highlighted the "original transvestite casting of Hippolito and Sy-corax—and frequently compound[ed] these disruptive aspects . . . by casting an actress as Ariel (so that at the play's conclusion Prospero appears to sanc-tion two pairings of women)."[27] The "disruption" caused by cross-gendered casting that enables an unorthodox pairing of women at the close of the play is the result of putting into play the dual signifying force of theatrical representa-tion—one that I have described as both ontic and mimetic. Thus the women's bodies, even while performing as male bodies, still have the status of being female and thus causing a kind of disruptive meaning to emerge. Dobson argues that "both the explicitly sexual content of *The Enchanted Island* and its 'low,' hybrid dramatic form could only result in its slow but inevitable demo-tion from the status of literature, and by the 1740s . . . is was already on its way to being banished from the legitimate theatres altogether." Indeed, Dobson states, the play was "driven out to less gentrified arenas," including "the illegal New Wells Theatre in Goodman's Fields," where the play was performed in 1745; the Bartholomew Fair; and subsequently "to even darker fringes of the theatrical world," including New York and Charleston.[28]

NEW WORLD DRAMA—TRANSPORTED

The Licensing Act of 1737 instituted a new regime of censorship in London theatres, following a general democratization of theatrical fare in the wake of the Glorious Revolution.[29] Passed largely through the efforts of Robert Walpole, the Whig prime minister who accrued vast political power follow-ing the South Sea Bubble scandal, the Licensing Act was aimed directly at censoring criticism of Walpole and his administration—an administration reviled by many for the depth of its engagement in the new financial world of credit, political patronage, bribery, and corruption. While the Whigs had used public theatre—in the form of pope-burning rituals in particular—to their own political benefit prior to the Glorious Revolution, the collectivizing force of theatricality, as perfected by D'Avenant himself, was subject to mobilization in a variety of directions, particularly in a world of increased social and geographical mobility. Indeed, Walpole himself was burned in effigy in the streets of London in the 1730s after proposing an unpopular excise tax.[30] However, Walpole was an astute manager of public opinion and publicity: he gained the nickname of the "Skreen-Master General" for his role in screening from sight the involvement of members of the court in the South Sea debacle, while garnering public support for his ability to manage the national financial crisis.[31]

As the metaphor of "screenmaster" indicates, managing public opinion in the era of popular sovereignty and the modern credit economy involved not simply accruing public sentiment to one's views, but segmenting the public—and public vision—such that opposition mobilization did not occur, and it is particularly in this direction that many of Walpole's policies were developed. The Riot Act of 1715, the brutal Black Act of 1723, and the Licensing Act of 1737 can all be seen as policies aimed directly at controlling the mob—and more particularly as policies designed to disperse assemblages that formed in the name of the commons to resist inequalities effected by the new regime of finance capitalism. That the Whigs had put this mob into motion and into the vernacular in 1663, as MacCaulay reports, is no small irony; moreover, the irony is compounded when we understand the extent to which new forms of mobility were necessary for the redistribution of labor and property required by capitalism as it took shape in this period.

However, what bears particular attention is the extent to which the political narrative of popular sovereignty—of the power of the commons and of British liberty—serves as something of a screen for an ongoing economic narrative involving the capitalist eradication of the commons and the increased conscription of labor in the Atlantic world. The decorative screen, as Paul Langford reports, became a fashionable item of furniture in the early eighteenth century, but it also became a central metaphor for the workings of the Walpole administration and the way in which the profits of finance capital benefitted the unseen hands of corrupt, behind-the-scenes financiers and politicians. Satirical political cartoons regularly depicted the deceptive "screen" that presented one image to the public while shielding from view the reality of corruption and unconstrained greed, particularly in association with the South Sea Company. Far from a Leviathan who embodies the people, this image of government-as-screen is one that is, itself, notably theatrical: the "screen scene" (later to be immortalized on stage in Richard Brinsley Sheridan's *School for Scandal*) represents the simultaneous construction of knowledge and nonknowledge as the work of government and capital in an age of popular sovereignty. More specifically, the screen (as depicted in the "Brabant Skreen" cartoon—see figure 3.1) places an economic scene and a politic one in

FIGURE 3.1. "The Brabant Skreen," from the *London Mercury: Or, Great Britain's Weekly Journal* (1721), picturing the disgraced cashier of the South Sea Company, Robert Knight, receiving a pass of safe conduct to Brabant Estates in Belgium, from George I's mistress, the Duchess of Kendal. Behind the screen, Walpole (visible in the mirror on the right) is concealed with other courtiers. The front of the screen displays scenes related to the South Sea Bubble, including the hanging of the poor and the rewarding of the rich. © The Trustees of the British Museum

a relation of nontransparency but great intimacy with one another. Thus, while a narrative of economic events appears on one side (depicting the South Sea Bubble), behind the screen, events are determined in wholly political terms (by Walpole and the king's minions).

As attention to the South Sea Bubble indicates, a key component of the development of finance capital was the new geography of Atlantic empire, but it was precisely the dislocations and distances of this Atlantic geography that enabled strategic erasures of its significance from the scene of local political mobilization.[32] The infamous South Sea Bubble involved massive private and public speculation in a company whose main activity was purchasing and transporting slaves from Africa to the New World. The South Sea Company was established in 1711 and granted exclusive trading rights to Spanish South America; but a key function of the company was to fund government debt, which was exchanged for publicly traded shares of the company. In 1713, with the conclusion of the Treaty of Utrecht, the South Sea Company was granted the *Asiento*—the lucrative contract to supply slaves to Spain in the New World. In subsequent years, the South Sea Company continued to take on a greater share of the government debt, and in 1720 rumors of the fabulous riches expected from trade in the New World (and specifically the slave trade) drove share prices to extraordinary heights and fueled widespread trading and frenzied speculation. When returns were not realized, share prices fell precipitously, bankrupting broad swaths of the English public, including wealthy and less-wealthy stock-holders, and unleashing a tide of criticism against the immorality of stock-jobbers and the profiteers of the new finance economy.[33]

While much critical attention has been devoted to the South Sea Bubble and the inauguration of a credit economy, as well as the literary ramifications of an economy based on speculative fictions, less consideration has been devoted to the extent to which the South Sea Bubble revealed the imbrication of the English state and economy in Atlantic capitalism and the slave trade.[34] Significantly, Walpole's rise to power and his efforts to contain anti-Whig opposition in the aftermath of the Bubble take place in relation to a new geography of Atlantic capitalism that is displayed and concealed by the "screen-master" in a shifting array of (competing) economic and political narratives or scenes that Walpole sought (often without success) to control. One effect of the South Sea Bubble was to generate a new anti-Whig coalition between wealthy Tories who had lost the prerogatives of landed gentry to the new economy and lower-class laborers who were similarly displaced by Whig policies of enclosure.[35] Although the Whigs had mobilized the crowd on their own behalf prior to the Glorious Revolution, Walpole clearly sought to limit the force of precisely such a crowd, mobilized (against him) in the name of the people or the "British commons" during the years of his ascendancy. The Riot Act of 1715, the Black Act of 1723, and the Licensing Act of 1737, as I argue at greater length below, might all be seen as efforts by Walpole to segment the commons—and thus to demobilize the mob. In every case, moreover, the language and the economics of Atlantic slavery and British liberty remain at stake—often in suppressed form—in the politically contested performances that stage and respond to Walpole's repressive efforts.

In its initial form, proposed in 1735, the Licensing Act aimed specifically at limiting the number of non-licensed theatres and thus controlling the presence of crowds in London neighborhoods—an act that appealed to a coalition of economic and religious interests in the House of Commons. When Walpole tweaked the bill such that it included provisions for royal censorship of all plays performed in the patent theatres, members of the House of Commons withdrew their support, in part because the bill was now aimed at securing the power of the king and of Walpole himself. However, two years later the Licensing Act of 1737 passed, with the provision of censorship, as parliamentary concern about crowds and riots increased.[36] One rationale for the Licensing Act, as John Loftis argues, was a claim that the quality of the material performed at the patent theatres had declined because the theatres increasingly catered to nonelite audiences. Specifically, pantomime, dancing, and musicals made up a larger share of the material performed in the eighteenth century, and this material was deemed "nonrational" and degrading rather than uplifting by critics of the theatre. The Licensing Act of 1737 was thus aimed at shoring up the "rational entertainment" offered in the patent theatres. Rather than eradicating pantomime and musical performance, however, the effect of the Licensing Act was to polarize highbrow and lowbrow theatrical forms, as "nonrational" forms were pushed to the margins of the London theatrical world and performed in theatres where "illegitimate" drama flourished.[37] Moreover, it is in this context—that is, in relation to the developing geographic margins of the London theatrical world—that English theatrical performers expanded their field of performance toward Anglophone colonial America.

Specifically, one can trace a direct link between the restrictive force of the 1737 Licensing Act in London and the creation of the first major touring company in the Anglophone Atlantic—namely, the Hallam Company that was led by Lewis Hallam and arrived in Virginia in 1752 and made its way to Charleston in 1754. The touring company was financed by Lewis and his brother, William, sons of an actor who had raised his children in (and into) the peripatetic life of the wandering player. William Hallam performed at venues such as Bartholomew Fair and Dublin before opening the Wells Inn Theatre in Goodman's Fields in 1739. The unlicensed theatre featured primarily rope dances, concerts, pantomime, and harlequinades—forms of marginal or unlicensed entertainment that flew beneath the radar of the Licensing Act. In 1744, however, Hallam began to attempt to perform legitimate drama by means of a not uncommon end run around the Licensing Act—namely, by advertising "'A Concert of Vocal and Instrumental Music,' between the halves of which a play would be offered 'gratis,' and to soothe the government by causing 'The Concert to conclude with the Chorus of Long Live the King.'"[38] And in 1745 Dryden and D'Avenant's *The Enchanted Island* appeared on Hallam's stage starring Hallam's wife in the role of Miranda. Ultimately, however, Hallam's ruses to skirt the Licensing Act were not entirely effective, and after several legal run-ins, Hallam's theatre closed in 1752.

Shut down and shut out in London, William and Lewis Hallam embarked on the plan of forming a traveling theatrical company that would tour America: the following year, Lewis arrived in Virginia with a small company and a repertoire of twenty-four plays. The Hallam company performed in Virginia, New York, and Philadelphia before arriving in Charleston for a brief season in 1754, after which they traveled to Kingston, Jamaica. In Jamaica, Hallam joined forces with David Douglass, a Scottish printer; upon Hallam's death a few years later, Douglass married Hallam's widow and formed the American Company of Comedians, which began touring North America in 1759, arriving in Charleston in 1763. In 1773, Douglass proposed a successful subscription plan that funded the construction of the first permanent theatre in Charleston—a theatre at which *The Enchanted Island* was performed repeatedly in the late eighteenth century.

The performance culture that Walpole and others sought to regulate in London thus migrated to other locations in the Anglophone world and assumed new forms there: one might thus view the Licensing Act as productive of new geographical and generic margins rather than as solely repressive. The marginalization of pantomime and "illegitimate theatre" in London aided the circulation and growth of a-linguistic theatre (pantomime, dancing, ontic-oriented performance) in provincial and colonial locations—locations where, in turn, new assemblages—what one might call creole publics—were formed.

The highly mobile and mobilizing force of theatricality is thus given new scope in the era of Atlantic capitalism, in part because of the centrality of mobility to capitalism itself. The Walpole administration participated in and championed the new capitalist economy *and* found itself struggling to control the representational energies unleashed by the motility of bodies, goods, and value—representations of which occurred in print and on the stage. Walpole's initial effort to control theatrical representation failed in 1735 but succeeded quite decisively in 1737 with the passage of the restrictive Licensing Act. Importantly, the debates over the 1735 and 1737 Licensing Acts, and the defining issues of vagrancy, property ownership, and government libel around which these debates revolved, arose in the context of the astounding success of John Gay's satirical opera *The Beggar's Opera*, which represented Walpole's administration as a pack of sturdy beggars—namely, as duplicitous, excessively mobile thieves.

THE BEGGAR'S OPERA AND
THE PERFORMATIVE COMMONS

In many respects, John Gay's *Beggar's Opera* was a prime mover in the history of the Licensing Act of 1737: novel in both form and content, the ballad opera took the London theatre world by storm in 1728, running for a record-breaking sixty-two consecutive nights. The populist force unleashed in the space of the theatre by the *Beggar's Opera* produced after-the-fact barriers erected by Walpole and others to mitigate the galvanizing effects of a theatrical tempest composed of popular ballad, political satire, and bawdy, hum-along, class-leveling festivity. Combining folk ballad with the depiction of a gang of thieves and the corrupt officials who oversee the circulation of the thieves and prostitutes in and out of the legal system, the play served to satirize both Italian opera and the Walpole administration. In its attack on the property-grasping legal regime of the Whigs, and in its explicit account of Whig legal practice as a form of thievery (property as theft), the ballad opera appealed to both aristocrats and the lower classes, whose prerogatives had been eclipsed and/or eradicated by the forces of capitalist growth. Accordingly, one might argue that—responding directly to the threat of the enclosure of the traditional English commons—*The Beggar's Opera* celebrates a revivification of the commons in theatrical form. In championing an ethos that is antiproperty, antimarriage, and anticontract, the play generates a performatively enacted commons that is articulated most fully in the spectacle of the communal pardon from death by hanging of the charismatic thief, Macheath, at the close of the play.

In contrast to *The Beggar's Opera*, which is set entirely in England, its sequel, *Polly*, is staged against an Atlantic geography as Macheath, Polly, and Jenny Driver are all transported (voluntarily and involuntarily) to the New World. And while *Polly* attempts to convoke an Atlantic commons, as I argue below, it ultimately fails to do so in part because the Atlantic commons (in the face of the ever-present threat of white enslavement) must be racially segregated to preserve British liberty. John Gay's two operas thus might be seen to point to two different responses to the crisis of Whig ascendancy and the new regime of absolute property: one proposes the performative revivification of the English commons, the second involves bringing into view the racial politics of transportation and social death in the Atlantic world. It seems significant that the second approach—that of naming the way in which race intersected with capitalism—was the one that failed to generate public interest and acclaim. The white, underclass Macheath of *The Beggar's Opera* captured the heart of the public, but when performing as a black in *Polly*, MacHeath sparked no collective desire among the English or white creole public in North America. The lack of shared interest in Macheath's blackface persona, Morano—in contrast to the collective swoon over Macheath—indicates the way in which the Atlantic economy of race, sovereignty, and labor cannot be animated as a political force—as a commoning force—precisely because it operates by way of naturalizing divisions among the populace. Indeed, Gay himself organizes the opera in such a way as to exclude Morano from becoming the object of collective desire: in this way, it would seem that once Gay seeks to represent the racial politics of Atlantic capitalism, he can no longer imagine a functioning cultural commons. Thus, despite his efforts to critique "Skreen-Master General" Walpole, Gay, too, reproduces an Atlantic screening of the racial divisions of labor, sovereignty, and liberty.[39]

Much of the striking novelty of *The Beggar's Opera* is embedded in the formal dimensions of the piece; indeed, Gay may be said to have invented the genre of the ballad opera with this work. While Italian opera was enjoying immense popularity on the English stage at the time, Gay turned to English folk ballads rather than Italian composers for the music that formed the core of his opera. Writing new lyrics for traditional melodies, Gay retained the ballad form of the folk music; more importantly, the music of the ballads consisted of a repertoire held in common by the English people. Given that audience members knew, in advance, the melodies of the songs performed in the opera, one might imagine that each musical piece served as something of an invitation to the audience to participate in the performance—to hum along (figuratively or literally) or, at the very least, to recognize the melody in question as one known to them, one belonging to the members of the audience.

Critics have tended to argue *either* that *The Beggar's Opera* is primarily concerned with the issue of musical form and the satire of Italian opera, *or* that the opera reserves its satirical force for a critique of the increasingly restrictive Whig legal system. On Michael Denning's reading, for instance, the extraordinary popularity of the play can be seen as a public pushback against the eradication of the commons and against an overarching Whig logic of enclosure, privatization of property, and emergent capitalism.[40] However, the issues of musical form and political content are intimately related insofar as both address the subject of the commons and the politics of privatization and enclosure. As E. P. Thompson argues, the notorious Black Act of 1723 criminalized the use of property which had previously been considered legally available for common use; the Black Act thus aimed to enforce a logic of enclosure or absolute property—a notion of property that was fundamental to capitalist development.[41] Thompson writes,

> During the eighteenth century one legal decision after another signaled that the lawyers had become converted to the notions of absolute property ownership, and that (wherever the least doubt could be found) the law abhorred the messy complexities of coincident use-right. The rights and claims of the poor, if inquired into at all, received more perfunctory com-

pensation, smeared over with condescension and poisoned with charity. Very often they were simply redefined as crimes: poaching, wood-theft, trespass.[42]

In taking a gang of thieves as its central subject, *The Beggar's Opera* focuses directly on matters of criminality, theft, and trespass, and, as Denning effectively argues, the reviled Black Act is the immediate historical context against which we can view this portrayal of criminality.

The Black Act was written in to law to punish those who continued to claim their right to use what was once common property in England. More specifically, the Black Act was designed to target organized resistance to the enclosure of the commons by singling out the so-called Waltham Blacks and other groups of men who blackened their faces in order to hunt, poach, trespass, and occasionally commit forms of mayhem at night without being seen. While the blackened face was a means of eluding capture, the performative quality of the use of blackface seems notable as well—not least because the epithet "Blacks" came to signal, in popular eighteenth-century usage, a social identity rather than simply a description of behavior. Moreover, the association between the disguise of blackness and racial identity was remarked and disported on by both observers of and participants in the outlaw political activity of Blacking. Thus, for instance, one eighteenth-century writer refers to the Blacks as "sham negroes."[43] More intriguingly, a published letter recounting the experience of a traveler who, by dint of circumstance, is unwittingly present to a meeting and feast of the Waltham Blacks, states that the traveler was "presented . . . with a humorous kind of Ceremony to a Man more disguised than the Rest who sat at the upper End of the Table, telling [the traveler] . . . he hoped [he] would not refuse to pay [his] Respects to Prince Oroonoko, King of the Blacks."[44] The performative quality of the Blacks' use of blackness is in full evidence at this moment: Oroonoko's heroic blackness is itself the product of the stage, and the Waltham Blacks—in this anecdote—rely on the vexed theatrics of enslaved, diasporic African sovereignty to stage their revolutionary, outlaw political order.

The blackness of eighteenth-century English "Blacks" was, however, indicative of a class-based rather than a racial identity: the "Blacks" were individuals who conjoined for the purpose of protesting bourgeois property regimes and thus were identified as laborers, artisans, and subsistence farmers—individuals whose livelihoods were associated with traditional village and feudal land tenure and labor. Nonetheless, the relation between the blackness of an English agrarian underclass and the blackness of diasporic Africans is more than nominal. Both groups were sentenced, by way of capitalism, to forms of social death in which the prerogatives of social identity and natality were forcibly removed and eradicated.[45] While the experience of kidnapped and enslaved Africans in the middle passage was a form of social death far more extreme than what agrarian Englishmen experienced in the eighteenth century, the comparison is nonetheless useful insofar as it brings into visibility the way in which capitalist property forms eradicated the birthright of individuals whose families had, for generations, lived on the land and made a living from it in traditional ways that were criminalized by the Black Act.

Further, E. P. Thompson points out that the moment at which organized resistance to new norms of bourgeois property ownership began to take shape— that is, when groups of people began to "associate . . . themselves under the name of *Blacks*"—coincided with the enforcement of the specific punishment of transportation against those who had committed crimes against property, most particularly the crime of poaching deer. The severity of this punishment, according to Thompson, caused foresters to band together in order to poach more safely and effectively in groups: "in short," writes Thompson, "the fear of transportation . . . gave rise directly to Blacking."[46] Forced transportation to the outer reaches of the British empire—including America—was certainly a means of enforcing social death on individuals, and indeed, it was a punishment that resembled, in certain ways, the experience of Africans who were transported to the New World against their will. The threat of transportation—enforced removal to and enslavement in the New World—thus turned English whites into "Blacks." In assuming the epithet of "Blacks," then, the Waltham Blacks made common cause with African conscripted laborers in the Atlantic world while not taking on the cause of enslaved Africans. Referencing, in cloaked form, the enslavement and transportation of blacks in the Atlantic world, Waltham Blacks protested their loss of access to English liberties and English commons.

A second historical aspect of the Black Act links the politics of English Blacking to the slave trade: according to one eighteenth-century anonymous history of the Blacks, the practice of Blacking began "in and about the Times of general Confusion when the late pernicious Schemes of the *South-Sea* Company bore all Things down before them, and laid Waste what the Industry and good Husbandry of Families had gather'd together."[47] The South Sea Bubble here exemplifies the cost that capitalist investment ultimately had for traditional communities from which wealth (the fruits of "good husbandry") had been extracted and continued to be extracted by new forms of capitalist ownership and accumulation.

For my purposes, however, what is particularly significant about the connection between the South Sea Bubble and Blacking is the link that it reveals between the slave trade and traditional "good husbandry" on English land: the extreme profits from the former (the slave trade) accrued to the new system of capitalism and bourgeois property ownership, and thus helped to eliminate the value and economic viability of the latter (traditional good husbandry on common land). Thompson remarks that labor became increasingly free during the eighteenth century, and property, rather than labor relations, became the focus of legal rights under a developing capitalist regime. However, this history does not take into account the fact that some forms of labor were becoming increasingly unfree during the eighteenth century—namely, slave labor in the colonies. The increased interest in protecting property and the "freeing" of labor in England is, I would posit, directly related to the development of the capitalist economy, which was based on profits from slave labor in the colonies. Thompson's account tends not to integrate crucial Atlantic (and racial) dimensions of Whig capitalism into an understanding of the history of the Black Act. Or, differently put, one could say that the workings of Marxist "primitive accumulation"—the "original" accumulation of wealth that jump-starts the investment structures of capitalism—effected the social death of both agrarian English workers who were dispossessed of property by policies of enclosure and of Africans whose labor was extracted by means of unprecedented structural violence and institutionalized forms of natal alienation and social death. The cultural representation of the Waltham Blacks thus reveals the eclipsed (screened) proximity of the enclosure of the commons in England and the workings of slavery and social death in the colonies of the New World.

How, then, does *The Beggar's Opera* respond to the threat of primitive accumulation and the new finance economy? Interestingly, the primary matter of the narrative concerns marriage rather than theft: from the outset of the opera, dialogue and song revolve around the question of whether Polly can, will, should, or has already married Macheath. In the context of the opera, however, marriage is clearly related to the same issues of property ownership that arise in relation to crime and theft. Macheath, in matters of marriage as well as real property, refuses to commit to a notion of absolute property ownership. Rather, when it comes to women, Macheath is committed to the "messy complexities of coincident use-right" that define the logic of the commons as outlined above by Thompson: Macheath, it seems, is more than willing to be held in common by many women, despite the plot complexities entailed therein. Further, the invocation of a musical commons in the form of folk melody and collective dance tends to signal, within the opera, a rejection of the logic of absolute property whether with regard to stolen pocket watches or would-be wives.

As the opera progresses, the ratio of ballad to dialogue tilts increasingly in the direction of ballad. The final scenes of the opera find the central character, Macheath, impeached, imprisoned, and facing a seemingly inevitable and immediate execution by hanging. In these fast-moving final scenes (eleven through sixteen), public sentiment is mobilized such that the obviously guilty Macheath is ultimately freed from execution by "the taste of the town." Significantly, much that occurs in this closing sequence suggests the crucial role of music and dance in generating Macheath's communal pardon. In scene eleven, for instance, Macheath is imprisoned and visited by Polly and Lucy, the two women who compete most prominently to attain the title of Macheath's wife. As each laments Macheath's impending death and pleads with him to be recognized as his wife, Macheath breezily demurs to decide between the two: "What would you have me say, Ladies?—You see this Affair will soon be at an end, without my disobliging either of you." Despite his effort to defer the question of the marriage contract in perpetuity, Polly's father notes that the legal consequences of his marital status will outlast his mortal coil: Peachum states, "But the settling this Point, Captain [Macheath], might prevent a Law-Suit between your two Widows." The question remains unanswered, however, because Macheath launches into song: to the tune of "Tom Tinker's My True Love," Macheath perseverates—"Which way shall I turn me—How can I decide?"[48] Macheath thus interrupts discussion with his song. Moreover, the interruption becomes permanent as dialogue within the scene ceases from this point forward, and only a series of ballads ensues: after Macheath sings, Polly performs a ballad, Lucy then sings, Lockit (Lucy's father) sings, and Macheath sings again; the scene concludes when Macheath is taken away to his execution without having resolved the issue of the marriage contract. In this scene, then, the music of the commons (folk melody and ballad) intervenes to defer the logic of contract, ownership, and law.

In the scenes that follow the debate between Polly and Lucy, the musical invocation of the logic of the commons becomes increasingly manifest. In scene 12 of the opera, Lucy and Polly, still standing in the prison that Macheath has just left, suddenly notice the strains of music—music arising from the prisoners who are celebrating a temporary legal reprieve. Lucy explains, "The prisoners, whose Trials are put off 'till next Session, are diverting themselves." The diversion of music, then, is directly correlated here with the deferral of legal decision: music and dance present themselves as a common, embodied scene of demurral, distance, and displacement from the law of contracts and individual ownership. The scene closes with "A Dance of Prisoners in Chains, &c"—a communal celebration of the banishment of legal judgment from the scene of collective embodiment and pleasure.[49] Scene 13 finds Macheath in another prison cell at the court, awaiting his execution: resorting to a logic that now seems clear, Macheath—in the face of the finality of the death sentence passed on him—begins to sing to the tune of communal English ballads. Indeed, the entire scene consists of Macheath singing ten separate folk tunes, each of which is severely abbreviated: six of the tunes are invoked for the space of two lines of ballad, and one tune for a single line of ballad. If the lines of the ballad are so brief, why does Gay choose to have them sung to ten tunes rather than one? Clearly what matters for Gay, in addressing the audience, is less the fact that Macheath is placing words to music, than the sheer number of shared tunes that his words are used to animate. The audience is repeatedly called on (ten times) to *recognize* Macheath's song—to name the tune that Macheath is singing in one line or two—and thus to participate in a visceral, shared ownership of Macheath's song.

Shortly after this scene (just after four additional women with children approach Macheath to demand legal status as his wives in scene 15), Gay stages a metatheatrical intervention in the plot—namely, a dialogue between a Player and the Beggar who introduced the opera as his creation at the outset of the performance. The Player insists that Macheath must not be hanged, nor must the other thieves be transported, "for an Opera must end happily." The Beggar agrees, and rewrites the script so that "the Rabble" demand, and accomplish, Macheath's reprieve from the sentence of the court. The Player concurs: "All this we must do, to comply with the Taste of the Town."[50] In the final scene, Macheath, his many wives, and the rabble dance together. Gay's direct reference to the frame of the opera—specifically, to the framing of the opera highlighted in the discourse between the Player and the Beggar—draws attention to the relation between the frame and audience consent. To invoke the terms discussed in the previous chapter, we might see this as an instance of frame alignment played out on the stage. The Player points to a misalignment between the epistemological frame of the play and audience consent: were the legal system to prevail in exacting Macheath's death, this would violate audience consent (the "Taste of the Town"), which has repeatedly been elicited over the course of the opera in the name of a competing episteme or frame—namely, that of the embodied commons as a force antithetical to individual ownership, absolute property, and legal title.

In the final scenes of the opera, a cultural commons achieves decisive force—the audience has been enrolled, by the visceral force of song and dance, in the commons. The strength of this audience position requires, according to the Player, a realignment of the action of the opera itself such that the commons triumph over Whig property law and Macheath is freed by means of a collective reprieve. The final scene relies heavily on music and dance—specifically, the folk ballad form—to generate a shared space of embodied belonging that evades the contractual terms of bourgeois marriage and Whig law. And thus, when Macheath is set free, the play arguably generates a new commons—a theatrical space organized around the spectacle of public hanging, in which Whig legal prerogative is reclaimed by the people in the collective space of festival. Notably, this commons is achieved by way of a "distribution of the sensible"—that is, by generating a new collectivity by way of the shared sensate experience of participating in folk ballad performance—an aesthetic operation explicitly defined as a matter of "taste" within the opera.

POLLY AND ATLANTIC BLACKFACE

Despite the phenomenal success of *The Beggar's Opera*, the failure of that success to touch Gay's sequel, *Polly*, is perhaps just as significant, particularly given that *Polly* takes as its setting the Atlantic world of English imperialism that lies outside the common ground of England. In *Polly*, Macheath turns Atlantic outlaw, donning blackface to become the pirate king, Morano, who is engaged in battle with Indians and white plantation owners for control of the riches of the New World. Polly, the sweetheart of *The Beggar's Opera*, has followed Macheath to the New World but ultimately fails to gain the last dance with her paramour in the sequel that bears her name. And indeed, the opera as a whole fails to generate the celebratory communal last dance, authorized by the voice of the rabble and the taste of the town, with which *The Beggar's Opera* concluded: in sharp contrast to its predecessor, *Polly* ends with a wedding dance, celebrating the union of Polly and the Indian chief's son, Cawwawkee, while Morano's lifeless body swings from a tree offstage. Significantly, *Polly* failed to generate an audience either in London or in the colonies. Critics have largely attributed this failure to the fact that *Polly* was censored by the Lord Chamberlain's office in 1728 and thus was not allowed to appear on stage in the early eighteenth century to capitalize on the success of *The Beggar's Opera*. But censorship can serve as a form of publicity, and in the case of *Polly*, sales of the printed script (which was not suppressed) were likely swelled by the performance ban.[51] Nonetheless, Morano never entered the cultural vernacular as did Macheath. Nor did a staged production of *Polly*, rewritten by Benjamin Colman and performed in 1777, ignite public engagement in the play, despite the continued success of *The Beggar's Opera* at the time. And it is telling that

Polly, performed only thirteen times in England (in Colman's version), was never transported to the stages of America.[52]

Why was Gay unable to animate the engagement in *Polly* that had succeeded so wildly in *The Beggar's Opera*? Despite the promising material—Macheath as romantic pirate, sweet Polly sold into New World prostitution, and Jenny Diver on deck as well—the Atlantic location of the play seemingly offers no clear common ground, no embodied commons, in the way that English tradition does. Or, at the very least, one could say that Gay repeatedly searches for, and fails to find, the common ground that might engage the taste of the town in visceral consent and pleasure. The lack of fusion in *Polly* is exemplified in the fact that Macheath and Polly, despite occupying the stage together, fail to recognize one another when in each other's presence. Macheath in black face paint is unrecognizable to Polly, and Morano sparks none of the unquenchable desire in Polly that Macheath ignited. Polly, sold into sex slavery when she arrived in the New World, has dressed as a young man to escape her owner, but when Polly meets Morano and asks to join his pirate band, Morano fails to recognize her in her masculine attire. Clearly, Morano has no desire for Polly when she is dressed in pants. The utter failure of chemistry between Macheath and Polly, even when they meet face to face, speaks to the eradication of the kind of visceral desire that infused the collective taste of the town in *The Beggar's Opera*. Moreover, it is significant that desire is eradicated in *Polly* by way of segmenting the commons along lines defined by race and gender.

When we first encounter Macheath as Morano in *Polly*, we learn two somewhat contradictory pieces of information about his new identity as a black pirate king. First, we are told that, upon being transported as a slave to the New World, he proceeded to rob his master and become a pirate. So far, so good: Morano's soul would seem to be very much that of Macheath insofar as the pirate king is clearly legible as the transfigured highway robber in an Atlantic idiom. But we also learn that Morano has donned blackface, *not* in order to escape capture while committing crimes against property ownership, but in order to remove himself from circulation as a potential partner to women—that is, to protect the marriage contract he has entered into with Jenny Diver. "Was it not entirely for you," Morano asks Jenny, "that I disguis'd my self as a black, to skreen my self from women who laid claim to me where ever I went? Is not the rumour of my death, which I purposely spread, credited thro' the whole country? *Mackheath* is dead to all the world but you."[53] On a note of pronounced discord with the overriding antimarriage and antibourgeois refrain of *The Beggar's Opera*, Morano here announces that he has deliberately removed himself from the commons: he has become the sole property of Jenny Driver and thereby has actively participated in generating the social death of Macheath.

There is a thus a confusion of signifiers clustered around Morano's blackness within the opera. On the one hand, the blackness of the English Blacks, which is literalized in Macheath's embodiment of Morano, serves as a means of leveraging social death into political revolt: in such a case, the disguise of blackness serves both to erase the Englishman's identity (to perform Macheath's social death), and to announce an identification with the socially dead African slave (or slave-prince such as Oroonoko) in order to reclaim the commons. In this respect, Morano's blackness represents a radical naming of the mechanisms of racialization and social death that lay at the foundation of the developing capitalist Atlantic world. On the other hand, by Morano's own account, his blackface disguise is a strategy (a "skreen") for entering into bourgeois marriage and accumulating property and, as such, does not in the least participate in a political critique of capitalism. Throughout the opera, both Gay himself and Morano—the black pirate king who dreams of outfitting his wife with a "coach and six"—seem caught in the contradiction of this double vision of blackness in the Atlantic world: the identification of white labor with black enslavement reveals unsavory truths about Atlantic capitalism; creating a black underclass is the primary means by which white wealth is accumulated in the Atlantic world—a wealth that Morano and Gay seem unwilling to forego.[54]

Morano's attachment to Jenny and to a bourgeois fantasy thus bears further scrutiny, as does his persona as an outlaw diasporic African Black. Ironically, as we have seen, Morano has willfully excluded himself from the realm of common desire by blacking-up, and he has done so in order to achieve bourgeois property ownership: "I conquer but to make thee great," he sings to Jenny. And specifically, the two share a vision of New World conquest that will fund a life of ease in England, where Jenny, "Like a city wife or beauty/ . . . shall flutter life away;/And shall know no other duty,/But to dress, eat, drink, and play."[55] Morano thus aims to parlay his Atlantic blackness into wealthy English whiteness. However, the version of social mobility that he imagines occurring by means of cross-racial performance is ultimately rendered impossible within the play: the racial barrier in the colonial world, even when fictive, apparently cannot be crossed. Captured by the opposition (Indians and white colonials) in battle, Morano is put to death without trial, lamenting his exclusion from an English commons that might have exonerated him: "This [death] sentence indeed is hard," complains Morano. "Without the common forms of trial! Not so much as the counsel of a new gate attorney! Not to be able to lay out my money in partiality and evidence! Not a friend perjur'd for me! This is hard, very hard."[56] Executed at the command of the Indian chief Pohetohee, Morano, as a black man, has no recourse to the impromptu court of public opinion—the voice of the rabble that redeemed Macheath from execution in *The Beggar's Opera*. Rather, the New World commons is divided among white Europeans (a group that includes both creoles and transported criminals in the play), diasporic Africans, and Native Americans—and, as such, it is no commons at all. Macheath has withdrawn himself, intentionally, from the space of common desire by donning blackface, and as a result, he has no recourse to the commons when he is captured and executed as a black pirate.[57]

At the close of the play, Polly agrees to marry Pohetohee's son, Cawwawkee, and the opera ends with a celebratory wedding dance. Yet with Morano/Macheath's lifeless body swinging from a tree off stage, the dance functions as the sign of an anodyne and even cruel calculus of property acquisition in contrast to the lusty, collective scene of pleasure that closed *The Beggar's Opera*. Notably, the marriage contract, so successfully evaded in *The Beggar's Opera*, is here consummated between the English Polly and the Native American Cawwawkee—a scenario of white and indigenous union often evoked (as discussed in chapter 6) in the service of settler colonialism in America. The revelatory link between the "blackness" of the English Blacks and that of diasporic Africans enslaved in the New World that *Polly* broaches is thus rendered invisible and inert at the close of the opera while settler colonialism and the marital contract serve to establish forms of ownership and enclosure.

Although Morano did not survive transportation to the New World, Macheath, it seems, did. Despite a certain amount of criticism concerning the immoral nature of the central characters in the play, *The Beggar's Opera* was immediately and enduringly popular in England, and, interestingly, spread at once to provincial venues including Bath, Bristol, and Dublin and subsequently to stages across the Atlantic. Adam Hallam, itinerant player and father of the two brothers who sent the Hallam touring company to North America, successfully published a French translation of *The Beggar's Opera* that was banned in Paris, but was performed in London.[58] And Hallam's son, Lewis, included *The Beggar's Opera* in the repertoire of twenty-four plays that he brought to the colonies of North America in 1755. Not surprisingly, the opera was tremendously popular in colonial North America as well: according to theatre historians Odai Johnson and William Burling, it was the fourth most often performed play in North America prior to 1774.[59] Another theatre historian describes the play as "the best drawing card of that age" in the colonies—a known favorite of performers and audiences alike.[60] Records indicate that both Thomas Jefferson and George Washington enjoyed a performance of *The Beggar's Opera* in Williamsburg in 1770.[61] In Boston in 1770, one Mr. Joan performed the entire play as a solo act, "personat[ing] all the characters, and enter[ing] into the different humours, or passions, as they change from one to another through the opera."[62] And in 1795, in Charleston, a notice appeared in the *South Carolina Gazette* requesting a performance of *The Ladies Folly or the Beggar's Opera Reversed*—a version of *The Beggar's Opera* in which the male characters are played by female actors and vice versa—which had debuted in London more than a decade earlier.[63]

The popularity of the play in London was due in part to the ability of the opera to make common cause across class divisions, most particularly among elite and plebian audience members. But the portability and fungibility of *The Beggar's Opera* indicates that the community-generating force of the play was not limited to an audience well versed in the politics of the Walpole administration or Londoners' taste for Italian opera. Indeed, the portability of the play suggests that it had the capacity to generate a community anywhere it landed—among children, among provincials, among Frenchmen, among cross-dressers, among colonials. In fact, we might say that this is the very trick of the play that is exploited in its outré variations: the play is set down in the midst of an unlikely community in order that one may watch it generate a likely common ground.

Thus, as much as the opera derides norms of bourgeois property ownership and the legal regime of Whig capitalism, it nonetheless has an important constructive aspect to it as well. The opera stages a scene of disorder—in its satirical portrait of thieves and corrupt officials—but it also enacts a scene of order in the construction of the new collectivity that is visible in the collective dance at the close of the play. We might conclude that if the play is biting with respect to capitalism, enclosure, and marriage, it is nonetheless celebratory of the possibilities of a communally generated order that informs and arranges the bodies of individuals into a shared scene of dance and music. The central thrust of the play is thus not necessarily anathema to the social order but rather generates the possibility of a performative social community that is arrived at by way of "taste" or embodied public consensus.

The alternative geographies where the theatrical traditions of pantomime, ballad opera, and melodrama did develop were part of a larger imperial culture in the provinces and the colonies; theatre, moreover, had an important role in generating a creole commons in New World locations such as Charleston, New York, and Kingston. The reading of *The Beggar's Opera* I have presented here thus points to an alignment of "the commons" as a geographical and legal space in England with the common space of the public sphere, particularly in relation to the larger Anglo-Atlantic world beyond London. In other words, a sort of transference may be said to have taken place, in which the "commons" became a performative and discursive site rather than the location of real property. And indeed, this is the overall trajectory of the plot of *The Beggar's Opera* as a whole, as we have seen: in response to a Whig regime that privatizes property and encloses the real estate of the commons, a new performative commons achieves political force in the opera through shared song, dance, and collective theatrical embodiment. The commons, one might say, was increasingly realized in the unreal space of the theatre during the eighteenth century. This formulation is one that has particular significance with respect to the circulation of culture in the imperial Atlantic world. In New World colonial locations, where little or no real property was held in common by whites and no real property served as a historical scene of collective belonging for European colonials, the community looked to different institutions for the embodiment of its collectivity—institutions that included, for example, the church, the courthouse, the marketplace, and the theatre. A commitment to eradicating the material commons—in the form of both Whig enclosure and settler colonial appropriation of Native American lands—helps to structure the presence of the performative commons in the world of Atlantic modernity. *The Beggar's Opera*, as we have seen, comments on the eradication of the commons in England, but insofar as the opera convenes a performative commons, it also instantiates a new form of theatrical cultural power that will have particular sway in the Anglo-Atlantic periphery. The double-edged nature of this performative commons is worth underscoring: on the one hand, such a commons is highly mobile, circulatory, and vagabond-like—as a performative collectivity untethered to any given location save that of its provisional materialization, it has the structure of a "promiscuous multitude." On the other hand, the point of representing and performing the collectivity is to generate order and meaning through shared engagement, to find common ground in articulating the entity of "the town" by way of aesthetics (by way of "taste")— hence the order-creating capacity of the performance.[64]

The Beggar's Opera is a highly mobile performance that tells the story of this new commons and its radical possibilities. Placed in relation to *Polly*, however, this same performance reveals a different aspect of the Atlantic public sphere—namely, the extent to which the localized and localizing nature of the embodied (performative) commons can function as a screen for the far-flung relations of economic and political interdependence that structure the Atlantic world. In particular, the commoning force of *The Beggar's Opera* serves as a screen for the segmenting (and specifically, the racialized segmenting) of an Atlantic world labor force. Performing the triumph of the English commons, *The Beggar's Opera* occludes from sight the relation between white "Blacks" and black "Blacks" in the Atlantic world; *Polly*, in turn, suggests that the possibility of this black commons is exactly what cannot constitute a collective scene of knowledge and pleasure in the capitalist geography of Anglo-Atlantic colonialism.

CHAPTER 4

CHARLESTON

COLONIAL INTIMACY AND BARE LABOR

The enslaved black body that appeared on stage in the figure of Oroonoko
in London and galvanized a weeping public there had a far different stage
life when (re)transported to the New World. In Charleston (as we saw in
chapter 1), Oroonoko was on the verge of materializing on stage in 1795, but
the production was banned by gubernatorial edict before he could make an
appearance there, and he never subsequently reappeared. In Kingston, Jamaica,
no record exists of Oroonoko's presence on stage, and in New York City,
Oroonoko first appeared for a four-night run in October 1783.[1] Notably,
London and New York City had majority white populations at the time of
Oroonoko's appearance before the public; Charleston and Kingston, on the
other hand, had majority black populations in the late eighteenth century. The
presence of a black body—even a white body performing as a black body—on
stage thus had a different meaning in the colonies of South Carolina and
Jamaica than in London or New York: moreover, that meaning had to do
with questions concerning the performance of a public collectivity—with the
performance of a public or commons at the embodied location of the theatre.[2]

As I have argued in the preceding chapters, the contradictions inherent in
the colonial relation—between British liberty and race slavery—were managed in the metropole, in part, by means of recourse to geographical distance
(invoked to attenuate and screen the force of contradiction); in the colony,
however, that strategy was not available. In a colonial polity such as Charleston, black, Native American, and white bodies lived in profound intimacy
with one another, separated by a distance defined in legal and juridical terms
rather than spatial ones. As such, the contradictions of the colonial relation
were sharpened and intensified in the colony. On the one hand, the political

discourse of English liberty had taken root on colonial ground and indeed, by 1776, had reconfigured itself as a revolutionary American politics of popular sovereignty. On the other hand, embodiments of the people—and, specifically, the racialized embodiment of the population of a city such as Charleston—directly contradicted the assertion that popular sovereignty was a guiding principle of order under the plantocratic dispensation of South Carolina. The need for the slave body to be present (economically, as labor) and absent (politically, as figuring the people) thus reached new heights of contradiction—and new pitches of display and erasure—in the early national southern state/colony.[3] Further, the stagings of white freedom and black social death masked and participated in the ongoing effort to erase Native peoples from the polity and to eradicate their claims to indigenous sovereignty.

In the previous chapter, I argued that capitalism engaged in a practice of "Blacking" to create the conscripted labor that fueled Atlantic modernity. This "Blacking" affected both Europeans and Africans but increasingly assumed the form of a racially codified economic and legal system that effected the social death of Africans who were transported to the New World as a source of lucrative and disposable labor. Insofar as the slave in this economy is disposable—debarred from political and social identity and from social reproduction—the slave is seemingly a figure of what Giorgio Agamben has called "homo sacer" or "bare life," namely, "life which ceases to be politically relevant . . . and can as such be eliminated without punishment."[4] Such a description applies, for instance, to Macheath, "blacked-up" as Morano, whose life is "eliminated without punishment" in *Polly* (in sharp contrast to the white Macheath in *The Beggar's Opera*, whose life is sustained by the collective "taste of the town"). But if the black pirate king can be killed offstage without ado, it is not the case that the laboring black slave can be eliminated without comment from the economy of Atlantic modernity. Given the centrality of black labor to the colony, I argue that the figure of the slave in the colony is less one of "bare life" than one of "bare labor." The slave is stripped of the prerogatives of social life—consigned to social death—while nonetheless providing labor that is central to the economic existence of the polity.

In the colony of Charleston, plantocratic authority sought both to "blacken" New World Africans and to deprive them of and debar them from the resources of sociality. Moreover, in the multiple assemblages in which the people manifested themselves as a polity in Charleston, the black population was rendered negligible, uncountable, invisible. The profound irony, however, as we will see, lies in the fact that the operations of erasure effected a new inscription of cultural identity and sociality: under the sign of social death, social life assumes new forms. Indeed, out of the effort to generate bare labor, what emerges is a form of intimacy—a public in which persons of color are not absent, but centrally present. Rather than a scene of bare life, we find a colonial scene marked by intimacy, violence, and erasure and a culture that takes place in the space of that erasure—a "second scene" of colonialism. The theatre, in particular, is a location at which the provisional community of the colony gathers and constitutes itself through performance, citation, and erasure. Traveling on imperial Atlantic routes, theatrical scripts and players cover great distances but generate, by way of insistently local performances, new colonial intimacies—newly assembled publics.

ERASURE AND ENUMERATION:
WHITE AND BLACK IN COMMON

Founded as a proprietary colony in 1670, South Carolina was colonized by wealthy planters from Barbados who brought with them enslaved Africans and ambitions to expand the lucrative plantation model of Barbadian agricultural production. Given the dense community of Native American tribes inhabiting the area that the proprietors sought to colonize, English colonizers survived in South Carolina only insofar as they negotiated with Native peoples, participating in the shifting arrays of affiliations and antagonisms between and among tribes and wielding the power of access to an Atlantic market of goods to trade for alliance and support. But access to the Atlantic trade opened another route to rapid profit for white colonials in South Carolina as well—namely, capturing Indians and selling them into slavery at other colonial ports including Massachusetts and the Caribbean. The earliest profits reaped from slavery in South Carolina were not those of labor extracted from New World Africans, but those based on extracting Native Americans from ancestral lands and transporting them into Atlantic servitude and social death. According to Alan Gallay, white colonials enslaved and exported as many as 51,000 Indians from South Carolina ports between 1670 and 1720. More Indians were exported from Charleston during these years, Gallay reports, than enslaved Africans were imported. The Indian slave trade, in its Atlantic dimensions, writes Gallay, "infected the South: it set in motion a gruesome series of wars that engulfed the region. For close to five decades, virtually every group of people in the South lay threatened by destruction in these wars. Huge areas became depopulated, thousands of Indians died, and thousands more were forcibly relocated to new areas in the South or exported from the region. . . . The trade in Indian slaves was at the center of the English empire's development in the American South."[5]

The Indian slave trade ultimately threatened the survival of the colony of South Carolina as well: during the Yamasee War in 1715, an array of powerful tribes, including the Catawbas, the Chocktaw, the Yamasee, and the Ochese Creek, united against the English and decimated white settlements, virtually destroying the colony. Notably, one of the first actions of the united tribes was to execute the white Indian traders in their midst: as many as ninety English Indian traders were killed during the first weeks of the war. Ironically, the colony of South Carolina survived only because the English were able to gain the support of the Cherokee, who aligned with the English against the Creek. Following the Yamasee War, however, the Indian slave trade largely disappeared; more importantly, English colonials turned to agricultural production, and a plantation model of production dependent upon enslaved black labor in particular, with new intensity. William L. Ramsey concludes that "the [Yamasee] war ended South Carolina's experimentation with Indian slavery and committed the colony to an exclusive reliance on African labor from 1715 onward."[6] The history of settler colonialism in South Carolina thus involved the eradication and export of Native Americans and the importation of Africans, as well as the "blackening" of Africans by way of an increasingly codified system of racialization that supported a regime of production based on bare labor.

Followng the Yamasee War, the Charleston public was fundamentally shaped by the fact that while whites wielded political power, blacks wielded numerical power. As Peter H. Wood demonstrates in his influential study of the development of the colony of South Carolina, blacks made up a majority of the population from 1708 forward—a fact that distinguished South Carolina from other slaveholding colonies in British North America.[7] The ramifications of the signal fact of the black majority were great for the slave regime of South Carolina: because blacks out-numbered whites, whites needed to develop and deploy strategies for maintaining power and masking their numerical insufficiency. Given the black majority and the repressive and violent nature of slavery, a constant, profound insecurity marked the workings of white power and the daily lives of white slave owners in South Carolina. Indeed, so strongly felt was the threat of a black majority that the colony repeatedly passed laws designed to limit the ratio of blacks to whites. In 1740, for instance, following the Stono rebellion (a quashed slave revolt), the colony passed a stringent new slave code aimed at preventing the possibility of slave revolt. The Negro Act of 1740 included provisions requiring a ratio of one white per ten blacks on any plantation and imposed high tariffs on newly imported slaves from Africa and the West Indies. However, the profitability of slave labor for white planters caused such provisions to be routinely ignored and/

or evaded. Thus the black majority in South Carolina persisted throughout the eighteenth century, carrying with it both the promise of white wealth and the threat of violent revolt.

Confronted with ocular evidence of a black majority, white visitors to South Carolina often announced themselves stunned at the sight of such blackness made visible. As both Wood and Robert Olwell note, visitors to eighteenth-century Charleston tended to consistently overestimate the black-to-white ratio of the population. In 1774, for instance, the German Lutheran minister Henry M. Muhlenberg stated of Charleston, "At first it strikes one as strange to see so many Negro slaves, for here, it is said, there are twenty blacks for every white man."[8] The ratio at the time was probably closer to fifty-fifty than twenty to one, but the severe overestimation of visitors such as Muhlenberg is an index of a certain visual shock, or visual threat that white visitors seemed to experience upon being in the presence of a population in which whites were not the majority: when they walked the streets of Charleston, what registered in their minds was clearly the predominant presence of black men and women.[9]

Implicit in the anxious enumeration of white and black bodies was a clear concern with slave rebellion; as a visitor from Massachusetts in 1772, Josiah Quincy, made evident in his account of life in South Carolina, fear of insurrection was both omnipresent and suppressed, thus making it the constant subtext of white life:

> Slavery may truly be said to be the peculiar curse of this land. . . . A few years ago, it is allowed, that the blacks exceeded the whites as seventeen to one. There are those who now tell you, that the slaves are not more than three to one, some pretend not so many. But they who talk thus are afraid that the slaves should by some means discover their superiority. Many people express great fears of an insurrection, others treat the idea as chimerical. I took great pains (finding much contrariety of opinion) to find out the true proportion. The best information I could obtain fixes it at about seven to one, my own observation leads me to think it much greater.[10]

Quincy's account indicates a simultaneous concern to enumerate—to count and thus *see* slave bodies and the threat that they might pose—and to *erase*, to eradicate the racial composition of the public for fear that seeing that composition or speaking of it might invite revolution. More specifically, Quincy notes that whites are most concerned that *blacks* not be able to attain knowledge of their numerical superiority, wary that such knowledge alone might serve as the grounds of revolt.

Thus, in addition to the mechanisms of physical coercion and punishment—of direct bodily harm and the theatrics of terror associated with physical violence—used to enforce the enslavement of blacks, whites relied on tactics of erasure and silence: by not allowing the black majority to see or hear of itself, Quincy's statement suggests, slave owners believed themselves to be controlling and containing the threat of revolution. One key effort exerted to prevent blacks from either "discover[ing] their superiority" or acting on that knowledge was the prohibition placed on the gathering of black publics. Newspapers often commented with concern on the presence of black publics on the streets of Charleston, and regulations were repeatedly enacted to prevent the visible conjoining of blacks into groups. The most extensive regulations concerning black assembly were codified in the Negro Act of 1740: the act not only fixed the permissible ratio of blacks to whites on plantations at ten-to-one, but it also prohibited more than seven blacks from traveling together on a road without a white person, and it authorized all justices to keep order by "dispers[ing] any assembly or meeting of slaves which may disturb the peace or endanger the safety of his Majesty's subjects." In addition, the 1740 law states that "all due care [must] be taken to restrain the wanderings and meetings of negroes and other slaves, at all times, and more especially on Saturday nights, Sundays, and other holidays, and their using and carrying wooden swords, and other mischievous and dangerous weapons, or using and keeping of drums, horns, or other loud instruments, which may call together or give sign or notice to one another of their wicked designs and purposes." Further, masters were forbidden by the act to allow "public meetings or feastings of strange negroes or slaves in their plantations."[11]

Of particular interest in the phrasing of this law is the connection it draws between the specter of black gatherings and music, feasting, and weaponry. Enacted directly following the Stono rebellion, the law is clearly written in response to the events that unfolded in the environs of Charleston in 1739, when roughly twenty slaves gathered and began attacking white warehouses and killing whites in order to acquire weapons. A rapidly amassing group of rebels began marching toward St. Augustine, Florida, possibly because they had heard that the Spaniards promised freedom to slaves deserting the English colony. According to an account of the events printed in London's *Gentleman's Magazine* in March 1740, the Stono rebellion began as slaves "calling out Liberty, marched on with Colours displayed, and two Drums beating, pursuing all the white people they met with. . . . They increased every minute by new Negroes coming to them, so that they were above Sixty, some say a hundred, on which they halted in a field, and set to dancing, Singing and beating Drums, to draw more Negroes to them, thinking they were now victorious over the whole Province, having marched ten miles & burnt all before them."[12] Accounts such as this sowed fear among whites about the activities of groups of blacks "dancing, Singing, and beating Drums"—that is, groups of slaves performing a black cultural commons and thereby displaying and giving voice to their political power as a collectivity.

As Richard Cullen Rath demonstrates, slave colonies in the Caribbean had repeatedly enacted legislation to outlaw drumming and blowing horns among slaves: white planters were concerned that horns and drums might function as calls to arms among slaves.[13] With the Negro Act of 1740, South Carolina followed in the footsteps of such efforts—efforts that aimed to prevent the communicative function of horns and drums. Further, such legislation points to the fact that dance and music were cultural forms with particular power and persistence—forms of "covert knowledge" to use Rath's term—that were exercised in the face of a system that sought to eradicate the communicative and collectivizing (i.e., social and human) capacities of New World Africans in order to more efficiently extract their labor for profit.[14] The accounts of the Stono rebellion thus suggest the power of music to help convoke a public with knowledge of itself—that is, these accounts indicate the way in which music can call into being a collectivity, much in the way that the folk ballad of *The Beggar's Opera* generated a collectivity with the ability to call forth a new epistemic framing that challenged Whig property regimes.

Attempts to stop the gathering of black collectivities in South Carolina failed: despite laws to the contrary, blacks gathered at a variety of sites in Charleston in the eighteenth century, including the street, the marketplace, and the racetrack, and in private spaces as well. Further, extant evidence demonstrates that whites were ineffectual in their efforts to eradicate large gatherings of blacks unmonitored by whites at which dancing, music, and festivity occurred during the eighteenth century. Consider, for example, a newspaper account from 1772, complaining about the lack of enforcement of laws against slave gatherings in Charleston:

> The [author of the letter] had once an opportunity of seeing a Country-Dance, Rout, or Cabal of Negroes, within 5 miles distance of this town, on a Saturday night; and it may not be improper here to give a description of that assembly. It consisted of about 60 people, 5–6th from Town, every one of whom carried something, in the manner just described: as, bottled liquors of all sorts, Rum, Tongues, Hams, Beef, Geese, Turkies and Fowls, both drest and raw . . . Moreover, they were provided with Music,

Cards, Dice &c. The entertainment was opened, by the men copying (or taking off) the manners of their masters, and the women those of their mistresses, and relating some highly curious anecdotes, to the inexpressible diversion of that company. Then they danced, betted, gamed, swore, quarrelled, fought, and did everything that the most modern accomplished gentleman are not ashamed of . . . They had also their private committees: whose deliberations were carried on in too low a voice, and with so much caution, as not to be overheard by the others . . . Whenever or wherever such nocturnal rendezvouses are made, may it not be concluded, that their deliberations are never intended for the advantage of the white people?[15]

The gathering is initially described as a "Country-Dance, Rout or Cabal"—a series of terms whose definitions, while equated with one another in this passage, cover a wide range of meanings, beginning with the social and recreational resonances of the term "dance," moving to the legal/military implications of the term "rout" (one definition of the word that seems germane in this instance is "an assembly of people who have made a move towards committing an illegal act which would constitute an offence of riot"[16]), and concluding with the politically resonant term "cabal." Dancing and feasting are thus closely associated with military and political engagement. Further, a certain theatrical quality informs the festivities described here; according to this account, the slaves begin by imitating white masters, suggesting an acute understanding of the codes of performance that structure white and black behavior in daily life and that inform white subjugation of blacks. Moreover, as the conclusion of the passage makes clear, for the white observer of this event, the gathering of blacks into a collectivity can only imply an assault on the white power structure.[17]

In South Carolina's Negro Act of 1740, blacks are primarily defined within the text of the law in terms of labor and are, furthermore, systematically deprived of access to sociality and communication: in effect, then, the law aims to generate blackness as a category of bare labor. The section of the law forbidding drumming and horn blowing also states that "masters, overseers and other persons whomsoever" (presumably such other "persons" are white) are granted authority to arrest any slave, away from his or her plantation, who does not have "a letter from their master, or a ticket." In this single section of the law, then, the communicative power of horns and drums is explicitly removed from blacks, and the communicative power of written letters and tickets (issued by whites) is given precedence and authority in their stead; as such, all communicative power is arrogated to white hands—collective communication itself becomes the prerogative of whiteness. Further codifying the eradication of representational powers by blacks, the Negro Act makes it a criminal act to teach slaves to write.

Eradicating drumming among blacks, eradicating writing among blacks, and placing the technology of writing solely in the hands of white owners cumulatively produces illiteracy as a quality of blackness; this production of illiteracy must be seen as a political strategy that is of a piece with eradicating sociality and the gathering of the black commons. Accordingly, it may be more useful to consider the illiteracy of slaves in South Carolina as a form of forced a-literacy—a term that I use to underscore the political nature of illiteracy insofar as it is a form of nonknowledge, or exclusion from knowledge, that is actively generated by the white legal structure and should not, as such, be confused with a form of educational insufficiency (as the term "illiteracy" tends to imply).[18] The Negro Act aimed to produce blacks as a different category of beings than whites for the purpose of generating a body of workers from whom labor could be extracted with the least possible cost. The enforcement of a-literacy and the criminalization of the black commons may be seen as two forms of social death associated with the legal production of blackness as labor and property. The response of white owners to the alarming reality of the black majority might thus be seen to assume two contradictory discursive forms: a discourse of enumeration on the one hand and a discourse of erasure on the other. Enumerating black bodies meant defining (counting up, counting on) a massive, laboring work force: making a body black—naming it as black and seeing it as black, according to the law—meant turning it into property and labor. But seeing blacks collectively meant, for white slave-owners, acknowledging the danger of a black majority and thus creating, as we have seen, a desire to erase blacks from representations of the collective body of the public.

ATLANTIC REVOLUTION AND
THE FREEDOM OF THE SCENES

At the Charleston Theatre, much of import occurred that bears no relation to the librettos and scripts of plays that were written and printed in London. First and foremost, the theatre (as in London) was a location at which the public performed itself in relation to what occurred on stage.[19] As such, the theatre was a key institutional location in Charleston where a creole commons or embodied public sphere was staged. Much like the church, marketplace, or courthouse, then, the theatre was an important site where racial domination—in the form of both enumeration and erasure—was performed. Unlike the church, marketplace, or courthouse, however, the theatre was a location where the public went in order to *explicitly* consume performance, as well as to perform itself and thus to debate its own self-constitution. To an extent, then, the theatre had a metacritical function with respect to forming a public, and most particularly with respect to forming a creole cultural commons—in other words, the public was self-consciously engaged in performing itself as a public and was thus also self-consciously engaged in debating the borderlines defining inclusion and exclusion as well as recognition and erasure of the members of the public.

When we look to the official transcript concerning the theatrical public in Charleston, it appears that blacks were summarily excluded from theatre attendance as well as from performing on stage: blacks, according to legal statute, were forcibly erased from the creole commons of Charleston.[20] In 1795, for instance, the city council passed an ordinance forbidding blacks from attending the theatre.[21] And one English visitor to the Charleston Theatre in the early nineteenth century reports that blacks were not allowed to be represented on stage or in the audience to prevent them from attaching any sense of significance to their presence there. John Lambert, writing in 1810, thus states unequivocally that blacks were banned from both stage and audience:

> I expected to find the Charleston stage well supplied with sooty negroes, who would have performed the African and Savage characters in the dramatic pieces to the life; instead of which, the delusion was even worse than on our own [English] stage; for so far from employing real negroes, the performers would not even condescend to black their faces, or dress in any manner resembling an African. This I afterwards learnt was occasioned by motives of policy, lest the negroes in Charleston should conceive, from being represented on the stage, and having their colour, dress, manners, and customs imitated by the white people, that they were very important personages; and might take improper liberties in consequence of it. For this reason also, Othello and other plays are not allowed to be performed, nor are any of the negroes or people of colour permitted to visit the theater.[22]

One might note, in this passage, the resonances between Lambert's account of a concern that public representation will enable blacks to conceive of their importance with respect to the larger public and Josiah Quincy's account (cited above) of the necessity (in the minds of white planters) of maintaining silence with regard to the demographic ratio of blacks to whites lest blacks acquire knowledge of their "superiority." In both cases, a strategy of erasure is advocated as a means of eradicating the threat of a black majority: in both cases, then, the embodied creole commons is restaged as white rather than primarily black in order to sustain white domination of blacks.

Scholars have tended to take this official transcript at face value, but the scripted nature of such representation (erasure being an activity of scripting) suggests that actual performances of the creole commons may not have adhered to this libretto.[23] And indeed, additional evidence suggests that, ordinances notwithstanding, blacks were admitted to the theatre on a regular basis and made up an active part of the audience that performed itself as a public there. Further, New World Africans and New World African culture appeared on the Charleston stage as well. In 1796, for example, a letter appears in the *South Carolina Gazette*, complaining that blacks are regularly attending the theatre in defiance of the ordinance passed the year before:

> *having* been for a length of time absent from the city and returned but a few days past, I resolved to partake of the pleasure arising from theatrical exhibitions, and attended at last night's performance. My pleasures were marred as well from the view of 65 blacks and people of color, situated in the gallery, whom I myself enumerated (a part of which I could only see, so that it may reasonably be concluded there were many more) as from the continual noise which proceeded from the gallery, and which myself among others, observed to be made by these people. If so salutary a regulation has been repealed [prohibiting blacks from attending the theatre], the police of this city deserve severe reproofs from their constituents; if it still exists, I pronounce it a scandalous reflection not only on the citizens, but on the intendant, the 13 wardens, the city sheriff, his deputy, the city marshall, and 26 city constables, amounting in all to 43 persons, intended for the preservation of peace and good order in this city, . . . I perhaps may be supposed . . . to be an enemy to the Charleston Theatre, but am absolutely an enemy to both [theatres operating in Charleston], because the companies acting therein, are not sufficiently good to entertain very rationally an enlightened city and seem intended to please the gallery company present last evening.[24]

EX. Ruled out

The letter, signed "A Native Citizen," explicitly names an alternative strategy or script of racial representation: namely, enumeration. Rather than erase the presence of blacks and the threat of a black majority within the Charleston public, the letter writer is thoroughly engaged in a different calculus—one of counting, and rendering visible, black and white bodies that appear in the theatrical public. In the face of the promiscuous public witnessed at the theatre, where blacks are intermingled with whites, and where blacks are a conspicuous and numerous portion of the public, "Native Citizen" proposes an alternative system of ordering the population—namely, a sort of Foucauldian grid of power comprising the hierarchical system of intendant, wardens, sheriff, marshals, and constables, all of whom are expected to surveil the population within their jurisdiction, and thus saturate the city with the gaze of white authority. Notably, however, "Native Citizen's" numbers do not add up in favor of white authority: ultimately, he counts sixty-five blacks and forty-three whites in this lengthy enumeration, and while the whites are in positions of power, the numerical insufficiency of white bodies is clearly part of what motivates the cry for a continued dedication to white-dominated order articulated in the letter.

It is worth noting that "Native Citizen" is not simply concerned that blacks are seated in the gallery at the theatre but is also worried that the actors on stage seem to be playing directly to them. Further, according to the letter, the gallery patrons were vociferous in their response to the play. In short, then, black audience members were clearly performing themselves as part of the public, and were *recognized* by the actors as part of the public. Another letter to the editor, complaining of the presence of blacks at the theatre in 1801, makes an interesting reference to the "rabble" in attendance at the Charleston Theatre. Specifically, the letter writer blames the "rabble" for routinely giving women headaches when they attend the theatre and concludes that "people of colour should be absolutely excluded" from the theatre.[25] This letter suggests, again, that black audience members were active participants in the creole commons gathered at the theatre. Moreover, the term "rabble," despite its derogatory connotations, also invokes a theatrical cultural commons: recall that the "taste of the town" in *The Beggar's Opera* was articulated as the voice of the "rabble" that demanded that Macheath be exonerated from execution. The invocation of a rabble comprising people of color thus ironically demonstrates the extent to which blacks were voting members, as it were, of the embodied public gathered at the theatre. While some patrons and managers clearly welcomed this state of affairs as a means of generating additional ticket sales and/or enlivening argument over the nature of the public itself—as conducive, that is, to the kind of promiscuity and debate that was a scene of pleasure at the theatre—others saw it, predictably, as a threat to the "rational" order of the theatre and the larger social order established by the white plantocracy.

Debates concerning the racial character of the embodied public sphere in Charleston assumed heightened visibility at the close of the eighteenth century because of the proximity of the Haitian Revolution, which began in 1791 and concluded with the creation of the first black republic in the Americas in

1804. Large numbers of refugees from St. Domingue, both white and black, arrived in Charleston during the 1790s, and while Charleston initially offered a sympathetic reception to white planters fleeing violence from slaves, the tide of sentiment in favor of the refugees began to shift as support for the French Revolution waned with the unfolding of the reign of terror in France and as concern about the spread of racial revolution increased. In fact, the politics of revolution in Charleston in the 1790s were extremely complex: Charlestonians supported the republican politics of the American Revolution and, initially, enthusiastically supported the republican politics of the French Revolution. The revolution in St. Domingue, however, mobilized discourses of political equality in terms of race (rather than class) in ways that challenged the white plantocracy's support for the French and for republicanism in general. As the revolution in St. Domingue progressed, metropolitan officers of the revolutionary French republic authorized the freeing of slaves in St. Domingue in 1792—a move that enraged white creole planters there. French officials did so in part to enlist blacks in St. Domingue in the French military's battle against the British, who sought to take control of the island. Thus, a third division that segmented the would-be republican populace (beyond race and class) in Charleston and St. Domingue was that separating creole from metropolitan interests—a fourth set of divisions (visible in the French decision to free slaves in order to rebuff the British) obtained among the European empires and U.S. alliances (or lack thereof) with these empires, including French, British, and Spanish imperial powers. The collective republican body of Charleston was thus riddled with dividing lines that constituted and segmented the population in competing and contradictory ways. Construed solely in terms of a U.S. geography, one might tend to consider the population of Charleston as divided primarily along racial lines, but viewed within an Atlantic geography, the issue of race becomes far more complicated, embedded as it was in the 1790s within a larger history of European empire, European republican revolution, and New World counterimperial revolution.

The activities of Charleston's Democratic-Republican clubs offer a useful example of just how complex the politics of revolution were in Charleston at this point. As Michael Kennedy reports, the French Popular Society was formed in Charleston in the early 1790s "at the height of pro-French feeling" and attracted more than one hundred members between 1792 and 1795, including both Frenchmen and white English creoles; the primary activity of the club was the performance of patriotic ceremonies that allied French and U.S. republican politics.[26] Kennedy describes the elaborate nature of these celebrations, which concluded with the unveiling of panoramic scenes or "transparencies" painted by Antoine Audin, a member of the French Patriotic Society who would become renowned as a skilled painter of theatrical scenery in the United States:

> The typical fete opened in the early morning with cannonades by French vessels in the harbor. About noon the celebrants assembled at the consulate or at Harris's café. Then, wearing tricolor cockades and singing patriotic anthems, they marched to the Huguenot Church for a solemn service and an oration.... Following the ceremonies at the church ... the company normally reassembled in the afternoon for a festive banquet.... At every dinner toasts were given [to Washington, Rousseau, Franklin, the Rights of Man, the Jacobin Societies, etc.].... Highlights of the festivals were the transparencies which Audin displayed in the evenings.... On [one] part of the transparency, France and America held the treaty of alliance of 1778, and Truth threw the hideous monster, Fanaticism, to the ground. As a last touch, Audin showed the ghost of Mirabeau, a French Revolutionary hero, being welcomed to the Elysian Fields by Franklin, Voltaire, and Rousseau.[27]

The primary activities of the French Popular Club were thus strikingly theatrical: the club repeatedly staged lengthy scenes of celebratory republicanism, aimed at uniting the iconographic figures of French republicanism with those of U.S. republicanism. The fact that the celebrations relied heavily on the work of Audin, a scene painter, demonstrates just how closely related to theatrical performance such celebrations were. Further, the citywide geography of these celebrations—moving from harbor, to church, to tavern, to banquet hall—gives an indication of the way in which such festivities aimed to generate a widespread integration of French and U.S. publics, embedded within multiple sites of life in Charleston.

The integrationist aims of the French Popular Society were severely challenged, however, by the influx of white St. Domingue planters who arrived in Charleston in increasing numbers following the burning of Le Cap Français by ex-slaves in St. Domingue in 1793. Blaming the French revolutionary government for freeing the slaves, the displaced colonial aristocrats "complained bitterly about French colonial policy," thus poisoning the well with respect to the wildly celebratory activities of the French Popular Club who hailed the leaders of the French revolutionary government as heroes and aimed to galvanize a Charleston public around the clarity of this republican truth. Frenchmen within Charleston were thus deeply divided over French policy in St. Domingue, and competing accounts of the activities of Citizens Sonthonax and Polverel, the French leaders who took charge of freeing the slaves in St. Domingue, were the subject of extensive newspaper coverage and debate.[28] Further, exiled planters from St. Domingue sought to impugn the French consul in Charleston, Michel-Ange-Bernard de Mangourit, explicitly arguing that he was attempting to spread antislavery revolution to the United States. Thus, for instance, a letter to the newspaper charges that the French revolutionary government had embraced principles that "tend visibly to the subversion of the political existence of the four southern [slaveholding] states of America, and to the destruction of the lives and property of their inhabitants"; Mangourit, in particular, was charged with planning to institute the "fierce execution of a certain law" in Charleston—namely, the abolition of slavery.[29] In addition, as Robert Alderson demonstrates, threats of a massive, interstate slave revolt, alleged to be orchestrated with assistance from black refugees from St. Domingue, reached Charleston in late 1793: some Charlestonians took this as definitive evidence of French efforts to export black republican revolution to the southern United States. Charleston, as Alderson argues, "was gripped by fear and suspicion," and in October 1793, the governor of South Carolina proclaimed that all free blacks who had arrived from foreign ports during the past year were required to leave the state—this in addition to laws that banned any ships from St. Domingue from landing in Charleston.[30]

The theatrics of race, republicanism, and revolution in the Charleston public sphere played out not only in the newspapers and on the streets of Charleston, but also, quite explicitly, on the stage of the theatre.[31] In 1794, John Sollee, a refugee from the French Revolution, opened the French Theatre in Charleston, which was largely staffed by white performers who were refugees from St. Domingue. The French Theatre did not, however, perform only or even primarily for French audiences in Charleston: rather, the majority of the performances were a-linguistic; that is, they did not require a shared spoken language between actors and audience because they consisted of ballets, acrobatics, pantomimes, rope dances, and harlequinades. Moreover, so popular were the a-linguistic performances of the French Theatre that the Charleston Theatre soon moved to adopt versions of the genres performed there in order to compete for audience share. And indeed, within a year of the opening of the French Theatre, Alexander Placide, a refugee from St. Domingue who initially managed the French Theatre, defected to the Charleston Theatre and later became its longtime manager, a trajectory indicative of the extent to which the influx of French refugees in Charleston became a permanent part of the theatrical public sphere.[32]

However, the infusion of French/St. Domingue theatricality in Charleston was not uncontroversial. By 1797, one letter writer complained that the "rage" for French theatre had permanently destroyed the integrity of the Charleston Theatre:

> From the first establishment of the Charleston Theatre to this period, we have witnessed a gradual falling off in the performers, until their neglect has become an insult upon the good nature of the citizens. . . . Had the citizens been resolute in their support [of the Charleston Theatre], we might now boast a respectable theatre; but numbers, from the laudable motive of encouraging the distressed theatrical performers from St. Domingo, gave so decided a preference to the French style, as to make it all the rage, and it became the ruin and destruction of the very theatre they would have promoted. . . . Can you allow the least merit to the [current] manager in procuring you a good company or retaining those actors that were tolerable? Has he ever been able in one instance to change the inapplicable scenes that have been hanging in a falling state without an interruption to the play? . . . Has he kept his theatre clear of people of colour, agreeably to the restrictions of your City Council, and his own proposals? Are not his scenes crowded with visitors of every description, to the entire interruption of the performance; and has he ever had the modesty to keep from being seen, even mulatto wenches?[33]

The overall tone of the letter bears remarking on: as with other letters published in the newspaper about the theatre in Charleston, this writer assumes that the theatre is a civic space—one that the citizens of Charleston should be expected to actively monitor insofar as it represents the city and its values. Indeed, the point of the letter as a whole is precisely to exercise this monitory function to insure that the theatrical public sphere is an ideal reflection of the polity (as conceived by the author of the letter). Though privately hired and paid, the manager of the theatre is regarded, in effect, as an elected public representative by the author of the letter. More specifically, the letter contends that the Charleston Theatre has been permanently and detrimentally infected by a contagious French culture, imported from colonial St. Domingue. Complaints leveled against the manager include his failure to successfully revise scripts performed at the Charleston Theatre to adequately suit a Charleston audience and, more significantly, allowing blacks both to attend the theatre and to appear on stage.

The final complaint of the letter writer concerns the appearance of "mulatto wenches"—mixed-race women—who, in violation of a standard of propriety ("modesty") invoked by the writer, have not been kept out of sight in the space of the theatre: in short, the theatre manager is accused of *failing to erase* (failing "to keep from being seen") women of color from the public space of the theatre. The suggestion in the letter is that the audience has been exercising what is known as the "freedom of the scenes"—a policy (or prerogative) dating to seventeenth-century English custom that allowed theatre patrons to stand on stage during a performance; the custom is very much of a piece with an understanding of the theatre as a location where the audience, as much as the players on stage, performed themselves for the public. Struggles over the freedom of the scenes were widespread in the eighteenth century in both England and the colonies, as managers and actors objected to having stages crowded with audience members, and audience members—particularly wealthy ones— insisted on their right to display themselves on stage.[34] The letter cited above complains that the manager of the Charleston Theatre has not managed to keep the stage free of audience members, but more particularly, the letter writer objects to the fact that "visitors of every description" have crowded the scenes. And most specifically, the letter writer states, the manager has allowed people of color—"even mulatto wenches"—to display themselves on stage. In short, then, women of color have evidently joined spectators on stage to view performances and in so doing have explicitly performed their own identity as audience members, and, by extension, have performed themselves as legitimate and visible members of the Charleston polity. The troubling presence of the black woman's body on stage is crucial here: on stage, the black spectator *performs* her identity as a member of the public and her body serves as a *sign* of the public and its capacity for consent.

THE FRENCH THEATRE AND
THE SECOND SCENE OF COLONIALISM

The ruination caused by the influx of refugees from St. Domingue would seem to consist in the introduction of an altered concept of the theatrical public sphere—one in which white domination and the erasure of black embodiment is not a guiding principle. But how and why did a mixed-race public manage to materialize in Charleston despite ordinances aimed specifically at preventing it from doing so? Why would whites, such as those managing the French Theatre and the Charleston Theatre, want to evade laws prohibiting black visibility? Further, why would whites fleeing racial revolution in St. Domingue embrace a seemingly more racially egalitarian notion of the public sphere than Anglo-Charlestonians? And why would large audiences pay to join this public if they did not approve of or find pleasure within it? To answer these questions, it seems useful to consider more closely the creole nature of the Charleston public, particularly in the 1790s. The discourse of liberty at stake within the performance of a consenting, embodied public in Charleston at this point was increasingly unaligned with that of *English* liberty, even for those who spoke English. Rather, at stake was a public constituted in relation to an evolving Atlantic politics of liberty—one that was articulated at the intersection of English liberty, American revolutionary republicanism, French revolutionary republicanism (and the backlash against it), antislavery revolution in St. Domingue, and creole anticolonial revolution (of both U.S. and St. Domingue varieties). As we saw in the last chapter, John Gay's *Polly* failed to generate a creole cultural commons because of the extent to which Gay's notion of English popular liberty relied on an Atlantic racialization of labor and power that segmented rather than convoked an Atlantic, creole cultural commons. A creole cultural commons, one might speculate, would need to be able to negotiate the contradiction between racial segmentation and popular embodiment—or rather, would need to negotiate that contradiction in terms quite distinct from those that worked successfully in London. In turning to the French theatre in particular, and its influence on the Charleston Theatre as well, one can see the emergence of precisely such a new negotiation—not one in which New World Africans or Native Americans become full and equal citizens within a creole public, but one in which the colonial relation assumes a new (creole) form that is simultaneously more inclusive and more internally repressive with regard to race.

Three years prior to the publication of the letter to the editor complaining about the influence of St. Domingue actors cited above, the French Theatre opened its doors in Charleston for the first time. In the early 1790s, white refugees from St. Domingue were warmly received in Charleston, including the actors seeking employment on the Charleston stage. The actors from St. Domingue initially performed in February 1794 at the Charleston Theatre, and the *City Gazette* notice of the performance gives a flavor of the extent to which politics and theatre were intricately linked:

> Some French play actors lately from St. Domingo, after having been plundered by privateers, and conducted to Providence, where they experienced a number of misfortunes, have at length arrived at Charleston, this hospitable city, where the French have been for several months welcomed and treated as brothers. These play actors, not withstanding the difficulties they foresee in exercising their profession in a country where their language is not generally understood, think they can, however, venture this resource, the

only one which is left to them to alleviate their present distress, in hopes, that being French and unfortunate men, these two titles will be sufficient to recommend them to the public benevolence.[35]

According to this notice, the public convoked around the performers from St. Domingue is one that is explicitly segmented by language but united along the lines of political brotherhood: the politics of this brotherhood remain somewhat underarticulated, shrouded in the dual appeal to French identity (and thus to a republican brotherhood) and the epithet "unfortunate"—the latter presumably a reference to suffering at the hands of both pirates and race revolution and, as such, an appeal to a brotherhood based on a shared white, creole status. Importantly, neither France nor Providence, Rhode Island, is considered a suitable haven for the refugees, whereas Charleston is: Charleston is thus represented as intrinsically linked to St. Domingue in a way that France and Rhode Island are not. Arguably, then, what sustains the bonds of sympathy between English-speaking Charlestonians and French actors from St. Domingue is the fact that both share a core identity (one that trumps language and nationality) as white, colonial creoles in plantation economies.

Shortly after an initial performance at the Charleston Theatre by the "unfortunate" men from St. Domingue, the French Theatre opened on a permanent basis, with the performers from St. Domingue forming the core of the company. Although the Charleston Theatre had welcomed the refugee actors for a benefit performance, the launch of a separate theatre inaugurated a direct and hard-fought competition between the existing English-speaking theatre and the theatre of the refugee actors, the opening shots of which involved the performance of a pantomime version of Daniel Defoe's novel *Robinson Crusoe*, this entitled *Robinson Crusoe or Harlequin Friday*.[36] Eleven days after an initial performance of the pantomime *Pygmalion*, the French Theatre advertised a performance of the pantomime of *Robinson Crusoe* in which Crusoe was to be represented: "In his island, and his return with Friday to Europe. A grand historic pantomime in two parts, with entire new scenery, and all the views of the island; with the landing of the savages, and their dance."[37] The scenery, the advertisement indicated, would be painted by the renowned Monsieur Audin. Just two weeks later, the Charleston Theatre countered by mounting a performance of *Robinson Crusoe* of its own, advertised as "The much esteemed pantomime entertainment of Robinson Crusoe, or Harlequin Friday. *With entire new scenery, dresses and decorations.* The scenery painted by Mr. Oliphant; and the pantomime got up with the greatest care and attention under the immediate inspection of Mr. Sully, and Mr. M. Sully."[38] Interestingly, then, the staging of *Robinson Crusoe*—a drama concerning shipwreck in the New World, and the reinvention of European identity in relation to the territory and peoples of the New World—became the subject of a war for theatrical patronage between the Franco-colonial and Anglo-colonial theatres in Charleston.

The "Crusoe wars" between the French and English theatres in Charleston thus serve as an intriguing case study in the relation of drama to the developing Atlantic creole public. In its concern with shipwreck and European settlement in the New World, *Crusoe* directly takes up the terms of the colonial relation; translated from the famous novel by Defoe to a stage performance—and more specifically, to a *pantomime* performance—*Robinson Crusoe or Harlequin Friday* serves as an explicit revision of earlier texts. Indeed, as a dramatic performance (rather than a written text), the Crusoe pantomime serves to revise not only Defoe's novel, but prior dramatic representations of the colonial relation as well, including, most pointedly, Shakespeare's famous drama of New World shipwreck and encounter, *The Tempest*. Intriguingly, this genealogy (from *Tempest* to *Crusoe*) is highlighted by the fact that the Charleston Theatre performed D'Avenant and Dryden's *The Tempest, or The Enchanted Island* in the midst of the Crusoe wars on the night of May 12, 1794, sandwiched between performances of *Robinson Crusoe*, which appeared on the nights of May 7, 9, and 14 of the same year. In what follows, I suggest that this genealogy—from *Tempest* to *Crusoe*—enables us to trace the Atlantic transformation of the performative commons: indeed, the *Robinson Crusoe* pantomime, I would suggest, serves the Charleston public as something of a creole *Tempest*.

The *Enchanted Island* was staged three times during the 1773–1774 theatrical season in Charleston—more than any other single play. The play's concern with performing white reproduction (as discussed in the previous chapter), one might speculate, would have met with a receptive audience in the colony given the fact that reproducing the white population of the colony in sufficient numbers remained an ongoing concern. Despite the fact that a costly tariff had been placed on the importation of slaves following the Stono rebellion, the effort to decrease the ratio of blacks to whites in the population had not yielded the desired results. In 1740, the low country area had a ratio of two blacks to one white, but by 1770, that ratio was three and a half to one; by 1780, the ratio was four to one. Evidence suggests that blacks were reproducing *and* increasing in numbers in the low country, but whites were not: the white population did not increase between 1740 and 1770, whereas the black population increased by 75 percent.[39] Despite concern among whites about the threat of black rebellion, the allure of profits from slave labor clearly trumped these concerns as the number of slaves kidnapped in Africa and sold in South Carolina continued to increase despite the tariff. Importantly, the world to which *The Enchanted Island* transported the audience was one in which white reproduction was unstoppable—a veritable force of nature—rather than unattainable.

Performed on stage in Charleston, *The Enchanted Island* engages in familiar strategies of erasure with respect to the representation of the black majority: if, outside on the streets, blacks are a numerical majority, inside the theatre, enslaved subalterns are "naturally" in the minority and seemingly will continue to be so. And yet, the strategy of erasure is not wholly successful, nor, perhaps, wholly desirable either. Notably, for instance, the enslaved laborer is not absent from the stage in *The Enchanted Island* but, rather, is visible as a subjugated minority in the figure of Caliban—a fact that suggests that it is not possible to imagine the colonial relation, even in the space of the colony, without the figure of the non-European body present. Indeed, one might say that it is precisely the point of the play to perform and manage this relation. Within the world of the colonial Atlantic, the black body cannot be ushered off the stage, off the street, or off the plantation because of the centrality of black labor to the economic and social fabric of the colonial world: as such, the representational strategy of erasure is, as we saw above, in tension with the need for representational presence. This dual representational strategy, in turn, serves to manage and produce the effects of the colonial relation, namely, white liberty.

In the colony, the paradox of the physical presence and social/epistemic absence of the laboring, non-European body intensifies even as (or perhaps, because) that paradox serves as the basis of the plantocratic, colonial order. Indeed, this paradox is embedded within the colonial relation from the outset: it is visible in Shakespeare's *The Tempest*, for example, when we observe that a certain form of ontic meaning is associated with Caliban's presence even as he is erased from the scene of linguistic meaning and social reproduction. Caliban's curse of Miranda's language lessons has been read as something of a primal scene of colonialism; Stephen Greenblatt, for instance, describes the scene as exemplary of "linguistic colonialism" or the conquest of New World peoples and territory by means of language. But if we listen to Caliban's curse, something more than subjugation and abjection is performed therein: notably, Caliban explicitly states that his "profit" on learning English is that of learning to curse.[40] In the face of Miranda's account of language as expressive and referential—as endowing purposes with meaning—Caliban thus chooses to locate value in a form of speech that is performative rather than referential.

A curse has a certain embodied, physical quality to it that is associated with its ability to make something happen—to perform something—in the world.

It is a kind of speech that hovers at the ontic edge of language, at the border of mere sound where mimesis is sheared away. As obscene (non-)language, the ontic force of the curse stands in tension with the mimetic agency of language, and thereby gestures to an alternative scene of meaning. This alternative scene of meaning is one that emerges "in the break" (to use the words of Fred Moten) of the epistemic contradiction between the imperative to be at once (socially) absent and (physically) present. This break consists, as Moten argues with respect to a black aesthetic tradition, in a "radically exterior aurality that disrupts and resists certain formations of identity and interpretation by challenging the reducibility of phonic matter to verbal meaning or conventional musical form."[41] Indeed, as I suggest at greater length below, this alternative scene might be understood as the *aesthetic* product of the colonial relation—one that emerges most particularly in the space of the colony because of the duality that must be managed there without recourse to physical and geographical separation. Caliban's curse offers an opening onto this creole aesthetic: his curse enables something new to emerge and take shape—something that is registered as presence rather than absence, and as a form of value (profit) rather than loss, albeit a form of profit that is unallied with the emergent calculus of capitalism.

How does this new *something*—the space opened by Caliban's curse—appear in Dryden and D'Avenant's version of the *Tempest*? In its focus on embodiment, *The Enchanted Island*, as we saw in the last chapter, heightens the ontic possibilities of relations between bodies—including relations arrayed under the sign of the unnatural or the obscene, such as sexual relations between Caliban and Miranda or Caliban and Sycorax. The scope given to the ontic force of physicality enables nonlinguistically ordered meanings to be generated around these bodies—a proliferation of comedic, antic, obscene possibilities that the audience is invited to enjoy (recall, for instance, Dorinda's "innocent" wish: "it would be finer, if we two/Had two young Fathers"). As such, *The Enchanted Island*, perhaps unintentionally, tends to suggest that white mastery of colonial space is linked to a second scene of coloniality—one that takes place at a physical, bodily level and one that potentially opens onto a different kind of knowledge and subjectivity than that adumbrated by Prospero, a space designated in the play as obscene—named at the sensual edge of language, as the aural, material excess of the curse or the reduplicative sound play of "tory rory and ranthum scanthum." Thus as much as the ideology of bare labor is articulated within the theatrics of the colonial relation—within Prospero's origin stories or Dryden and D'Avenant's fable of white bodily reproduction—in this very articulation (and particularly in its theatrical form), the ideology of bare labor is belied. What springs up between bodies placed in proximity to another are *social* relations imbued with meaning and desire: as rapidly as such meanings are eradicated or controlled—think of Prospero's labor to decisively erase and control the meaning of the sexual desire between Caliban and Miranda—so too are new relations and means of expressing them generated. Creole embodiment—and the creole public—is *composed* in the space of this obscene and ontic scene, in a location where bare labor is never just bare labor, but is constantly *reconstructed* as such out of the disavowed intimacy of colonial bodies.

The embodied creole public of colonial America inhabits the physical world of Caliban and Miranda—a world in which the intimacy of black and white bodies is a condition of existence but is nonetheless disavowed in legal, social, and epistemic registers. Josiah Quincy's remarks on interracial sex in eighteenth-century South Carolina give an example of the lived contradictions of such an ethos as it appears in the daily life of planters and slaves:

> It is far from being uncommon to see a gentleman at dinner, and his reputed offspring a slave to the master of the table. I myself saw two instances of this, and the company very facetiously would trace the lines, lineaments and features of the father and mother in the child, and very accurately point out the more characteristick resemblance. The fathers neither of them blushed or seem[ed] disconcerted. They were called men of worth, politeness and humanity. Strange perversion of terms and language! ... An African Black labors night and day to collect a small pittance to purchase the freedom of his child: the American or European White man begets his likeness with much indifference and dignity of soul sees his progeny in bondage and misery, and makes not one effort to redeem his own blood. Choice food for satire—wide field for burlesque—and noble game for wit! unless the enkindled blood inflame resentment, wrath and rage, and vent itself in execrations.[42]

Quincy's shock coalesces in particular around the fact that biological paternity by white men of enslaved offspring is not denied, but publicly acknowledged and even enjoyed. The "likeness" of father and child is traced in the physiognomy of faces, and yet this likeness is officially (socially, legally) taken to have no bearing on the matter of the child's status as free or enslaved, white or black, recognized citizen or chattel property. The likeness is seen and unseen at once—recognized with pleasure and unrecognized with devastating consequences. Note, too, that Quincy is fairly explicit as to the way in which this disavowed set of sexual relations disorders linguistic relations as well: he associates the disavowal of sexual and social relations across racial lines with a "strange perversion" of language. In other words, we see here the proximity of linguistic and genealogical elements of the colonial relation and its (daily, lived) paradoxes. Quincy's diagnosis of the likely results of this paradox is worth noting as well: he names two possibilities that may eventuate from the intensity of this contradiction—"burlesque" or "enkindled blood . . . wrath, and rage"—namely, revolutionary violence.

The proximity of burlesque and revolution in Quincy's statement is intriguing: both burlesque and revolution embody social disorder, critique, and subaltern knowledge, but these similarities tilt in the direction of radically different practices—one of laughter, one of bloodshed. The white performers from St. Domingue who arrived in Charleston were fleeing a scene of revolution—a revolution in which enslaved blacks had seized control of political and military power from white colonials, most palpably in the burning of Le Cap Français in 1793. On stage in Charleston, these performers presented satire and burlesque of the colonial relation and the vicious nature of its paradoxical distribution of social life and death. Performance offers, as I have suggested, a particularly powerful means of engaging the structures of visibility and disavowal at stake in the colonial relation. Further, the performance of burlesque or satire enables an engagement with social contradiction that both remarks on and potentially defuses the explosive power of that contradiction—that both courts revolution and transforms its violence into comedic and collective pleasure. The "Crusoe wars" that broke out between the French and English theatres in Charleston are situated at precisely this creole node in the Atlantic network of coloniality and political revolution. *Robinson Crusoe or Harlequin Friday*, as we will see, both testifies to and satirizes the contradictions of the colonial relation in an ontic/antic performance that stands in a line of theatrical genealogy that looks back toward Caliban and forward to Jim Crow and blackface minstrelsy.

⌐ROBINSON CRUSOE OR HARLEQUIN FRIDAY⌐

The performance histories of *The Enchanted Island* and *Robinson Crusoe* suggest that Charlestonians were actively engaged in restaging the colonial relation in both its mimetic and ontic dimensions. The theatre, then, was not a location where nonwhite bodies were wholly prohibited from appearing (on stage or in the audience) but one where the relations of whiteness and blackness—and the meanings of whiteness and blackness—were performed, shaped, and enjoyed in their mutability and complexity, and in their staged appearance and disappearance. To be clear, laws and regulations in place in

Charleston in the 1790s did forbid blacks from attending the theatre, but as we have seen, these rules were, in practice, routinely flouted; moreover, the appearance of blacks on stage and in the audience was not, I would argue, the result of a lapse in vigilance on the part of the state but an indication that representations of racialization were central to the cultural work engaged in by the performative creole commons.

In its exploitation of the pantomime form, *Robinson Crusoe or Harlequin Friday* capitalizes fully on the linguistic evasion and a-linguistic performance that is hinted at in the visual economy of *The Enchanted Island*; in so doing, however, *Robinson Crusoe or Harlequin Friday* effectively restages the colonial relation in terms that give wide scope to the play of what I have called the second scene of colonialism. While *The Enchanted Island* attempts to imagine the naturalness of white reproduction, the Crusoe pantomime explores more clearly the unspoken story of the colonial relation and, in particular, the creole possibilities of New World culture. Indeed, as we will see, the harlequinade, in some respects, reverses the plot of *The Tempest*: in the traditional plot of the harlequinade, the black-masked character of Harlequin pursues the white Columbine while Columbine's father, Pantaloon, seeks to keep the two apart. Unlike Caliban and Miranda, who are decisively separated by Prospero—and, notably, are separated by means of a scene of language instruction—Harlequin always evades the paternal prohibition of Pantaloon and succeeds in uniting with Columbine. In mapping the plot of the harlequinade onto that of Defoe's *Robinson Crusoe*, the French Theatre thus opens the possibility of an alternative relation—namely, the possibility of an isle that is peopled otherwise than by Prospero's language and English sexual union. Further, the pantomime promotes Caliban to a far more central role as he eventually becomes Harlequin Friday, sharing a title role in the Crusoe drama, and includes "savages" as participants in collective dances. As such, the Crusoe pantomime does not engage in the erasure of blackness or indigeneity; rather, I would suggest, it represents both under the *sign* of erasure—that is, under the sign of a formal prohibition of the (mimetic, linguistic, legal) representation of blackness. Further, indigeneity does not disappear in the pantomime, and certainly does not disappear in terms of an erasure that is historically prior to the emergence of blackness; rather, indigeneity appears in tandem with blackness in the complex figure of Harlequin Friday. Harlequin Friday, we might say, is Caliban brought back to the stage after he has foresworn to speak: if Caliban's profit on acquiring knowledge of Prospero's language was learning to curse, in the guise of Harlequin Friday, he has given up language altogether in favor of a new vocabulary of stunning activity, or what the *Crusoe* libretto describes as "pantomimical revolution."

The pantomime of *Robinson Crusoe or Harlequin Friday* is not itself of creole origin: rather, it was written by Richard Brinsley Sheridan, and it first appeared on stage in London in 1781. Because pantomime is, by nature, not closely tethered to a written script, it is a highly mutable dramatic form. To an even greater degree than other forms of drama, pantomime is subject to local revision and to the interactive relations that characterize embodied performance. The performances of *Crusoe* in the 1790s in Charleston are a case in point: as we will see, they varied tremendously from the Sheridan script as well as from one another. The first act of Sheridan's pantomime is a serious rendition of Crusoe's life on the island, including his encounter with the "savages," his rescue and seemingly benevolent enslavement of Friday, and his return to Spain; in the second act, Friday becomes Harlequin and a new plot ensues, ending, as the libretto states, when "Harlequin, after many fanciful distresses, and the usual pantomimical revolutions, receives his final reward in the hand of Columbine."[43]

Two innovations found in Sheridan's version of *Crusoe* are particularly notable: First, the English harlequinade, as a genre, typically presented a serious plot in the first act followed by an unrelated comic plot in the second act. While Sheridan's written version of the pantomime suggests only the most tenuous link between the figure of Friday and that of Harlequin, nonetheless, Sheridan's *Robinson Crusoe* is the first harlequinade in which the serious and comic plots are linked (in the character of Friday/Harlequin), rather than merely juxtaposed.[44] Moreover, in mapping the black-masked figure of Harlequin onto the native figure of Friday, Sheridan is the first author to decisively attach the signifier of Harlequin's blackness to the racial economy of the Atlantic world—in other words, Sheridan is the first to make Harlequin *racially* black. What is most significant about Sheridan's script then, is the fact that it weds Defoe's novel and, specifically, the figure of Friday, with the stock figure of Harlequin and the genre of the harlequinade, thereby attaching new significations to both the Harlequin and the Crusoe texts.[45] Moreover, Friday's blackness is not that of bare labor so much as that of what one might call extravagant relationality: Friday's relation to Crusoe speaks to forms of intimacy and belonging that are extravagant to white genealogy, albeit intrinsic to coloniality. Friday's blackness, moreover, does not erase indigeneity so much as partake of it: both native of the island and slave to Crusoe, Friday is a condensed figure of coloniality.

The harlequin tradition derives from the Italian Commedia, but it is decisively transformed in the British tradition, most notably by the fact that the Anglophone harlequinade is a pantomime, performed without words, unlike the Italian harlequinade from which it derives.[46] The English harlequinade relies on a stock set of comic characters, with a loose plot that involves Harlequin's pursuit of his beloved, Columbine, and the efforts of Columbine's father, Pantaloon, to prevent that union. Typically, the plot of the harlequinade is nonnarrative and depends primarily on the transformative nature of Harlequin as an embodied figure, rather than on the unfolding of a series of causally linked events. Harlequin is an intensely physical character, but he also defies physical laws insofar as he can transform himself into other characters and other entities, including animals and even inanimate objects such as clocks or pieces of furniture, and then transform himself back again: because of this transformative capacity, Harlequin is always able to escape Pantaloon's patriarchal prohibition to unite with Columbine.

Enormously popular in England from 1720 forward, the pantomime, like the ballad opera, was viewed as dangerous in its physicality and its appeal to a broad swath of the public. In particular, as John O'Brien notes, because the pantomime eschewed language, its turn to the ontic force of theatricality posed a threat to the organizing force of language itself: "to specify the particular order of threat that pantomime posed, we might . . . think of it as a 'crime *against* writing,' an action that undercut the theater's desire to define itself as a space of language; . . . a corresponding fear [was] that the theater's materiality—its use of costumes, scenery, and the bodies of performers—interfered with the transparency of its language and compromised its claim to be a site whose rules were those of the word, in particular of the written word."[47] Notably, then, the pantomime turns explicitly away from the mimetic force of narrative, such as that wielded by Prospero in *The Tempest*, and toward the force of physicality itself. And as O'Brien points out, this turn toward physicality in the pantomime often cuts against the organizing conceptual force of language rather than operating in concert with it.

It is particularly significant, then, that at the center of Daniel Defoe's novel, *Robinson Crusoe*, we find a scene of pantomime that is directly followed by a scene of language instruction: when Crusoe first encounters Friday in the novel, the two do not share a common language and thus speak to one another by way of gestures—gestures which, according to Crusoe's narration, announce Friday's desire to be a lifelong servant to Crusoe. More specifically, Crusoe encounters Friday when he is fleeing from a group of natives who are intent on killing him. After Crusoe assists Friday in escaping from his pursuers, Friday indicates—by way of pantomime—his "submission" and desire to serve Crusoe "as long as he liv'd."[48] And on the heels of this performance, Crusoe teaches Friday two key words in English: he names his new servant

"Friday" after the (English) day of the week on which Crusoe met him, and he instructs Friday to call him "Master." Just as in Shakespeare's *Tempest*, then, the scene of language instruction is also a staging of the colonial relation—one in which Friday's identity as a figure of bare labor is linguistically established.

Pantomime is necessary in the novel because Friday and Crusoe do not share a common language: at the edge of empire in the New World, a bodily language must suffice at the scene of encounter. But, as we have seen, that bodily language is rapidly overwritten by a scene of language instruction in the novel. In the staged version, however, the gestural language of encounter is the *only* language used in the entire unfolding of the narrative; moreover, no linguistic gloss is provided to supply an official transcript of the meaning of Friday's performance. On stage, then, no language is provided to secure the epistemology of Crusoe's relation to Friday—no days of the week are at hand, and no nomination occurs in which Friday's subjugation is inscribed. Without an official transcript in place, then, other possible readings of Friday's performance emerge. In other words, a gap opens between the novel's assertion of Friday's desire to be a slave for life and the staged performance of Friday's submission. And indeed, the pantomime seems organized around exploring precisely this gap. Notably, in the pantomime version, Friday does not remain Crusoe's slave forever: rather, in the second half of the pantomime, Friday becomes his own master and becomes master, as well, of an a-linguistic capacity for endless transformation and transmutation—a capacity that seems to be the antithesis of any enduring state of being, including lifelong submission. The pantomime thus opens the possibility that Friday's "act" of submission is but a posture—one among a number of such postures that change and evolve, in a series of antic revolutions, within the pantomime.

The French Theatre in Charleston performed a pantomime advertised as *Robinson Crusoe* on April 21, 1794, just two weeks after opening its doors for the first time. Transposed from the London stage to that of Charleston, the *Crusoe* pantomime as performed by the French Theatre not only does not follow Defoe's novel particularly closely; it also does not follow the Sheridan script insofar as the French Theatre version does not include Harlequin Friday as a character in the drama. In the newspaper account of the French Theatre pantomime, readers are informed that the first act will include Crusoe: "In his island, and his return with Friday to Europe. A grand historic pantomime in two parts, with entire new scenery, and all the views of the island; with the landing of the savages, and their dance." The brief account of the action does not include any mention of the enslavement of Friday, as does the Sheridan version. More striking, however, is the divergence between the French

Theatre's second act of the pantomime and that performed in England. The "Second Part" of the pantomime at the French Theatre, readers are told,

> Will be composed of a grand entertainment given to Robinson Crusoe, with dances, songs, &c., &c. by madame Placide, daughter of the captain, madame Val in the character of Lisette, master Duporte, 13 years of age, being his first appearance, he will dance the Grand Folie Despagne, with variations; Lover, Monsieur Dainville; Taylor, Monsieur Val; Hair Dresser, Signior Spinacuta; a negroe dance, by Mr. Francisqui, a dance by madame Val; another dance; by Mr. Francisquie.... The whole to conclude with Minuet de la Cour, by Mr. and Madame Placide. The scenery will be painted by Mons. Auden.[49]

This description of this "second scene" is interesting on a number of accounts: First, there is no explicit mention of Harlequin, nor of Friday for that matter. The second part of the pantomime would seem to consist almost entirely of dances, although a number of interesting characters are cast as well: among others, the characters of the "Lover," the "taylor," and the "hair dresser" are mentioned, all of whom would seem to be more at home in the landscape of the harlequinade than the desert isle. In addition, Monsieur Francisqui, a renowned dancer, performs the role of Friday in the first half of the pantomime and performs "a negroe dance" in the second part, thus indicating that he may not entirely break character from one half to the next—in other words, as a dancing negro/Friday, Monsieur Francisqui may come close to embodying Harlequin Friday even if he is not named as such. There is some evidence that the "Friseur" or French hair dresser was a stock comic character in the harlequinade, as was the figure of the tailor (sometimes named "Snip").[50] Harlequin and company, like Shakespeare's mechanicals in *A Midsummer Night's Dream*, were stock characters who transformed their rude occupations into humor and masquerade.

The second part of the French Theatre's *Crusoe* thus conjoins an interest in mechanical occupations, stock comic characters, and a variety of dance forms. In doing so, it looks much like the final scene of *The Beggar's Opera*, in which the "rabble" join hands for a collective dance. This scene, then, might be viewed as the dance that does not occur at the close of *Polly*—a dance that includes a host of characters, conjoined together in a "grand pantomime" of musical, a-linguistic performance, transposed into a creole key—that is, including both a "negroe dance," a "grand folie d'Espagne," and a "minuet de la cour," all of which follow upon the "dance of the savages" in the first part of the pantomime. The specificity of the French Theatre's situation here is worth considering: the Haitian Revolution has forced white French colonials into a relation of nonbelonging—into an a-linguistic relation with English-speaking Charleston; into a community in which what is shared is not language, even colonial language. What is shared between the white French colonials of St. Domingue and the white English colonials/U.S. citizens of Charleston is a certain spatial geography, namely that of settler colonialism and racialized labor.[51] This geography, moreover, is one that the dance inhabits or claims as the site of social life (rather than social death) for a series of nonspeaking figures who are banned from access to a language of their own. In Charleston in the 1790s, those without access to the dominant language of English include white French colonials together with Native Americans and African slaves—"Friseurs" as well as Fridays.[52] The dance of the French Theatre establishes the centrality of a creole identity that links French white colonials to Anglophone white colonials by means of their shared relation to the subaltern body of color. Burlesque or revolution—dance or violence—the "pantomimical revolution" places white and nonwhite bodies in relation to one another and claims a certain power and pleasure in doing so *without* securing linguistic control of this scene—that is, without translating the creole scene into a metropolitan tongue. In doing so, then, the French Theatre pantomime opens up transformative creole possibilities embedded within the colonial relation.

The Crusoe pantomime performed by the French Theatre references a set of colonial Atlantic bodies and signifiers that constitute common ground among audience members, and it is this broadly creole commons (rather than a British or French colonial one) that they so effectively convoke in their pantomime. Significantly, then, the French Theatre is able to access an alternative imaginary—one that reconfigures the obstacles of segmentation that beset John Gay in his efforts to imagine a creole commons. Further evidence of the French Theatre's method in this regard appears in the highly successful performance of the "Grand, Historical, and Tragic-Heroic Pantomime" titled *Mirza and Lindor*, which was adapted by the St. Domingue refugees from a French ballet first performed in 1779.[53] According to the advertisement for the French Theatre's performance of the pantomime in June 1794, the three-act pantomime concerned the love of Lindor, a French colonel, for Mirza, the daughter of the governor of "an island in America." Mirza and her loyal slave woman are captured by a Spanish privateer, who forces his unwanted attentions on Mirza; Mirza is saved from the Spaniard by Lindor, and her father ultimately blesses their union; the third act of the pantomime consists of a series of dances that celebrate the wedding of Mirza and Lindor. The embodied, creole nature of this performance is difficult to mistake. The

Charleston newspaper reports that the third act of the pantomime consists of the following dances:

> MINUET DE LA NATION, By Francisqui and Mrs. Placide.
> A Savage Dance.
> A Negro Dance, by Mrs. Val.
> A PAS DE CINQ by Master Duport and the Savages.
> A CREOLE DANCE, by Mrs. Placide.
> A SAVAGE DANCE, by Mr. Placide.
> A PAS DE DEUX by Mr. Francisqui and Mrs. Placide.
> A Military Exercise.
> The whole to conclude with a GENERAL DANCE.

The similarity between this final act and the series of dances with which the *Crusoe* pantomime concludes indicates that the French Theatre has settled on something of a successful formula in convoking an embodied creole commons. Given that the series of dances is, in this instance, quite literally in celebration of a wedding, the comparison with the failed collective dance performed in *Polly* is particularly striking. Further, should there be any doubt about the extent to which the audience was part of the embodied collectivity that authorized and participated in this dance, the French Theatre advertisement notes that audience members literally did perform in the dances: the three acts of the pantomime, according to the notice, are "Intermixed with DANCES, FIGHTS, and MILITARY EVOLUTIONS, By Military Citizens of this City."[54] The integrative note that is struck by the final line of the advertisement—"The whole to conclude with a GENERAL DANCE"—delineates a New World space in which "savage," "negro," "creole," "military," and European bodies inhabit the same space in unison, forming a collective body that moves in step together, as a single ensemble.

The success of the French Theatre's efforts to generate an embodied creole commons is evident not only in their repetition of the (improvised, local) collective dance in the final act of both the *Crusoe* pantomime and that of *Mirza and Lindor*. It is also evident in the rapidity with which the Charleston Theatre adopted the representational strategies that debuted on the stage of the French Theatre in order to compete for audience members. As theatre historian Julia Curtis notes, the Charleston Theatre swiftly recalibrated its repertoire following the opening of the French Theatre to include many more pantomimes than in previous seasons—an indication that the form of the pantomime, as well as its content, seemed to have particular appeal to the Charleston public.[55] Further, as we have seen, at least one member of the Charleston public subsequently described the "rage" for the "French style" of the actors from St. Domingue as the source of an unfortunate infection that ultimately corrupted the Charleston Theatre—a corruption indexed by the presence of nonwhite bodies in the public sphere. Yet rather than view the influence of the St. Domingue actors as a "corruption" that is specifically French, as does the Charleston letter writer, I would suggest, as the readings above indicate, that the shift in the commons generated by their presence in Charleston might better be described as intercolonial and creole than as French.

In the case of the Crusoe pantomime in Charleston—in which we find blackness represented under the sign of linguistic and narrative erasure—the "second act" of colonialism emerges as something of a new representational economy, or a new set of relations that eschew the language lessons and narrative force of the colonial relation in order to explore new forms of signification and new forms of relation. The second act of *Harlequin Friday*, one might argue, restages the colonial relation outside the reach of the epistemic force of colonial narrative, beyond the gaze and linguistic control of Robinson Crusoe. It is difficult to know precisely what occurs on stage in the second act of *Robinson Crusoe or Harlequin Friday* as it was later performed at the Charleston Theatre, given that, as one advertisement states, "Surprizing Tricks and Changes, [occur] Which the limits of an advertisement will not permit us to enumerate."[56] Nonetheless, we can make a number of observations based on the descriptions that do exist. First, Harlequin succeeds in uniting with Columbine at the end of the second act—an event which, while wholly in keeping with the formula of the harlequinade, is nonetheless a radical one on the Charleston stage, particularly when Harlequin's blackness is explicitly associated with the New World blackness of Friday. This, then, explicitly reverses the plot of *The Tempest*, in which Caliban and Miranda are separated by Prospero's narrative control. Moreover, it suggests that Harlequin Friday, unlike Caliban, may be able to succeed in "peopling the isle" with nonwhite bodies. Yet given that the force of the pantomime is nonnarrative and nongenealogical, it is perhaps more accurate to see Harlequin Friday as fantastically mutable rather than reproductive: in the descriptions of the second act of the pantomime that we do have, every emphasis is placed on the transformative powers of Harlequin Friday.

Not only does he transform himself from Friday to Harlequin, but he is also able to transform the objects around him: each transformation enables Harlequin Friday to access new forms of mobility, and these forms of mobility, in turn, allow him to secure his "escape" with Columbine. His transformative capacity, then, is less one that generates new narratives than one that creates new relations (most importantly, the sustained relation of Harlequin and Columbine), and surprising juxtapositions that refigure, as it were, the terms of the colonial relation that are set forth in the language lessons of Prospero and Crusoe. Harlequin Friday's hypermobility and mutability enable him to people the world differently—to "change the joke and slip the yoke" of the colonial relation, to use the words of Ralph Ellison. If Friday, as a figure of bare labor, was forcibly relegated to an a-linguistic status by Crusoe, when he assumes the form of Harlequin, Friday capitalizes, as it were (finds "profit" in, to use Caliban's term), on this a-linguistic status by deploying its associative, nonlinear logic to reassemble the colonial relation in a new form—a form that gives him access to desire, pleasure, the power of self-fashioning while paradoxically not a self, and social belonging as his body is united with that of Columbine.

Performed on stage in Charleston in 1794, the pantomime of *Robinson Crusoe or Harlequin Friday* decisively reconfigures the colonial relation as it was staged in London. This new creole relation is one that is produced from within the rupture of a colonial topography—from within the contradictory logics of embodied presence and mimetic absence that structure the colonial relation. Thus, we view a new "distribution of the sensible" that forms a creole sensus communus. In opening the second scene of colonialism as the space of collective meaning making, the French Theatre and later the Charleston Theatre as well generate a new distribution of the sensible that is decidedly creole—that indicates the centrality of bodies of color to the making of the New World public.

By 1806, another version of the Crusoe pantomime appears at the Charleston Theatre, billed as "The Grand Pantomime of Robinson Crusoe; Or, HARLEQUIN FRIDAY." Ever mutable, the cast and plot of the pantomime are slightly changed, but Harlequin Friday's creole identity remains pronounced. "In the course of the Pantomime," the advertisement states, "Harlequin will make several leaps. The Metamorphose of Harlequin to an old woman, with the comic Dance, called FRICASSEE. A Corn Field will change into Cupid's Palace; with a variety of other tricks too numerous to insert."[57] The "Fricassee" is a traditional French country dance that mimics a lover's quarrel and involves rhythmic stomping and slapping of one's own body parts. As such, the dance is very close to the New World African dance tradition of "patting Juba." The leaping, stomping Harlequin Friday thus here begins to resemble the jumping figure of Jim Crow, whose antic form will be pronounced the "original" American theatrical tradition when T. D. Rice assumes the blackface role roughly twenty years later.[58] Harlequin Friday, then, stands in a creolized performance tradition that is linked to Shakespeare's Caliban, on the one hand, and blackface minstrelsy, on the other hand.

This genealogy of Harlequin Friday—looking forward to Jim Crow—is one that must give one pause. If I have described the creole harlequinade as one that opens aesthetic, representational, and even political possibilities for New World peoples of color, the proximity of this tradition to Jim Crow and blackface minstrelsy points toward the simultaneity of modes of degradation and dehumanization that are also embedded in the same theatrical forms. It is worth remembering, for instance, that Southerne's *Oroonoko* was cancelled in eighteenth-century Charleston by order of the mayor. The heroic figure of Oroonoko was external to the existing "distribution of the sensible" that configured the embodied theatrical public sphere in Charleston. Harlequin Friday, on the other hand, is exiled from language but accedes to power under the ruse of powerlessness and inaugurates a signifying regime that stands beneath the sign of disavowal and thus is only intermittently legible, and functions as much as a scene of oppression as liberation, at the fine line between the two. What breaks out, in the break, may be more aesthetically radical, but is also absent from the official transcript. This divided legacy is nonetheless important and is particularly significant when contrasted with accounts of the print public sphere from the same period—accounts that have little space for the centrality of peoples of color to the public sphere and which cannot address the duality of the colonial relation. The embodied public sphere in Charleston is thus fundamentally different than that found in London. It is not in the least exclusive with respect to bodies of color, but it is poised at the intersection of revolution and burlesque.

CHAPTER 5

KINGSTON

OROONOKO, RUNAWAY

When the word "Oroonoko" appeared in Jamaica's *Royal Gazette* in 1809, it did not advertise an upcoming performance of the play by Thomas Southerne but rather, named a runaway slave who had been arrested and imprisoned in the St. James workhouse: on a long list of runaways we find "Oroonoko, a Congo, 5 feet 1 3/4 inches, marked TY right shoulder, to Mr. Thomas Yates, Westmorland, July 7."[1] The naming of this Jamaican slave neatly reverses the tale of nomination that appears in Aphra Behn's novel: in the novel, "Oroonoko" is the title character's African name—a name that is replaced by the Anglophone "Caesar" when he is enslaved in Surinam. Evidence suggests that "Oroonoko" was not, in fact, a name of African origin, but one chosen by Behn to sound suitably foreign; David Eltis's extensive database of African names does not include the name "Oroonoko."[2] "Orinoco" is the name of a major river in Venezuela and the word "orinoco" is derived from Amerindian languages. Accordingly, it seems likely that Behn borrowed the Amerindian word to serve as the African name of her title character. But as an Anglophone slave name, "Oroonoko" appears multiple times in the pages of colonial Jamaican newspapers. By 1809, then, "Oroonoko" had *become* an Anglophone name: the widespread popularity of Southerne's play had caused "Oroonoko" to enter into the English vernacular. Like the names of other runaway slaves appearing in the same 1809 *Royal Gazette* advertisement—Romeo, Julius, Hercules, Dublin, Plato, and Cupid, among others—"Oroonoko" was an English slave name that erased and replaced the unfamiliar African name of a newly arrived conscript into race slavery; moreover, embedded within the name one might hear, as well, the echoes of an eclipsed Native American presence.[3]

And yet, despite the fact that the name "Oroonoko" evidently came trippingly off English tongues in Jamaica, extant evidence indicates that Southerne's play of that name, *Oroonoko: A Tragedy*, was never performed there in the eighteenth or early nineteenth centuries. Jamaica had a lively theatre scene and was a key node linking the routes of colonial performance traversed by touring actors and acting companies between such sites as London, Charleston, and New York City. Lewis Hallam, who left London in the wake of the Licensing Act, arrived in Jamaica in 1755 just after performing in Charleston. Following his death, Hallam's touring company was reconstituted in Jamaica under the leadership of David Douglass and Hallam's son, Lewis Hallam Jr.: Douglass's American Company began touring the northern colonies in 1758 and built a permanent theatre in Charleston in 1773. The company returned to Jamaica in 1775, shortly after theatre was outlawed in the North American colonies by an act of Continental Congress in 1774, and made Jamaica its home for the following nine years.[4] Many of the actors who appear in Charleston thus were present on the Jamaica stage as well; but as was the case in Charleston, Oroonoko was not among the characters performed for the colonial audience, despite his prominence on the London stage.

The effacement of the play *Oroonoko* from the stage in Jamaica and the presence of the slave name Oroonoko in the pages of the *Royal Gazette* point together to a history of memory and forgetting—of denomination as erasure and embodiment. Although the tragedy of the royal slave does not appear before a Jamaican audience, the slave name "Oroonoko" simultaneously references and suppresses this story. Moreover, the runaway advertisements themselves point to related questions of embodiment and nomination. The pages of eighteenth-century Jamaican newspapers are crowded with advertisements of slaves for sale and notices of runaways being sought by owners. Indeed, given the preponderance of such advertisements within the pages of these newspapers, it is difficult not to surmise that the newspapers were in large part sustained by the commerce in human flesh that these notices detail in stunningly prosaic and formulaic terms. The print public sphere in Jamaica is thus arguably erected on the backs of the slave bodies it seeks to capture within an economic and linguistic system of appropriation and possession.[5]

In the ubiquitous advertisements of slaves for sale, Jamaican newspapers display and exercise the signal technology of slavery: namely, the imposition of social death by way of the destruction of natal nomination and the restructuring of identity and value around what I have described (in the last chapter) as bare labor. The social death that slavery sought to effect by stripping slaves of genealogical identity and kinship structures did not aim to eliminate life altogether but to transform life into units of labor unfettered by the friction of human connection and sociality. In these advertisements, markers of slave identity are wholly articulated in relation to labor: "TO BE SOLD, Upon a Valuation with a warranted Title," announces a 1793 advertisement in Kingston's *Royal Gazette*, "TEN NEGROES, counting of an equal number of each Sex, who are all accustomed to work in the Field."[6] A "Young, healthy NEGRO WOMAN, who is an exceeding good Sempstress and Pastry Cook," is advertised for sale in Kingston, as are "299 CHOICE YOUNG *Coromantee, Fantee, and Ashantee* NEGROES, IMPORTED IN THE Ship HESTER, Capt. J. LANGLEY, *From the Gold Coast*, By JOHN TAYLOR."[7] As the latter advertisement indicates, "New Negroes" from Africa were identified by their African ethnicity, an ethnicity correlated by plantation owners with the capacity to labor in the colony: Coromantees, for instance, were valued as particularly strong field laborers.[8]

Notably, these advertisements do not refer to slaves by name; in the advertisement for slaves imported from Africa cited above, the ship on which the slaves arrive is referred to by name ("Hester"), as is the captain of the ship ("J. Langley") and the importer ("John Taylor"); however, none of the 299 souls who have made the crossing in the hold of the *Hester* are named. In contrast to "New Negroes," "Seasoned Negroes" are typically described in terms of their experience in plantation labor: they are advertised as "used to jobbing" and "used to a Sugar Plantain," or they are characterized in relation to particular skills: "THIRTY-EIGHT Seasoned Negroes," for sale in 1780 are described as "valuable, trusty people; [who] have been for some years past employed in the Brick–making Business & are many of them Proficient at that Trade."[9] Stripped of nomination, sociality, and genealogy—rendered fit only for labor and confinement like Caliban imprisoned in his rock—the newspaper as nexus of capitalist exchange renders New World Africans as commodified units of bare labor. In 1780, another typical advertisement identifies a slave woman for sale, together with farm animals, only in terms of her capacity to labor: "TO BE SOLD, For Cash, good Bills of Exchange, or Produce, A COMPLETE WASHER-WOMAN and SEMPSTRESS, AND Two excellent Saddle–Horses." Just above this announcement appears another one: Lewis Hallam Jr. will be performing the following week in *The Tempest* at the Kingston Theatre.[10]

However, as much as the advertisements selling slaves portray diasporic Africans as figures of bare labor, this effort is often undermined in adjacent columns of print that advertise rewards for the apprehension of runaway slaves. In this genre of advertisement, the plantocracy enumerates every characteristic of its "property" in order that it may be reclaimed as property: in the process of this enumeration, however, what emerges is an account of richly social, rather than socially dead, beings. Consider, for instance, the advertisement for the runaway slave, Flora:

> RUN AWAY from the Subscriber, on the 11th of August last, a Negro Woman, named FLORA, born in Kingston; remarkable for having what is called a Scald Head, not having the smallest appearance of hair on it.—Also, Her Daughter PHIBA, Calls herself often CUBA and ABBA.—She is marked on both shoulders AW, raised in lumps, from endeavouring to take them out: She is also marked on both cheeks and breast, if narrowly examined. PHIBA was seen in company with a Negro Man, CUFFEE (who resides on the parsonage of this parish), on the road leading to One-Eye Estate, and supposed gone towards town, where they have relations, and at Mr. William Clarke's.—On Mr. Keymiss's estate, to windward, lives a son of Flora, called Johney.—They are all well acquainted with Bessy Barrow, who left this parish to live in town, at the same time Phiba and Flora run away.[11]

Not only does "Flora" have a name in this advertisement, but she has a place of birth, a daughter named Cuba or Phiba with a male partner and relations, a son named Johnny, a friend named Bessy, and a uniquely hairless scalp. In comparison with the concise advertisements of slaves for sale, the runaway advertisement (as a genre) is lengthy and replete with proper names and kinship connections. In this instance, it is clear that Flora is deeply embedded within a system of relations that identify her as a social individual rather than a unit of labor. Moreover, these social relations offer Flora a form of egress from slavery, which the "subscriber," in turn, seeks to track and eradicate.

Couched beneath the generic "Ran Away" heading—among advertisements for "Lost, Stolen, and Strayed" livestock—a rich range of signifiers thus proliferates to name the putatively generic and nameless laboring slave. Not only do many runaway individuals bear the marks of their owners seared into their skin and the scars of whippings that have lacerated their bodies, but they also display forms of identity that tether them less closely to the scene of enslavement. A "Young NEGRO MAN, named SHARPER," for instance, "had on when he went away, a Pompadour Coat, with Frogs of the same colour." The advertisement warned, "It is probable, that he may attempt to pass as FREE, having already, under an imposition of that kind, taken a cruize in one of his Majesty's ships of war by the name of TOM JONES."[12] Sharper, we thus learn, is given to cruising aboard ship in a pink coat with matching pink ornamental fastenings. Quashie, who calls himself Lawrence, "is an artful, cunning chap and passes for a free French Negro, as he can speak a little French."[13] The escaped slave named "Kingston" speaks no English but sports "a blue jacket and black velvet breeches"; his companion, "Jamaica," wears "a green jacket and a pair of Russia duck trowsers."[14] The range of skills, costumes, languages, predilections, social and familial relations, and narrative histories that appear in these texts point in a distinctly different direction than the advertisements for slaves as laborers: as David Waldstreicher notes, runaway advertisements bespeak individuals who are "actor[s] in the world of goods, manipulating possessions and perceptions to make and remake" themselves. Runaway advertisements, then, give the lie to the ideology and technology of social death and bare labor.[15]

In the contradiction that emerges between these two genres—the slave sale advertisement and the runaway slave advertisement—we see conflicting imperatives articulated concerning embodiment, nomination, and the performance of social value. In this chapter I argue that, while slavery operates by way of technologies aimed at the production of social death, there is, ultimately, no such thing as social death.[16] In other words, in the face of a system that works insistently to produce black bodies as a form of commodified bare labor, black sociality and cultural production proliferate under the sign of their own erasure. The hyperbolic contradiction between an ideology of bare labor (effected by mimetic strategies of erasure) and practices of sociality (effected by embodiment as well as new mimetic forms) emerges in a variety of ways—in scenes of violence and in colonial "screen scenes" that expose epistemic rupture around the knowledge and nonknowledge produced by way of the intimacies and contradictions of colonialism. If we have tended to accept that the print public sphere in colonial America is the location in which civic life is carried forward as a project of popular sovereignty in the form of reasoned debate, we find in the figures of slaves who appear in pages of Jamaican newspapers a very different narrative—one which is highly material, sonic, and performative, located in display and erasure rather than in the discourse of reason and argument—located, then, in the realm of the aesthetic.

THE IMPOSSIBLE COMMONS AND RADICAL AESTHETICS

In late eighteenth-century Charleston, South Carolina (as seen in the previous chapter), a creole commons emerged in the space of the theatre—one that develops a more national shape in the early to middle decades of the nineteenth century (as we will see in the next chapter, concerning New York City). In this same period, however, Jamaica remained under the colonial control of Great Britain: indeed, imperial oversight of the colony increased as British military engagement in the Caribbean expanded in relation to the Haitian Revolution and inter-European warfare in the area. Rather than developing in a postimperial direction (creole, then national), the "commons" in Jamaica was itself an intensely vexed site: indeed, as I argue in this chapter, Jamaica might be understood as the scene of an impossible commons.

Economically, Jamaica stood at the center of the Anglo-Atlantic empire.[17] Exports from the West Indies accounted for more than 60 percent of the annual value of commodities shipped from British America in the late eighteenth century, and Jamaica was by far the wealthiest of the British colonies in the West Indies. Further, many North American colonies were dependent on West Indian markets for their economic growth: as Barbara Solow concludes, "The commodity exports of Britain's American colonies were to a remarkable extent either the outputs of or the inputs into slave colonies."[18] If we tend not to include Jamaica on our mental map of the American colonies, it is because this map has been retroactively revised by the history of U.S. nationalism: on the eve of the American Revolution, there were twenty-six British colonies in the Americas, and Jamaica was the wealthiest and most economically significant among them.[19]

Jamaica was distinct from colonies such as South Carolina in other ways as well, notably, in the far higher ratio of blacks to whites in the colony—a ratio of nine to one in the late eighteenth century.[20] However, given the brutality of the labor regime and living conditions to which slaves were subject, the slave population in Jamaica was not only unable to sustain itself by means of reproduction during the eighteenth century, but it declined even in the face of continued massive importation of slaves from Africa.[21] The enforced labor system of slavery was maintained only by way of a regime of spectacular violence and terror; Jamaica was, in effect, a "garrison society" in which an implicit (and quite often explicit) state of war obtained between free whites and enslaved blacks.[22] Historian Mary Turner reports that a slave rebellion "of some dimension" broke out roughly every five years; as the pages of Kingston-based periodicals and planters' diaries detail, slaves were routinely in revolt against slavery and were, just as routinely, subject to violent public punishment including whipping, maiming, burning, hanging, and decapitation.[23]

The racialized labor regime that formed the basis of the plantation economy in the sugar islands of the West Indies was thus remarkably and singularly extractive—extractive of sugar and profits for British planters and extractive of labor and life itself from enslaved workers. As Sidney Mintz has argued, the sugar plantations of the Caribbean might be viewed as the first factories of Western modernity insofar as labor was mechanized, laborers were rendered interchangeable with one another, and the plantation was devised to maximize production and profit.[24] Characteristically, one Jamaican planter opined in Kingston's *Columbian Magazine* in 1797, "A plantation ought to be considered as a well constructed machine, compounded of various wheels turning different ways, & yet all contributing to the great end proposed ... and in conducting the whole business, if any one part runs too fast or too slow in proportion to the rest, the main purpose will be defeated."[25] A key "wheel" in the machine of the plantation was the labor of slaves, coerced from individuals stripped of social identity in order to serve as bare, mechanical labor. Just a month earlier, the same journal included the following item—one among a list of miscellaneous local events: "Last week a stout negro man, carelessly feeding the mill, which was turning with considerable velocity, at Constant-Spring-estate, in Liguanea, was drawn in by the arm, and in a few seconds the body was crushed almost to atoms."[26] As such "Domestic Occurrences" indicate, the mechanized production of the plantation was predicated on the optimization of the movements and, ultimately, the disposability of the workers whose labor fueled its operations. In its structures of labor and production, as Sibylle Fischer and others have argued, the Caribbean plantation system might thus be seen to stand at the heart of capitalist modernity: "Far from being a remnant of precapitalist practices, slavery in the Caribbean was one of the first and most brutal appearances of modernity." In the sugar colonies, then, African slaves were forcibly conscripted into the developing capitalist system of economic and social relations that defines modernity as we know it.[27]

In addition to the segmentation of the population in relation to labor, a key aspect of the development of capitalist modernity in the Atlantic world involves the geographical separation of sites of production from those of social reproduction.[28] Capitalism, by definition, entails the economic dominance of the market: the primacy of the market dictates the separation of production from consumption, given that production under capitalism is no longer aimed at generating use value (and thus is not immediately linked to consumption) but at generating market (exchange) value.[29] Enslaved workers in Jamaica, for instance, were not forced to cultivate sugar cane for the purpose of eating it (indeed, they were often subject to corporal punishment for consuming sugar cane), but in order to produce sugar that was sold and consumed in England. A signal feature of the Anglo-Atlantic plantation economy is thus the vast geographical separation of the site of production—Caribbean sugar plantations—from the site of consumption and social reproduction—England. Further, I would contend, this separation had enormous consequences for individuals living in the colony insofar as *social reproduction* was normatively proscribed in the name of defining the colony as a site of *production* alone.

According to colonial ideology, then, labor and production occur in the colony, and social reproduction normatively occurs in the metropole. If, following Cindi Katz, we define social reproduction as "the material social practices through which people reproduce themselves on a daily and generational basis and through which the social relations and material bases of capitalism are renewed," we see that resources for social reproduction are amassed in the metropole and largely eradicated in the colony.[30] Hence, for instance, in the eighteenth century, white or free black creoles were typically sent from the colony to the metropole in order to be educated and trained as recognizable social subjects, whereas slaves in the colony were deprived of access to forms of social and genealogical identity—subject, then, to technologies of social death.[31] For enslaved blacks in the colony, this deprivation took the form of barred access to a range of material and abstract goods, from clothing and food to education, citizenship, marriage, freedom, and the legal right to own and inherit property. Slaves in the sugar colonies were literally worked to death, replaced as wheels in the plantation machine with "new negroes" brought from Africa. As Vincent Brown concludes, "Until the end of the transatlantic slave trade, Jamaican planters essentially externalized the costs of raising children to villages in Africa."[32] In short, then, in Jamaica, the production of commodities such as sugar and coffee systematically occurred at the expense of the sustenance and reproduction of human life in accordance with the new geography of capitalist modernity.

The ideological proscription of social reproduction in the colony extended to whites as well: white creoles were viewed, from the metropole, with disdain and derision. White creoles were typically seen to have imbibed a sort of infection from their colonial birth—one that might be eradicated if sufficient time were spent in the metropole. Their birth in the colony, however, was seen as infusing them, in the words of Jamaican planter Edward Long, "with a degree of supineness and indolence" that "frequently hurt their fortune and family." Indeed, Long describes creole identity in quasi-biological terms: "The effect of climate is . . . remarkable . . . in the extraordinary freedom and suppleness of [creoles'] joints, which enable them to move with ease, and give them a surprising agility, as well as gracefulness in dancing. Although descended from British ancestors, they are stamped with these characteristic deviations." Nonetheless, Long maintains, the creole body can be reformed if sufficient time is spent in the metropole; those creoles "who leave [Jamaica] in their infancy, and pass into Britain for education, where they remain until their growth is pretty well completed, are not so remarkably distinguished either in their features or limbs." Good at dancing, bad at working; good at extramarital sex, bad at fidelity; "fickle and desultory" white creoles (male and female) were viewed as unsuited for the work of furthering European empire precisely because of their intimacy with the extranational space of the colony.[33] The white creole who lacked a metropolitan veneer was thus regarded as morally and socially degenerate—that is, unfit for regeneration and incapacitated for normative social reproduction.

Despite this derision, whites in Jamaica clung fiercely to their sense of identity as British subjects. Unlike colonists in the thirteen northern colonies that broke with England in 1776, white Jamaicans remained loyal to the crown, in part because they required the backing of the British military to prevent slave revolt against plantocratic rule by a white minority. Further, as an agricultural monoculture, Jamaica's economic fortune was tightly tethered to the British market, where sugar prices were protected by government embargos on competing imports from other countries. White planters in Jamaica thus could not afford to loosen their ties to Britain in the way that northern colonists had by the close of the eighteenth century. Close ties to Britain were maintained by the strong West Indies lobby in Parliament, as well as patterns of absenteeism that kept the wealthiest planters in England rather than Jamaica. But the effort to remain British in the Caribbean environs of Jamaica was one with perverse consequences: while insisting on their British identity and British liberty, white planters in Jamaica developed a legal system and cultural practices that diverged dramatically from those in England, in large part because of the racialized divisions that structured plantocratic society. Jamaican whites were thus, as Michael Craton argues, "reluctant creoles" or, one might say, creoles for whom creolism was a vexed signifier.[34] While they "forcefully staked claims that they should be seen and accepted as British subjects," writes Christer Petley, white Jamaicans "helped to create a creolized slave society in Jamaica, and their conflicts and interactions with enslaved people helped to ensure that they adopted distinctively local practices and attitudes."[35] While insisting on their Britishness, white creoles lived colonial lives—lives whose material practices were necessarily not British, particularly in relation to the institution of slavery.[36]

The segmenting of the population, the institution of agricultural monocultures in the islands of the Caribbean, and the inauguration of an economy based on the geographical separation of sites of production and consumption are hallmarks of the enclosure of the commons on a global scale. Indeed, the distancing of production from social reproduction is, according to the social theorists Maria Mies and Veronika Bennholdt-Thomsen, a signal indicator of the destruction of the commons: "A commons regime, as long as it functions, is part of a subsistence or *moral economy* . . . In a commons regime [production and consumption] are not two separate economic spheres but are linked to each other. Production processes will be oriented towards the satisfaction of needs of concrete local or regional communities and not towards the artificially created demand of an anonymous world market."[37] In its orientation toward the market rather than toward the needs of the community, the plantation economy might be described as fundamentally un-commoning. And in its structural and ideological disavowal of the creole commons inhabited by whites and blacks in the colony, Jamaica might be described as the scene of an impossible—an "unthinkable"—commons. Two contradictions thus inform the impossible commons in Jamaica: first, British liberty remains linked to a notion of popular sovereignty—thus, British colonials endorsed concepts of representation and liberty while straining to eradicate the representational capacities of nine-tenths of the population of Jamaica. Second, despite the un-commoning structural violence of capitalism with regard to social reproduction in Jamaica, social reproduction nonetheless did occur on the island, and the sociality of the island was necessarily creole, for both blacks and whites. The impossible commons of Jamaica is thus also an ineradicably material commons, one whose presence registers—when it obtrudes into figurative space—as obscene with respect to British imperial norms.

At sites where crowds of bodies (the people as a commons) gather in Jamaica, a contradictory staging is thus pronounced—one in which governmentality (the biopolitical control of bodies, and the erasure of some bodies, in the name of state power) contends with the insistent and "obscene" nature of the colonial relation materialized in creole form. A satirical cartoon from 1802 of a dance in Jamaica, "A Grand Jamaican Ball! Or the Creolean Hop a la Mustee; as exhibeted [sic] in SPANISH TOWN," published in London is emblematic in this regard (see figure 5.1). In this image, blacks and whites crowd into a ballroom: in its center, white creoles dance, and black slaves wait on young white creole women and aging male planters; at its edges, large groups of both whites and blacks observe the dance, black musicians and white soldiers play instruments, and two older white men lasciviously embrace/attack younger white women. In keeping with the ideas of creole anatomy expressed by Edward Long, the white creoles appear to have developed a looseness of the joints that enables them to dance in antic postures with, for instance, legs and arms arrayed akimbo, distended at stark angles rather than in bended fashion. The clear suggestion of the image is that the white dancers have adopted African forms of movement: as the title of the image indicates, the white creoles dance "a la Mustee"—that is, like "octoroons" or persons of mixed race.

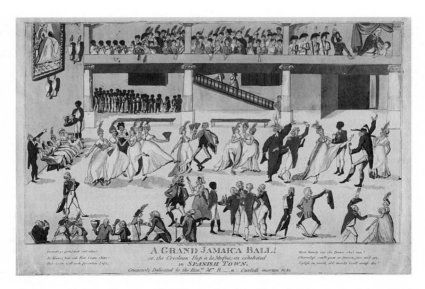

FIGURE 5.1. "A Grand Jamaican Ball! Or the Creolean Hop a la Mustee; as exhibeted [*sic*] in SPANISH TOWN." Published in London, 1802. Courtesy of the Library of Congress, British Cartoon Collection.

And indeed, the proclivity for dancing, and dancing in an African-inflected manner, among white creoles is a standard subject of metropolitan derision. One eighteenth-century writer describes the typical white creole woman as "a paper-faced skeleton, romping, or stretching and lolling, from sofa to sofa, in a dirty confused hall or piazza, with a parcel of black wenches, learning and singing obscene and filthy songs and dancing to the tunes." The creole white man, in turn, is described by this author as a "presuming, negroefied, aukward, ignorant guegaw" who, although "languishing on his deathbed" would at "the sound of the gumbay or violin . . . get up and dance till he killed himself."[38] Used to signal racialized debasement, such language suggests that the embodied nature of dance betrays the mixed-race physicality of creole life in the colony. In the cartoon of "A Grand Jamaican Ball," the text below the image offers a warning to young white creole women about such behavior: "But soon will each forsaken Lass,/Most keenly rue the Dance she's run!/Charmless you'll grow in person, face and eye,/Joyless in youth, old maids you'll useless die!" The debasement of white creoles by the proximity of blacks, on this account, entails a compromised capacity for reproduction; creole lasses will become old maids. The mixed-race creole commons that gathers at the dance is thus figured as obscene—in violation of the bounds of English social reproduction—with respect to metropolitan sensibilities.

Like the ballroom, the theatre was a site at which large numbers of Jamaicans gathered with regularity; moreover, mixed-race audiences were common in the eighteenth century.[39] At the close of the eighteenth century, Kingston had an active theatrical calendar; in the 1780s, Hallam's company presented up to twenty-four plays in Kingston in a given season.[40] In this regard, Kingston was of a piece with other wealthy colonial cities around the Atlantic littoral that were able to support a commercial theatre. As distinct from locations such as Charleston or Philadelphia, however, the Kingston theatre was more closely associated with the British military and the Society of Freemasons. Indeed, the soldiers of the king's army lodged in Kingston regularly took to the stage, occasionally performing benefits for Douglass's company rather than vice versa.

The interpenetration of the military, the theatre, and the print public sphere (Douglass held the title of the king's printer as well as the master of revels and was the editor of the *Royal Gazette*) implicates the theatre in a logic of governmentality—that is, within a colonial regime that sought to shape bodies into a governable, colonized population. It is precisely along these lines that Kathleen Wilson describes British theatre in Jamaica as "part of the emergent governmentality of eighteenth-century colonial societies that ... sought to enact and confirm the national difference and modernity that distinguished English or British people from non-British." According to Wilson, "theatre in the colonies and outposts of empire was a central component of ... the 'national performative': a term that refers to both the efforts to perform national difference in ways that established or stabilized colonial structures of rule, and the continual contestation and subversions of colonized subjects who rejected or reinterpreted metropolitan practices."[41] Yet even as the theatre served to perform models of British identity intended to stabilize colonial rule, the very presence of the audience—and the materialization of a creole commons therein—brought to the fore contradictions within the ideology of British liberty and colonial modernity.

In October of 1780, for instance, soldiers in the British army performed Thomas Otway's popular she-tragedy, *Venice Preserved*, for the benefit of the American Company. The prologue of the play, reprinted in the *Royal Gazette*, apologetically seeks audience support: the soldiers ask for forbearance, explaining that they are neither professional, nor seasoned actors. The prologue is typically used to situate a performance in its local context, and in this case, the character of Pierre takes to the stage to literally map the play and audience onto the landscape of Jamaica. Specifically, the prologue draws a succinct analogy between the geography of the theatre—upper boxes, side boxes, and the pit—and the (plantocratic) geography of Jamaica—mountains, cane fields, and savannah: "Now let me see—where shall our Work begin,/Sure that fine Mountain [marked with asterisk indicating upper boxes] can't be Rock within;/All round the' Enclosures [asterisk indicating side boxes] sweet strait Canes I view,/A fine Savannah that, [asterisk indicating pit] well watered too—/May still such Harvest's drooping Merit prop,/And each Night's Labour bring as fine a Crop.—[Going]/[Return]/But hold,—one Word, as we're New Negroes here,/Kind Overseers be not too severe."[42] The military officer speaking this line thus compares the actor-soldiers to slaves and specifically to "New Negroes," who are beginning the work of entertaining the audience. Even as the speaker of the prologue seeks to impose a stratified order on the audience and the landscape, his effort to situate the play in Jamaica ironically involves the invocation of the terms of colonial embodiment that are insistently racialized. The "labor" of performance, inscribed into the landscape of Jamaica, thus "blackens" the performing soldiers who become "New Negroes" working to please the audience. The materiality of the performance and its specific location in Jamaica, thus, in a comic register, renders British bodies black and enslaved rather than white and free.

Additional accounts of the theatre in Jamaica indicate that audiences there assumed the representative shape of the "town" just as they did in locations such as New York City and Charleston—that is, the audience was a corporate body inclusive of diverse elements of the community. Michael Scott, a Glaswegian living in Jamaica during the first decades of the nineteenth century, describes the audience in the theatre at Jamaica as broadly inclusive of all strata of society, albeit located in seats stratified accordingly. Scott describes seating himself at the Kingston Theatre in "the second row of a *buccra* box, near the stage" and observes the "neatness of the house . . . and the comical appearance the division of the castes produced"—a caste division that he describes in strikingly racialized terms:

> The pit seemed to be almost exclusively filled with the children of Israel as peculiar in their national features here as everywhere else; the dress boxes contained the other white inhabitants and their families; the second tier the brown *ladies*, who seemed more intent on catching the eyes of the young buccras below, than attending to the civil things the males of their own shade were pouring into their ears above; the gallery was tenanted by Bungo himself, in all his glory of black face, blubber lips, white eyes,

and ivory teeth—this black parterre being powdered here and there with a sprinkling of white sailors, like snowdrops in a bed of purple anemones; Jack being, as usual on such occasions, pretty well drunk.[43]

As in accounts of the New York theatre, each section of the seats represents a sector of the "town." However, as the grotesquely caricatured features of the black, brown, and Jewish audience members indicate, Scott's account of the racially mixed audience is one that attributes to this embodied commons less the force of a representative collectivity than of satire and obscenity.

In related terms, Lady Maria Nugent, the wife of the British governor of Jamaica, General George Nugent, describes being disturbed by the mixed-race audience she encounters upon attending a theatrical performance. Nugent reports viewing the performance of a comedic show in Spanish Town in 1803:

> We all drove to Spanish Town, to see Mr. Cussans's exhibition. It was a performance something in the style of [Charles] Dibdin. We could not help laughing at the nonsense; but, at the same time, it made me melancholy to think, that the folly and extravagance of a person who had been brought up as a gentleman, and who is really of a respectable family, should compel him to expose himself in that way to the public. The audience were of all colours and descriptions; blacks, browns, Jews, and whites.[44]

J. P. Cussans, a performer who adopted the format of one-man song and dance shows developed by well-known English actor Charles Dibdin, was something of a wastrel: born in Jamaica into the wealthy Cussans family (owners of the Amity Hall plantation), he was educated in London and evidently achieved some renown there as a showman and general hell-raiser. But the distaste that Cussans animates in Nugent has less to do with his scandalous behavior than with his appearance in public—specifically, she is discomfited by his exposure "*in that way* to the public" (emphasis added). Nugent is evidently disturbed that Cussans appears on stage in order to earn money (hence the reference to compulsion): such an engagement bespeaks a downward class mobility that disturbs demarcations between "respectable" people, such as white "gentlemen," and individuals who labor in the colony, such as black slaves. But in addition, as Nugent more pointedly underscores in this passage, Cussans's appearance in public is upsetting because of the kind of public before which he appears—namely, a public in which an audience is promiscuously gathered, forming a creole commons of blacks, browns, Jews, and whites.

Intriguingly, Cussans was most famous for writing and performing a song titled "O! Poor Robinson Crusoe!" As one memoirist reports, "In this song,

[Cussans] had as many encores as he pleased," when he regularly performed it at Saddler's Wells in London.[45] In the well-known ballad, the singer chants the tale of his grandfather, Robinson Crusoe, who, like Cussans himself, seems to have transgressed the limits of British identity while inhabiting a not fully deserted isle. The eighth and ninth stanzas of the song record that, after Crusoe makes a house for himself on the island,

> his man Friday
> Kept the house snug and tidy;
> To be sure was his duty to do so;
> They lived friendly together,
> Less like servant than neighbor,
> Did Friday and poor Robinson Crusoe
> Oh, poor, &c.

> Then he wore a long cap
> And a coat without nap,
> And a beard as long as a Jew, so,
> That by all that is civil,
> He looked like a devil,
> Rather than poor Robinson Crusoe.
> Oh, poor, &c.[46]

Like the pantomime of *Robinson Crusoe or Harlequin Friday*, which was performed in Jamaica as well as Charleston, the Cussans song exposes the ligatures of the colonial relation. It reveals the cohabitation of white and non-white bodies in colonial space and conjures a degraded British genealogy (the song is a tale of a lost grandfather) in which patrimony derives not from "all that is civil" but from a colonial adventurer who has come to resemble a Jew and a devil. Notably, Jamaica had a large Jewish community, as both Nugent's and Scott's comments indicate, and Jews were not infrequently taken to stand as figures of what we might call "becoming unwhite"—or a threatening loss of British whiteness.[47] The creole commons that appears in the mixed-race audiences gathered in Jamaica is insistently figured as obscene by white metropolitans precisely because it brings into view the materiality and significance of the colonial relation—the extent to which British liberty is dependent on the racialized labor systems of colonialism, and the intimacy of white, black, and brown bodies.

While it is not clear whether Cussans performed his signature "O! Poor Robinson Crusoe!" on the evening Nugent attended his performance in Spanish Town, he did perform the song a year earlier at the Kingston Theatre. The *Daily Advertiser* indicates that "between the first and second acts," of a benefit performance of *Richard Coeur de Lion* for one Miss Tessier, "Mr. J. P. Cussans (from England) will chaunt his Robinson Crusoe, concluded by a hornpipe danced by Mr. Frederick."[48] Interestingly, the actors sharing the bill, Miss Tessier and Miss Francisqui, are refugees from St. Domingue who appear with a French troupe led by Augustus Tessier. Less than two weeks earlier, Tessier advertised that he had "erected a vast and commodious amphitheatre for the accommodation of people of colour, to which he has added a row of the second boxes adjoining the circus, by which means the people of colour will have a very spacious, airy and distinct place to which they ascend by a separate passage."[49] Tessier's advertisement clearly appeals directly to people of color, indicating his commitment to attracting white and black audiences.[50] Intriguingly, one of the performances Tessier's company mounts in the following month is that of *Shipwreck or Azémia*, evidently based on a French comic opera by the librettist Auguste Étienne Xavier Poisson de La Chabeaussière and composer Nicolas Dalayrac: *Azémia* debuted in France in 1786 with the title *Azémia ou le Nouveau Robinson* and appeared there again the following year with the title *Azémia ou les Sauvages*.[51] As its original title indicates, the opera revisits the tale of Robinson Crusoe; and indeed La Chabeaussière stated that he "wanted to write a dramatic novella after the style of Shakespeare's *The Tempest*, and of Dryden, the story of *Robinson Crusoe*, and the various histories of voyages . . . [with] variety, picturesque effect, surprise, everything that seemed likely to diversify a musical score."[52] Specifically, the opera concerns the plight of a young woman, Azémia (something of a cross between Crusoe and Miranda), who has grown up on a deserted island with her father; by the close of the opera, she is united in marriage to the young Englishman, Prosper—an event that is consecrated by a grand dance with the island's savages. Like the pantomime version of *Robinson Crusoe* performed by the French Theatre in Charleston, then, *Azémia* stages a creole commons in its final scene—one in which a New World commons performs as an embodied collectivity. Nonetheless, the astounding success of the Charleston performance of Crusoe was not replicated in Jamaica: rather, within three weeks of this performance, the Grand Jury declared the French Theatre a public nuisance and prohibited further performances "by the company at present acting therein."[53]

It is not clear that either the subject of Robinson Crusoe (in the form of Cussans's song or the comic opera *Azémia*) or the mixed-race audiences that Tessier courted were the reason the French Theatre was shut down; it is more likely the case that riots occurred at the theatre and that actors from St.

Domingue were regarded with suspicion given anxiety in Jamaica about the proximity of the events of the Haitian Revolution unfolding nearby. Indeed, in late March, a "Frenchman (supposed to be one of Mr. Tessier's Company from his having taken refuge behind the scenes)" was sought for a "gross, infamous, and daring assault . . . on the person of an inhabitant of this town, at the Theatre."[54] Such events may, indeed, have been the immediate cause of the closing the French Theatre in Kingston; however, the riotous and combustible nature of the theatre is not unrelated to its function as an embodiment of the commons, and in the case of Jamaica, to its status as a creole commons. Riots in the space of the theatre are quite often disputes over the participatory and representational presence of individuals and groups within the collectivity of what does (or does not) register as a "people."

Michael Scott's description of the racially stratified theatrical audience in the early nineteenth-century Kingston Theatre (cited above), for instance, also narrates the unfolding of a theatrical riot that occurs in the form of a pitched battle between white and Jewish members of the audience after two spectators seated on either side of him begin to brawl. And in April 1815, the military was called in to quell a riot at the Kingston Theatre that resulted when people of color protested a proposal to create a separate entrance and set of steps to the gallery for blacks. "At the opening of the Theatre of this City of the present season," reports the *Royal Gazette*, "a mob, composed of persons of colour, assembled on the Parade, and committed many violent outrages, by pelting the house with brick-bats, hissing at females and others who wished to attend the performance, and pulling down the steps leading to the Upper Boxes, &c." Martin Halhead, a free black, together with five other men, was investigated by the "Corporate Body" of Kingston and subsequently charged with being a ringleader of the event.[55] Halhead had been arrested two years earlier for a similar action—namely, a publicly staged protest against racial segregation—when he refused to vacate a pew in church after being told it was reserved for whites only.[56] In that incident, Halhead challenged the right of the government—specifically, the right of the "Corporate Body"—to regulate the corporate body of the people in church, in effect staging his own body as a visible component of the commons and insisting on the mixed-race nature of that corporate body. Charged with "resisting, and grossly insulting, a Magistrate in the execution of his duty," Halhead was summarily declared guilty following his protest of segregation in church.[57]

The material convening of the people as a collective body was thus a fraught act in Jamaica insofar as it brought into visibility the non-British (creole) and nonwhite nature of that public even as the colony operated in the name of

British liberty and popular sovereignty. The colonial relation that sustains metropolitan British economic and political life is not mediated by geographical distance in the colony: rather, its contradictions are insistent and material. Further, although the creole commons in Jamaica are unthinkable, it is nonetheless the case that a collective body obdurately materializes in the colony—at the theatre, in the pews of churches, in dance halls. Despite the ideological proscription of social reproduction in the colony, then, sociality does not disappear, nor can it be wholly erased or screened from public view. Moreover, in the face of technologies of social death, the social life and representational capacities of New World Africans do not disappear but take on new forms.

These new forms might be understood in terms of what Édouard Glissant describes as "forced poetics," or a poetics that is created in relation to a prohibition on expression. For Glissant, the hallmark of forced poetics is a sort of creative violence—a dissensus that violates the system of language itself: forced poetics emerges as a "cut across one language in order to attain a form of expression that is perhaps not part of the internal logic of this language."[58] Speech thus takes on a materially sonic form, abrogating the sense-making qualities of language in the name of shaping a new sensorium—a "verbal delirium [at] the outer edge of speech" in the words of Glissant: "improvisations, drumbeats, acceleration, dense repetitions, slurred syllables, meaning the opposite of what is said, allegory and hidden meanings."[59] What is worth underscoring here is the sensate nature of such a poetics and, thus, its aesthetic nature. Indeed, it is significant that this "speech" is one that takes the shape of poetics rather than speech precisely because speech is forbidden. "Dispossessed man," writes Glissant, "organized his speech by weaving it into the apparently meaningless texture of extreme noise." Turning to scenes of noise and materiality—specifically New World African Jonkonnu, dance, and dress—in the subsequent sections of this chapter I argue that such "noise" opens out into the space of a new shared sense (a poetics) among the dispossessed (the "part of no part") and thus reframes a sensus communis. This reframing, in turn, inaugurates a performative commons at the scene of impossible commoning.

A range of embodied, sonic, scenic, and material practices thus appear as forms of New World African aesthetic commoning in Jamaica. This is a radical aesthetic tradition born of the extreme conditions of race slavery and the structural violence of colonial modernity—one that can subsequently be traced in performance traditions that become central to Atlantic culture as well as British and U.S. national culture. Importantly, eighteenth-century Jamaica seldom appears in accounts of the history of Anglophone theatre, culture, or aesthetics: Jamaica did not become wholly independent from Great Britain until 1962 and, as a result, has been written out of nationally oriented accounts of British and American literature and culture, despite the fact that Jamaica stood at the center of the Anglophone Atlantic colonial system. However, positioned at the origin of capitalist modernity in its dehumanizing systems of labor and racialization, Jamaica might also be seen to stand as an originating site of a politico-aesthetic innovation of cultural commoning in its most radical form.

In her recent capacious account of black culture, Hortense Spillers proposes a formulation by which we might understand the originating force of such an aesthetic. "It is striking," writes Spillers, "that precisely because black cultures arose in the world of normative violence, coercive labor, and the virtually absolute crush of the everyday struggle for existence, its subjects could imagine, could *dare* to imagine, a world beyond the coercive technologies of their daily bread. . . . Because it was set aside, black culture could, by virtue of the very act of discrimination, *become* culture, insofar as, historically speaking, it was forced to turn its resources of spirit toward negation and critique."[60] Spillers here suggests that culture emerges most forcefully from negation and critique—that it moves toward creation and innovation on the basis of what is not or what is and should not be. Subject to systemic violence and erasure that would reduce bodies to sheer materiality—to bare labor—by colonial and capitalist technologies, enslaved black peoples fashioned from the denuded materiality of their lives rich modes of signification—namely, culture itself and a performative commons, in its starkest, and perhaps most stunning form.

COLONIAL TRAFFIC IN WOMEN: SCENES OF PRODUCTION AND REPRODUCTION

In October 1780, the *Royal Gazette* reported that Hallam's American Company suffered a major theft from its men's wardrobe. Gone missing are "a great Number of valuable dresses," including: "A Scarlet Coat and Waistcoat with blue Cuffs and Collar, richly laced with Silver, with soil stone Buttons. A Pompadour Suit with a broad Gold net Lace. A Suit of Scarlet Cloth with a broad Gold Lace. . . . A purple Cloth Suit trimmed with a narrow Silver Lace," and thirteen additional similarly richly rendered suits. A fifty-pound reward is offered for the apprehension of "the perpetrators of this villainy."[61] As the size of the reward implies, the value of these costumes was significant: the sumptuous array of material here—lace, scarlet cloth, and silver and gold trim—was not easily or inexpensively come by in Jamaica, nor in other eighteenth-century colonial locales. And the signifying capacity of such clothing was essential to theatrical performance, particularly for an acting troupe that included plays such as Shakespeare's *Richard III* and *The Merchant of Venice*, Richard Sheridan's *The School for Scandal*, and Nicholas Rowe's *The Fair Penitent* as staples of its repertoire.

The historian Roderick McDonald reports that on Peeke Fuller's plantation in Jamaica, "the standard allotment for adult slaves in the clothing distribution of 1800 was a cap, seven yards of osnaburg, and three and a half yards of baize."[62] Osnaburg—the fabric widely used for clothing made for slaves—was a coarse, unbleached linen, largely imported from Scotland. The rough weave of osnaburg offered scant warmth or protection; further, it scratched the skin of those who wore it. Baize, in turn, is a coarsely woven woolen cloth. The 1792 Consolidated Slave Acts of Jamaica required that masters supply slaves with "proper and sufficient clothing"—an indication that some masters were negligent in clothing their slaves even minimally. Stripping Africans who survived the middle passage of their clothing was a significant act—a literal denuding of the newly enslaved individual. And the signifying capacity of osnaburg was important as well insofar as it performed the visible segmentation of the labor force in racialized terms. As McDonald points out, "Clothing was one of the most important instruments planters had in the acculturation process that asserted and defined slave status. The clothes that slaves arriving in Jamaica received were foreign to all their previous experience. . . . Although the material and style were European, the osnaburg trousers, frocks, shifts, and coats were the clothing of slaves and slaves alone."[63] In the hands of planters, osnaburg was plied as a technology of social death.

A significant exception to the plantocratic system of disrobing slaves and clothing them in baize and osnaburg emerged in the years surrounding the 1807 closing of the slave trade. With the prohibition of the importation of "new negroes," planters were no longer able to "outsource" the biological reproduction of slaves to Africa: as such, the fact that the slave population did not and could not reproduce itself in Jamaica was newly perceived as a crisis for the plantocracy. The axiom among planters that it was "better to buy than breed" was replaced with a set of strategies and policies aimed at encouraging reproduction. The procedures of so-called amelioration during this period by planters—aimed to both increase sugar production in the West Indies and to quell criticism from English abolitionists about slavery—included efforts to improve the rate of reproduction among slaves.[64] To do so, planters offered clothing to women as an inducement for "breeding." The West Indian planter Matthew "Monk" Lewis reports, for instance, that in addition to giving slave mothers a dollar "for every infant which should be brought to the overseer alive and well on the fourteenth day," he plans to provide mothers with "a

The driver's whip unfolds its torturing coil.
"She only Sulks___go lash her to her toil."

FIGURE 5.2. Production versus reproduction: an abolitionist image of an overseer forcing a mother to leave her child. Drawing originally published by the Female Society, for Birmingham, West-Bromwich, Wednesbury, Walsall, and Their Respective Neighbourhoods, for the Relief of British Negro Slaves (1828). Courtesy of the Library of Congress, Prints and Photographs Division.

present of a scarlet girdle with a silver medal in the center [for her] to wear . . . on feasts and holidays, when it should entitle her to marks of peculiar respect and attention."[65] Further, he proposes, each additional child will earn the slave mother another medal for her belt, thus creating an "order of honour" for mothers. Lewis was not alone in such efforts to use clothing as an inducement to increase the number of his enslaved laborers: indeed, the British Parliament recommended such a course of action as well.[66]

Efforts to increase the birthrate among slaves in Jamaica did not succeed: attempts to redress/dress up the conditions of bare labor that slave women endured had little effect given the sustained commitment of the plantocracy to production over reproduction. Abolitionists seized on gender roles as a means of impressing the cruelties of slavery on an English public: extracting the labor of production negated the possibility of reproduction and violated codes of femininity (see figure 5.2). As Hilary McD. Beckles and Verene Shepherd succinctly report, "the pro-natalist policies of the post-1807 ameliorative period were doomed to fail as long as the majority of the enslaved women labored in the field. Women's productive capacity was not to be sacrificed for reproduction; thus there was a clear incompatibility between production and reproduction."[67] As Beckles and Shepherd point out, then, the effort to add the labor of reproduction to that of production for slave women failed because of the inherent contradiction between the two in the landscape of plantation slavery.

In order to generate bare labor, slavery worked to strip black women not just of clothing but of a fundamental aspect of social identity—namely, gender itself. As Spillers has argued, the conditions of the middle passage were ones in which Africans were "culturally 'unmade.'" Under such conditions, writes Spillers, "one is neither female, nor male, as both subjects are taken into account as quantities."[68] This "unmaking" with respect to gender extended to the conditions of labor on the sugar plantation. The most physically demanding work performed on the sugar plantation was that of field work—"digging cane holes, planting, trashing, cutting, tying, loading and carting." Rather than placing women in less physically arduous jobs, women were, in effect, ungendered so as to perform the most brutal labor not only alongside men, but in greater numbers than men: as Lucille Mathurin Mair documents, "in the extraction of this labour, no distinction is made between men and women." The racialization of slave workers thus enables an ungendering that serves the purposes of providing planters with a more flexible (and disposable) work force. Indeed, as Mair points out, not only were slave women tasked with performing the most physically demanding work on the plantation, but it was most particularly African-born women—not creole or mixed-race blacks— who bore the brunt of this work: "Racism eased the process by which black women, and black women only, were massively drafted into the assembly line of the field."[69] Black women, in this sense, were ungendered by a racist calculus elaborated in conjunction with the geography of capitalist modernity: in the colony, black women were not viewed as women, but rather as units of labor generating the production of sugar.

In such a colonial geography, gender is thus thoroughly reconfigured in relation to race: black women become ungendered while white women, in contrast, become highly gendered figures who embody reproductive possibility. Given that the status of a child followed that of the mother with respect to enslavement or freedom, white women's bodies were the sole location in the colony for the reproduction of "British liberty" and thus, in the words of Cecily Forde-Jones, white women were "reproducers of the human state of freedom" in the colonial Caribbean.[70] On colonial ground, however, any reproduction was vexed, even that of whites. Given that the social reproduction of Britishness was a metropolitan, rather than colonial prerogative, the reproduction of British liberty in the colony was fraught with the possibility of going awry: in such a context, the white woman's body, too, was a contested site of reproduction.

Evidence of the difficulty of reproducing British (rather than creole) identity in the colony appears in Lady Nugent's account of the christening of her firstborn child, George Edmund Nugent or "Georgy." Born in the colony, Georgy was, in fact, a creole: in the pages of her journal, however, Nugent attends carefully to the staging of Georgy's christening—his naming and recognition as a new Christian subject—in order to insist on his *British* rather than creole identity. Nugent writes:

> My dear baby looked beautiful in his christening dress, and was wrapped, by way of mantle, in a beautiful muslin handkerchief, embroidered in gold sent me by Madame Le Clerc. I am much flattered by the pleasure all the Members of the Assembly, &c. expressed, on the birth of our little boy. He is, it seems, the first child that has been born in this situation; for none of the former Governors have had children. . . . Old [Jamaican planters] Mr. Simon Taylor and Mr. Mitchell could never say enough upon the subject, and they seemed to think that he should now be so attached to the island, and should become quite one of themselves. I own, although I am grateful for their kindness, I could not carry my gratitude so far.[71]

As the passage indicates, debate over Georgy's new identity emerges at the naming ceremony: Nugent notes that she is flattered by the pleasure taken in Georgy's birth by the colonial elite, but she also notes that the two wealthiest and most powerful plantation owners in the colony—Simon Taylor and William Mitchell—are particularly excited because they view Georgy as "one of themselves"—that is, a creole. Rejecting the claim that Georgy is a creole— she "cannot carry [her] gratitude so far" as to endorse Mitchell and Taylor's views—Nugent instead wraps Georgy in the mantle of metropolitan identity—specifically, a gold-embroidered muslin mantle supplied by the dazzling figure of metropolitan aristocracy, Pauline LeClerc, the sister of Napoleon and the wife of General Charles LeClerc.[72] The first lady of colonial St. Domingue, Madame LeClerc was the French colonial counterpart to Lady Nugent, first lady of British colonial Jamaica. In announcing and performing the intimacy of her relation to Madame LeClerc at the christening—in wrapping her baby in the luxury linen of a gold muslin handkerchief—Lady Nugent distances her son from the proximity that Taylor and Mitchell claim, wrapping Georgy within a genealogy of metropolitan elites who visit and rule over, but do not belong to, colonial climes. Ironically, then, Lady Nugent resorts to *French* support to establish her capacity to reproduce *British* identity in the space of the colony: she does so in order to dissemble—to mantle over, one might say—the unbearable creolism of her infant son.

There is some irony in this gesture. First, Nugent was evidently unaware when she wrote this passage that General LeClerc had died of yellow fever in St. Domingue five days before her son was christened. As such, she wraps her son in a mantle that might be considered a shroud of imperial rule in the West Indies: not only was LeClerc dead, but French imperial rule in St. Domingue would shortly be abolished by revolutionary slave forces, resulting in the first free black republic in the hemisphere. Second, the article of clothing in question is a muslin handkerchief, albeit one embroidered in gold—an item with a distinctly colonial heritage. The muslin handkerchief was a garment worn as a turban, to great effect, by women of colour in the West Indies. In St. Domingue, as one writer explains, "[the Mûlattresses'] favourite coiffure is an India handkerchief, which is bound round the head: the advantages they derive from this simple ornament are inconceivable; they are the envy and despair of the white lades, who aspire to imitate them."[73] The head coverings that women of colour were required to wear as signifiers of a degraded status were thus transformed by means of an embodied aesthetic into signifiers of the opposite—that is, into markers of an elevated status as objects of desire. Pauline LeClerc's purported adoption of the madras headscarf, noted in Leonora Sansay's novel, *The Secret History; or, The Horrors of St. Domingo*, thus implicitly announces a creolization of desire on the part of the metropolitan elite. The muslin handkerchief in which Nugent wraps her infant does not, then, ward off intimacy with the colonial relation so much as embody it.

The scraps of cloth changing hands and changing bodies in all of these instances—pompadour suits, yards of osnaburg, scarlet girdles adorned with silver medals, gold embroidered muslin handkerchiefs, and madras headscarves—thus bear with them a great deal of meaning. Clothing and adornment are used, in each case, to materialize not just identity but forms of kinship and access (or lack thereof) to kinship systems. Spillers, again, is helpful here in pointing to the particular valences of kinship in the African diasporic world: New World slavery, writes Spillers, creates a condition of "kinlessness" among slaves, given that it systematically deprives slaves of genealogical identity: "kinship loses meaning" with regard to the identity of the enslaved, "since it can be invaded at any given and arbitrary moment by the property relations" of the master's ownership of the slave. In short, the affiliative bonds of kinship are abrogated under slavery in favor of an affiliation construed in terms of property ownership: "It is this rhetorical and symbolic move that declares primacy over any other *human and social claim*, and in that political order of things, kin, just as gender formation, has no decisive legal or social efficacy [for the slave]."[74] Gender and kinship are thus erased by slavery in favor of capitalist production and property accumulation. And indeed, as we have seen, the genealogical/signifying function of maternity in the colony is placed under pressure by the capitalist geography of modernity—a condition that is experienced in an acute form by enslaved black women, but in some different degree by colonial white women as well: maternity, in the colony, presents itself as something of a category crisis.

In this landscape—one scoured of social and juridical resources for sustaining kinship, gender, and social reproduction—a primary resource for the creation of kinship becomes the aesthetic realm, and specifically, the mobilization of the force of dissensus, located at the intersection of the ontic and the mimetic. As I suggest in what follows, in the performative commons of the theatre in Kingston, dramatic performance is marshaled toward reimagining the reproductive capacity of white women, as well as reconfiguring patriarchy within a colonial geography. But dissensus emerges from this space as well— a dissensus that produces an alternative theatricalization of kinship, one in which the ontic force of the material becomes the resource for new mimetic possibilities of kinship and affiliation that revise the script of bare labor and social death for New World Africans. The scraps of cloth in which bodies are wrapped serve as ineluctable signifiers of the relations that bind people to one another, across and despite the structural violence of race slavery. Turning to the material of cloth itself, and tracing the way in which its ontic status as mere textile comes to assume mimetic shape through acts of performative commoning, we can trace the way in which material passes from hand to hand, creating relations that belie the bareness of bare labor, and that offer aesthetic egress from kinlessness.

THEATRICAL PRODUCTIONS OF ENGLISH LIBERTY

On stage in Jamaica, quite a number of popular plays appear that arguably aim to script the reproductive role of white women in relation to the geography of colonialism. The plays I consider here include *The Duenna or the Double Elopement*, a comic opera by Richard Brinsley Sheridan that first appeared in London in 1775, and was the first play to be printed in Jamaica (1779); a related Sheridan play that was popular in Jamaica, *School for Scandal* (1777); and one of the first original plays written and performed in Jamaica, *A West-India Lady's Arrival in London* by Margaret Cheer (1781).[75] Such plays dramatize what Gayle Rubin has called the "traffic of women"—that is, cultural rules for the exchange of women in the formation of kinship systems and the sexual division of labor.[76]

While Sheridan's *School for Scandal* debuted in London and has no specific colonial setting, its relevance to colonial Jamaica appears in the centrality of its concern with establishing rules for the exchange of women in the new conditions of the Whig ascendancy—that is, in a world where money, and a new capitalist geography, rather than lineage have begun to rescript ideals of marital alliance. *The School for Scandal* was among the most often performed plays of the late eighteenth century, in Jamaica as well as London. Though ostensibly about the pitfalls of high society gossip and scandal mongering, the play also concerns the infusion of new colonial money into established English social hierarchy. Specifically, the drama hinges on the matter of which of two brothers with elevated social status and dwindling cash—Joseph or Charles Surface—will inherit the riches of Sir Oliver, an uncle who has been absent for many years amassing wealth in the East Indies. In order to establish who is worthy of the inheritance, Sir Oliver poses in two disguises: as a needy relative ("Mr. Stanley") and as a moneylender ("Mr. Premium") affiliated with the "friendly Jew," Moses. Thus, like Robinson Crusoe in J. P. Cussans's famous song, Sir Oliver's colonial adventuring seemingly eventuates in his appearance in the figure of a Jew in contrast to "all that is civil": in the play, Oliver must masquerade as a moneylender in order to test the character of his nephews and to reintroduce his colonial capital into the English social system. In his guise as "Mr. Premium," Sir Oliver is ultimately able to divine that Charles is willing to sell off almost the entirety of his family portraits to Moses and his fellow "moneylender" but insists on retaining ownership of the portrait of Sir Oliver for sentimental reasons: it is this action—insisting on the nonexchange value of a paternal male relative—that insures his ultimate success over his brother in claiming Sir Oliver's colonial wealth.

Significantly, the climactic scene of *The School for Scandal* is the famous "screen scene"—one in which the chief gossipmonger and would-be adulterer, Lady Teazle, secrets herself behind a decorative screen and listens to a conversation taking place on the other side in order to both hide her own indiscretion with Joseph Surface and to learn the true sentiments of her husband about their marriage. The screen creates an epistemic break within the circulation of knowledge on the stage: the audience, in viewing the scene, is asked to place itself in the position of both knowing and not knowing that Lady Teazle is behind the screen, just as the audience is asked to see and not see that the moneylender "Mr. Premium" is the rich uncle Oliver, returned from colonial climes. Like the "Skreenmaster General," Robert Walpole, Sheridan here both exposes and screens the colonial relation from sight, all while he launders new money through a second narrative—one that concerns the fidelity of metropolitan English women to their husbands.[77] When the screen is removed in the famous screen scene, revealing the false Lady Teazle behind it, what is dramatically exposed, then, is not the danger of the colonial relation (on which the social system is dependent for its renewal), but the need to school white women against sexual infidelity to their husbands. In broad terms, then, the play might be seen to concern the issue of new capitalist modes of accumulation and their effects on existing social structures. The displacement of concern with forms of extranational colonial sociality—figured in the proximity of English and non-English peoples such as Jews—onto a concern with the scandal of metropolitan women's sexuality serves to screen/disavow the (obscene) relation of the inside of English society from its apparent outside.[78]

And indeed, an explicit concern with the access of nonwhite persons to the scene of English social reproduction (and, specifically, to the reproductive body of the white woman) is the more pronounced subject of *The Duenna*, the Sheridan play that David Douglass and his partner, William Aikman, printed in Kingston in 1799 and that was performed repeatedly there as well. The plot of *The Duenna or the Double Elopement* (published in Jamaica under the title *The Comic Opera of the Duenna*) turns on matters of marriage and elopement—issues that resonate with concerns of social reproduction and genealogy that haunt Jamaican public discourse. Moreover, despite its original subtitle, the play ends with a triple elopement and a triple marriage, yet pointedly, only two of those marriages rise to social intelligibility, while the third (which takes place between a Jew and an aging governess) is erased from legibility. The play is set in Seville, Spain, and features a nobleman by the name of Antonio, who is in love with the beautiful Louisa. However, Louisa's father, Don Jerome, is forcing her to marry a Portuguese Jew named Isaac Mendoza for his wealth. Louisa's duenna or governess, Margaret, contrives to switch places with Louisa, allowing Louisa to elope with her beloved Antonio and duping Isaac, the "over-reaching" Jew, into marrying the aging and unattractive Margaret. Further, Louisa's brother, Ferdinand, is in pursuit of a woman named Clara, whose father has destined her for the nunnery. With Louisa's assistance, Ferdinand and Clara are able to elope as well. Hence three marital couples are generated at the close of the play: the noble-born Louisa and Antonio (Antonio is noble but poor), the noble-born Ferdinand and Clara, and the lowly but wealthy Isaac together with the lowly and unlovely Margaret. All three are married by means of strategies that involve the manipulation of knowledge and nonknowledge, including extended impersonation, trickery, and shifting sight lines staged throughout the play by means of the machinery of concealment, veils, masquerade, and deceptive missives.

The central emotional force of the play lies in uniting the obviously deserving Antonio with Louisa, while keeping Louisa out of the hands of the grotesquely caricatured, "cunning little Isaac." Represented as grasping, hairy, and avaricious, Sheridan's Jew becomes a stock figure of the English stage in this period, as Michael Ragussis demonstrates. Although the play is set in Spain, Ragussis suggests that a figure such as Isaac is "used on the stage to locate and secure the boundary between Englishness and otherness." At the theatre, writes Ragussis, "learning how to be English often meant learning how to exclude Scots, Irish, and Jews."[79] Like the Jewish moneylender in *School for Scandal*, Isaac thus serves as something of synecdoche for the disruption caused by the social mobility and colonial provenance of capitalist accumulation that supported the growth of the English bourgeoisie. On stage in Jamaica, one might expect that Isaac's performance would resonate strongly with the concerns of an audience pressed by the experience of coloniality and the injunction to reproduce Englishness by way of the ejection of non-English figures—including individuals who were Jewish, brown, or black. Further, as we have seen, Jamaica had a large Jewish population at the time, and Jewishness often served as something of an intermediary signifier in debates concerning black/white racial formations in the colony.

In Isaac's case, more so than that of Moses in *School for Scandal*, a rhetoric of race—and specifically one of color—appears as a prominent means of delineating between English and non-English bodies. In *The Duenna*, Isaac is described at one point as: "a body that seems to owe all its consequence to the dropsy—[with] a pair of eyes like two dead beetles in a wad of brown dough. A beard like an artichoke, with dry shrivell'd jaws that would disgrace the mummy of a monkey."[80] Manifestly, then, Isaac's face is brown, and he is, moreover, compared unfavorably to a primate. The governess Margaret, to whom the play will consign Isaac as a suitable partner, is similarly portrayed as money-seeking and lacking in physical charm. Although there is no indication that she is Jewish, Margaret is described, like Isaac, as less than fair of face. While Louisa's father has told Isaac that his daughter has "dimity skin" with a "lovely bloom," Isaac finds that the Louisa to whom he has been introduced (namely, Margaret rather than Louisa) "is the very reverse" of what he has been promised: "As for the dimity skin you told me of, I swear 'tis a thorough nankeen as ever I saw; for her eyes, their utmost merit is in not squinting—for her teeth, where there is one of ivory, its neighbour is pure ebony, black and white alternatively, just like the keys of an harpsicord."[81] "Dimity" is a kind of white cotton cloth, imported to England and the West Indies from India, whereas "nankeen" is a beige or buff-colored cloth typically made in China from undyed cotton; further, the evocation of ivory and ebony suggests associations with African trade. In short, then, Margaret's nonwhiteness is figured in terms of global commerce—that is, the very colonial commerce that shaped every aspect of colonial life in Jamaica, but that also needed to be screened from recognition in order to enable nationalized scenes of English social reproduction.

Although Margaret and Isaac marry at the close of the play, the double elopement of the play's title evidently refers to the marriages of Antonio to Louisa and Ferdinand to Clara. This fact is clarified when these two marriages are celebrated with a grand closing dance, in the manner of *The Beggar's Opera*, at which Isaac and Margaret are not present. Indeed, *The Duenna* was often compared to *The Beggar's Opera*, both because it followed in the generic footsteps of Gay's ballad opera, and because it was the first play to surpass the opening run of *The Beggar's Opera*. But whereas *The Beggar's Opera* closes with a collective dance (as discussed in chapter 3) that embodies an antimarriage and anticontractual ethos of performative commoning, *The Duenna's* final dance serves the opposite purpose: namely, it celebrates a form of genealogical enclosure in which white Englishness is sanctioned as a locus of social reproduction and nonwhite persons are screened from view. Indeed, it seems worth noting that the nankeen-colored Margaret is able to secure access to the marriage contract (even that with Isaac) only because her real identity is screened from view in her disguise as Louisa. As such, social order is established in the final scenes of the play both by celebrating the correct placement of noble-born Europeans in marriage with one another, but also by expelling a foreign, nonwhite couple from the frame of the play. Given the extent to which gender was itself a matter of racialization in Jamaica, a play such as *The Duenna* would thus school men and women in the reproduction of whiteness despite the colonial promiscuity of white and nonwhite bodies.

The concern with controlling white women's reproductive capacity in relation to colonialism is mirrored in another play that found success on the Jamaica stage, namely, Nicholas Rowe's *Fair Penitent*. In Rowe's tragedy, the wayward daughter, Calista, violates the marriage contract to which her father has consigned her, engaging in sex with the gay Lothario before her marriage to Altamount. Calista, who is anything but penitent in the play, nonetheless ultimately commits suicide, enabling the play to insist on patrilineal reproductive prerogative: rather than reproducing herself, Calista's suicide reproduces her father's authority by eradicating her own extramarital desire and the intimacies thereby produced. As Kathleen Wilson argues, the play "provided a site for negotiations about sex, gender, class, and English national identity" that had particular purchase in a colonial location such as Jamaica.[82] In each of these plays, then, the extranational intimacies of colonialism—particularly as embodied in the creole—are restructured in terms of genealogical erasure. Social distance is thus established (by way of colonial screen scenes) in the face of the physical intimacy engendered by colonialism, thereby discursively separating that which, in practice, is collectively constituted.

An additional play, one both written and originally performed in Jamaica, points to just how significant and complex the erasure of creole intimacy was for white women in particular. The play in question, titled *A West-India Lady's Arrival in London*, was evidently written by the popular actress Margaret Cheer. The script of the play is not extant, but some indication of its content—and a controversy associated with it—appears in a newspaper notice announcing its pending performance in Kingston in October 1781. Specifically, "Miss Cheer" preemptively defends the use of West Indian dialect by the title character of the play. In a paid notice she states:

> MISS CHEER . . . hears it has been objected, that the Heroine of the Farce . . . should even for a short time assume the dialect peculiar to a few in this Island; but when she recollects the success the "Irish Widow" met with in Dublin, who assumes the brogue in order to disgust a disagreeable love . . . ; as she is persuaded that the public of Jamaica yield to none in candour and discernment, so she has no doubt but they will, without disapprobation see the 'WEST-INDIA-LADY' for a time lay aside the elegance of her character, and assume an awkwardness by which she is to get rid of three English Sharpers, and reward the passion of a countryman of her own with a large fortune.[83]

Evidently Cheer has learned that Jamaican audience members do not wish to hear white West Indians speaking in creole dialect on stage. Such a dialect, presumably, contributes to a derogatory image of white West Indians as, precisely, creolized rather than wholly British in their appearance and tone. Cheer's defense against such a charge is not a defense of creolism, but a defense of the performative nature of creole intonation: speaking in creole dialect is merely a mask, she suggests, that enables the West Indian lady to retain control of how (and in whom) she invests her offshore funds in the metropole. As Cheer's citation of Garrick's popular play *The Irish Widow* indicates, dialect was a common marker of identity used on stage in the late eighteenth century and served as a means of disguise as well. In Garrick's play, for instance, the widow Martha Brady affects an Irish brogue to ward off the attentions of an unwanted suitor. Yet as Cheer's notice in the paper suggests, even the use of creole dialect as a ruse by a white woman on stage caused alarm in Jamaica. In short, then, even the clever reversal Cheer proposes—in which the performance of creole dialect serves as a screen for elegance and wealth—is one that troubles the staged terms in which the colonial relation covertly supports English social reproduction.

Careful as such productions are to manage the reproduction of whiteness and the laundering of colonial wealth, the physical act of commoning—that of gathering a multitude of bodies—at the theatre in Jamaica produced counterevidence to the governmentality performed there. As we have seen, mixed-race audiences were commonplace at the theatre, and audiences assumed a representative force—one that engendered disgust, riot, and pleasure. The creole commons that gathered at the theatre took shape, as I have argued, in insistently material terms. The ontic nature of this materiality appears, as well, in the very plays that seemingly work to eradicate the representational force of this materiality. Two specific instances of such resistant materiality appear in the plays described above: one in the form of cloth—of fabric itself—and a second in sonic form. The governess's not-quite-white skin color in *The Duenna*, as we have seen, is described by way of analogy to the beige color of the cotton cloth, nankeen. At the close of the eighteenth century, nankeen was not only a product of imperial commerce, but it was a textile with strong West Indian associations. It was often used for making light but sturdy pants, and nankeen trousers were the uniform of sailors as well as West Indian planters and tradesmen. Indeed, by the early nineteenth century, nankeen trousers were considered stereotypically West Indian: a short story published in a Philadelphia journal, for instance, describes a man impersonating a West Indian as "dressed in all the importance and loose nankeen trowsers [*sic*] of a warm West Indian."[84] Domestic slaves, who were provided with more expensive clothing than enslaved field workers, were also likely to wear pants of nankeen.[85] When the word "nankeen" was spoken on stage to refer, metaphorically, to the color of the governess's skin, it also would have served to name the material in which a good portion of the audience was clothed.

In related terms, the sound of the creole dialect that Margaret Cheer was evidently cautioned against presenting on stage was an aspect of the material sensorium that white, black, and brown West Indians inhabited together. As travel narratives written by Europeans indicate, the Jamaican creole dialect was one that whites as well as blacks spoke, often to the dismay of whites intent on maintaining a distinction between the two. Edward Long describes the creole dialect as a "sort of gibberish" that "infects many of the White Creoles, who learn it from their (black or colored) nurses in infancy, and meet with much difficulty, as they advance in years, to shake it entirely off, and express themselves with correctness."[86] And Lady Maria Nugent expresses her revulsion for such sounds in even stronger terms: "Many of the [white] ladies . . . speak a sort of broken English, with an indolent drawing out of their words, that is very tiresome if not disgusting."[87] The creole dialect that could not be spoken on stage was thus undoubtedly spoken in the audience. The creole commons that the plays seemingly banish takes shape in material form—in sound and cloth we see creole kinship emerge in material terms. As this materiality threatens to tip into legibility as a signifying system—that is, not as "dissonant gibberish" but as the grounds of shared meaning making—so too does the creole commons threaten to stage a dissensus that reconfigures the sensus communis and the politics of the community itself. The commonwealth is thus reformed here, not in relation to the people who make up a public but in relation to the res publica—that is, in relation to the ontic *thing* (res) that constitutes the public sensorium.

THE CREOLE SENSORIUM: DISSENSUS AND NEW FORMS OF KINSHIP

If the insistent materiality of the creole sensorium requires screening from imperial view, it serves the opposite function for those consigned to social death—that is, it becomes the source of new kinship and forms of social life precisely because it cannot be wholly erased. The material kinship embedded and embodied in clothing, for instance, is a key source of social being and meaning for the enslaved population of Jamaica. The ontic nature of fabric—its very thing-ness—tends to serve as something of an alibi within the plantation economy because clothing can seem to have little function other than the utilitarian provision of protection and covering. But like theatrical performance itself, clothing participates in mimetic and figurative regimes as much as that of the ontic: which is to say, fabric fashioned into clothing serves as *both* stuff and signifier, textile and text.[88]

Notwithstanding the osnaburgh, penniston (blue woolen cloth), and baize that were standard-issue fabrics for slave clothing, European writers commented at length on the textiles and clothing in which slaves and free blacks dressed in Jamaica that did not conform to this uniform. Two conflicting accounts predominate: slaves are described as dressed in clothing that is pitiably ragged, *or* they are viewed as dressing in excessive finery. Each of these accounts is subject, as well, to conflicting interpretation. Abolitionists, for instance, portray the scraps of rough cloth in which field slaves dress as evidence of deprivation imposed by planters; slavery advocates describe tattered clothing as an indication of impropriety, irresponsibility, and lack of civility and morality on the part of slaves. And in the case of elegant attire worn by blacks, apologists for slavery adduce two further conclusions: elaborate dress is viewed as evidence of, on the one hand, an excessive, imitative, and childish sensibility on the part of blacks or, on the other hand, the beneficence of the plantocracy in providing for slaves and the general happiness and contentment of the enslaved.

Thus despite the fact that many planters provisioned slaves in the most miserly fashion, deficient clothing among slaves was often viewed as a sign of "savagery." An article in the *Columbian Magazine* reported, "Many negroes, while in their owners employ, totally neglect their dress; wearing the most ragged cloaths in their possession, sometimes until they fall off, which however they protract as long as they can, by knotting their drapery to keep it hanging together. . . . Nakedness is considered as matter of little reproach . . . a coat or breeches being often the whole dress."[89] In related terms, the memoirist A. C. Carmichael explains that the poorly clothed slave is not a victim of want, but rather a victim of his or her own lack of civility: "When I first landed in the West Indies," she writes, "I was shocked at the unclothed state in which I saw many negroes; but a few months' careful observation shewed me that it was not the want of clothes, but the dislike to their burden that occasioned this." Slaves, she reports, would rather not wear clothes in the heat, and refuse to do so given that "a sense of decency is scarcely known to the savage." Somewhat in contrast to this view, however, Carmichael also reports on the love of fine clothing exhibited by many slaves and suggests that their lack of work clothing may be caused by an interest in acquiring alternative dress: "[Improvident] negroes . . . either take no care of their clothing, or they sell it to hucksters, who give them fine showy clothes instead, not at all suitable for a working dress. Such people are often improvident enough to exchange all their blue Pennistowns for some article of jewellery."[90]

Carmichael's suggestion that slaves are "improvident" in their interest in "fine showy clothes" is widely echoed in accounts of West Indian slave culture by European travellers. One visitor, for instance, reports happening on a scene of slave recreation, and finding himself "amazed at the profusion of silks or fine linen in which numbers of the females were arrayed, besides gold trinkets and jewellery in abundance; most of the males too were decent, many fine: strutting in their silk hose and ruffled shirts, pert and proud as so many country squires at a farmer's wedding."[91] The planter William Beckford, in turn, describes the dress of mulattoes at a ball, commenting that "it will hardly be credited how very expensive their dress and ornaments are, and what pains

FIGURE 5.3. "Offended Dignity." The black dandy on the left states, "Dem Buckra say darra you, Missy Leah Tomlin," as he displays an abolitionist image of a half-naked slave woman being whipped. Missy Tomlin responds, "Dem Buckra tell big Lie, Massa Richard Tanton, and you an Buckra be one great fool." Etching by William Heath (1830). Courtesy of the Lewis Walpole Library, Yale University.

they take to disfigure themselves with powder and with other unbecoming imitations of European dress."[92]

As the language of such passages indicates, slaves who dressed themselves in sumptuous clothing were subject to ridicule and disdain; rather than viewed as exhibiting civility when dressed in such attire, they were seen as performing failed imitations of whiteness. The broadside cartoon image titled "Offended Dignity" (see figure 5.3) satirizes both images at once—that of the seminaked supplicant slave whose figure appeared in abolitionist literature in England, and that of the imitative black dandy. In the cartoon, a black man dressed in the attire of a West Indian dandy—striped trousers, yellow waistcoat, cravat, hat, and blue jacket with brass buttons—speaks to a "Missy Leah Tomlin," who, in turn, is bedecked in a ball dress with elaborate bows, jewelry, earrings, a feathered hat, and yellow shoes with red ornamentation. Upon being told that "Buckra" (in this case, abolitionist literature) represents her as a half-naked woman dressed in rags, Miss Tomlin takes offense: "Dem Buckra tell big Lie, Massa Richard Tanton, and you an Buckra be one great fool." The broadside thus presents the divergent—and equally white-centric—images of black dress circulated in European accounts of slavery: that of the imitative dandy, and that of the seminaked slave on bended knee.

But an alternative reading of the "fantastic" and "gaudy" appearance of such dress and the "inordinate . . . love of dress and finery" displayed by black creoles suggests that an aesthetic performance is at stake that is far from imitative.[93] Rather, in relation to a colonial geopolitics of bare labor and imperial technologies of social death, the superfluity of adornment would not figure as poor imitation but as an intentional performance of excess—staged not in order to establish a claim to civility as the opposite of savagery, but in order to perform an exuberant and nonutilitarian presencing that flies in the face of bare labor and social erasure. Extravagant adornment might be understood, then, as precisely that which exceeds the bareness to which the slave is consigned. Moreover, in such a case, the nonutilitarian aspect of excess would be exactly what is at stake: dress, then, has value as "showy finery" rather than in suitability for labor. Thus, when Carmichael complains that "improvident" slaves exchange their Penniston work clothes for jewelry and finery, we might understand such slaves to be engaged in an act of resistance to the geopolitics of coloniality: rather than dressing for the labor of production, they are clothing themselves for an unrestrained staging of sociality.

At stake in the ridicule directed at the black dandy is a debate over the meaning of slave clothing: does it lie in its function as part of a system of production, or its function as part of a system of signification? On the part of the slave who imitates European white dress by exceeding its codes, we might discern not failure but a dissensus enacted in the form of an aesthetic engagement in the performativity of dress. Consider the following instance of such a dissensus—a debate waged at the ontic level—in which Carmichael laments the excessive money spent on clothing domestic servants: "I recollect B——, a head servant of ours, who was sent to a store in quest of shoes for himself, and brought home a pair which cost 14s. 4d. sterling. I ventured to tell him that I disapproved of his choice, as they were light thin dress shoes, which would not serve him many weeks;—but his answer was given with great nonchalance in these words:—'Misses, me could not dance in tick shoes; they too heavy and hot.' In fact, this man would not have deigned to wear such shoes as I wore every day in walking out."[94] The shoes that Carmichael imagines should serve to further the slave's labor on her behalf are, instead, purchased by the slave in order to dance: they do not serve, then, in the production of sugar and plantocratic power, but in the aesthetic engagement in a creole commons—in the collective scene of social reproduction, the dance. Excess and improvidence, on such an account, are aesthetic and political acts of the creative destruction of plantocratic order.

The signifying force of elaborate dress emerges most powerfully in relation to the Christmas revelry of Jonkonnu plays and the highly codified "set girl" dances and parades in eighteenth-century Jamaica. Set girls—teams of enslaved and free black women—regularly performed spectacular competitive dances in matching costumes during the Christmas holiday. As one typical account of their performance indicates, set girls are distinguished, above all, in their elaborate and sumptuous dress:

> At Christmas the negroes are altogether without restraint, and go over the country feasting, dancing, and drinking. Many of the girls form themselves into what they call sets, in which the dresses are nearly alike; these sets travel, preceded by flags, drums, and other music, from estate to estate, dancing at the house of the white people, and in the negro villages, where they are given money, and very often entertained. Their dresses on these occasions are often very expensive, hats that cost a doubloon (sixteen dollars), and blue or white kid shoes at fifteen shillings per pair are by no means uncommon; those that wish to be particularly smart carry parasols.[95]

The account of the set girls is somewhat contradictory: on the one hand, the writer begins by stating that blacks "are altogether without restraint" at Christmas, but the details that follow suggest that a great deal of preparation, organization, and (indeed, excessive) expense are involved in the performance staged by the set girls. Far from unrestrained, or "baby-like" as Lady Nugent would have it, the set girls' performance suggests regimental precision.[96]

What is most significant about the set girls, then, is not simply their dress, but the fact that they are organized into assemblages or sets: as such, their elaborate dress announces not only splendor and beauty but a form of social belonging as well. As an 1808 account indicates, the dress colors identified members of a set: "negro girls of the towns (who conceive themselves far superior to those on the estates, in point of *taste, manners,* and *fashion*) exhibit themselves in all the pride of gaudy splendor, under the denomination of *blues* and *reds*—parties in rivalship and opposition to each other, and distinguished by those colours."[97] In this description, a distinction is drawn not only between "blues" and "reds"—families of set girls made up of well-dressed women from the town—but membership in such sets serves to distinguish town women from country slave women.

Notably, however, the principle on which the sets were organized varies markedly from one account to the next: in the text accompanying his well-known watercolor of the French set girls (see figure 5.4), the artist Isaac Belisario describes sets comprised of refugees from St. Domingue who, "on becoming

FIGURE 5.4. French Set-Girls, by Isaac Belisario (Kingston, 1838). Courtesy of Yale Center for British Art, Paul Mellon Collection.

fixed residents [of Jamaica] . . . formed themselves into three Bands or Sets at Christmas, denominated 'Royalists,' 'Mabiales,' and 'Americans.' The former was composed wholly of Creoles of St. Domingo, who considered themselves on that account of the highest grade—the 2d, of Africans from Congo, and the latter of a portion of both." Other accounts, such as that of Monk Lewis, describe a red set representing an English allegiance and a blue set representing a Scottish allegiance. An account in the *Columbian Magazine* describes seemingly arbitrary groupings defined "by various names, as the Golden Set, the Velvet Set, the Garnet Ladies, &c." Finally, the account of Glaswegian Michael Scott emphasizes difference of skin color among the members of the sets: the set girls "danced along the streets, in bands of from fifteen to thirty. There were brown sets, and black sets, and sets of all the intermediate gradations of colour. Each set was dressed pin for pin alike, and carried umbrellas or parasols of the same colour and size, held over their nice showy, well put on *toques*, or Madras handkerchiefs, all of the same pattern, tied round their heads, fresh out of the fold."[98] If the principal of assemblage is variable, however, what is much less so is the performance of belonging within the set: as Scott's passage notes, the dresses of the set girls are "pin for pin alike," and it is on this family resemblance that the aesthetic force of their performance rests.

The clothing of the set girls might thus be seen to establish something of a kinship group—one that is not genealogical in nature (not aimed at establishing provenance and descent) but, rather, one that stages a form of siblinghood, a lateral form of belonging and social identity. If slavery aimed to render slaves kinless, without the social support of kinship groups, the performance of the set girls directly contradicted such a claim, generating a kinship group out of the ontic resource of material itself. As Ann Rosalind Jones and Peter Stallybrass argue, clothing is mimetic of social belonging: "Clothing is a worn world: a world of social relations put upon the wearer's body."[99] Social death is here countered by textile and color in the blue, garnet, or gold of sumptuary display that links one body in voluntaristic, flexible belonging to another. As Sara Johnson argues in her compelling account of the French Set-Girls and trans-Caribbean culture in this period, "the flourishing of a regional counter-plantation aesthetic during the Age of Revolution" occurred during "an era that necessitated the constant renegotiation and restructuring of black community life." Members of the French Set Girls, Johnson demonstrates, were able to deploy diverse aspects of their identities in their performances, "alternatively emphasiz[ing] their African ethnicities (Congolese, Dahomeyan), their creole pedigrees (Jamaican, Cuban, Haitian) or one of many colonial labels (British, Spanish, French) depending on the circumstances."[100] Thus, the flexible formation of the set itself bespeaks a resourceful kinship, constructed in the contested space of kinlessness. Wielding the ontic force of clothing as a mimetic source of kinship and aesthetic possibility, the set girls performed anew an affiliative logic of social reproduction in the shadow of a colonial regime of social death.

The performance and play of Jonkonnu, which also occurred during the days of Christmas holidays on which Jamaican slaves were annually released from work, stages social reproduction as well but does so in terms that are more radically aesthetic than those of the set girls. A performance with evident African roots, Jonkonnu involved plays, parade, and dance led by a "whimsical character" wearing a mask and costume: "Sometimes [the Jonkonnus] wear two faces, different from each other; as usually they have but one, which is often rendered hideous by beards and boar's tusks." As this 1797 account indicates, in addition to the "ugly mask," the Jonkonnu might wear, "a close waistcoat and trowsers, chequered like a Harlequin's coat, or hung with shreds of various coloured cloth dangling like a loose shag; . . . many of their present figures claim attention for the fantastic modern cut of their cloaths, often of silk and sometimes enriched with lace; a quantity of hair on the head as preposterously dressed as some European beaux."[101] Notable in this account is the sense, as Simon Gikandi argues, that Jonkonnu wears two faces: literally, at times, the Jonkonnu figure wears a two-faced mask, but more figuratively, the Jonkonnu performance operates in dual registers of Europeanized and African culture, and of play and resistance: "John Canoe had two faces and functions: one imitated the culture of taste; the other mocked it. . . . One face imitated the measured manner of the European court; the other face, which was notable for its hideousness, was a distortion of the symmetrical form of the accepted aesthetic."[102]

When seen as dual-faced, the Jonkonnu performance, so often described by European observers as failed imitation, veers rather conspicuously into parody. "At Christmas," writes visitor Peter Marsden in his account of Jamaica, "the prime negroes and mulattoes pay a visit to the white people during the festivity, and are treated with punch; one of them attends with a fiddle, and the men dress in the English mode, with cocked hats, cloth coats, silk stockings, white waistcoats, Holland shirts, and pumps. They dance minuets with the mulattoe and other brown women, imitating the motion and steps of the English but with a degree of affectation that renders the whole truly laughable and ridiculous."[103] Marsden's description would seem to suggest that the dancers are ridiculously inept, but it seems equally plausible that the reverse is true: namely, that they are not imitating but mocking the "steps of the English." In another account, the satirical force of the performance is not lost on the English observer Cynric Williams, who relates that at the dance he witnessed, "the merriment became rather boisterous as the punch operated, and the slaves sang satirical philippics against their master, communicating a little free advice now and then."[104] Thus, the Jonkonnu performance clearly partook of the saturnalia, registering a degree of protest by inverting the rigid power dynamic of master over slave. As Stuart Hall writes, "The doubling of registers, the complex symbolic reversals by which the terrors of servitude are simultaneously 'normalized,' rehearsed, and 'replayed' as violent parodic masquerade, signifies a complexity of meaning-making" embedded in Jonkonnu.[105]

But English observers also note with some regularity that the sense and meaning of Jonkonnu eludes them, particularly with respect to the central, masked and costumed Jonkonnu figure. Williams, in the description of the Christmas festivity noted above, describes the central Jonkonnu scene thusly: "A new ceremony was to be exhibited. First came eight or ten young girls marching before a man dressed up in a mask with a grey beard and long flowing hair, who carried the model of a house on his head. This house is called the Jonkanoo, and the bearer of it is generally chosen for his superior activity in dancing. He first saluted his master and mistress, and then capered about with astonishing agility and violence. The girls also danced without changing their position, moving their elbows and knees, and keeping tune with the calabashes filled with small stones. . . . The custom is African and religious, although the purpose is forgotten."[106] Williams's description indicates that a sense is embedded in the performance to which he does not have access: the purpose of the ceremony is not one that he can discern. To a large extent, such resistant or inaccessible meaning might be understood as cultural difference—as the performance of an African ritual that English observers did not understand. And indeed, critical debate over the issue of African cultural retention versus Europeanization within Jonkonnu performance has guided much of the discussion and analysis of Jonkonnu by critics and historians.[107] But it seems important to ask what Jonkonnu performance meant in the context of plantation slavery—not only what it remembered, but what it enacted for those who performed it and those who watched.

Such enacting might be understood as a form of parodic resistance, as we have seen, but also, and perhaps more significantly, as a presencing of something else—of both a remembered African culture and an Africanization, or an indigenization of the colonial ground. I borrow the term "indigenization" from Sylvia Wynter's analysis of Jonkonnu; specifically, Wynter uses the term to describe the establishment of an alternative, non-Europeanized and anticapitalist relation between and among people, culture, and the earth. Her analysis is worth citing at length here:

> With the discovery of the New World . . . the process which has been termed *"The reduction of Man to Labour and of Nature to Land under the impulsion of the market economy . . ."* really had its large-scale beginning. For the European, alien to the New World, Nature became land; and land, if it were to be exploited, needed not *men* essentially, but so many units of labour power. . . . If the European presence in the New World represented the techniques of civilization by which Nature is utilized . . . by which man enters into a relation of land-labour-capital, the African presence represented a paradox and contradiction. . . . [For the African] land was always the Earth, the centre of a core of beliefs and attitudes, [out of which] would come the central pattern which held together the social order. In this aspect . . . the African slave represented an opposing process to that of the European, who achieved great technical progress based on the primary accumulation of capital which came from the dehumanization of Man and Nature. . . . The African presence . . . *"rehumanized Nature,"* and helped to save [the slave's] own humanity against the constant onslaught

of the plantation system by the creation of a folklore and folk-culture . . . Folklore represents the attempt to prolong and recreate a system in which the community and the society and the social order is primary; folklore is not only the relation of Man to Nature but of Man to himself. Folklore was the cultural guerilla resistance against the Market economy.[108]

Wynter's analysis is complex: she suggests that the presencing of African culture in the form of Jonkonnu and, more broadly, folklore, is a means of resisting the core structuring relations of capitalism in the colony. These relations involve, to use the terms of my analysis, the reduction of New World Africans to the status of bare labor, and the reduction of social relations to relations of production. Establishing an alternative relation to the earth—one that is not instrumental and extractive but relational—and performing modes of social recognition between and among men and women that divorces them from a status as "units of labour" thus serve to uproot and vitiate the geography of capitalism and the attendant premises that sustain race slavery. The "rooting of the African in the New World" is thus defined by Wynter as an "indigenization" that reconfigures the relation of the New World African to the colonial ground—one that, importantly, does not construe that relation as one of labor to land but as one of man to earth. The deinstrumentalization of both man and earth brings into visibility a set of relations that are social and reproductive—relations that slavery seeks to eradicate.

In its invocation of a relation between people and earth, Wynter's account of indigenization is also one of commoning; indigenization, as Wynter describes it, is a process that works against the capitalist enclosure of the commons toward a moral economy of collective sustenance. As I have argued, Jamaica's colonial position in the geography of capitalist modernity is one that positions it as the scene of an impossible—an "unthinkable"—commons. Jonkonnu, understood in terms of Wynter's analysis of indigenization, might be seen as enacting the unthinkable—as performing a presencing of the African on colonial ground such that the privatizing and dehumanizing epistemology of capitalism is disrupted and reconfigured by a new aesthetic of commoning.

If we read Jonkonnu, then, as reaching well beyond a satirical reappropriation of English performance traditions toward an aesthetic of indigenization, the "plays" embedded in Jonkonnu take on a new cast. As Belisario's account of Jonkonnu notes, strolling companies of "self-styled Performers . . . dared to perpetrate 'murder most foul,' even on the plays of Shakespeare" during the Christmas revelries. His account, like others we have seen, is one that attributes to New World Africans a limited ability to correctly mimic English performance:

"Richard the Third" was a favorite Tragedy with [the Jonkonnu performers]; but *selections* only were made from it, without paying the slightest regard to the *order* in which the 'Bard of Avon' had deemed it proper to arrange his subject: Pizarro was also one of their Stock pieces; but whatever might have been the performance, a Combat and Death invariably ensued, when a ludicrous contrast was produced between the smiling mask, and the actions of the dying man. At this Tragical point, there was always a general call for music—and dancing immediately commenced—this proved too great a provocative usually to be resisted even by the slain, and he accordingly became resuscitated, and joined the merry throng.[109]

Belisario's account of *Richard III* is particularly intriguing because it is echoed rather precisely in other Jonkonnu descriptions, which remark on the fact that the slain Richard immediately comes to life following his death and joins in an energetic collective dance. In Monk Lewis's account of a Jonkonnu performance of a scene from Rowe's *Fair Penitent*, the action is identical: "As soon as Lothario was fairly dead, and Calista had made her exit in distraction, [the Jonkonnu performers] all began dancing reels like so many mad people."[110] Although Belisario describes the resuscitation of the slain Richard as a mimetic break with Shakespeare's script (and thus as a performance failure), the repetition of this scenario across Jonkonnu performances indicates that it may be less a failure to understand and enact English scripts than a considered effort to revise the shape and meaning of the plays.

And indeed, two aspects of such Jonkonnu revisions are notable: first and most obviously, we see the return to life of a slain character in an animated closing dance, but second, and significantly, Belisario and others mention that a revision in the order of the scenes of Shakespeare's play occurs as well. Although some reports indicate that the dialogue in such plays was performed to perfection, with "no need of a prompter," the accounts nonetheless all indicate that only some scenes of the plays are performed and/or that the scenes are performed nonsequentially.[111] Again, rather than view this as a sign of incompetence, we might posit that the order of the scenes was not germane to the meaning of the Jonkonnu performance. With respect to the two plays mentioned here—*Richard III* and *The Fair Penitent*—nonsequential performance is particularly significant given that both plays revolve around the relation between paternal/political authority and genealogical descent. A nonlinear performance of such plays would thus serve to undermine, confuse, and/or dilute the force of the narrative concerning lineage embedded within each play.

If we return to the staging of *The Fair Penitent* in the Kingston Theatre, we might recall that its meaning there was linked to the precarious production of a genealogically British/white identity effected through the control of the daughter's body. In the face of unauthorized sex across dynastic lines, Calista kills herself and Lothario (her illicit lover) is slain as well. *Richard III*, in turn, is a play that explores the intersection of dynastic descent and just rule, reconciling the two in the final sword fight where Richmond triumphs over the tyrannical Richard III, who has usurped the throne by murdering all those who stood in line before him. However, as Kathleen Wilson comments regarding the Jonkonnu performance of *The Fair Penitent*, the actors "turned the civilizing effect of English theatre on its head" and thereby "dispens[e] neatly with concerns for lineage or legitimacy."[112] When Calista and Lothario join the collective dance at the close of the performance, the effort to structure genealogical identity as a form of racialized enclosure is utterly confounded.

The dead body of Richard—not to mention those of Lothario and Calista— reanimated in a collective dance points not toward the authority of lineage to secure social order, but toward the kind of commoning we have seen in the closing dance of a play such as *The Beggar's Opera*. In contrast to the "dual elopement" of *The Duenna* or the sacrificial dead daughter in *The Fair Penitent*, both of which enact the reproduction of whiteness and the segmenting of the commons, the Jonkonnu dance partakes of a *Beggar's Opera* form of resuscitation from death. Just as Macheath is pardoned from the gallows to engage in uncoupled collective dance at the close of the ballad opera, so too is the Jonkonnu performance one that pushes against the contractual logic of marriage, genealogy, and descent in favor of the materially embodied presencing of dance itself. And the return from death, too, is suggestive of the resource of dance in relation to the technologies of social death to which slaves were subject: the dance performs and enacts an aesthetic return from death/enclosure to collective sociality. To borrow the words of Monk Lewis in describing one such a performance, what emerges into visibility is the "rapture of the black multitude" rather than the authority of white genealogy.[113]

The nature of the dissensus produced by such a performance is thus lodged not in mimesis (the narrative concerning genealogy) but in the ontic force of performance and, most particularly, sound. Indeed, much of what registers most forcefully as unseemly, unaccountable, or dissident for English observers of Jonkonnu performance (in addition to dress and dance movements) appears in sonic form. Belisario, for instance, describes the Jonkonnu figure who balances a pasteboard house on his head "whilst going through many strange contortions of body and limbs, *miscalled* dancing. . . . A *rather* discordant chorus of female voices, added to the stunning and harsh grating sounds produced by the instruments in the band, constitute the only *music*. . . . It would appear, that *sound*, without the slightest attention to harmony, delights these personages, for they are in no way annoyed, should the vibration of a drum even be destroyed by a fracture in the parchment."[114] Here, Bellisario is aware that the music performed with the Jonkonnu dance is music, and yet he is resistant to categorizing it as such. We might recall that Rancière's definition of the aesthetic turns on the "distribution of the sensible," or the degree to which elements of the sensorium constitute collective sense or its opposite. The sonic horizon of Jonkonnu produces just such a rift at the level of sound itself and, in performance, effects a redistribution of the sensible, or a reconfiguration of the sensus communis as the ontic force of sound asserts itself as music and as meaning.

For metropolitan whites, such evidence of social reproduction in the colony manifested itself as obscene—as that which could not be spoken but obtruded on knowledge nonetheless. Thus, when Lady Nugent hears the sound of Jonkonnu performance, she alternatively delights in the music and "thousand anticks" of the "blackies" and complains of the "noise" that intrudes on her in her bedroom: "Noise all night, and if possible, today worse than ever"; "Much noise of tom-toms etc. all the morning"; "Noise of rude music, etc. etc., all night . . . [I] am particularly unwell."[115] The sound of Jonkonnu performance registers, on the one hand, as playful music and on the other hand as noise—as an irritating, nonsignifying, and vaguely threatening disruption of Nugent's daily routine. What is unspeakable, but nonetheless heard, within this noise is the sound of revolution—the possibility of a black collectivity that may be mobilized against the regime and episteme of "British liberty." In 1804, when news of the success of the Haitian Revolution and the proclamation of the birth of Haiti as an independent republic ruled by blacks reached Jamaica, Nugent was again bothered by intrusive noise: "The negroes appeared to be inclined to riot," she reported, "and to make a noise in the streets, when the troops marched out, but they were soon dispersed by the militia. The black servants here seem to rejoice at the bustle, but, as they profess to hate the French, their pleasure is only that of change; for, like children, they are fond of fuss and noise, and have no reflection."[116] Despite Nugent's studious efforts not to see what is before her, it seems clear that, try as she might, she cannot quite rid herself of the (obscene) sound of the black commons—the noise/ music of black revolt against the system of slavery.

An original poem—a parody of a passage from Shakespeare's *Tempest*— appears in a Kingston journal in 1799 that conveys how deeply disturbing the non-English soundscape of Jamaica felt as it pressed itself on those who sought to be British:

PARODY OF SHAKESPEARE

Sayings, ca iras, drums, flags, twanging instruments,
A thousand different cries, sometimes riots,
Do stun my ears by day; unruly horses,
And scoffing negroes, break my rest at night;
Or, if I sleep, in dreaming I awake
With shrieks of fire; methinks I see the street
In horrid blaze around me, that I long
To quit this isle for Britain once again.[117]

The poem revises a passage spoken by Caliban in Shakespeare's play—a passage in which Caliban offers a poetic ode to the sweet sounds of the island that is his home: "Be not afeard: the isle is full of noises,/Sounds and sweet airs, that give delight, and hurt not./Sometimes a thousand twangling instruments/ Will hum about mine ears; and sometime voices,/That, if I then had wak'd after long sleep, / Will make me sleep again: and then, in dreaming,/ The clouds methought would open and show riches/Ready to drop upon me; that, when I wak'd/ I cried to dream again" (3.2.130–38). Caliban's aesthetic sensibility is thus the subject of parody in the Kingston poem; however, what the poem conveys is less parody than anxiety and fear. Moreover, it is the sensorium itself that causes profound dissonance and unease for the author of the poem. The disturbing sounds of the island speak to the author's repressed knowledge of a revolutionary scene—one involving slave revolt on the order of that occurring in nearby St. Domingue (fire, French republican sayings, and insubordinate slaves): the sound and knowledge of this black collective is lodged in the music/noise of a sensorium that the author can hear and yet refuses to know—a performative sensus communis that is obtruding on the author even as he/she disavows knowledge of it.

What emerges here as dissensus—as an insistent material sensation hovering at the intersection of meaning and nonmeaning—is powerfully theorized by Fred Moten as the core of a black radical aesthetic. Moten defines the disavowed speech of the slave/commodity as a sonic presence that disrupts "the Enlightenment linguistic project." The new materiality of such a sonic presence, in turn, becomes a "rematerializing inscription" with signifying force: "There occurs in such performances a revaluation or reconstruction of value, one disruptive of the oppositions of speech and writing, and spirit and matter."[118] Moten thus locates the scene of black aesthetic production as one of performance—a performance whose materiality cuts against Enlightenment regimes of knowledge with an ontic force that rematerializes itself "in the break"—in the break of the epistemic contradiction inscribed within the colonial relation. If the commons is eradicated in the name of segmentation of the labor market, and not reconstituted in the name of the people as a political ideal, it is only by way of the aesthetic, that is, by way of the sensorium, that it is created. Jonkonnu, then, is a form of radical aesthetic commoning generated at the heart of capitalist modernity.

JONKONNU'S LIVES: RAISING CANE AND EATING IT

The performance that announces itself in excess of the Enlightenment project of plantocratic knowledge is thus both obscene and compelling insofar as it speaks of the extraordinary liberatory force of the aesthetic—the power of culture itself—to emerge from the scene of social death and negation. To what extent, however, does this aesthetic commons assume cultural or political force in the face of its unthinkability within capitalist modernity? I want to point briefly to two divergent effects—one cultural and one political—that are related to the aesthetics of the impossible black commons in Jamaica. The first is the figure of the black dandy, one whose origins, I would posit, are in the performative excess called forth as a counterspirit to ideologies of bare labor and technologies of social death. And the second is a scene of revolutionary origins that serves as the prelude to the British emancipation of New World Africans enslaved in Jamaica—a brief anecdote that involves raising cane and eating it as well.

Among Belisario's set of well-known images of Jamaican blacks is the figure of "Lovey, alias Liverpool," a fifty-one-year-old native of Congo who is familiar on the streets of Kingston as a vendor of bouquets and a puppet-show performer. The song that Lovey sings while his puppets dance begins with the lines, "Tang ding, ding dang, tiggi dang, ding dang/John-crow pick me dandy eye out."[119] "John Crow" was the name given to the black turkey vulture native to Jamaica and serves, by extension, as a somewhat derogatory term for a man who is especially dark-skinned and perhaps ragged: John Crow, in short, is the opposite of the dandy. As a Jamaican proverb has it, "John Crow seh him a dandy man but same time him hab so-so feather." By the time of Belisario's 1837 drawing, if not far earlier, the black dandy had thus found its double in the figure of John Crow—a doubling evident, as well, in the U.S. blackface minstrel pairing of the dandy Zip Coon and the raggedy slave Jim Crow. The opposition between the underdressed Crow and the overdressed dandy repeats the epistemic break occasioned by the divergent materialities of slave clothing—the ragged black slave is the fantasy produced by technologies of bare labor; the dandy is a refutation of social death and bare labor made manifest in the signifying play of sheer and irrepressible ontic/mimetic possibility.

Within Belisario's collection of images, Lovey himself (dressed in osnaburg) plays John Crow in relation to "Koo Koo or Actor-Boy," the quintessential figure of the black dandy (see figure 5.5). Belisario's image of the Jonkonnu "Actor Boy" represents him clothed in elaborate dress of silk, satin, muslin, and lace, together with a plumed headdress and a white mask. According to Belisario, during the holiday, Jonkonnu actor boys strutted the main street of the town, competing with one another for the title of most spectacular: "The vanity of excelling in costliness of attire . . . may be annually seen, when a struggle for superiority in that respect amongst these 'Actor Boys,' takes place on the Parade. . . . Gentlemen who may be passing, are requested to decide which is the smartest dressed. . . . The Band consists of drums and fifes only, to which music the Actor stalks most majestically, oftentimes stopping to afford the by-standers a fair opportunity of gazing at him. In this position he is represented, with a whip and a fan, the former is useful in clearing his path of intruders, and the latter proves serviceable in cooling his face, to effect which the mask is of necessity raised."[120] Voguing before the assembled public, competing actor boys engage, as Belisario's description indicates, in a performance of performance itself: a contest over being seen in which what matters most is not an ability to imitate anything, but a presencing of exuberant, spectacular, and lavish materiality. And although Belisario ascribes utilitarian value to the whip and the fan in the actor boy's hand, it is difficult not to see the symbolic import of their appropriation by the subaltern slave, transformed from labor-associated instruments of violence into scepters of aesthetic sovereignty. Returning the gaze of the public from beneath the mask of whiteness, the actor boy parades a black aesthetic in the Kingston commons.

The stylized éclat of the black dandy appeared not only on the Kingston Parade, but on the London stage as well. In theatrical form, the material excess of the costumed West Indian slave famously takes the stage in the character of Mungo in Isaac Bickerstaff's drama *The Padlock*. As Monica Miller has argued, Mungo, who speaks in West Indian dialect, had an "electrifying effect" on London audiences when he debuted there in 1768.[121] Notable for his comedic back-talking and his outrageous striped suit, Mungo was the first blackface figure to speak in West Indian creole on stage. Miller makes a persuasive case that, in his exuberant red and white silk attire, Mungo is the progenitor of the black dandy—a figure who emerges more fully in later decades when, Miller suggests, he evolves into the eighteenth-century "macaroni" and thereby shifts

FIGURE 5.5. Koo, Koo or Actor-Boy, by Isaac Belisario (Kingston, 1838). Courtesy of Yale Center for British Art, Paul Mellon Collection.

"from being stylized to self-stylization."[122] According to Miller, Mungo's remarkably lavish clothing reflects a penchant among wealthy metropolitans to attire slaves as showy accessories dressed to display their owners' wealth. But it seems equally possible to trace an alternative provenance and/or reference point for Mungo's "glittering striped suit"—namely in the West Indian self-styling of the Jonkonnu performer. Belisario's Jonkonnu performer, for instance, sports an elaborate replica of a plantation house on his head, as well as showy striped red-and-white pants. Other images of black men dressed for show in Jamaica (see figures 5.4 and 5.5) also display characteristic red-and-white striped trousers. This textile genealogy is difficult to trace with precision: Belisario's images, for instance, significantly postdate Mungo's first appearance on stage in London. However, the iconography of the striped suit is enduring: as Miller notes, when Ira Aldridge appeared as the first black actor to play the role of Mungo on stage in London in the nineteenth century, he too wore a red-and-white striped suit. Like Mrs. Carmichael's less than fully subordinate dancing domestic slave, then, Mungo dresses for show rather than labor, invoking and participating in a tradition that in colonial Jamaica, as we have seen, is one of radical and resistant black self-styling.

In addition to the enduring figure of the black dandy, the aesthetic commoning of Jonkonnu takes a second, political form in Jamaica itself. The Jonkonnu festivities were widely recognized by planters as a time when social disorder might prove threatening to the white power structure. Tellingly, as we have seen, Jonkonnu is repeatedly associated with the threatening radicalism of the Haitian Revolution, and specifically with the political threat of black assemblage and the overthrow of white rule. Thus, as Richard Burton points out, it is no surprise that organized acts of collective resistance to slavery in Jamaica were repeatedly timed to coincide with Christmas: given "how readily the rituals of slave life—funerals, 'plays,' . . . possibly Jonkonnu—and acts of resistance could flow into each other, the first providing both inspiration and cover for the second; it is also abundantly clear that Christmas was the optimum time for launching an uprising."[123] During Christmas of 1831, an organized uprising that would come to be known as the Baptist War was staged—one that involved one in five slaves in the western part of Jamaica. A catalyst for the uprising occurred just before Christmas: an estate attorney, James Grignon, met a slave woman on the road with a piece of sugar cane in her hand. Grignon accused the woman of stealing the cane and whipped her; he then ordered the head driver to whip her again. The driver refused to whip his wife; following his refusal, all of the slaves on the estate revolted. On December 27, multiple estates went up in flames and other slaves refused to work in the fields. Although the rebellion was quickly suppressed, the uprising arguably hastened the passage of the 1833 Abolition Act, which ended slavery in Jamaica.[124] Not only in refusing to work—in refusing to serve as wheels in the plantation machine—but in the decision to eat cane as well, the slaves performed an act of commoning: they enacted a resistance to the logic of the market that rendered colonial Jamaica an impossible commons. These two examples—that of the black dandy and a politics of revolt related to eating sugar cane—are both linked to Jonkonnu. Jonkonnu, then, must be understood as a performative intellectual act: one that made the commons thinkable in both aesthetic and political terms.

CHAPTER 6

NEW YORK CITY

FROM OROONOKO AND JONKONNU TO JIM CROW

After Richard III was slain on stage at the Bowery Theatre on the night of November 25, 1832, he did not, evidently, rise from the dead to join in a grand, collective dance as did his predecessors in Jamaican Jonkonnu performances. Junius Brutus Booth, appearing in the role of Richard III that night, may, nonetheless, have found himself somewhat distracted by the presence of more than three hundred audience members who joined him on stage, participating in the battle, cheering in the swordfight, and, ultimately, staging a collective dance after Richard's death. At the center of this dance, however, was neither Booth as Richard III nor a Jonkonnu player in a white face mask, but a well-known actor—Thomas Dixon Rice—in black face paint. And when T. D. Rice sang and wheeled about in the role of Jim Crow, the audience that surrounded him on the stage that night was so enthralled that they "made him repeat it some twenty times."[1]

The scene is striking for a number of reasons. First, it is somewhat difficult to countenance at all because it strays so far from our current norms of theatrical spectatorship. According to the newspaper report of the performance, "gallery spectators amused themselves by throwing pennies and silver on the stage, which occasioned an immense scrambling among the boys, and they frequently ran between King Richard and Lady Anne to snatch a stray copper." In Richard's dream scene, "several curious amateurs went up to the table [on stage], took up the crown, poised the heavy sword, and examined all the regalia with great care, while Richard was in agony from the terrible dream; and when the scene changed, discovering the ghosts of King Henry, Lady Anne, and children, it was difficult to select them from the crowd, who thrust their faces and persons among the royal shadows." Finally, in the battle scene, "the audience mingled with the soldiers and raced across the stage, to the shouts of the people, the roll of the drums, and bellowing of the trumpets; and when the fight between Richard and Richmond came on, they made a ring around the combatants to see fair play, and kept them at it for nearly a quarter of an hour."[2]

The newspaper report suggests that this was "a ludicrous scene"—that is, far from the usual performance of Booth in *Richard III*. Published by William T. Porter in his *Traveller and Spirit of the Times*, this particular report evidently aims to poke fun at the patrons of the Bowery Theatre, a New York City venue that established itself in the 1830s as the home of boisterous working-class audiences—dominated by the so-called Bowery b'hoys, who attended the theatre in an extraordinarily active and participatory fashion.[3] At the Bowery, a historical sense of audience rights combined with an egalitarian politics to produce a particularly strong sense of what Richard Butsch has defined as "audience sovereignty."[4] Or, as the British actress Fanny Kemble noted in less favorable terms, "the mixture of the republican feeling of equality peculiar to this country and the usual want of refinement common to the lower classes of most countries, forms a singularly felicitous union of impudence and vulgarity to be met with no where but in America."[5]

The populist sensibility of theatre in the early nineteenth-century United States (and particularly at the Bowery) was conjoined, in this instance, with a play that might be seen to enact the triumph of popular sovereignty. The version of *Richard III* most often staged in the United States during this period was Colley Cibber's redaction—one that sometimes went by the title *The Fall of Tyranny*. As the revised title suggests, Cibber's version offered a more direct critique of British monarchical sovereignty than did Shakespeare's play. Whereas Shakespeare's play hinges on the question as to which dynastic line will rightfully succeed to the throne of England (York or Lancaster), Cibber's version stages a movement from tyranny (in the fall of Richard) to something far closer to popular sovereignty (in the ascension to the throne by Richmond). When Richmond slays Richard III at the close of the play in Cibber's version, his claim to authority is staged as one based on the consent of those he will govern: "Farewell Richard," he states, "and from thy dreadful end/May future kings from tyranny be warned." Richmond, in his moment of victory, then turns to the soldiers on the stage around him and states, "Next to just heav'n, my noble countrymen, I owe my thanks to you, whose love I'm proud of, And ruling well, shall speak my gratitude."[6] One might imagine that these lines, which do not appear in Shakespeare's play, would have lent force to an enactment of popular sovereignty when directed to a stage populated by audience members as well as actors.

Cibber's *Richard III* at the Bowery thus serves to enact a scene of Jacksonian democracy in both ontic and mimetic terms. In participating in the slaying of a tyrannical king, the audience stages a performative commons—one in which the working people of New York assume the force of a triumphant demos as they vanquish the figure of monarchical authority.[7] In this sense, the performance enacts a familiar story—one in which Americans declare independence from antiquated British models in an assertion of democratic vitality. And indeed, the history of nineteenth-century theatre in the United States has been rehearsed in precisely these terms: only by midcentury, according to this history, did Americans begin to assert an interest in developing a national culture of their own as distinct from British cultural parentage. The Astor Place Riot that occurred in New York City in 1849 has been taken as an inaugural scene in this narrative: the riot at the Astor Place Opera House left twenty-six men and women dead in the streets following a violent clash over the relative merits of two actors (one British, one American) who were performing the lead role in Shakespeare's *Macbeth* at competing theatres. The British actor William Charles Macready reportedly had an "effete" and "cerebral" acting style that was the object of both scorn and rage among working class white "Nativists," who were ardent supporters of the American actor, Edwin Forrest. Known for his masculine and muscular acting style, Forrest's most famous role was that of the Wampanoag Chief Metamora—a role that, as one nineteenth-century critic wrote, enabled Forrest to "stand forth as a gorgeous figure of the red man."[8] On the day of the riot, bills posted around the city called for protesters to attack Macready's performance at the Astor Place Opera House with the rallying cry, "WORKING MEN, SHALL AMERICANS OR ENGLISH RULE IN THIS CITY?"[9] In the wake of this staged opposition of British and American performance, critics have viewed the riot as emblematic of a desire for a nationalized American culture—one that seemingly emerged with explosive force in the nineteenth-century United States in populist "theatre of the mob" and riots associated with stage performance.[10]

But if the replacement of the tyrannical British king by the sovereign audience at the Bowery Theatre makes sense in these terms—as an enactment of Americanization and democratization—we might still wonder why Jim Crow is so central to this scene. The newspaper account of the events on stage segues seamlessly from the battle scene to T. D. Rice's dance, with no sense that there is a pause between the two performances. The scenarios of regicide and blackface minstrel performance appear to be almost of a piece—an impression that is furthered by evidence that the final two acts of *Richard III* were, with some regularity, performed on New York stages without the rest of the play but together with a performance of Jim Crow.[11] This staging, then, shows a surprising similarity to Jamaican Jonkonnu performances of *Richard III* (selective and nonlinear performance of scenes, followed by a concluding collective dance). However, the Jonkonnu performer at the center of Jamaican stagings of the play is a far cry from the figure of Jim Crow: or better put, we might say that the two figures resemble one another by way of antithesis. If the Actor Boy is a stylized dandy, performing an excess of material presence in a display of aesthetic intensity, Jim Crow is a figure whose excess has been subject to degradation. Significantly, Jim Crow dresses in rags, but the rags are not osnaburg—rather, images of T. D. Rice on stage show him wearing "showy finery" in a state of disrepair and filth (see figure 6.1.).

Jim Crow, then, is a figure whose performance both replicates and erases that of the Jonkonnu dancer: specifically, he assists in defining U.S. nationalism by way of the erasure of a prior, Atlantic history. While U.S. independence is typically imagined in terms of a break with England, the new geopolitical formation of the United States is one that, in the nineteenth century, was also decisively influenced by the Haitian Revolution and the closing of the British slave trade—events that generated profound changes in U.S. labor structures and culture and that inaugurated a new geographical imaginary for the nation. In the wake of the Haitian Revolution, the United States turned away from an Atlantic/colonial history and economy toward a westward-facing account of the nation and the "manifest destiny" of U.S. expansionism.[12] More than just a break with England, then, U.S. nationalism entailed a break with a previous colonial formation in which North American and Caribbean colonies had comprised portions of an integrated imperial geography with political, economic, and cultural ligatures binding the whole. If the dead body of Richard III indicates a break with England, the figure of Jim Crow—in taking the place of the spectacular figure of the extravagantly well-dressed New World African—indicates a break between the United States and an Atlantic imaginary that included Africa and the Caribbean as well as England.

Four nights after Booth performed the role of Richard III at the Bowery Theatre in November 1832, he assumed the role of another royal figure on the same stage: that of the African prince, Oroonoko. Although there is no record as to whether the audience joined Oroonoko on stage as he fomented slave revolt against the English in Surinam, we do know that the play was not warmly received. A notice in the *New York Mirror* pans the play, and interestingly, it is not Booth's performance that provokes criticism, but the script itself. "Southerne's tragedy of Oroonoko has been got up after considerable preparation," reports the review. "Mr. Booth, in the principal character, cer-

FIGURE 6.1. Jim Crow, from the cover of sheet music produced in London (circa 1835). Courtesy of the Library of Congress.

tainly makes all that can be made out of it; but besides the piece being faulty throughout, the plot is most unreasonable. The loves of Oronooko, a sooty negro, and an accomplished white, Imoinda, are positively unnatural. Their meeting after a long separation in a foreign land, in slavery, is a stretch of the imagination something beyond the admission even of a 'poet's license,' and the catastrophe is quite *too* horrible in approach as near the sublime as it does the ridiculous."[13] Theatre historian Joseph Norton Ireland reports that this was the first performance of Southerne's *Oroonoko* in New York City; a second performance followed on December 15, 1832, but the play disappeared thereafter from the Bowery stage.[14] In contrast to the fortunes of Oroonoko on stage, an alternative "sooty" figure who debuted in the same month did quite well, according to Ireland: "Mr. T. D. Rice made his Ethiopian *début* on the 12th [of November, 1832], in his song of 'Jim Crow,' which attained a popularity unequaled by anything of the kind before or since, and 'wheeled about' its lucky chaunter from poverty to fame and fortune." T. D. Rice, concludes Ireland, "probably drew more money to the Bowery treasury than any other American performer in the same period of time."[15]

The distaste exhibited here for the figure of Oroonoko, in sharp contrast to the taste of the town that animated Jim Crow's stunning popularity at the Bowery, points, again, to the eclipse of an Atlantic sensus communis in favor of a U.S. nationalist one. Oroonoko is a black man who has a royal lineage, hails from Africa, and is enslaved in the Caribbean by the English. Jim Crow is a black man who hails from "Kaintuck"—a raggedy slave who is, in the words of one fictive autobiography, "de blackest nigger [Massa] ebber see."[16] Locating the 1776 image of Oroonoko on stage in England (see figure 6.2) next to that of Jim Crow in 1835 (see figure 6.1), we might even imagine that Jim Crow has worn the clothes of Southerne's Oroonoko for seventy years until they have become shredded rags. Placing Jim Crow in a performance lineage with Oroonoko as well the Jonkonnu Actor Boy underscores the way in which Jim Crow's performance of U.S. national blackness circumscribes and overwrites an earlier Atlantic diasporic history in which blackness had a more extensive geography and lineage—and far more multivalent cultural meanings—than it would come to have in the racialized landscape of the mid-nineteenth-century United States. The performance of Jim Crow accrues its meaning not just in antic dance and display, but in the act of erasure it simultaneously performs.

The shift, in a location such as New York City, from a public that performed itself as colonial and creole to one that assumed a national shape thus required the erasure of a prior formation—an Atlantic imperial one. The array of colonial relations (traced in previous chapters) that inhabited the American

FIGURE 6.2. Actor John Horatio Savigny as Oroonoko in Thomas Southerne's *Oroonoko* (1776). Courtesy of Rare Book and Manuscript Library, University of Illinois at Urbana-Champaign.

colonies—white upstart colonial creoles, royal slaves, and Indian kings—were required to shed their colonial relationality in order to perform in a new drama of U.S. nationhood. However, an Atlantic history remains embedded within the performative commons of U.S. nationalism and, indeed, is required to construct that nationalism. Specifically, the performance of what would become white U.S. nationalism, as I argue below, involved a theatrics of indigenization that placed a variety of suppressed colonial relations on display: not only the minstrelized slave, but the Indian king became key figures on the New York City stage in the early nineteenth century. In order for the white creole to become an (indigenous) white national, histories of settler colonialism and Atlantic race slavery are both evoked and erased by means of renewed and revised performances of the Indian king (D'Avenant's tortured Inca prince, as we will see, becomes Edwin Forrest's Metamora) and the royal African slave (Southerne's Oroonoko becomes T. D. Rice's Jim Crow).

In turning to the theatrics of indigenization, I also return to the history of commoning and the relation of the performative commons to a material commons—to the communal occupation and use of land in America. In the North American colonies, and later the United States, little or no property was held in common among European settlers or the creole whites who established themselves as a Lockean, property-owning citizenry from the mid-seventeenth century forward. No legally sanctioned physical commons took enduring form in colonial America because the land grab by European imperialists in America coincided with the privatization of property under the advent of capitalism.[17] Historians have thus suggested that, because there were no traditional rights to be violated by the new regime of property ownership, the "moral economy" described by E. P. Thompson—the performed community demand for collective sustenance in acts such as price riots—did not take shape among creole whites in the United States, or, at least did not take shape in the same ways. Forms of collective action in the name of economic justice occurred with regularity during the early national period, but these demands were not framed in relation to historical rights to the use of common property for communal sustenance; rather, as Ruth Bogin argues, petitions and crowd actions by "America's free working people . . . began to transform the moral content of their economic outlook from acceptance of a hierarchical structure [in which the wealthy bear an obligation to the poor] to invocation of political rights."[18] Such a formulation, however, points to precisely the translation of material commons (the use of land for collective sustenance) into a virtual commons (the right to representation as a member of a virtually constituted collective) that is at the heart of a Lockean notion of contract theory—one that equates exclusive rights of property ownership with forms of citizenship.[19] It is this regime of property and politics that forms the basis of settler colonialism and that subtends a delimited popular sovereignty in the United States—one that, in turn, operates to enclose and privatize the commons and to exclude the multitude from political and material forms of sustenance.

Stepping back from a history of white nationalism in the United States, then, we might note that although no traditional rights linked white creoles or early nationals to American land, there were nonetheless people who had lived on the land in America from time immemorial—namely, Native Americans. In a larger Atlantic frame, colonialism itself is visible as a form of wholesale enclosure involving the disappropriation of land held in common by native peoples. Thus, as historian Daniel Vickers points out, "If the strict English definition of private property right was a cultural weapon in the conquest of [North America], then the spirited Indian defense of their lands across the centuries can well be termed the only pure expression of moral economy in American history."[20] Vickers's equation of Native American protest with the performance of moral economy and the right to the commons is one that, I suggest in this chapter, was embedded in the cultural unconscious of the eighteenth- and nineteenth-century United States and emerged spectacularly on stages throughout the country in the form of performances of Indian-ness, often, ironically, in the service of constructing a white indigeneity. In this chapter, I argue that theatrical performances of melancholic Native American sovereignty play a particular role in constructing the performative commons in the United States, in part because of the alternative relationship of commoning (rather than Lockean ownership) that Native Americans held to the land. The invocation of this collective relation to the land often took the form of whites "playing Indian," and served to construct a right of (white) commoning and indigeneity, even as Native peoples were written out of political representation and evicted from lands they had inhabited from time immemorial.

In the chapter that follows, I trace the array of colonial relations (including Richard III, Jim Crow, and Metamora) that are invoked to perform white "Nativism" during the period of Jacksonian democracy. I do so by turning to a sequence of theatre riots in New York City—a sequence that culminates in rather than originates with the Astor Place Riot. In tracing these riots, I propose a new account of theatre history in the United States—one that is colonial and Atlantic in scope rather than solely national and one that focuses on scenes of representation, embodiment, and erasure in theatrical spaces as well as the layered and contrapuntal performances of colonial relations therein. The history of riotous performance I trace in this chapter indicates the extent to which, for an American public, on-going enactments of imperialism and colonialism held center stage—indeed, formed the basis of nationalism—in the period of Jacksonian democracy and beyond.[21]

THE AFRICAN THEATRE RIOTS: 1822

A less-noted theatre riot occurred in the hotel adjacent to the famous Park Theatre in New York some two and half decades prior to the Astor Place Riot. During a performance of *Richard III*, the actors in the newly founded African Theatre Company were arrested midperformance and "escorted, in their tinseled robes, to the watch house" for the apparent crime of performing Shakespeare. According to a newspaper report, the actors "pleaded so hard in blank verse, and promised never to act Shakespeare again, that the Police Magistrates released them at a very late hour."[22] Freed from jail, the African American actors soon thereafter performed an original play by William Alexander Brown, *The Drama of King Shotaway*, on the incendiary topic of the 1795 Carib insurrection on the island of St. Vincent in the West Indies.[23] According to Marvin McAllister, Brown's play is the first drama written by an African American performed in the United States.[24] And indeed, the African Theatre Company, which performed from 1821 to 1824 in New York City, is described by critics as the first professional theatre founded by African American actors in the United States. The riot and closure of the theatre was apparently occasioned by the intervention of the manager of the well-established Park Theatre, who sought to eradicate competition by calling for the arrest of the actors in the African Theatre. Theatre audiences at the Park were racially mixed at the time, although black spectators were typically segregated to seats far from the stage; mixed-race audiences would be the financial mainstay of the African Theatre Company during its subsequent years of operation.

Despite the arrest of his actors, William Brown vowed not to bow to intimidation and subsequently built a new theatre in Greenwich Village to house his successful company. Yet within weeks of the opening of the new theatre, a second, far more destructive riot occurred. In August 1822, a group of fifteen to twenty white men bought tickets to the evening performance of the African Company. Once within the theatre, they strategically cut down the circle of lamps illuminating the stage and audience, and in the chaos and darkness that ensued, stripped the actors of their costumes, destroyed benches, sets, and scenery, and severely beat William Brown as well as other actors. Police were again called, and in this instance, they arrested the white rioters rather than the black actors. The so-called Bellmont riot was orchestrated in part by

George Bellmont, together with other performers from a nearby circus.[25] The exact causes and aims of the riot are by no means clear: certainly the rioters were bent on physically destroying the theatre and Brown's assets including the scenery, benches, lighting, and costumes, and the actors themselves. Yet despite the clarity of these destructive aims, historians have been divided over whether to attribute the Bellmont rioters' actions to theatrical competition alone or to racism directed against the African Company in particular and anti-abolitionist sentiment in general.[26]

The riots at the African Theatre are significant for two reasons: first, they cast a different light on the politics of the violence at Astor Place, indicating that the white nationalism on display at the Astor Place Riot emerged out of a contentious and improvisational mix of Atlantic representational practices and not solely out of the emancipation of American actors from English scripts. Indeed, the white working class versus white upper class dichotomy that critics have identified as central to the Astor Place Riot is one that relies on the dynamics of racialization—specifically, on the real and implied presence of nonwhite bodies for the creation of (white) Anglo-American genealogies. Second, and perhaps more importantly, the African Theatre riots indicate the wider scope and significance of theatre riots in general. While it is plausible that white theatre managers and actors sought to put the African Theatre out of business for financial reasons, the stakes for the community at large would seem to be greater than mere financial competition. More than a business with primarily economic ramifications, theatre, as we have seen, is an enterprise that involves forms of cultural prestige and representational authority with particular import for the politics of popular sovereignty. Insofar as the African Theatre convened a mixed-race public and sought audience participation in New World African embodiments of creole nationalism, it visibly engaged questions concerning the nature of the U.S. commons and the cultural and racial foundations of nationalism itself.

One of the earliest public notices concerning the entertainment offerings of William Alexander Brown, founder of the African Company, appeared in the *National Advocate* in August of 1821. Before opening a theatre, Brown had presided over one of the first public gardens for African Americans— an outdoor commercial venue called the African Grove, at which ice cream and drinks were sold and music was performed. Reporting on the novelty of Brown's public garden, the writer for the *National Advocate* offers an account of the social gathering at the African Grove that indicates an interest in and concern for the way in which public entertainment venues *create* and authorize audience members as a kind of public:

A garden has been opened somewhere back of the hospital called *African Grove* ... and it was not an uninteresting sight to observe the entree of a happy pair. The gentleman, with his wool nicely combed, and his face shining through a coat of sweet oil ... cravat tight to suffocation, having the double faculty of widening the mouth and giving a remarkable protuberance to the eyes; blue coat fashionably cut; red ribbon and a bunch of pinchback seals; wide pantaloons; shining boots, gloves, and a tippy rattan. ... Thus accoutered and caparisoned, these black fashionables saunter up and down the garden, in all the pride of liberty and unconsciousness of want. In their address; salutations; familiar phrases; and compliments; their imitative faculties are best exhibited. After a vile concerto by the garden band, a company of four in a box commenced conversation, having disposed of a glass of ice cream each.

"You like music, Miss? Can't say I like it much. ... Did you ever hear Phillips sing, 'Is dare a heart dat neber lov'd,'? I sing xactly like him; Harry tell us some news. De Greeks are gone war wid de Turks. Oh! dat's bery clever; and our gentlemen said at dinner yesterday, dat de Greeks had taken Constantinople, and all de wives of de Dey of Algiers. O shocking! Vell, Miss, ven is de happy day; ven vill you enter de matrimony state? ... Harry, who did you vote for at de election? De fedrilists to be sure; I never wotes for de mob. Our gentlemen brought home tickets, and after dinner, ve all vent and woted. Miss how you like to go to de Springs? I shouldn't like it; too many negers from de suthard, and such crowd of folks, that decent people can get no refreshments."

Thus they run the rounds of fashion; ape their masters and mistresses in every thing; talk of projected matches; reherse the news of the kitchen, and the follies of the day; and bating the "tincture of their skins," are as well qualified to move in the *haut ton*, as many of the white dandies and butterflies, who flutter in the sun shine. They fear no Missouri plot; care for no political rights; happy in being permitted to dress fashionable, walk the streets, visit African Grove, and talk scandal.[27]

The tone of the piece is on its face ambivalent: the article both makes a case for the status of free blacks as social citizens of the town and undermines this claim by describing the civility of blacks as essentially imitative, parodic, and ultimately ineffectual. The markers of civility mentioned in the article are in themselves intriguing: the black patrons perform their status as members of the public by reference to aesthetics, dress, manners, recreation, politics, news, and marriage. The pleasure garden becomes the site for displaying this civility and thus for exercising a form of citizenship and inclusion in the New York polity: at the African Grove, black patrons exercise "all the pride of liberty and unconsciousness of want." That is, they exhibit their status as both free and propertied individuals. And while the author concludes dismissively that this veneer of cultivation is imitative and thus not political (blacks "care for no political rights"), the article also touches on the question of political enfranchisement quite directly in its mention of blacks who vote for the Federalist Party. In the conversation reported here, voting is of a piece with other forms of social enfranchisement, including vacationing at Saratoga Springs, exchanging news of world events, and articulating musical preferences. According to the reporter of this article, the African Grove was a space in which black patrons sought to *perform* their social and civic fitness, although the author is at pains to indicate the shortcomings of this performance and thus to demonstrate the incapacity of blacks to achieve cultural and political enfranchisement.

The racist ridicule of the black patrons of the African Grove at the heart of the article suggests an awareness of the performative nature of public citizenship and seeks to conjure in the reader an anxiety about the possibility of an "unauthorized" or merely "imitative" performance of this citizenship. Shortly after the African Grove opened, William Alexander Brown opened the Minor Theatre at the same location in New York City for a performance of *Richard III*, therewith opening the doors to the first theatre company of black actors performing in the United States.[28] As a number of historians have argued, the opening of Brown's theatre in 1821 was intimately related to issues concerning the public and political status of free blacks in New York City.[29] In 1817, the New York legislature had passed a law to manumit all slaves at the end of ten years, in 1827. By the early 1820s, only roughly five hundred enslaved blacks lived in New York City, together with a population of more than ten thousand free blacks. The early 1820s were thus a liminal moment for the black population of New York City—a moment at which the status of blacks was in transition between a history of enslavement and a promise of liberation. With respect to the position of the free black in the political and cultural life of the city, the future was unclear and thus a matter of energetic improvisation and contestation. Taking to the stage to perform Shakespeare was a means of both enacting a public status and forming a public in which New World Africans were legitimate participants. In January 1822, Brown staged the performance of a play he had written himself, causing a writer for the *Commercial Advertiser* to comment, "Thus it seems that these descendants of Africa, are determined to carry into full practice the doctrine of *liberty and equality*, physically by acting plays, and mentally by writing them."[30] For white observers and attendees at the African Theatre, the theatre was thus decisively linked to the demonstrative embodiment of freedom and citizenship; the presence of blacks on stage performing before mixed-race audiences and sitting in theatres as members of mixed-raced audiences legitimated their visibility within and belonging to a nationalized U.S. performative commons.

Yet as indicated by the excerpt from the *National Advocate* article printed above, the white press was often derisive of the efforts of the African Theatre. Indeed, according to historian Samuel Hay, the derision was directly tied to concerns of white newspapermen about the potential voting power of free blacks. In 1821, when the African Theatre opened its doors, the question of the enfranchisement of poor whites and free blacks was open for debate at the New York state constitutional convention being held in Albany. A proposal had been circulated at the convention to restrict the franchise according to race rather than according to property requirements: the roughly two hundred blacks who met the existing property requirement and who had previously been eligible to vote would have thus been disenfranchised by the new proposal. At the same time, factions were lobbying to eliminate the property requirements for white men altogether. If property requirements were eliminated for both whites and blacks, thousands of black men would be able to vote in New York state.[31] The *National Advocate*, edited by Mordecai Noah, covered both the franchise debates at the constitutional convention and the opening of the African Theatre in language that indicated a clear sense of connection between the creation of the two publics—namely, the public convened at the African theatre and the public voice constituted by the voting citizenry of the state.

An article in the *National Advocate* from September 1821 makes the anxiety about black enfranchisement and its links to the African Theatre quite clear. Under the title "African Amusements," the notice in question prints an announcement of a performance of *Richard III* by Brown's theatre, but the announcement is preceded by the following commentary: "gentlemen of *colour* . . . now assemble in groups; and since they have crept in favour with the convention, they are determined to have balls and quadrille parties, establish a forum, solicit a seat in the assembly or in the common council, which, if refused, let them look to the elections. They can out vote the whites, as they say. One black gentleman most respectfully insinuated, that he thought 'as how he mout be put on the grand jury!'"[32] In both this article and the one cited above, a significant use of dialect is deployed to de-authorize blacks as eligible for full political and cultural citizenship: the fractured speech of black dialect is produced in order to serve as evidence of an incapacity to engage in the work of citizenship, including voting for considered reasons and serving as a member of a jury. Noah's articles are among the earliest to engage in a print version of minstrelization in the United States—that is, the caricature of black speech, song, and performance that would subsequently take American stages by storm in the form of blackface minstrelsy performed by white actors. Indeed, Hay credits Mordecai Noah with the title of "father of Negro minstrelsy" insofar as his derisive reportage of black dialect in descriptions of the patrons of the African Grove and the actors of the African Theatre assumed a paradigmatic status in public representations of African Americans for years to come.[33] Noah's characterization of these performances as merely imitative—and the development of the trope of poor imitation of whiteness as central to blackface minstrelsy—serves to undermine the claim of black citizenship in the U.S. nation.[34]

The first play performed by the African Company and one of the most popular was evidently *Richard III*, a play that, as we have seen, had transcultural currency in Jamaica as well as in the United States, yet press reports from the start derided the black actors' abilities by way of minstrelized dialect: according to Noah, the lead actor who performed the role of Richard III pronounced, upon entering the stage, "Now is de vinter of our discontent made glorus summer by de son of New-York."[35] As we have seen, it was commonplace to modify a script, including one by Shakespeare, to reflect the local occasion of its performance. The African Theatre's modification of the line, despite its cleverness (in elaborating on the pun of son/sun already in place in the play, the revised line extends to include the "new" son of York—referring to both the actor as the son of the city of New York, and the figure of Edward IV within the play as the son of the House of York), is nonetheless cited by Noah, and subsequently by many others, as evidence of an inability to understand and perform Shakespeare. Noah thus assists in inaugurating a tradition in which the evident threat of New World Africans performing Shakespeare is transposed into scenes of comedic ineptitude.

COMPETING CREOLES: BLACK AND WHITE
INDIAN KINGS IN AMERICA

The trope of poor imitation advanced with such energy in Noah's account of the African Theatre is one that he explicitly links to an incapacity for citizenship. It is worth remarking, then, that the horizon of legibility for such an argument is that of U.S. state belonging. On the one hand, Noah's reporting on the African Theatre participates in an increasingly binary account of black and white racial identity in this period—a binarization that is often articulated in terms of concerns about miscegenation. On the other hand, this binarization itself effects a certain erasure—the erasure of a history (and an on-going present) of settler colonialism on which the U.S. state is founded. Both blacks and whites, in the United States, were creoles; however, the shift to white nationalism required the erasure of the creole status of whites—a shift effected through newly articulated claims to white American "Nativism" in the early nineteenth century as well as by the eradication of an Atlantic framing of the culture and politics of collectivity.[36] What Mark Rifkin describes as "settler common sense" (sensus communis) relies upon a naturalization of the frame of nationhood such that its horizons are determinative at the level of everyday feeling and affect: "The imposition and reproduction of [U.S. state] legal geography is less a background feature of private feeling and public sentiments than a central enframing condition for both (and the relations among them) at all scales. Such sensations of individual selfhood and collective belonging are predicated on shifting forms of incorporation, superintendence, regulation, and erasure of Native polities and their homeland."[37] In attending to, and constructing, a binary divide between competent white citizens and incompetent black would-be citizens, Noah's language implicitly imposes a national frame on personhood in the New York polity. Thus, one effect of eradicating the extranational frame of the Atlantic world (and its histories of colonialism, unsettlement, transportation, and diaspora) from the horizon of popular sovereignty in the United States is that of embedding a politics of settler colonialism within the structure of national feeling—even a national feeling fractured along a black/white binary. Indeed, as Aileen Moreton-Robinson points out, "the question of how anyone came to be white or black in the United States is inextricably tied to the dispossession of the original owners and the assumption of white possession."[38]

It is in this context that we might make sense of the astounding number of performances in the nineteenth-century United States of the figure of the Indian King on stage: more than seventy-five plays on the topic of Native Americans were written in the United States in this period, indicating that the business of what Philip Joseph Deloria describes as "playing Indian" was important theatrical work in the era of Jacksonian "democratization."[39] And significantly, the performance of indigeneity occurred in New York not only on the stages of the Park Theatre and the Bowery Theatre, but at the African Theatre as well. The African Theatre Company's interest in performing indigeneity is evident in their dramatization of Richard Sheridan's well-known historical tragedy *Pizarro*. Brown's company performed the play or scenes from it on at least four separate occasions between 1821 and 1824, in productions starring both James Hewlett and Ira Aldridge as the Inca warrior, Rolla, who heroically resists the invasion of Peru led by the Spanish conquistador Pizarro. Sheridan's play was an adaptation of a translation of August Von Kotzebue's play *Die Spanier in Peru, oder Rolla's Tod* (1796), which was also translated for performance in the United States by William Dunlap. Sheridan's play debuted in London in May 1799 and shortly became the most popular play of the decade in England. Within months, it appeared on the U.S. stage and in multiple print editions; it was subsequently performed every season save one in New York City from 1800 to 1863.[40] Brown was thus far from singular in his interest in this play; indeed, *Pizarro* was a stock play for many companies by 1822 and appeared in Jonkonnu performances in Jamaica as well. In the drama, Rolla is aided in his defense of his native land by Alonzo, a Spaniard who has deserted Pizarro's ranks and joined the Inca at the instigation of the humanitarian Spanish friar Bartholomé de las Casas—a historical figure who appears in Sheridan's play. Las Casas was the author of a famous text concerning the Spanish massacre of the Indians in America, *Brevísima relación de la destrucción de las Indias* (1552–1553), translated, as we saw in chapter 2, into English by John Phillips as *Tears of the Indians* (1656). Phillips's text helped to establish the "Black Legend" in England, the tale of Spanish atrocity that supported the claim that English colonial efforts were—in stark contrast to those of the Spanish—characterized by humanity and Christian benevolence rather than by rapacity, murderousness, and greed.[41] Like William D'Avenant's *Cruelty of the Spaniards in Peru*, the play offers both a version of humane conquest in the figure of Alonzo (seemingly that of an English settler colonialism), as counterposed to the inhumane conquest of the Spanish "Black Legend" represented in the figure of Pizarro.

As a number of literary critics have suggested, the popularity of Sheridan's *Pizarro* in England and the United States was in part contingent on the adaptability of its political message to a variety of contexts. Rolla's famous speech, delivered to the Inca soldiers prior to their battle against the Spanish invasion, is a paean to patriotism framed in broadly humanitarian and republican terms. Rolla tells the soldiers,

> You have judged as I have, the foulness of the crafty plea by which these bold invaders would delude you—Your generous spirit has compared as mine has, the motives, which, in a war like this, can animate their minds, and *ours*.—*they*, by a strange frenzy driven, fight for power, for plunder and extended rule—*we*, for our country, our altars, and our homes. . . . They offer us their protection—Yes, such protection as vultures give to lambs—

covering and devouring them! . . . The Throne *we* honour is the *people's choice*—the laws we reverence are our brave Fathers' legacy—the faith we follow teaches us to live in bonds of charity with all mankind, and die with hope of bliss beyond the grave. Tell your invaders this, and tell them too, we seek no change; and, least of all, such change as they would bring us.[42]

In his emphasis on "the people's choice," Rolla makes the case that Inca government is a form of indigenous popular sovereignty—one that the cruel Spaniard (Pizarro) seeks to destroy and that the indigenized Spaniard (Alonzo) seeks to support. Moreover, in its opposition of "WE" and "THEY," counterposing the value of homeland, family, and the people to those of the invaders' motives of plunder, the speech is remarkably adaptable to a variety of political moments.[43] In the U.S. context, the play aroused patriotic sentiment; as one writer opined in the *Massachusetts Mercury* in 1799, "the vivifying speech of ROLLA, previous to encountering the enemies who had invaded his country, might be pronounced by every American with equal propriety, on the menaces which have been uttered by our foes."[44] Further, as this writer's identification with Rolla indicates, Rolla's speech facilitates the mapping of white creole popular sovereignty onto American indigeneity—neatly reversing, we might note, the usurpation and foreclosure of Native sovereignty being performed in U.S. courts at the time.

Like D'Avenant's *Cruelty*, then, *Pizarro* aids in constructing an account of popular national sovereignty. But in distinction from *Cruelty*, the settler colonial aims of the play are more pronounced: specifically, popular sovereignty takes the overt form of indigenization in *Pizarro*. Whereas the torture the Spaniards inflicted on the Inca in D'Avenant's opera helped to consolidate a consenting national polity in the theatres of England in relation to English claims to New World sovereignty, the sovereign feelings constructed in *Pizarro* occur on a more intimate level. In Sheridan's play, the indigenization of Alonzo is enacted by way of family feeling. Rolla is the tragic hero of the play, but the force of Rolla's heroism is ultimately lodged, in a quasi-genealogical fashion, in the European figure of Alonzo and his creole offspring. Although Alonzo is a Spaniard, he has repudiated the Spanish cause in favor of that of the Inca because of his commitment to humanitarian ends and disgust with Pizarro's dishonorable aims and tactics; importantly, moreover, Alonzo is married to the fair-skinned Inca Cora, whose affections he has managed to steal from Rolla. And the Inca warrior, Rolla, in his innate nobility, has ungrudgingly ceded claim to Cora despite his continued love for her.

Much of the drama of *Pizarro* hinges on Alonzo's disappearance in battle with the Spaniards and Cora's subsequent distress on behalf of herself and their infant child. Rolla initially offers to serve as a substitute father for the child—an offer that Cora violently rejects. Subsequently, Rolla discovers that Alonzo is being held captive by the Spaniards and that Pizarro is planning to torture Alonzo to death for his defection. Rolla then valiantly substitutes himself for Alonzo as a prisoner of the Spanish (rather than as father of Alonzo's child and husband to Cora), allowing Alonzo to return to Cora. Just as Cora and Alonzo are reunited, Spanish soldiers abduct their infant. In the spectacular penultimate scene of the play, Rolla recovers the infant and is fatally wounded while escaping from the Spanish camp. He flees across a bridge over a precipice, foiling Spanish pursuit by destroying the bridge after he crosses it, and dramatically deposits the infant, unharmed, into Cora's waiting arms. Cora is distraught at the sight of blood on the infant, but Rolla reassures her, with this dying breath, "'Tis my blood, Cora!"[45] Although Alonzo is the father of the creole child, it is Rolla's blood that literally sustains the infant's life and Rolla's death that enables Alonzo to reunite with Cora, thereby sanctifying (with native blood and with the seeming nobility of natural law) Alonzo's title to Peruvian land. In short, while Rolla dies a noble death, the prestige of this nobility accrues to Alonzo and to the creole child produced by settler colonialism. Insofar as Rolla hands Alonzo the right, not simply to be a ruler of the Inca (as in *Cruelty*), but to take his desired position as the father of Cora's child, a genealogical possession is effected: and in changing places with Alonzo, Rolla voluntarily assumes the position of the tortured Indian and places the mantle of indigeneity on Alonzo. The performance of settler colonialism that took the shape of operatic heroism in D'Avenant's *Cruelty* thus assumes the form of melodramatic (familial) embodiment in Sheridan's *Pizzaro*.

For U.S. audiences, it seems probable that this account of creole legitimacy would have had powerful appeal, although the relations triangulated in the play would not be those of Spaniards, English, and Native Americans but those of metropolitan English, creole Americans, and Native Americans. Indeed, the cultural purchase of just such a narrative in the United States is indicated in the success of the play *Metamora* (1829), a play that effectively translates the triangulations of *Pizarro* onto U.S. soil in such as a way as to ordain creole Anglo-Americans as the legitimate settlers of North American land. *Metamora* is a tragic melodrama that recounts the demise of its eponymous Indian chief hero, a figure based on the Wampanoag leader Metacom, who was defeated by the colonists of Massachusetts Bay Colony in King Philip's War in 1670.[46] The play was written by John Augustus Stone and had been commissioned by Edwin Forrest (the "native" of the American stage whose cause was advanced by rioters at Astor Place) by way of a contest Forrest sponsored in order to encourage the development of American drama.[47] In 1828, Forrest proclaimed that he was "desirous that dramatic letters should be more cultivated in my native country" and offered to "the author of the best Tragedy, in five acts, of which the hero or principal character shall be an aboriginal of this country, the sum of five hundred dollars."[48] Forrest thus proposed that American drama would be developed (as separate from a European dramatic tradition) by recourse to representations of Native Americans. Stone, who had apparently seen Forrest perform the part of Rolla some years earlier, penned *Metamora* for the contest and won the prize; Forrest's rendition of the lead role filled theatres around the country for twenty-five years and became central to his embodiment of a muscular, American masculinity (see figure 6.3).[49]

As does *Pizarro*, Stone's *Metamora* proposes a triangulation of positions in early America among Native Americans, white Americans (creole British), and English aristocrats. While the "English" are unabashedly evil (effeminate, aristocratic, and acquisitive), the white creole character of Oceana (who is born shipboard, crossing the Atlantic) emerges as the heroic intermediary between Metamora and the duplicitous English elite. Dubbed "Maiden of the Eagle Plume" by Metamora for her kindness in binding a wound of his, she ultimately survives a double attack—that of the English rake, Lord Fitzarnold, who wishes to marry her for her money, and that of Metamora, who intends to use her as a hostage but relents because of what one might call her innate goodness. As Metamora dies, Oceana and her true beloved, Walter, are preserved from both English and native hostilities by Metamora's protection: Metamora's blessing of the pair thus sanctions Oceana and Walter's union as wholesome and American, rather than English and corrupt. The American audience of the play effectively views an origin myth of white nationalism that produces the United States as the consecrated future of a contentious native and English heritage.

Metamora thus exemplifies rather concisely the U.S. penchant for "playing Indian" as described by Philip J. Deloria—a penchant that dates to the nation-founding symbolics of the Boston Tea Party. Deloria writes, "In playing Indian, Americans invoked a range of identities—aborigine, colonist, patriot, citizen—all of which emerged from the categories of Indian and Briton. In the process they created a new identity—American—that was both aboriginal and European and yet was also neither. . . . There was, quite simply, no way to conceive an American identity without Indians."[50] Forrest's representation of white nativism by way of the Native American chief Metamora attained iconic status in the United States: a biographer writing at the close of the nineteenth

FIGURE 6.3. Edwin Forrest in the role of Metamora. Courtesy of Rare Book and Manuscript Library, University of Illinois at Urbana-Champaign.

century contends that the figure of Metamora, as performed by Forrest, was as recognizable as that of George Washington: "Many of the little speeches which the great actor pronounced from the lips of the Indian king were so finely and truthfully inflected that they dwelt with much force and meaning in the memory of the hearer and became at the time constant quotations, and were as familiar upon the public's tongue as the name of Washington."[51]

Deloria emphasizes the synthetic effects of playing Indian—in which white Americans emerge as U.S. nationals out of a history of British and Indian conflict—, but an additional dimension of playing Indian concerns the history of the commons in the United States. Specifically, performances of Indian identity in the nineteenth-century United States might be seen as invocations of moral economy. The relation of playing Indian to invoking an account of the commons is visible in an insurgency in Maine that occurred in the early nineteenth century against the juridical property regime of the U.S. state—an insurgency that involved a rag-tag band of white squatters who styled themselves "White Indians." The White Indian emerged as a performative identity (like that of the Waltham Black in England, discussed in chapter 3) in central Maine in relation to disputes over property use and ownership. Many poor whites migrated to central Maine following the American Revolution because of an expectation that land owned by British proprietors and loyalists who had fled during the revolution would be granted to U.S. citizens. In fact, the Maine courts ruled otherwise, enforcing pre-revolutionary land ownership claims, and the result was a series of uncertain claims by absentee proprietors (on the part of royalists who had fled to England) who insisted that the land the settlers inhabited did not belong to them. The fairly substantial armed resistance of the settlers to the writs of proprietorship and efforts of the courts to enforce them took the form of a full blown military organization, albeit one mustered in disguise. As Alan Taylor reports, the insurgents, "cultivated the myth that [they] were actually nearby Indians intervening out of disinterested sympathy for their oppressed white brethren."

Notably, however, the White Indians appeared to be deeply invested in the performance of Indian identity in a way that seems to exceed an interest in mere disguise. Taylor relates that "each 'White Indian' donned a uniform of moccasins, an Indian blanket, and a masked and elaborately decorated hood that usually ended in a conical peak. To disguise his voice, the insurgent affected a gutteral, broken English that he sometimes enhanced by placing a wood chip in his mouth. What began as a simple need for an effective disguise developed into a detailed new identity complete with songs, flags, effigies, speeches, and rituals designed to proclaim rebel 'laws' and to degrade local men regarded as turncoats."[52] Returning to Vickers's comment that Indian protest is the purest evocation of moral economy in the early United States, I would suggest that playing Indian here serves to enact a right to the commons—to property held outside of the juridical authority of the United States; to property held in collective use, for time immemorial. Thus the performative commons enacted here is one that asserts the political power of the people in relation to an anti-Lockean regime of land ownership in which Native Americans become central claimants. In order to evoke a material commons in the United States, then, it is literally necessary to make common cause with Native Americans against the U.S. state. Embedded in the act of "playing Indian" by creole whites is thus a deep irony: creole whites enact Indian relations to land in the name of claiming a popular sovereignty that evicts Indians from their land.

As theorists have argued, settler colonialism is quite distinct from colonialism insofar as its aim is self-erasure: rather than maintaining the distinction between colonizer and colonized, as is the case in colonialism, settler colonialism aims at a horizon of extinction. The colonized subject is expected to disappear according to what Patrick Wolfe has called a "logic of elimination." And as many scholars have noted, the culturally iconic figure of the melancholic "vanishing Indian" performs just this role—namely, that of becoming extinct.[53] But as Wolfe also points out, elimination is complex and ongoing: "settler colonialism does not simply replace native society *tout court*. Rather, the process of replacement maintains the refractory imprint of the native counter-claim . . . The native repressed continues to structure settler-colonial society."[54] We might view this "native repressed" as appearing in the activity of playing Indian: playing Indian both invokes the Indian as the figure of indigeneity with the right of occupation, and places that right into the hands of white settlers. The "logic of elimination" requires the presence of the native whose vanishing becomes the work of the present in creating a fictive past—one that includes the death of the Indian.

Metamora, as we have seen, is one such vanishing Indian whose presence was particularly forceful and enduring on the nineteenth-century stage. Edwin Forrest's self-proclaimed identity as American's "Native Tragedian" owed much to his performative identification with Metamora.[55] Somewhat intriguingly, biographers and critics habitually note the muscular presence—the sheer ontic force—of Forrest when praising his life-like impersonation of Metamora. Forrest boasted that he lived with the Choctaw tribe for a month in an effort to get what his biographer William Rounseville Alger describes as an "accurate knowledge of the American Indian." Alger reports that Forrest was particularly interested in what we might call Indian embodiment: one night in the woods with the Choctaw Chief Push-ma-ta-ha, "Forrest asked him to strip himself and walk to and fro before him between the moonlight and firelight, that he might feast his eyes and his soul on so complete a physical type of what man should be."[56] Despite this emphasis on physicality, it is worth underscoring that the storied force of Forrest on stage, in embodying Metamora, is directed toward the act of elimination: his excessive presence accounts for the éclat achieved by Metamora's compliant vanishing in the final act—an act during which his young son is killed, he murders his own wife, and he is subsequently brought down in a hail of English bullets.

An 1833 newspaper account of Forrest's performance of Metamora indicates both the physicality of Forrest's presence, and its value in assisting with the affect produced by the vanishing of the Indian:

> Mr. Forrest's personation of the Indian hero is one the most perfect pieces of histrionic art ever exhibited on any stage. There never was a more complete identification of the actor with the assumed character. He is Indian throughout, from the crown of his head to the sole of his foot, in every look, tone, gesture, and action. This personation was witnessed, we are told, a short time since, in Boston, by a company of Penobscot Indians and their squaws; and the tears of the latter attested the fidelity and touching pathos of the scene, where the hunted Metamora returns to his wigwam, and finds his Nameokee weeping over the lifeless body of his child.[57]

In this article, we find an additional set of performers introduced, namely, a group of Penobscot Indians who affectively endorse the poignancy of Metamora's death with the evidence of their tears. The presence of real Indians, witnessing the death of the staged Indian, thus ratifies the ever vanishing presence of the Native American. This somewhat contradictory staging of presence and absence suggests the way in which the "logic of elimination" of settler colonialism has written into it a strange temporal recursivity. The Indian is supposed to have already vanished in order to bequeath indigeneity upon white creoles, and yet, the Indian must also be materialized—forcefully (if we take Metamora as an example)—in order to continue the act of vanishing. Moreover, the Indian in the audience who is asked to witness this vanishing both seems to attest to the affective and mimetic force of such a history (particularly if weeping, as newspaper accounts such as the one above report) while ontically refuting it simply by means of being present—by means of having not yet vanished.

Efforts to stage this complex recursivity, by means of displaying Native Americans as members of theatrical audiences, were commonplace in the nineteenth century. Perhaps most well-known is the enforced "defeat tour" of the Sauk warrior Black Hawk in 1833: after surrendering to the U.S. military at the close of the so-called Black Hawk War in Prairie du Chien in 1832, Black Hawk was paraded through the cities of the east coast as a prisoner and brought to the theatre to appear as an audience member in Baltimore, Philadelphia, and New York.[58] Crowds thronged to the theatre to view Black Hawk; moreover, Black Hawk's tour closely followed on the heels of visits of then President Andrew Jackson. Indeed, in Baltimore the two attended the theatre on the same night, and, as one newspaper reported, "generally divided the attention of the citizens [of Baltimore] between them."[59] The presidential architect of Indian removal thus relied upon the presence of Black Hawk to assist in performing the popular sovereignty of white nationalism. In the performative commons of U.S. nationalism, then, the vanishing Indian is resolutely present.

Called upon to stoically subside into a romantic past, such an Indian presence seemingly lends force to the narrative of creole indigeneity; nonetheless the presence of the Indian body itself offers counter-evidence to such a narrative and is occasionally mobilized as such. When performed in Augusta, Georgia, in 1831, for instance, *Metamora* met with a hostile reception: James E. Murdoch reports that Forrest was greeted with yells and hisses because his performance of Metamora seemed to dignify the claims of Cherokee peoples to land in Georgia—claims being actively prosecuted at that moment. Rather than ushering such claims into an historical past, the play—when performed in Georgia—gave scope to the real presence of Cherokee people on their ancestral lands rather than to a fiction of creole indigeneity.[60] The mimetic force of the vanishing Indian thus gave way, in such a case, to the ontic force of Indians present within the commons. The dissonance of Native American (mimetic) absence and (ontic) presence registers as well in a further anecdote concerning Black Hawk's attendance at the theatre—one relating his reputed response to a performance of Jim Crow in Philadelphia. According to an article in the *Nantucket Enquirer*, Black Hawk paid no attention to what occurred on the stage, save when forced to listen to four encores of Jim Crow: "Black Hawk being carried to the theatre at Philadelphia managed to sleep through the play, until the applause of the audience at the song of 'Jim Crow,' waked him up. He endured the first repetition with tolerable resignation; but on its being encored for the fourth time louder than ever, cried out 'Peecabogo agankitchigamink pilchilazo'—When these barbarians come to visit me, I shall treat them to a concert of wild cats."[61] In this anecdote, the noble savage is shown to find the racialized sensus communis of the Philadelphia theatre to be intolerable: the music of Jim Crow is noise to Black Hawk's ears. The dissensus that the anecdote portrays points to the difficulty of placing two temporally distinct lines of the nationalizing narrative (colonization and racialization) into the same time and space. Within the article, however, the dissensus is cast as comedic rather than disruptive: Black Hawk's words of protest are described as amusing noise to the presumed readers of the paper rather than a challenge to either colonization or racialization. In a more somber vein, the *Boston Courier* reported that Black Hawk's experiences at the theatre impressed upon him the evidence of his own impending extinction: "During the evening [after a day on tour], when ruminating upon the fatigues of the day, Black Hawk said, 'I have seen the braves of our great father, and many white men to-day—we have all seen them; before to-day I thought the Americans were like musquitos, to be found at certain places and at certain seasons but now I am convinced they are like spears of grass, they grow everywhere.'"[62] At the theatre, a white performative commons is thus amassed to enable Black Hawk to participate in mourning his own extinction; at the theatre, however, Black Hawk's very presence also speaks to dissensus and the potential mobilization of ontic force against narratives of colonization and racialization.

If the terms of embodiment register within the performative commons as both ontic and mimetic, what might be the force of the Native American King performed on stage by a black actor? Although William Brown directed four productions of *Pizarro* between 1821 and 1824 at the African Theatre, no reviews of these performances exist. However, we might speculate that a black actor performing in the character of Rolla would contribute to a strategy of black creole indigenization—that is, to a politics in which New World Africans are understood as rightful occupants of New World lands, and as embodying forms of natural sovereignty with respect to those lands. Such a performance, then, would be identifiable, following the argument of Jodi A. Byrd, as a mode of anti-racist performance that is nonetheless built on a colonizing foundation: "imperialism has forced settlers and arrivants [such as conscripted slaves and immigrants] to cathect the space of the native as their home."[63] Black creole indigeneity, despite its discursive engagement in a critique of white nationalism, nonetheless might be seen as embedded within the larger project of settler colonialism. As Byrd suggests, then, we might "understand colonial discourses not only as vertical impositions between colonizer and colonized but also as horizontal interrelations between different colonized peoples within the same geopolitical space."[64] Importantly, Byrd's critique illuminates the friction between anti-racist and anti-colonial struggles, but I would also suggest that the specific framework of the nation state—precisely the frame of geographical and cultural nationalism so forcefully imposed in the early nineteenth-century United States—creates and/or significantly intensifies this friction. The performance of indigeneity on stage at the African Theatre, I want to suggest, participates in a different geopolitical frame—namely, that of the Atlantic world—and thereby *links* anti-colonial and anti-racist performance rather than substitutes one for the other.

Brown's company performed plays by Shakespeare, including *Richard III*, *Macbeth*, *Hamlet*, and *Othello*, but in addition, the company performed a number of plays that dealt specifically with New World topics including African and Native American anti-colonial revolution in *Pizzaro* as well as in a play written by Brown himself, *King Shotaway*. The latter play concerned the insurrection of the so-called Black Caribs in the West Indies: the Caribs of St. Vincent were descendants of Carib Indians and African maroon slaves who rebelled against British colonizers of the island in 1795 under the leadership of the Carib chief Joseph Chatoyer with the assistance of French republican forces.[65] Chatoyer lost his life in the battle, and the British, upon gaining control of the island, deported more than five thousand Black Caribs to the island of Roatan off the coast of present-day Honduras.[66]

The Carib insurrection of St. Vincent was certainly less well-known in the early decades of the nineteenth century in the United States than was the Haitian Revolution. Indeed, for a U.S. audience, reference to rebellion on St. Vincent would undoubtedly invoke the more successful revolution that had transpired in Saint Domingue at the close of the eighteenth century. While no script of *King Shotaway* is extant, the first known reference to Brown's play appears in the New York *Commercial Advertiser* of 1822 and gives the full title of the play as "*Shotaway; or the insurrection of the Caribs*, of St. Domingo. King Shotaway, Devillee."—thus effectively transposing the location of the play from St. Vincent to St. Domingo.[67] A second reference to the play by the theatre historian George C. D. Odell, citing a playbill from 1823, gives the title as "the Drama of King Shotaway, Founded on facts taken from the Insurrection of the Caravs in the Island of St. Vincent, Written from experience by Mr. Brown."[68] Although Marvin McAllister speculates that Brown himself mistakenly located the play in St. Domingo, given the competing evidence of the playbill and the newspaper account, it seems likely that the writer or typesetter at the *Commercial Advertiser* substituted "St. Domingo" for Brown's "St. Vincent" because of the currency of the Haitian Revolution in the mind of the U.S. public.[69] Further evidence of a typesetting transposition is indicated by the fact that the substance of the play, as indicated in the cast list, clearly refers to the St. Vincent uprising (i.e., "Caribs" and historical figures such as Joseph Chatoyer—"King Shotaway"—and his brother, Duvalee, "Devillee") and not to events in St. Domingo. The confusion within the popular press over the historical origin of the rebellion staged at the African Theatre is thus significant insofar as it transposes the failed insurrection of Joseph Chatoyer in St. Vincent into the successful insurrection of Toussaint L'Ouverture in St. Domingue, and thereby would seem to speak to an on-going U.S. concern with slave rebellion and, perhaps, with the potential "contagion" of Caribbean insurrectionary racial politics. Indeed, the first performance of *King Shotaway* predates by several months the discovery and prosecution of Denmark Vesey for planning a slave rebellion in Charleston, South Carolina, in the summer of 1822. As a slave, Vesey had served as a ship's steward and had visited islands in the West Indies, including St. Domingue. While the alleged conspiracy was discovered prior to its implementation, it engendered panic in South Carolina and extensive coverage in the northern press, including the *National Advocate*, during the summer of 1822.[70]

According to the somewhat speculative accounts of Brown's background, the theatre director and entrepreneur was a native of the West Indies who had served as a (free) steward on passenger ships on the Liverpool line before retiring to live in New York City. Brown's own history, then, is not that of the former southern U.S. plantation slave who has moved northward in the model of the minstrel show character that is familiar in the national U.S. imaginary. Like Denmark Vesey, Brown circulated as a ship's steward in the Atlantic world—a world that included the Caribbean as a central (rather than extranational) scene of colonial and anti-colonial repertoires of meaning. Brown thus resembles the Atlantic figure of Olaudah Equiano, for instance, or the sailors described by Jeffrey Bolster in *Black Jacks*; like Equiano, Brown evidently parlayed the capital he acquired in plying the Atlantic into forms of freedom—in Brown's case, into the creation of a theatre house in New York City.

A second play performed at the African Theatre, *Obi; or Three-Finger'd Jack*, also deals with insurrection in the West Indian colonies of England and further indicates the contours of the Caribbean/Atlantic tradition in which Brown's performances were located. The text of *Obi* is evidently based on the story of Jack Mansong, or "three-fingered Jack," who was introduced as the "terror of Jamaica" in an epistolary novel written by William Earle, published in London in 1800 and republished in Massachusetts by Isaiah Thomas in 1804. A theatrical version of the novel, written by John Fawcett, was performed in London in 1800, and was later staged in New York and Philadelphia as well.[71] In the Earle novel, Jack is the son of an African couple, Amri and Makro, who are cruelly betrayed into slavery by a duplicitous English sea captain. Jack's father dies during the middle passage, and his mother vows to raise her unborn child as the instrument of her revenge. Once in Jamaica Jack emerges as a heroic figure, much like Aphra Behn's Oroonoko. Jack, too, attempts to lead a slave rebellion; while the other slaves fail to follow his courageous example, he himself escapes and terrorizes both whites and blacks in Jamaica until he is ultimately killed in a dramatic fight at the close of the novel.

The play of *Obi* existed in both a pantomime version by Fawcett with a score by Samuel Arnold and a later melodrama by William Murray. The racial politics of the pantomime and the melodrama differ significantly from the novel: in the melodrama, the account of the cruelties and betrayal suffered by Jack's parents in Africa and the middle passage are eradicated altogether and much of the dramatic action focuses on the character of Rosa, the plantation-owner's daughter, who seeks to free her lover from imprisonment by Jack. Jack is presented as an exotic warrior who is clearly doomed to violent death and the emotional emphasis of the performance is placed on the reunion of the white lovers as well as the conversion of the slave Quashee from African Obeah (Obi) to Christianity, which enables him to triumph in slaying Jack. Whereas the novel emphasizes the failure of Enlightenment ideals in the institution of slavery, the pantomime sutures the alliance of Enlightenment and the slave economy by performing Christian triumph over savagery and excess. Fawcett's pantomime premiered in London in July 1800 at the Haymarket Theatre with Charles Kemble starring as Jack; it received popular acclaim and was performed thirty-nine times in its first season. It debuted at the Park Theatre in New York in May 1801 and subsequently was performed in Boston and Philadelphia as well, remaining in repertoire in the U.S. for the next twenty-five years.[72]

Interesting textual evidence linked to the African Theatre's performance of *Obi* indicates that Brown's production may have significantly revised the racial politics of Fawcett's pantomime. In December of 1821, a short-lived literary journal, *St. Tammany's Magazine*, published a piece titled "Soliloquy of a Maroon Chief in Jamaica," that was described as "Lately spoken at the African Theatre." In the speech, the Maroon chief eloquently argues for the humanity of New World Africans and threatens violence on behalf of those unjustly enslaved: "We are men,/As I said first, and as I say agen,/Men like yourselves. I'll prove it by my word,/And just Gods! Avouch it by my sword."[73] According to Michael Warner and his co-authors, it is likely that the speech was authored by William Alexander Brown or the leading actor of the company, James Hewlett, and delivered on stage in a performance of *Obi*. The African Theatre version of *Obi* would seem to significantly echo portions of Earle's novel in which, for instance, Jack's father Makri demands of the callous Captain Harrop, "Are we not men? . . . men as ye are? We vary in nothing but in color; we feel as you do, and are awake to the same sense of pain; but still are we disposed by and among you like cattle."[74] In the soliloquy, the Maroon Chief argues against the rhetoric of racialization that was ascendant in the United States during this period. Specifically, he critiques the notion of a binary color line separating white and black by arguing that New World Africans are less "black" than "red," or the color of "primeval man" and "red Adam" who "from virgin earth's red breast . . . rose." Whites, in contrast, are described as "the whitewashed race" whose "chalky sires . . . lost [Nature's] hue" and "lost her vigour and her sweetness too!" And rather than "white," the Maroon Chief describes Europeans as of a variety of colors: "Ye whites, browns, yellows, iron grey, /All call yourselves cream-white, and so ye may, /Brag of the symbol of your own disgrace, /And wear your mealy infamy in your face!" Thus the soliloquy deconstructs both whiteness and blackness, suggesting that men of a variety of colors cannot use the binary opposition of white versus black skin as descriptive in any effective way, and particularly not as a means of legitimizing European supremacy.[75]

In its emphasis on refashioning racial blackness as primeval redness, the speech of the Maroon Chief serves to perform an indigenizing of New World Africans. Unlike the creole indigenizing performed in a play such as *Metamora*, however, maroon indigeneity is not predicated on the vanishing of the Indian so much as the positing of a new relation between man and earth—namely, one of shared substance. In the case of the Black Caribs, whose anti-colonial revolt was the subject of Brown's own play, resistance to colonization is the shared work of native peoples and escaped slaves who have banded together in opposition to the extractive plantation economy that appropriates both land and labor for European profit. Similarly, the maroons of Jamaica inhabited the land in a mode that was resistant, above all, to the plantocratic regime of racialization and bare labor. Constellating the figures of the Maroon Chief, the Black Carib revolutionary, and primeval man, the performances of the African theatre do, indeed, perform a mode of indigenization, but one that has an anti-colonial engagement that aligns it with the performance of indigenization described by Sylvia Wynter (as seen in chapter 5)—an indigenization that aims less to eradicate native peoples in the name of anti-colonial nationalism than to eradicate a colonial relation to land and labor.[76] Significantly, the Atlantic framing of such an indigenization (visible in the repertoire of the African

Theatre) distances it from a settler colonial sensus communis that imposes the U.S. nation state as its horizon of meaning.

THE FARREN RIOT: 1834

Although the African Theatre Company and William Alexander Brown may have aimed to perform an African American commons by reference to an Atlantic history of indigeneity, this performance ironically had the effect of eliciting among some of its white observers a counterperformance of a degraded African American identity in the form of blackface minstrelsy. That the African Theatre stands as one powerful, originary catalyst of blackface minstrelsy is attested to by numerous specific connections between early practitioners of minstrelsy and the African Theatre. As we have seen, Mordecai Noah's print minstrelizations were among early formations of blackface minstrelsy, as were those of the British actor Charles Mathews, whose (fabulated) representations of the African Theatre's performance of *Hamlet* and the song "Opossum up a Gum Tree" became well-known set pieces. Indeed, as a genre, blackface minstrelsy has one foot firmly planted in the burlesque of Shakespeare; as Charles Haywood reports, "Nearly every minstrel troupe . . . exploited the Shakespearean canon for hilarious burlesque and comic opera travesty."[77] This was in part due to the popular currency of Shakespeare in the period of minstrelsy's ascendance; nonetheless, the African Theatre stands as a historical referent and origin point for black performance of Shakespeare, as was widely reported in the New York City press at the time.

A number of later minstrel productions hint at the legacy of William Alexander Brown within blackface performance: for instance, in *The Darkey Tragedian* (1874), a "black" actor (performed by a white actor in blackface) named "Mr. Forrest," dressed in the costume of Richard III, insists to his director, "Mr. Brown," that he will play only the high tragic roles of Shakespeare and not low comedy or burlesque. "Mr. Brown" laments, "Here's every member of my company fancying that he was cut out for a tragedian and turning up his nose at burnt-cork, as though disposed to quarrel with the steps by which he had ascended." "Mr. Forrest," when asked to perform burlesque, responds "I's got above dat now. Don't do anything but de fust-class legitimate. Hamlums, and Richard Number Two, and Skylark, and dem t'ings."[78] He proceeds, then, throughout the play, to perform one Shakespearean monologue after another in a minstrelized dialect with attendant malapropisms. In another "Ethiopian sketch," titled *Black Forrest*, a black actor longs to play tragedy and impersonates Edwin Forrest; he then attempts the role of Metamora and predictably demonstrates his incapacity for filling Forrest's shoes.[79] Both of these minstrel plays emphasize the apparent pretensions of unskilled black actors to perform the American masculinity of Edwin Forrest and to speak in the cadences of Shakespearean English—to inhabit, for instance, the role of Rolla, Richard III, or Hamlet as did James Hewlett.[80] In *The Darkey Tragedian*, the theatre manager's name—"Mr. Brown"—seems to refer directly to William Alexander Brown's African Theatre. One might note, as well, that in this sketch the black actor, "Mr. Forrest," begins his career by performing burlesque and comedy and then, in a misbegotten fashion, seeks to "ascend" to tragedy; this scenario effectively rewrites, by way of reversal, the theatrical history of minstrelsy such that the Shakespearean drama of the African Company is a pretentious afterthought to comic burlesque rather than the *precursor* of blackface minstrelsy's particular genre of Shakespearean burlesque. As such, blackface minstrelsy functions quite literally to erase the performance of black popular sovereignty that the African Theatre attempted to embody.

The opposition between the two lines of geopolitical representation that I have been delineating—an Atlantic colonial and a U.S. national one—emerges starkly in the early career of T. D. Rice, the originator of the role of Jim Crow. In Rice's earliest U.S. performances, he played the character of the Kentucky slave "Jim Crow" in which much of his performance involved dancing or "jumping" Jim Crow, and singing wildly improvisational lyrics as he danced. In 1834, at the Bowery Theatre, his dance evolved into a play, *Oh! Hush!* based on the song "Coal Black Rose," which pitted the Jim Crow character "Gumbo Cuff" against a Zip Coon/black dandy character named "Mr. Samuel Johnson, Exquire" in a competition for the affections of a woman named Rose. The character of Samuel Johnson bears a remarkable resemblance to Mordecai Noah's description of the black dandy in the African Grove: Johnson first appears on stage, ostentatiously reading a newspaper, to the "unintellumgent bracks" whom he invites to "hear de news ob de day discoursed in de most fluid manner."[81] Johnson, who is reading the newspaper upside down, was once a boot black himself, but having won the lottery, has gotten beyond his place and pretends to a status to which he is not equal. In this play and others such as the *Virginia Mummy* and *Bone Squash*, T. D. Rice plays the character of a former slave from Virginia or Kentucky who is something of a trickster figure—a character who antagonizes figures of authority with a punning lack of compliance to their plans with the persistent aim of filling his stomach and obtaining a drink of whiskey.

T. D. Rice's performances, as we have seen, took the United States by storm, and he subsequently traveled to England in 1836 where he outdrew Edwin Forrest and other well-known actors in his London performances. However, numerous of the plays he performed in England were written for him by English writers, and their account of Crow's genealogy was significantly different than that of the U.S. plays in which Rice had previously performed. Specifically, in almost every extant play written for him in England, the "Jim Crow" character Rice performed had (or pretended to) a *royal* African or Native American lineage.[82] In *The Foreign Prince*, for instance, Jim Crow is the son of African royalty and the play lampoons the desire of British middle-class characters to prostrate themselves before such "royalty," thus playing on the dissonance between a politics of aristocratic status and one of racial status. In *The Peacock and the Crow*, the title of the play refers to the conflict between two possible identities of the Jim Crow character—that of the "Crow" from the U.S. south, or that of the "Peacock" from England and the West Indies, namely the lost grandson and only male heir of the wealthy (and deceased) Nehemiah Peacock, whose son is reported to have married a woman "of colour" in South America. Jim Crow is cajoled into pretending to the title of the missing "Peacock" heir, and his co-conspirator, Quickset, enjoins him to dress in the theatrical garb of *Pizarro's* Rolla in order to perform his role as "Peacock." As Quickset reasons, "Mr. Crow must be a native chieftain at least, and there's a Rolla's dress that will be the very thing for him."[83] In *The Peacock and the Crow*, Jim Crow is the alter ego of "Peacock"—a figure who embodies the condensed colonial relations of the wealthy West Indian creole (Belcour) and the Native prince (Rolla), as well as an Atlantic blackness. The figure of Peacock brings to the fore the relations between and among colonization, racialization, and capitalism—and cannily indicates that Jim Crow is one and the same figure. On the English stage, then, Jim Crow stands in direct relation to an Atlantic performative commons, not solely a U.S. national one.

Two "autobiographies" of Jim Crow confirm this distinction. In the U.S.-published *The Life of Jim Crow* (1835), Jim Crow is born on a plantation in Kentucky: as the narrator reports, his skin was so black at his birth that his master "christened me Jim Crow."[84] Alternatively, in *A Faithful Account of the Life of Jim Crow, The American Negro Poet*, published in London in 1840, Jim Crow is the son of "Oulamou," a "celebrated . . . hunter and warrior" of the Six Iroquois Nations and his mother is Native American as well.[85] The literary and theatrical tradition into which Jim Crow is written in England is thus that of the "royal slave"—a tradition invoked in the repertoire of the African Theatre in the performance of characters such as King Shotaway, the Maroon Chief, and Rolla. In his reading of T. D. Rice's English performances, W. T. Lhamon, Jr. suggests that the English insist upon a more restrained position for Jim Crow than do the American scripts. By granting Jim Crow the status of royalty, Lhamon argues, the English scripts also dilute his anarchic energies and thus dilute Jim Crow's challenge to existing systems of authority as well: "Emerging [in the English Jim Crow scripts] is a conflict between the demotic impulse, as it existed in the early American plays, and the dilution of the demotic when the scripters insist on a preapproved honor: African royalty in rags."[86] Lhamon thus grants primacy (in both temporal and political terms) to the American Jim Crow scripts, suggesting that the English overwrite and domesticate Jim Crow's "demotic" force by scripting him into an existing class system. In contrast to Lhamon, however, I would posit the temporal priority of an Atlantic performance tradition and argue that American minstrelsy overwrites a history of colonialism and anti-colonial revolt as well, replacing and erasing this broader geopolitical frame with one of nationalism and racism in which a white/black binary secures the force of white creole nationalism.

Ironically, both nineteenth-century blackface minstrel performers and twentieth- and twenty-first-century scholars of blackface minstrelsy have emphasized minstrelsy's status as one of the earliest *indigenous* American musical and theatrical forms. As an antebellum book of minstrel "plantation songsters" announces, the "cry was that we have no NATIVE MUSIC . . . until our countrymen found a triumphant vindicating APOLLO in the genius of [blackface minstrel performer] E. P. Christy who . . . was the first to catch our *native airs* as they floated wildly, or hummed in the balmy breezes of the sunny south."[87] Yet the nationalist genealogy of the stage African American is a "faux" southern account of black identity that arises less from an urge for accurate *American* drama than from shifting race and class politics that supplanted cultural tropes of colonialism with those of nationalism. Charles Haywood, for instance, emphasizes that the blackface performer was "the creation of Northern minstrelmen who had little contact with the Southern plantations, and know less of the true life and habits of the black slaves. But that did not stop them from calling themselves 'the perfect representatives of the Southern Negro character;' claiming that they were singing 'authentic Negro songs,' and 'truly presenting the speech and manners' of the black folk."[88] Blackface minstrelsy, as fabulation, worked to efface the legacy of the colonial Atlantic and the colonization of America in favor of a circumscribed politics of racialized nationalism.

A rich vein of scholarship has emerged around minstrelsy in which critics have demonstrated the shifting and multilayered politics of race and class that informed minstrelsy and its varied incarnations and historical formations. Eric Lott in particular has emphasized the intersection of white working-class masculinity and early blackface performance in terms of a dynamic of "love and theft": for a white working-class population in the throes of becoming an industrialized labor force, minstrelsy demonstrated a "combined fear of and fascination with the black male" that was related to defining a new class position for whites.[89] Working-class whites both sought to identify with a perceived transgressive vitality and masculinity embodied in blackness that was pitched against white elite authority *and* sought to distance themselves from and elevate themselves above blackness as equated with forced labor, incivility, and failed autonomy. Lott explains the pronounced ambivalence of minstrelsy in terms of the intersection of race and class dynamics: "Sandwiched between bourgeois above and black below, respectable [white] artisans feared they were becoming 'blacker' with every increment of industrial advance, and countered with the language and violence of white supremacy. But the very vehemence of their response indicated the increasing functional and discursive interchangeability of blacks and working-class whites. . . . Blackface minstrelsy . . . was founded on this antinomy, reinstituting with ridicule the gap between black and white working class even as it reveled in their (sometimes liberatory) identification."[90] Lott thus emphasizes the ambivalence of minstrelsy, as compared, for instance, to scholars such as Lhamon and Dale Cockrell who describe the early blackface minstrel performances of T. D. Rice as carnivalesque, transgressive, and subversive of existing class and race divisions insofar as they aligned working-class whites with the anti-authoritarian energies of blackness.[91] Other readings of early minstrelsy, however, view the white working-class engagement in lampooning blacks as an effort to bolster white status by demeaning blacks and thereby substituting a racial opposition for a class one.[92] None of these accounts of the politics of minstrelsy, however, speaks to the layered colonial history of racial and colonial representation that precedes and underwrites minstrelsy. Imposing a racial binary in and through blackface performance serves to overwrite and naturalize the violence of settler colonialism that remains embedded within racialized nationalism. In other words, the imposition of a black/white binary by way of minstrel performance might be seen to assist not only in racialization, but also in the cultural work of making the Indian vanish into the past of U.S. nationalism.

The intersection between and among performances of race, class, citizenship, and the legacies of Atlantic colonialism in the United States is most evident in the Farren Riot, which occurred at the Bowery Theatre in New York City in July 1834—a theatre riot that both mirrors the Astor Place "scenario" of Americans declaring cultural independence from England *and* relies on blackface minstrel performance as well as playing Indian in order to articulate this independence.[93] George P. Farren was a British stage manager at the Bowery Theatre who, according to a newspaper report, "cursed the Yankees, and called them jackasses" and was called to task for doing so by handbills posted around the city on the morning of an evening performance scheduled to benefit him at the Bowery.[94] The performance was to star Edwin Forrest in *Metamora*. Anti-abolitionist rioters converged on the Bowery Theatre during Forrest's performance, having gathered earlier in the evening at the evangelical Chatham Street Chapel, where an abolitionist group had been scheduled to meet. Racial tensions were high in the area because of economic and social pressures on white working-class skilled and unskilled laborers, and rumors circulated that blacks and abolitionists were threatening to take over white neighborhoods and "mullatoize" them.[95]

As the mob at the Bowery Theatre swelled to over four thousand protesters, the crowd then broke into the theatre and drove Edwin Forrest from the stage, demanding justice from Farren. Forrest himself was unable to quell the crowd, and the announcement of Farren's dismissal together with American flag-waving by the Bowery manager, Thomas Hamblin, did not seem to suffice either. As the *Commercial Advertiser* reported, "notwithstanding the entreaties of Messrs. Hamblin and Forrest, [the mob] succeeded in putting an end to *Metamora*, without waiting the tragic conclusion to which he was destined by the author."[96] Yet while neither the American acting of Forrest nor the American flag waved by Hamblin could pacify the crowd, a different act succeeded where Forrest and Hamblin failed. According to the *New York Sun*, "Mr. Dixon, the singer (an American,) now made his appearance. 'Let us have Zip Coon,' exclaimed a thousand voices. The singer gave them their favorite song, amidst peals of laughter,—and his Honor the Mayor . . . delivered a short speech, made a low bow, and went out. Dixon, who had produced such amazing good nature with his 'Zip Coon,' next addressed [the mob]— and they soon quietly dispersed."[97] Why did a performance of Zip Coon (see figure 6.4) mollify a crowd seemingly enraged by anti-American sentiment from a British stage manager? How are colonial relations reperformed in the nationalized stylings of Zip Coon, Metamora, anti-British rage, and white working-class mob violence?

In many respects, the Farren Riot was epiphenomenal with regard to a wave of race riots that swept through New York City and other parts of the country in the 1830s. Indeed, the Farren Riot occurred in the middle of four days of violent anti-abolitionist rioting in New York City in which churches, businesses, black residences, white reformers' homes, and black people themselves were attacked by mobs. The riots occurred in relation to the increased activities and visibility of the New England Anti-Slavery Society, a group that had launched a frontal attack on slave laws as well as on northern colonization

FIGURE 6.4. Zip Coon, from the cover of sheet music. Endicott and Swett (1834). Courtesy of the Library of Congress.

societies that aimed to export free African Americans to colonies in Africa and the Caribbean. The New England Anti-Slavery Society was led by Arthur Tappan and William Lloyd Garrison and worked directly with British abolitionists Charles Stuart and George Thompson, in part to capitalize on the successful 1833 British law abolishing slavery in British West Indian colonies. The British connection was regarded with deep suspicion by anti-abolitionists: conspiracy theories flourished among white working-class factions that abolitionists and English aristocrats were aiming to destroy American liberty. As one historian of the riots reports, "Northern anti-abolitionists concluded that British aristocrats, with the aid of English merchants and manufacturers, had launched a conspiracy against the American republic. By abolishing slavery in the West Indies and raising a clamor against Southern slavery, these conspirators hoped to placate their own downtrodden masses with a false issue. Then, as years passed, they hoped to destroy American vigor either by fomenting war and carnage or by debilitating American manhood through widespread miscegenation."[98] Anti-abolitionist anger was thus directed both against white reformers such as Tappan and Garrison, and against the British; arguments both against the British and in favor of white supremacy were wrapped in the rhetoric of patriotism and American nationalism.

The question as to why anti-abolitionist violence broke out into large-scale mob violence in New York City in the summer of 1834 has led historians to point to a number of complex, intersecting social forces animating white working-class protesters at the time, including anxiety about miscegenation, labor competition between poor whites and blacks, economic and social insecurity on the part of white workers during a period of rapid industrialization and deskilling of labor, and white reaction to an increased visibility and strength of black community institutions.[99] Despite the richness of these accounts of the riots, they do not fully address the particular nexus of cultural forces that produced the simultaneous call for George Farren's head and Zip Coon's song and dance as voiced by a crowd of thousands at the Bowery Theatre. In focusing on the explicit and contentious demand for specific forms of cultural representation that occurred during the riot, one can see the importance of theatrical performance in relation to the politics of class, race, and nationalism, and more particularly, one can see the way in which the performative production of white indigeneity (and white nationalism) relied on representations of anti-elite Anglophobia, the presence of the vanishing Indian, and staged blackness (see figure 6.5).

The New England Anti-Slavery Society was committed to putting an end to slavery in the United States, but slavery had already been abolished in the

FIGURE 6.5. Interior of the Bowery Theatre, from *Frank Leslie's Illustrated Newspaper*, 1856. Courtesy of the Library of Congress.

state of New York in 1827. The activities of the New England Anti-Slavery Society that provoked violent response from New Yorkers were less attempts to free slaves in the U.S. South than the critique leveled by the society against the activities of colonization societies. Arguing for "immediate emancipation without expatriation" as against colonization was tantamount to proposing a racially integrated nation—a society in which free blacks would coexist civilly, politically, and economically with whites in the United States. A newspaper account of the 1834 riots from the *Commercial Advertiser*, for instance, blames the violence on the activities of "Fanatics" who advocate amalgamation:

> We have long been of the opinion . . . that the Abolitionists are the worst enemies the blacks of this city have. They are holding out to them the prospect of amalgamation, feeding their pride with impracticable hopes, exclaiming and denouncing the prejudice against color, leading them to believe that they are unjustly and cruelly treated by the whites by denial of equal political and *social* privileges, fomenting their passions . . . inviting them to sit with the whites indiscriminately, nolens volens, in public

assemblies and social parties, and thus attempting to break down the barriers which nature had set up between the races, and of which the guardian sentinel is TASTE.[100]

Although the newspaper article presents the work of abolitionists as that of breaking down existing barriers between the races, one might reverse this claim to say that the anti-abolitionists are themselves working to *establish* a barrier between the races—a barrier previously secured by slave laws but at the time very much up for question as free blacks in New York City lived, worked, voted, and performed Shakespeare shoulder-to-shoulder with whites. In fact, the Five Points area of New York City, like other working-class neighborhoods in northern cities, was racially integrated; one historian suggests that "this time and place found the races living together as easily as any before and perhaps more so than any since."[101] Precisely the reality of social integration came to seem threatening as members of the white working class sought to define themselves as "freemen" rather than "wage slaves" in an industrializing economy. David Roediger thus argues that "much popular energy was in fact expended to make the literal legal title of freeman absolutely congruent with *white* adult maleness."[102] In the article from the *Commercial Advertiser* cited above, the energy of anti-abolitionists is exerted not in legal terms but in cultural ones: maintaining the "natural" barrier between the races, the article opines, is a matter of "TASTE"—a term associated both with norms of civility (such as seating arrangements) and aesthetics (such as theatrical performance). The taste of the town here works to establish a national sensus communis by means of decisively separating entitled whites from degraded blacks.

The Farren Riot began at the Chatham Street Chapel—an auditorium with thirteen hundred seats that was more theatre than church, having originally served as the working-class Chatham Theatre prior to its purchase by the evangelist reformer Lewis Tappan (brother of Arthur Tappan). Indeed, George Washington Dixon had debuted early versions of his blackface play *Coal Black Rose* at the Chatham Theatre. When Tappan purchased the theatre in 1832, he evidently imagined that the force of theatricality would be a boon to his evangelist and abolitionist efforts: "The *sensation* that will be produced by converting the place with slight alterations into a church will be very great," wrote Tappan to a friend.[103] The transition of the theatre from a scene of blackface performance to a platform for "immediate emancipation" and anticolonization did not occur without contest. A riot broke out at the Chatham Street Chapel in May 1834, shortly before the Farren Riot, when abolitionists sought to interview a black carpenter from Liberia to demonstrate the failures of colonization schemes, and another disturbance occurred on July 4 of the same year during a celebration of the anniversary of "Abolition Day," which had occurred on July 4, 1827, in New York state.

The July 10 riot that later moved to the Bowery Theatre thus began on the boards of the former Chatham Theatre and was occasioned by the announcement that a mixed-race crowd would be gathered there for a meeting of the Anti-Slavery Society. When the meeting did not materialize, anti-abolitionists broke into the chapel and engaged in their own performance of anti-abolitionist rhetoric. Specifically, William H. V. Wilder took the stage and "gave a sketch of the miseries brought on the slaves of St. Domingo—which he himself witnessed, by the too sudden abolition of slavery on that Island."[104] Wilder's discussion of Caribbean revolution at this juncture is intriguing because it points to the extent to which the Caribbean remained part of a U.S. public's consciousness of racial slavery and race politics in the early nineteenth century, as well as the extent to which U.S. whites sought to distance themselves from this example. Although Wilder evidently discussed the miseries of free blacks in the Republic of Haiti, the miseries of free whites who were massacred during the revolution—widely reported on and decried in the U.S. press—would have been the more immediate point of reference for a white U.S. public. Further, the renaming of the French colony of St. Domingue with the title Haiti (or Hayti) by the revolutionaries in 1804—a name taken from the indigenous Arawak Taino inhabitants of the island—is an act that effectively claimed indigenous status for New World Africans on the Caribbean island.[105] Notably, the *Commercial Advertiser*, and presumably Wilder, eschew the indigenous name "Haiti" in favor of the colonial title, St. Domingo (as did most newspapers in the United States). In effect, then, Haiti appears as the foil or antitype for U.S. white nationalism: New World Africans (creoles) claimed indigenous status in Haiti and took full political possession of the island in a revolution against colonial powers. In the United States, New World whites (creoles) also sought to claim indigenous status and secure full political possession of the country following a revolution against colonial powers, and they sought to transform whiteness into an index of their legitimate possession of the land rather than to follow the signifying racial practices that had so alarmingly been instituted in another former European colony in the Atlantic world. White creole nationalism is thus constructed here in relation to the specter of Haitian black creole nationalism.

With the cautionary example of "St. Domingo" before them on one stage, the anti-abolitionist rioters turned their attention toward another stage and demanded a performance that would enact the eradication of aristocratic British (colonial) authority (in the figure of William Farren) together with the performance of blackface minstrelsy—and specifically, of Zip Coon and his "Opossum up a Gum Tree" sensibilities that registered, above all, as sheer incompetence for Shakespeare, leadership, speech, citizenship, or authority. Zip Coon, quite clearly, is no Toussaint Louverture. When the crowd initially broke into the Bowery Theatre, Forrest was performing the role of Metamora—a role that, as we have seen, stages the white creole claim to indigeneity that the crowd sought to establish for themselves. One newspaper account of the riot indicates that the crowd did not simply prevent the performance of *Metamora* but rather themselves assumed the stage by collectively playing Indian:

> A sudden rush was then made upon the doors, which were broken open, and the Theatre, from top to bottom, stage and all, was taken possession of by the crowd, just as the war dance in Metamora was in course of exhibition—the performers of which were driven from the board by yells and contortions, more extravagant than theirs. This irruption was achieved without any personal contests, and, indeed, without any very striking demonstrations of anger; but there was noise enough, and a most appalling demand for "Farren! Farren!"[106]

According to this account, the rioting crowd took possession of the stage by *performing* as Indians—indeed, by outperforming the actors on the stage in this regard. Like the patrons joining in the sword fight on stage during Richard III, the mob here performed their sovereignty as creole indigenes. Having taken the stage themselves, the crowd then obtained a promise that Farren had been dismissed; subsequently they called for "Zip Coon," a performance that one might view as replacing the specter of St. Domingo on the Chatham Street stage with the theatricalized failures of the black dandy.

According to Sean Wilentz, the protestors expressed a double antipathy toward British aristocracy and African Americans in order to stake out a claim to white working-class identity: "In their own way the crowds . . . were protecting their neighborhoods . . . from those they deemed external threats, while they vindicated the American workingman's honor from the insults and abuse of English aristocrats and meddlesome, evangelical entrepreneurial reformers."[107] Although Wilentz is correct with respect to working-class antipathy for British elites and for American blacks, he may be less accurate in his suggestion that whites were protecting "their" own neighborhoods. At the time, 12 percent of the neighborhood in question was made up of blacks, and 40 percent was made up of immigrants, primarily from Ireland: the neighborhood being thus composed, what was at stake in these acts of "protection" was the production of Irishness as American and white, and the eradication of black citizenship.[108] If Zip Coon is an "indigenous" American production, he is also designed to uproot black ownership in favor of white possession while erasing all history of Native American habitation, and this is literally performed at the Bowery Theatre as Farren and Hamblin, and then Forrest, are set aside for George Washington Dixon, the self-described "National Melodist," to perform Zip Coon and keep the peace. White indigeneity was thus established in relation to the multiple figures of the Atlantic world—Britons, Indians, and New World Africans—while simultaneously this palette was reduced to that of white against black. White U.S. nationalism emerged out of an Atlantic commoning and a racial segmenting, performed as an act of presencing and erasure at once.

The famous Astor Place Riot took place fifteen years later and, like the Farren Riot, starred Edwin Forrest as its "Native Tragedian," albeit not in the role of Metamora, but as himself—the heroic apotheosis of American cultural nationalism. On the evening of May 10, 1849, a restless crowd of more than ten thousand men and women congregated outside the Astor Place Opera House; inside, well-heeled patrons took their seats for a performance of Shakespeare's *Macbeth*, starring the leading British actor of the day, William Charles Macready. Macready's aristocratic acting style had become a lighting-rod for working-class, nationalist critique by those who favored the muscular acting style of Forrest. Only three days before, Macready had been driven from the same stage by a jeering audience of Bowery b'hoys who hurled chairs and debris from the cheap seats above onto the boards below. Yet Macready had been immediately petitioned to return to the Astor Place Opera House by a public letter (signed by Washington Irving and Herman Melville, among others) asserting that "good sense and respect for order" could and should prevail on the "American Stage."[109] Thus primed for a repeat showdown, on the evening of May 10, Mayor C. S. Woodhull called in a large police force to protect the opera house and alerted the military to stand ready for violence while the working-class crowd of protesters was assembled by organizers including Isaiah Rynders, a Tammany Hall ward heeler, and the dime-novel writer and Nativist agitator Ned Buntline (E. Z. C. Judson). As the crowd outside began to throw bricks and paving stones at the unarmed police guarding the opera house and to light fires in the street, inside Macready was assaulted by hisses and groans directed at him by a small but vociferous group of Forrest supporters who had infiltrated the "kid-glove," pro-Macready audience. With the police under attack, the governor called in the militia and the crowd was dispersed with gunfire: twenty-six protestors and bystanders were killed in the streets by the militia, and more than one hundred were wounded.[110] As newspapers reported, twice as many were killed in the riot as in the Battle of New Orleans, and five times the number of civilians were gunned down as in the Boston Massacre.

Accounts of the riot by historians emphasize the involvement of white working-class, anti-immigrant Nativists who rallied against English-identified elite members of New York's "Upper Tenth" who attended theatre at the exclusive opera house venue. However, as I suggested at the outset of this chapter, the notion that the riot concerned primarily a yearning for American cultural independence from England and class antagonism between poor and wealthy whites occludes the centrality of colonial relations to the construction of white nationalism that was at stake in the riot. As the very term "Nativist" indicates, the rioters sought to perform their status as indigenous claimants to American identity. If this claim was overtly framed in terms of a desire to excise the presence of British bodies from the performative commons, it was less overtly framed in terms of a related desire to excise the presence of Native American bodies from the performative commons and from the material commons of North America. Further, during the riot, white nativists drew overtly on a binary racialization between white and black to perform their sovereignty: during Macready's performance on May 7 at the opera house, hecklers reportedly yelled: "Three cheers for Macready, Nigger Douglass, and Pete Williams"—a cry that drew explicit links between British support for abolition, recent reports that Frederick Douglass had walked down Broadway with a white woman on each arm, and the activities of the African American manager (Pete Williams) of a Five Points bar at which blacks and whites danced together.[111] Rioters thus sought to perform their claim to the commons by way of erecting an opposition between whites and blacks as well as by claiming indigenous right to American sovereignty.

Significantly, Ned Buntline, who was ultimately arrested and imprisoned for his role in the Astor Place Riot, penned the sensational stories and stage plays that established "Buffalo Bill" (William F. Cody) as a mythic figure of the American frontier later in the nineteenth century. Like Davy Crockett, Buffalo Bill was a frontier fabulation whose tales of Indian fighting served to discursively eradicate the rights of Native Americans to inhabit their own lands and glorify U.S. expansionism. As Lara Langer Cohen has demonstrated, Jim Crow and Davy Crockett often shared the stage in the mid-nineteenth century: the tandem of "backwoods and blackface" performance, Cohen argues, provided complementary stagings in support of an emerging fiction of literary nationalism.[112] Although seemingly unrelated, the twinned performances of white frontiersmanship and black minstrelsy speak to the complicity of the work of colonization and racialization in shaping white nationalism. As the riots discussed in this chapter unfolded in the first half of the nineteenth century in New York City, as blackface minstrelsy emerged with spectacular success on American stages, and as Edwin Forrest embodied the vanishing Indian, the Supreme Court issued the Marshall trilogy of decisions (*Johnson v. McIntosh*, 1823; *Cherokee v. Georgia*, 1831; and *Worcester v. Georgia*, 1832) that defined Native American tribes as "domestic dependent nations," thus eradicating Native American independent sovereignty and enacting a new level of colonial violence.[113] At the same time, the Mississippi Valley lands forcibly taken from Native tribes were placed in the hands of wealthy white owners who would transform the land into the "Cotton Kingdom"—a kingdom whose prodigious wealth was generated by the labor of the more than one million slaves "sold down the river" in the internal slave trade between 1820 and 1860. As Walter Johnson argues, "White privilege on an unprecedented scale was wrung from the lands of the Choctaw, the Creek, and the Chicksaw and from the bodies of the enslaved people brought in to replace them."[114] The performance of white popular sovereignty at the theatres of New York City relied upon Native American and African American bodies as well, and specifically upon staging newly nationalized accounts of these bodies such that the repertoire of colonial relations that once inhabited an Atlantic performative commons were eclipsed from sight.

The Astor Place Riot serves as a closing point of sorts for the history of the Atlantic performative commons insofar as it enacts a resolutely nationalized theatrics. But it marks the closing of the performative commons in another regard as well—namely, insofar as the theatre was no longer a space for public debate over the representation of the collective taste of the town. In 1805, one U.S. critic wrote, "The public, in the final resort, govern the stage": after the Astor Place Riot, this statement ceased to be true.[115] After the Astor Place Riot, two methods of audience control subsequently interceded to change the face of theatre in the United States considerably: first, external control over behavior exerted in the form of police intervention (as at the Astor Place Riot) was stepped up considerably, and second, internal control of audiences increased as the experience of attending the theatre became privatized—that is, individuals ceased to attend as members of a public (with a public voice) and more often attended theatre as private (and more passive) consumers of entertainment whose behavior (and self-performance) was regulated by codes of middle-class propriety.[116] The mid-nineteenth century thus saw the enclosure of the performative commons in the space of the theatre: theatre was no longer the location at which the multitude congregated to debate and enact its self-representation. Audiences were both segmented, according to venue, and privatized, according to new codes of behavior. In the immediate wake of the Astor Place Riot, the *Morning Courier and New York Enquirer* lauded the military force used to put down the riot: "The promptness of the authorities in calling out the armed forces and the unwavering steadiness with which the citizens obeyed the order to fire on the assembled mob, was an excellent advertisement to the Capitalists of the old world, that they might send their property to New York and rely upon the certainty that it would be safe from the clutches of red republicanism, or chartists, or communionists of any description."[117] State military intervention at the Astor Place Riot made the theatre safe for capitalism if not for acts of commoning and dissensus.

The sense in which audience members and actors together performed scenes of popular sovereignty and commoning—scenes of the moral economy of collective belonging—in theatres around the Atlantic world has been the subject of this book. The concept of the performative commons explored is not, it should be clear, a romantic or normative ideal; rather, I aim to have traced a history that the concept of the performative commons helps to make visible—a history at the intersection of the privatizing force of capitalism and the public-making and collectivizing force of popular sovereignty as both took shape in the eighteenth-century Atlantic world. Commoning involves a set of relations—relations of sustenance enacted between land and people in the material commons and relations of representation aimed at collective sustenance in the virtual commons. However, the performative commons that emerged in theatres around the Atlantic world, as traced in the chapters of this book, are historically racializing and colonizing—engaged in acts of erasure as much as representation. Nonetheless, the performative nature of this commoning does include resources for thinking beyond and outside of coloniality. Resistance to settler colonialism involves making the history of settler colonialism visible rather than allowing the logic of elimination to erase this history and its persistence into the present. The history of the performative commons brings into visibility the colonial relations shaped by capitalism, colonization, and racialization, that structured the eighteenth-century Atlantic world. As I have suggested, the ineluctably material and representational nature of commoning allows dissensus to emerge at sites of embodied performance—a dissensus that speaks to the non-identity of the state and the people, for instance, or to the non-identity of the body of the people and its mimetic substitutions. The materiality and figurality of performance—its ontic and mimetic nature—thus opens possibilities for mobilizing new scenes of visibility even in the shadow of a colonial biopolitics of social death. If the theatre is no longer the location at which we can routinely expect to find such performances, it is nonetheless the case that the theatrical history of the performative commons enables us to see modes of commoning that continue to wield force and hold possibility today.

INTRODUCTION: THE PERFORMATIVE COMMONS
AND THE AESTHETIC ATLANTIC

1. January 1649, *Journals of the House of Commons*, vol. 6: 1648–1651 (1802): 125–26. Emphasis added.

2. Karl Marx, *Capital: A Critique of Political Economy*, trans. Ben Fowkes, vol. 1 (London: Penguin, 1990), 885.

3. William Edward Tate, *English Village Community and the Enclosure Movements* (London: Gollancz, 1967), 88. Although enclosure had been going on for centuries, Parliament became actively involved in the business of enclosure in the eighteenth century; see Leigh Shaw-Taylor, "Parliamentary Enclosure and the Emergence of an English Agricultural Proletariat," *Journal of Economic History* 61, no. 3 (September 2001): 640–62.

4. On representing the "people" in the early U.S., see Jason A. Frank, *Constituent Moments: Enacting the People in Postrevolutionary America* (Durham, NC: Duke University Press, 2010).

5. Lewis Hyde, *Common as Air: Revolution, Art, and Ownership* (New York: Farrar, Straus and Giroux, 2010), 31.

6. The concept of commons as a set of practices involving people, resources, culture, and social relations is elaborated by Dana D. Nelson in her forthcoming book, *Commons Democracy*; my account is indebted to this work. On "assemblage," see Bruno Latour, *Reassembling the Social: An Introduction to Actor-Network-Theory* (Oxford: Oxford University Press, 2005).

7. "Theatrical," *Columbian Centinel* [Boston], November 17, 1804, 2.

8. Of eighteenth- and early nineteenth-century audiences in the United States, Richard Butsch writes, "Fitting the revolutionary rhetoric of egalitarianism, the audience was conceived as a body of equal citizens, all of whom held rights. These were fiercely asserted as rights of a free citizen, linking rights in theatre to larger political rights. Thus the theatre was defined as a public space in which the body politic deliberated" (*The Making of American Audiences: From Stage to Television, 1750–1990* [Cambridge: Cambridge University Press, 2000], 14).

9. "Evacuation at the Bowery Theatre," *Traveller and Spirit of the Times* [New York], December 1, 1832, 2.

10. "Freedom of the scenes" was a custom dating to the seventeenth century according to which audience members were allowed to stand on stage during performances; this custom was largely eradicated by the mid-nineteenth century but persisted in various forms until that date. For further discussion see chapter 4.

11. The version of *Richard III* that was most often staged in the United States during this period was Colley Cibber's redaction of Shakespeare's play—one that often went by the title *The Fall of Tyranny*. Cibber's revision offers a far more direct critique of tyrannical monarchy than does Shakespeare's play and more clearly stages the fall of Richard III at the hands of popular sovereignty. For further discussion, see chapter 6.

12. Peter Buckley, "To the Opera House: Culture and Society in New York City, 1820–1860" (PhD diss., SUNY Stonybrook, 1984), 123.

13. Buckley, "To the Opera House," 124.

14. E. P. Thompson, "The Moral Economy of the English Crowd in the Eighteenth Century," *Past and Present* 50 (February 1971): 78–79.

15. Michael Hardt and Antonio Negri, *Commonwealth* (Cambridge, MA: Harvard University Press, 2009), 50–51.

16. Hardt and Negri, *Commonwealth*, 9.

17. Hardt and Negri do not wholly ignore the history of colonialism and empire in the early Atlantic world; however, they attend to it primarily in passing. See, for instance, Hardt and Negri, *Empire* (Cambridge, MA: Harvard University Press, 2000), 70.

18. Hardt and Negri, *Empire*, 255.

19. Jacques Rancière, *On the Shores of Politics*, trans. Liz Heron (London and New York: Phronesis and Verso, 1995), 32–33.

20. *Jacques Rancière*, http://multitudes.samizdat.net/Entretien-avec-Jacques-Ranciere. "Entretien avec Jacques Rancière," *Dissonance* 1 (2004) as translated and cited by Peter Hallward, "Staging Equality: Rancière's Theatocracy and the Limits of Anarchic Equality," in *Jacques Rancière: History, Politics, Aesthetics*, ed. Gabriel Rockhill and Philip Watts (Durham, NC: Duke University Press, 2009), 142. Hallward's essay contains a useful account of the centrality of theatricality to Rancière's work.

21. For a critique of this Habermasian notion of the subject, see Elizabeth Maddock Dillon, *The Gender of Freedom: Fictions of Liberalism and the Literary Public Sphere* (Palo Alto, CA: Stanford University Press, 2004).

22. Julia Curtis, "The Architecture and Appearance of the Charleston Theatre: 1793–1833," *Educational Theatre Journal* 23, no. 1 (1971): 4. For further discussion of the Charleston theatre and racial demographics, see chapters 1 and 4.

23. "Congress. House of Representatives," *New-York Daily Gazette*, December 15, 1790, 1194. Emphasis added.

24. Benjamin H. Irvin, *Clothed in Robes of Sovereignty: The Continental Congress and the People Out of Doors* (New York: Oxford University Press, 2011), 14.

25. Peter P. Reed, *Rogue Performances: Staging the Underclasses in Early American Theatre Culture* (New York: Palgrave Macmillan, 2009). I cite the term "conscripts of modernity" from David Scott, *Conscripts of Modernity: The Tragedy of Colonial Enlightenment* (Durham, NC: Duke University Press, 2004).

26. Jürgen Habermas, *The Structural Transformation of the Public Sphere: An Inquiry into a Category of Bourgeois Society* (Cambridge, MA: MIT Press, 1989); Benedict R. O'G. Anderson, *Imagined Communities: Reflections on the Origin and Spread of Nationalism*, rev. ed. (London: Verso, 1991); Michael Warner, *Letters of the Republic: Publication and the Public Sphere in Eighteenth-Century America* (Cambridge, MA: Harvard University Press, 1990); Dillon, *The Gender of Freedom*; Joanna Brooks, "The Early American Public Sphere and the Emergence of a Black Print Counterpublic," *William and Mary Quarterly* 62, no. 1 (January 2005): 67–92; Trish Loughran, *The Republic in Print: Print Culture in the Age of U.S. Nation Building, 1770–1870* (New York: Columbia University Press, 2007).

27. I use the term "a-literate" in preference to "illiterate," to underscore that lack of literacy in English is less the result of failure than force; for further discussion, see chapter 4.

28. Much of the most powerful work in African American studies looks to the broader field of performance studies rather than to print alone. For recent work on performance culture in African American studies, see especially Daphne Brooks, *Bodies in Dissent: Spectacular Performances of Race and Freedom, 1850–1910* (Durham, NC: Duke University Press, 2006); Soyica Diggs Colbert, *The African American Theatrical Body: Reception, Performance, and the Stage* (New York: Cambridge University Press, 2011); Jacqueline Denise Goldsby, *A Spectacular Secret: Lynching in American Life and Literature* (Chicago: University of Chicago Press, 2006); Saidiya V. Hartman, *Scenes of Subjection: Terror, Slavery, and Self-Making in Nineteenth-Century America* (New York: Oxford University Press, 1997); Koritha Mitchell, *Living with Lynching: African American Lynching Plays, Performance, and Citizenship, 1890–1930* (Urbana: University of Illinois Press, 2011); Fred Moten, *In the Break: The Aesthetics of the Black Radical Tradition* (Minneapolis: University of Minnesota Press, 2003); Tavia Amolo Ochieng' Nyongó, *The Amalgamation Waltz: Race, Performance, and the Ruses of Memory* (Minneapolis: University of Minnesota Press, 2009); and Diana Rebekkah Paulin, *Imperfect Unions: Staging Miscegenation in U.S. Drama and Fiction* (Minneapolis: University of Minnesota Press, 2012).

29. David Armitage provides a useful three-part taxonomy of methodologies in the field of Atlantic history in "Three Concepts of Atlantic History," in *The British Atlantic World, 1500–1800*, ed. David Armitage and M. J. Braddick (New York: Palgrave Macmillan, 2002), 11–27. For a recent account of Atlantic world history that is not focused through the lens of European empire, see James Sidbury and Jorge Cañizares-Esguerra, "Mapping Ethnogenesis in the Early Modern Atlantic," *William and Mary Quarterly* 68, no. 2 (2011): 181–208. On work in Atlantic studies in the field of history versus literary studies, see Eric Slauter, "History, Literature, and the Atlantic World," *William and Mary Quarterly* 65, no. 1 (2008): 135–66.

30. Aníbal Quijano and Immanuel Wallerstein, "Americanity as a Concept, or the Americas in the Modern World-System," *International Social Science Journal* 134 (1992): 549.

31. Kerry Ward, *Networks of Empire: Forced Migration in the Dutch East India Company* (Cambridge: Cambridge University Press, 2009), 56.

32. Lauren Benton, *A Search for Sovereignty: Law and Geography in European Empires, 1400–1900* (Cambridge: Cambridge University Press, 2010), xiii.

33. Paul Gilroy, *The Black Atlantic: Modernity and Double Consciousness* (Cambridge, MA: Harvard University Press, 1993), 57.

34. Édouard Glissant, *Caribbean Discourse: Selected Essays*, trans. J. Michael Dash (CARAF Books. Charlottesville: University Press of Virginia, 1989), 123–24.

35. Joseph R. Roach, *Cities of the Dead: Circum-Atlantic Performance* (New York: Columbia University Press, 1996), 5.

36. Orlando Patterson, *Slavery and Social Death: A Comparative Study* (Cambridge, MA: Harvard University Press, 1982). For a valuable recent discussion of slavery and social death, see Vincent Brown, "Social Death and Political Life in the Study of Slavery," *American Historical Review* 114, no. 5 (2009): 1231–49.

37. Jeffrey H. Richards, "Politics, Playhouse, and Repertoire in Philadelphia, 1808," *Theatre Survey* 46, no. 2 (2005): 199.

38. Loren Kruger, "Our Theater? Stages in an American Cultural History," *American Literary History* 8, no. 4 (1996): 699. Susan Harris Smith articulates a related set of concerns about the persistent denigration of drama in the United States as a literary form in *American Drama: The Bastard Art* (New York: Cambridge University Press, 1997). Recent work in early American theatre has begun to revise this mode: see Jeffrey H. Richards, *Drama, Theatre, and Identity in the American New Republic* (Cambridge: Cambridge University Press, 2005); Jason Shaffer, *Performing Patriotism: National Identity in the Colonial and Revolutionary American Theater* (Philadelphia: University of Pennsylvania Press, 2007); Reed, *Rogue Performances*; Heather S. Nathans, *Early American Theatre from the Revolution to Thomas Jefferson: Into the Hands of the People* (Cambridge: Cambridge University Press, 2003) and *Slavery and Sentiment on the American Stage, 1787–1861: Lifting the Veil of Black* (Cambridge: Cambridge University Press, 2009); and Odai Johnson, *Absence and Memory in Colonial American Theatre: Fiorelli's Plaster* (New York: Palgrave Macmillan, 2006).

39. As Jonathan Elmer argues with respect to literary representations of sovereignty in the Americas, "The ideological space of the new world that [literary] texts depict is not . . . a solution to, or 'exoneration' of, a European problematic [of sovereignty], but that problematic's more intense and volatile expression" (*On Lingering and Being Last: Race and Sovereignty in the New World* [New York: Fordham University Press, 2008], 14).

40. Tice L. Miller and Don B. Wilmeth, *The Cambridge Guide to American Theatre*, 2nd ed. (Cambridge: Cambridge University Press, 2007), 87.

41. Richardson Little Wright, *Revels in Jamaica, 1682–1838: Plays and Players of a Century, Tumblers and Conjurors, Musical Refugees and Solitary Showmen, Dinners, Balls and Cockfights, Darky Mummers and Other Memories of High Times and Merry Hearts* (New York: Dodd, Mead, 1937), 2.

42. For further discussion of colonial matrix of power underlying Western modernity, see Walter Mignolo, *The Darker Side of Western Modernity: Global Futures, Decolonial Options* (Durham, NC: Duke University Press, 2011), and Anthony Bogues, *Empire of Liberty: Power, Desire, and Freedom* (Hanover, NH: University Press of New England, 2010).

43. I use the term "bare labor" with reference to and in distinction from Giorgio Agamben's well-known concept of "bare life." Agamben defines "bare life" with respect to the Roman concept of "homo sacer"—someone who can be murdered without the

killer being regarded as a murderer: "bare life" is not granted juridical protection as human life. On bare life, see Agamben, *Homo Sacer: Sovereign Power and Bare Life* (Palo Alto, CA: Stanford University Press, 1998). However, I use the term "bare labor" rather than "bare life" to describe the position of slaves in the Atlantic economy of capitalist modernity because, despite receiving inhuman treatment, slaves were assigned economic and juridical value—albeit value according to which they registered as "units of labor" alone. Slaves, as Sylvia Wynter argues, were seen as "not *men* essentially, but so many units of labour power" in the colonial Caribbean (Wynter, "Jonkonnu in Jamaica: Towards the Interpretation of Folk Dance as a Cultural Process," *Jamaica Journal* 4, no. 2 [June 1970]: 36). For further discussion of bare labor see chapters 4 and 5.

44. I use the term "archive" in reference to Diana Taylor's powerful account of performance as a material archive in *The Archive and the Repertoire: Performing Cultural Memory in the Americas* (Durham, NC: Duke University Press, 2003).

CHAPTER I: THE COLONIAL RELATION

1. On English liberty, see Jack P. Greene, "Introduction: Empire and Liberty," in *Exclusionary Empire: English Liberty Overseas, 1600–1900*, ed. Jack P. Greene (Cambridge: Cambridge University Press, 2010), 1–24.

2. I use the term "colonial modernity" not in distinction from metropolitan modernity but as something of a synonym insofar as I am asserting that modernity—defined in economic and political terms—is constitutively entwined with colonialism. My thoughts on colonial modernity in relation to the Atlantic world are informed by C. L. R. James, *The Black Jacobins: Toussaint L'ouverture and the San Domingo Revolution*, 2nd ed. (New York: Vintage Books, 1963); David Scott, *Conscripts of Modernity: The Tragedy of Colonial Enlightenment* (Durham, NC: Duke University Press, 2004); Aníbal Quijano and Immanuel Wallerstein, "Americanity as a Concept, or the Americas in the Imaginary of the Modern World-System," *International Social Science Journal* 134 (1992): 549–59; Arif Dirlik, "The End of Colonialism? The Colonial Modern in the Making of Global Modernity," *Boundary 2* 32, no. 1 (2005): 1–31; and Sibylle Fischer, *Modernity Disavowed: Haiti and the Cultures of Slavery in the Age of Revolution* (Durham, NC: Duke University Press, 2004).

3. This contradiction implicitly and explicitly informs a great deal of scholarship on slavery and freedom in the Atlantic world. Works that articulate this contradiction with particular clarity include David Brion Davis, *The Problem of Slavery in the Age of Revolution, 1770–1823* (Ithaca, NY: Cornell University Press, 1975) and David Eltis, *The Rise of African Slavery in the Americas* (Cambridge: Cambridge University Press, 2000).

4. Recent work by Simon Gikandi, *Slavery and the Culture of Taste* (Princeton, NJ: Princeton University Press, 2011), as well as Catherine Molineux, *Faces of Perfect Ebony: Encountering Atlantic Slavery in Imperial Britain* (Cambridge, MA: Harvard University Press, 2012), indicates how central slavery was to metropolitan culture in the eighteenth century. See also Susan Dwyer Amussen, *Caribbean Exchanges: Slavery and the Transformation of English Society, 1640–1700* (Chapel Hill: University of North Carolina Press, 2007).

5. For related discussion of the displacement of regimes of punishment to the colonies, see Colin Dayan, *The Law Is a White Dog: How Legal Rituals Make and Unmake*

Persons (Princeton, NJ: Princeton University Press, 2011), 39–70; as well as Caleb Smith, *The Prison and the American Imagination* (New Haven, CT: Yale University Press, 2009), 11; and Gikandi, *Slavery and the Culture of Taste*, 183. More generally, see the work of Ann Laura Stoler (including *Carnal Knowledge and Imperial Power: Race and the Intimate in Colonial Rule* [Berkeley: University of California Press, 2010] and *Race and the Education of Desire: Foucault's History of Sexuality and the Colonial Order of Things* [Durham, NC: Duke University Press, 1995]), which has mounted the most effective challenge to Foucault's occlusion of colonialism from the scene of modernity.

6. Message from Investigating Judges (Vernon, Gilbert, Arbuthnot, Warner) to Governor, Antigua Council Minutes, National Archives of the UK, Public Record Office, Colonial Office 9/10, 2–3. My thanks to Jason T. Sharples for generously providing this information and that in note 7 below. For additional discussion of the Antigua trial, see Jason T. Sharples, "Hearing Whispers, Casting Shadows: Jail-house Conversation and the Production of Knowledge during the Antigua Slave Conspiracy Investigation of 1736," in *Buried Lives: Incarcerated in Early America*, ed. Michele Lise Tartar and Richard Bell (Athens: University of Georgia Press, 2012), 35–59.

7. Anonymous representation to the Governor, January 17, 173[7], Council Minutes, National Archives of the UK, Public Record Office, Colonial Office 9/10, 93, 97.

8. Southerne's *Oroonoko* was performed at Drury Lane on January 10 and March 1, 1736; at Lincoln's Inn Fields on April 2, 1736; and at Covent Garden on April 8, 1736, and on October 12, 1736, by royal command. See *The London Stage, 1660–1800: A Calendar of Plays, Entertainments & Afterpieces. . . . Compiled from the Playbills, Newspapers and Theatrical Diaries, Part 3: 1729–1747*, ed. Arthur H. Scouten, 2 vols. (Carbondale: Southern Illinois University Press, 1961), 1:542, 1:557, 1:569, 2:606.

9. John Dryden's *Indian Emperor* appears at Lincoln's Inn Fields on December 20, 1736, and at Goodman's Fields on April 8, 1736 (Scouten, *London Stage, Part 3*, 2:624, 1:570).

10. Karl Marx, *Capital: A Critique of Political Economy*, trans. Ben Fowkes, 2 vols. (London: Penguin, 1990), 1:915.

11. Marx is not entirely inattentive to slavery; nonetheless, his account of slavery tends to locate its force in the past and in the margins, particularly with respect to industrial labor in England. See Ken Lawrence, *Karl Marx on American Slavery* (Tougaloo, MS: Sojourner Truth Organization, 1976) and Robin Blackburn, *The Making of New World Slavery: From the Baroque to the Modern, 1492–1800* (London: Verso, 1997), 511–18.

12. A number of theorists have argued, in related terms, that primitive accumulation is ongoing within capitalism. See Silvia Federici, *Caliban and the Witch: Women, the Body and Primitive Accumulation* (New York: Autonomedia; London: Pluto, 2003), and David Harvey, *The New Imperialism* (Oxford: Oxford University Press, 2003), which describes contemporary forms of "accumulation by dispossession" within the global economy.

13. On the relation of sentimentalism, race, and colonialism in the eighteenth century, see Lynn M. Festa, *Sentimental Figures of Empire in Eighteenth-Century Britain and France* (Baltimore: Johns Hopkins University Press, 2006).

14. According to Schmitt, legal "amity lines" defined the space of colonial expansion as beyond the realm of political toleration and mutual respect for territorial sovereignty established by the Treaty of Westphalia; the colonies thus afforded a space for un-

regulated violence, which, in effect, helped to preserve the "sphere of peace and order" established in Europe (Carl Schmitt, *The* Nomos *of the Earth in the International Law of the* Just Publicum Europaeum, trans. G. L. Ulmen [New York: Telos Press, 2003], 97). For further discussion of lines of amity in the eighteenth-century Atlantic world, see Eliga H. Gould, "Zones of Law, Zones of Violence: The Legal Geography of the British Atlantic, circa 1772," *William and Mary Quarterly* 60, no. 3 (2003): 471–510.

15. Historically, notions of "English liberty" develop well before a politics of popular sovereignty, dating (in the popular imagination if not in fact) to those liberties articulated in the Magna Carta. In the period covered by this book, liberty is increasingly associated with modes of popular sovereignty. For the history of the Magna Carta and its relation to English liberty, popular sovereignty, and concepts of the commons, see Peter Linebaugh, *The Magna Carta Manifesto: Liberties and Commons for All* (Berkeley: University of California Press, 2008).

16. On the Royal African Company, see K. G. Davies, *The Royal African Company* (London: Longmans, 1957), and James A. Rawley, *The Transatlantic Slave Trade: A History* (New York: Norton, 1981).

17. The foundational and subsequently much-debated work on the economic relation of Caribbean slavery and British capitalism is Eric Eustace Williams, *Capitalism and Slavery*. For recent contributions to this debate, see Solow and Engerman, eds., *British Capitalism and Caribbean Slavery*; Blackburn, *The Making of New World Slavery, 1492–1800*; Carrington, *The Sugar Industry and the Abolition of the Slave Trade, 1775–1810*; Carole Shammas, "The Revolutionary Impact of European Demand for Tropical Goods," in *The Early Modern Atlantic Economy*, ed. John J. McCusker and Kenneth Morgan (Cambridge: Cambridge University Press, 2000), 163–85; and in a more literary-philosophical vein, Ian Baucom, *Specters of the Atlantic: Finance Capital, Slavery, and the Philosophy of History* (Durham, NC: Duke University Press, 2005). Much of this work does not focus specifically on the changes occasioned in England by the influx of money from imperial endeavor. Kathleen Wilson offers a succinct account of the direct and widespread effects of colonial trade on English culture and politics: "The colonial trade visibly changed English economic and cultural as well as political life, both because of the proliferation of luxury goods in shops and households across the country and because the broad social base of investment in overseas and colonial trade gave the empire an immediacy to those in England that supplemented and reinforced its cultural and political significance" (Wilson, *The Sense of the People: Politics, Culture, and Imperialism in England, 1715–1785* [Cambridge: Cambridge University Press, 1995], 56). See also, more generally, the essays in *A New Imperial History: Culture, Identity, and Modernity in Britain and the Empire, 1660–1840*, ed. Kathleen Wilson (Cambridge: Cambridge University Press, 2004).

18. In speaking to the relation of modern sovereignty and colonialism, I am indebted to the example of Jonathan Elmer's *On Lingering and Being Last: Race and Sovereignty in the New World* (New York: Fordham University Press, 2008), a book that brilliantly illuminates a set of relations between postmonarchical European sovereignty and discourses of racialization in the New World. As Elmer points out, the seeming Eurocentrism of modern sovereignty involves less a disregard for locations outside of Europe/the West than an encrypted dependence on them. See Elmer, *On Lingering*

and Being Last, 2–3, as well as his discussion of arguments in a related vein by Edward Keene in *Beyond the Anarchical Society: Grotius, Colonialism, and World Order in Politics* (Cambridge: Cambridge University Press, 2002); and Antony Anghie in *Imperialism, Sovereignty, and the Making of International Law* (Cambridge: Cambridge University Press, 2005).

19. For a discussion of Leveller proposals concerning the extent of the franchise from 1646 to 1649, see C. B. Macpherson, *The Political Theory of Possessive Individualism: Hobbes to Locke* (Oxford: Clarendon Press, 1962). In 2011, debate over whether prisoners should be allowed to vote was taken up in Parliament and made headlines in the UK; see Bagehot, "Prisoners' Voting Rights: Britain's Mounting Fury Over Sovereignty," *Bagehot's Notebook*, *Economist* (blog), February 10, 2011. Accessed November 30, 2013. www.economist.com/blogs/bagehot/2011/02/prisoners_voting_rights.

20. Dudley Diggs, *A Review of the Observations upon some of his Majesties Late Answers and Expresses* (Oxford: Leonard Lichfield, 1643), 4, also cited by Edmund S. Morgan, *Inventing the People: The Rise of Popular Sovereignty in England and America* (New York: Norton, 1988), 61.

21. Morgan, *Inventing the People*, 49, 58. On the relation between the fiction of the people and the politics of representation in the early United States, see Eric Slauter, *The State as a Work of Art: The Cultural Origins of the Constitution* (Chicago: University of Chicago Press, 2009), and Jason A. Frank, *Constituent Moments: Enacting the People in Postrevolutionary America* (Durham, NC: Duke University Press, 2010).

22. Jack P. Greene, "Introduction: Empire and Liberty," 22.

23. See Jack P. Greene, "Liberty and Slavery: The Transfer of British Liberty to the West Indies, 1627–1865," in *Exclusionary Empire*, 50–76, as well as Larry Daly Gragg, *Englishmen Transplanted: The English Colonization of Barbados, 1627–1660* (Oxford: Oxford University Press, 2003), and Catherine Hall, *Civilising Subjects: Metropole and Colony in the English Imagination, 1830–1867* (Chicago: University of Chicago Press, 2002).

24. See H. Trevor Colbourn, *The Lamp of Experience: Whig History and the Intellectual Origins of the American Revolution* (Chapel Hill: University of North Carolina Press for the Institute of Early American History and Culture, 1965); Bernard Bailyn, *The Ideological Origins of the American Revolution* (Cambridge, MA: Harvard University Press, 1967); and Forrest McDonald, *Novus Ordo Seclorum: The Intellectual Origins of the Constitution* (Lawrence: University Press of Kansas, 1985). On competing discourses of liberty in the British North American colonies, see Elizabeth Mancke, "The Languages of Liberty in British North America, 1607–1776," in *Exclusionary Empire*, 25–49.

25. On the transmutation of a doctrine of Anglo-Saxon liberty into an Atlantic politics of race, see Laura Doyle, *Freedom's Empire: Race and the Rise of the Novel in Atlantic Modernity, 1640–1940* (Durham, NC: Duke University Press, 2008). On the relation between territorialization, deterritorialization, and racialization in the Atlantic colonial world, see Elmer, *On Lingering and Being Last*. For a detailed account of the transmutation of English laws of servitude and civil death into a racializing colonial legal apparatus see Colin Dayan, *The Law Is a White Dog: How Legal Rituals Make and Unmake Persons* (Princeton, NJ: Princeton University Press, 2011).

26. Jack Rakove, "Review of *Exclusionary Empire: English Liberty Overseas, 1600–1900*, edited by Jack P. Greene," *Journal of Interdisciplinary History* 41, no. 3 (2011): 444.

Note that Rakove's comments here summarize claims made concerning English liberty in the essays in the volume he is reviewing and point to what Rakove describes as a lack of attention paid to non-English colonial peoples in these essays.

27. On the uncertain status of the English body in colonial climes, see Joyce E. Chaplin, *Subject Matter: Technology, the Body, and Science on the Anglo-American Frontier, 1500–1676* (Cambridge, MA: Harvard University Press, 2001); and Kathleen Donegan, "'As Dying, yet Behold We Live': Catastrophe and Interiority in Bradford's *Of Plymouth Plantation*," *Early American Literature* 37, no. 1 (2002); 9–37. On geo-humoralism, the development of discourses of race, and the early modern English body, see Mary Floyd-Wilson, *English Ethnicity and Race in Early Modern Drama* (Cambridge: Cambridge University Press, 2003).

28. Edward Long, *The History of Jamaica or, General Survey of the Antient and Modern State of the Island.* . . . 3 vols. (London: T. Lowndes, 1774), 1:9.

29. Long, *History of Jamaica*, 1:11; see also Long, *History of Jamaica*, appendix B, 1:194–213. On the history of English liberty in Ireland, see James Kelly, "'Era of Liberty': The Politics of Civil and Political Rights in Eighteenth-Century Ireland," in *Exclusionary Empire*, 77–111.

30. Discourses of race are not absent from the history of the colonization of Ireland by England; however, as Luke Gibbons argues, race does not operate as a (purportedly) immediate visual index of difference (as was the case with race slavery in the Americas); rather, the Irish were, over time, discursively racialized in terms that equated them with Native American "savages": see Luke Gibbons, "Race against Time: Racial Discourse and Irish History," *Oxford Literary Review* 13, no. 1 (July 1991): 95–117.

31. Hobbes first published *Leviathan, or, the Matter, Form, and Power of a Common-Wealth Ecclesiastical and Civil* in 1651. The frontispiece of the first edition was engraved by the Parisian artist, Abraham Bosse, with consultation from Hobbes, after a drawing by the well-known Czech émigré Wenceslaus Hollar. See Keith Brown, "Thomas Hobbes and the Title-page of 'Leviathan,'" *Philosophy* 55, no. 213 (1980): 410–11.

32. "Theatre, Church Street, Mr. Edgar," *Daily Evening Gazette: And Charleston Tea-Table Companion*, February 18, 1795, 3.

33. According to extant calendars of the London theatre, *Oroonoko* was performed for only a handful of nights in its first season (1695) on the stage. Reports at the time did indicate, however, that the play met with "uncommon success" (*The London Stage: 1660–1800: A Calendar of Plays, Entertainments & Afterpieces.* . . . *Compiled from the Playbills, Newspapers and Theatrical Diaries, Part 1, 1660–1700*, ed. William Van Lennep [Carbondale: Southern Illinois University Press, 1965], 454–55). It is correct to say, nonetheless, that *Oroonoko* was one of the most popular plays of the eighteenth century: Laura J. Rosenthal reports that Southerne "became one of the century's most respected dramatists, largely as a result of his appropriation of *Oroonoko*," which appeared at least once a year from 1695 until 1829 and was one of the "two or three most popular plays of the eighteenth century" ("Owning *Oroonoko*: Behn, Southerne, and the Contingencies of Property," in *Troping Oroonoko from Behn to Bandele*, ed. Susan B. Iwanisziw [Burlington, VT: Ashgate, 2004], 83).

34. "From a correspondent," *City Gazette and Daily Advertiser*, February 27, 1795, 3.

35. *Columbian Herald*, February 17, 1795. Emphasis in the original.

36. *The Daily Evening Gazette: And Charleston Tea-Table Companion*, February 11, 1795.

37. Heather McPherson points out that eighteenth-century audiences in London became increasingly heterogeneous and active as the century progressed, as evident in orchestrated public riots that occurred in the theatre ("Theatrical Riots and Cultural Politics in Eighteenth-Century London," *Eighteenth Century* 43, no. 3 [2002]: 236–52). On theatre riots, see also Vincent J. Liesenfeld, *The Licensing Act of 1737* (Madison: University of Wisconsin Press, 1984) and Helen M. Burke, *Riotous Performances: The Struggle for Hegemony in the Irish Theater, 1712–1784* (Notre Dame, IN: University of Notre Dame Press, 2003).

38. Richard Butsch, *The Making of American Audiences: From Stage to Television, 1750–1990* (Cambridge: Cambridge University Press, 2000), 10.

39. *The Daily Evening Gazette: And Charleston Tea-Table Companion*, February 2, 1795.

40. *The Daily Evening Gazette: And Charleston Tea-Table Companion*, February 2, 1795.

41. *South Carolina Gazette*, July 26, 1773, and August 9, 1773.

42. *City Gazette and Daily Advertiser*, January 27, 1794.

43. *South Carolina Gazette and Timothy and Mason's Daily Advertiser*, April 24, 1797.

44. *Columbia Herald and Patriotic Courier*, April 7, 1785.

45. *South Carolina Gazette and Timothy and Mason's Daily Advertiser*, March 19, 1794.

46. *Columbia Herald and Patriotic Courier*, April 14, 1785.

47. The Charleston Theatre on Broad Street, built by Thomas Wade West and John Bignall, was opened on February 11, 1793. According to Julia Curtis, "The boxes, side and back, accommodated about 1000, or the major portion of the audience, while the pit and gallery could seat up to 400 patrons, if they squeezed together" ("The Architecture and Appearance of the Charleston Theatre: 1793–1833," *Educational Theatre Journal* 23, no. 1 [1971]: 4).

48. Thomas Hobbes, *Man and Citizen: De Homine and De Cive* (Indianapolis: Hackett, 1991), 174.

49. As Malcolm Bull explains (citing Hobbes), "Hobbes . . . us[es] the word multitude to refer to a plurality of individuals in the same place, and the word people to refer to a civil person. However, . . . the people and the multitude are not distinct or opposing forces; they are actually the same individuals: . . . When exercising power, 'the multitude is united into a body politic, and thereby are a people'; but when something is done 'by a people as subjects,' it is, in effect, done 'by many individuals at the same time,' i.e. by a 'multitude'" ("The Limits of Multitude," *New Left Review* [September–October 2005]: 23).

50. Michael Hardt and Antonio Negri are here describing Rousseau (*Multitude: War and Democracy in the Age of Empire* [New York: Penguin, 2004], 242–43), but the description extends to Hobbes as well.

51. Hardt and Negri, *Multitude*, 340. Hardt and Negri have been criticized for the idealism of their account of the radical possibilities of the multitude. For further discussion of Hobbes, Spinoza, and the multitude, see Warren Montag, "Who's Afraid of the Multitude? Between the Individual and the State," *South Atlantic Quarterly* 104, no. 4 (2005): 655–73; Antonio Negri, *The Savage Anomaly: The Power of Spinoza's Metaphysics and Politics* (Minneapolis: University of Minnesota Press, 1991); Étienne Balibar, *Masses, Classes, Ideas: Studies on Politics and Philosophy before and after Marx* (New York: Rout-

ledge, 1994); and Paolo Virno, *A Grammar of the Multitude: For an Analysis of Contemporary Forms of Life* (Los Angeles and Cambridge, MA: Semiotext(e) and MIT Press, 2004).

52. Jacques Rancière, *The Politics of Aesthetics: The Distribution of the Sensible*, trans. Gabriel Rockhill (London: Continuum, 2004), 12. For additional discussion of Rancière, theatre, politics, and aesthetics, see the introduction.

53. Rancière writes: "A dissensus is not a conflict of interests, opinions, or values: it is a division put in the 'common sense' a dispute about what is given, about the frame within which we see something as given; . . . a dissensus [involves] putting two worlds in one and the same world. A political subject, as I understand it, is a capacity for staging such scenes of dissensus" ("Who Is the Subject of the Rights of Man?" *South Atlantic Quarterly* 103, nos. 2–3 [2004]: 304).

54. Bert O. States, *Great Reckonings in Little Rooms: On the Phenomenology of Theater* (Berkeley: University of California Press, 1985), 20.

55. States, *Great Reckonings in Little Rooms*, 20. Note that States is here implicitly citing the work of Peter Handke, who writes "In the theater light is brightness pretending to be other brightness, a chair pretending to a chair and so on" (*Kaspar and Other Plays* [New York: Farrar, Straus, 1969], 10).

56. On the signification of things, themselves, on stage, see Andrew Sofer, *The Stage Life of Props* (Ann Arbor: University of Michigan Press, 2003).

57. See Peter H. Wood, *Black Majority: Negroes in Colonial South Carolina from 1670 through the Stono Rebellion* (New York: Knopf, 1974).

58. See Bernard Edward Powers, *Black Charlestonians: A Social History, 1822–1885* (Fayetteville: University of Arkansas Press, 1994) and further discussion of black publics in Charleston in chapter 4.

59. Whether Edgar would have performed in blackface is difficult to determine: on the one hand, reports such as that by English traveler John Lambert in 1810 indicate that blackface performance was forbidden in Charleston, precisely because of its potentially politically mobilizing force. However, other evidence indicates that performers did wear blackface, particularly at the close of the eighteenth century; moreover, Edgar, whose performance training was British, might have adopted the English custom of performing Oroonoko in blackface. For further discussion see chapter 4.

60. As Diana Taylor suggests, "The frictions between plot and character (on the level of narrative) and embodiment (social actors) make for some of the most remarkable instances of parody and resistance in performance traditions in the Americas" (*The Archive and the Repertoire: Performing Cultural Memory in the Americas* [Durham, NC: Duke University Press, 2003], 30). Not only does this friction exist in terms of what occurs on the stage (embodied actor/narrative), but it also extends to the audience (embodied people/sovereign public).

61. For an insightful discussion of *The Recruiting Officer*'s career on colonial American stages, see Jason Shaffer, *Performing Patriotism: National Identity in the Colonial and Revolutionary American Theater* (Philadelphia: University of Pennsylvania Press, 2007), 72–78.

62. For further discussion of racial representation and *The Padlock*, see Julie A. Carlson, "New Lows in Eighteenth-Century Theater: The Rise of Mungo," *European Romantic Review* 18, no. 2 (2007): 139–47, and Monica L. Miller, *Slaves to Fashion: Black*

Dandyism and the Styling of Black Diasporic Identity (Durham, NC: Duke University Press, 2009), 27–76, as well as chapter 5.

63. Richard Cumberland, *The West Indian: A Comedy: As It Is Performed at the Theatre Royal in Drury-Lane* (London: W. Griffin, 1771), 5.

64. See Julie A. Carlson, "Race and Profit in English Theatre," in *The Cambridge Companion to British Theatre, 1730–1830*, ed. Jane Moody and Daniel O'Quinn (Cambridge: Cambridge University Press, 2007), 175. In related terms, Jeffrey N. Cox writes that "a regular London theatergoer would have seen depictions of African characters or of slavery during perhaps every season of the eighteenth and early nineteenth century" ("Introduction," in *Slavery, Abolition, and Emancipation: Writings in the British Romantic Period. Vol. 5 Drama*, ed. Jeffrey N. Cox [London: Pickering and Chatto, 1999], ix). Jane Moody comments that toward the end of the eighteenth century, "hit plays such as Cumberland's *The West Indian*, Inchbald's *Such Things Are* and Sheridan's *The School for Scandal* represented the most valuable stock for provincial [British theatre] managers. It is notable that all these dramas explore characters who migrate from the colonies to Britain or vice versa" ("Dictating to the Empire: Performance and Theatrical Geography in Eighteenth-Century Britain," in *The Cambridge Companion to British Theatre, 1730–1830*, ed. Jane Moody and Daniel O'Quinn [Cambridge: Cambridge University Press, 2007], 31).

65. Kathleen Wilson, "Empire of Virtue: The Imperial Project and Hanoverian Culture," in *An Imperial State at War: Britain from 1689 to 1815*, ed. Lawrence Stone (London: Routledge, 1994), 143.

66. In addition to the works cited above, important work on the theatrical representation of empire on the British stage includes that of Laura Brown, *Ends of Empire: Women and Ideology in Early Eighteenth-Century English Literature* (Ithaca, NY: Cornell University Press, 1993); Mita Choudhury, *Interculturalism and Resistance in the London Theater, 1660–1800: Identity, Performance, Empire* (Lewisburg, PA: Bucknell University Press, 2000); Bridget Orr, *Empire on the English Stage, 1660–1714* (Cambridge: Cambridge University Press, 2001); Daniel O'Quinn, *Staging Governance: Theatrical Imperialism in London, 1770–1800* (Baltimore: Johns Hopkins University Press, 2005); David Worrall, *Harlequin Empire: Race, Ethnicity and the Drama of the Popular Enlightenment* (London: Pickering and Chatto, 2007); and Michael Ragussis, *Theatrical Nation: Jews and Other Outlandish Englishmen in Georgian Britain* (Philadelphia: University of Pennsylvania Press, 2010). My understanding of theatre and empire is indebted to this scholarship, and I draw implicitly as well as explicitly on these important titles in what follows.

67. While the vast majority of materials that treat the development of the public sphere in England concern print publication and/or the coffeehouse, some literary critics and historians do consider the theatre integral to the development of the public sphere. For useful theoretical considerations, see Jeffrey C. Alexander, "Cultural Pragmatics: Social Performance between Ritual and Strategy," *Sociological Theory* 22, no. 4 (2004): 527–73. For consideration of the public sphere and theatre in the early modern period, see Douglas Bruster, *Shakespeare and the Question of Culture: Early Modern Literature and the Cultural Turn* (New York: Palgrave Macmillan, 2003); Jeffrey S. Doty, "Shakespeare's *Richard II*, 'Popularity,' and the Early Modern Public Sphere," *Shakespeare Quarterly* 61, no. 2 (2010): 183–205; Paula Backscheider, *Spectacular Poli-*

tics: Theatrical Power and Mass Culture in Early Modern England (Baltimore: Johns Hopkins University Press, 1993); and Paul Edward Yachnin, "Hamlet and the Social Thing in Early Modern Europe," in *Making Publics in Early Modern Europe: People, Things, Forms of Knowledge*, ed. Bronwen Wilson and Paul Edward Yachnin (New York: Routledge, 2010), 81–95. In relation to eighteenth-century England, see John O'Brien, *Harlequin Britain: Pantomime and Entertainment, 1690–1760* (Baltimore: Johns Hopkins University Press, 2004); O'Quinn, *Staging Governance*; and David Worrall, *Theatric Revolution: Drama, Censorship and Romantic Period Subcultures 1773–1832* (Oxford: Oxford University Press, 2006). In relation to Europe more broadly, see James Van Horn Melton, *The Rise of the Public in Enlightenment Europe* (Cambridge: Cambridge University Press, 2001). Two considerations of theatre and the public sphere in France focus in particular on issues of democratization and popular sovereignty: Jeffrey S. Ravel, "La Reine Boit! Print, Performance, and Theater Publics in France, 1724–1725," *Eighteenth-Century Studies* 29, no. 4 (1996): 391–411; and Susan Maslan, *Revolutionary Acts: Theater, Democracy, and the French Revolution* (Baltimore: Johns Hopkins University Press, 2005). Finally, Loren Kruger, in *The National Stage: Theatre and Cultural Legitimation in England, France and America* (Chicago: University of Chicago Press, 1992), considers the Habermasian dimensions of national theatre in England, France, and the United States in the eighteenth through twentieth centuries.

68. "Contemporary Comment," January 25, 1707, cited in *The London Stage, 1660–1800, Part 2, 1700–1729*, ed. Emmett L. Avery, 2 vols. (Carbondale: Southern Illinois University Press, 1960), 2:338.

69. An account of this incident appears in *Gentleman's Magazine* 19 (February 1, 1749): 89–90. For additional discussion, see Wylie Sypher, "The African Prince in London," *Journal of the History of Ideas* 2, no. 2 (1941): 237–47, and *Guinea's Captive Kings: British Anti-slavery Literature of the XVIIIth Century* (Chapel Hill: University of North Carolina Press, 1942), 166–67; Gretchen Gerzina, *Black London: Life before Emancipation* (New Brunswick, NJ: Rutgers University Press, 1995), 11–14; David Brion Davis, *The Problem of Slavery in Western Culture* (New York: Oxford University Press, 1988), 472–82; and Srinivas Aravamudan, *Tropicopolitans: Colonialism and Agency, 1688–1804* (Durham, NC: Duke University Press, 1999), 250–53.

70. On the non-English-speaking population, and the non-English press in early America, see Colleen Glenney Boggs, *Transnationalism and American Literature: Literary Translation 1773–1892* (New York: Routledge, 2007).

71. As Sandra M. Gustafson argues, "Discussions of the public sphere in American literary scholarship commonly overemphasize the role that print plays in defining public discourse, neglecting the persistent importance of verbal arts such as oratory, and at the same time assuming a sharp divide between printed texts and oral performances" ("American Literature and the Public Sphere," *American Literary History* 20, no. 3 [2008]: 465). For a useful collection of essays tracing relations between print and performance in early America, see Sandra M. Gustafson and Caroline F. Sloat, eds., *Cultural Narratives: Textuality and Performance in American Culture before 1900* (Notre Dame, IN: University of Notre Dame Press, 2010).

72. Thus, for instance, when a new theatre was under construction in Charleston in 1792, the newspaper fawningly noted the resemblance of the architecture to that of

the London theatre: "The frontispiece, balconies, and stage doors, will be similar to those of the Opera House, London. The theatre is to be built under the immediate direction of Mr. West. When it is considered, that this gentleman has had near thirty years experience in many of the first theatres in England, and that he is to be assisted by artists of the first class . . . we may expect a theatre in a style of elegance and novelty" (*Charleston Gazette and Daily Advertiser*, August 14, 1792).

73. On Anglophilia in the United States, see Elisa Tamarkin, *Anglophilia: Deference, Devotion, and Antebellum America* (Chicago: University of Chicago Press, 2008); and Leonard Tennenhouse, *The Importance of Feeling English: American Literature and the British Diaspora, 1750–1850* (Princeton, NJ: Princeton University Press, 2007). On the predominance of British scripts in eighteenth-century North American theatre, see Jeffrey H. Richards, *Drama, Theatre, and Identity in the American New Republic* (Cambridge: Cambridge University Press, 2005); and Shaffer, *Performing Patriotism.*

74. Trish Loughran, *The Republic in Print: Print Culture in the Age of U.S. Nation Building, 1770–1870* (New York: Columbia University Press, 2007), xvii–xix.

75. Christina Elizabeth Sharpe, *Monstrous Intimacies: Making Post-slavery Subjects* (Durham, NC: Duke University Press, 2010), 3.

CHAPTER 2: LONDON

1. Charles I, *King Charles His Speech Made upon the Scaffold at Whitehall Gate Immediately before His Execution, on Tuesday the 30. Of Jan. 1648. With a Relation of the Manner of His Going to Execution. Published by Spetiall Authority* (London: Peter Cole, 1649), 6.

2. On the demise of the concept of sacred kingship in relation to the execution of Charles I as well as the inability of Charles II to revivify it, see Robert Zaller, "Breaking the Vessels: The Desacralization of Monarchy in Early Modern England," *Sixteenth Century Journal* 29, no. 3 (1998): 757–78.

3. January 1649, *Journal of the House of Commons*, vol. 6: 1648–1651 (1802): 125–26.

4. See Ernst Hartwig Kantorowicz, *The King's Two Bodies: A Study in Mediaeval Political Theology* (Princeton, NJ: Princeton University Press, 1957). For discussion of the advent of "the people's two bodies" in the wake of the English Civil War, see Edmund S. Morgan, *Inventing the People: The Rise of Popular Sovereignty in England and America* (New York: Norton, 1988), 78–93.

5. Stephen Orgel, "The Poetics of Spectacle," *New Literary History* 2, no. 3 (1971): 367. See also the essays in David Lindely, ed., *The Court Masque* (Manchester, UK: Manchester University Press, 1984); David M. Bevington and Peter Holbrook, *The Politics of the Stuart Court Masque* (Cambridge: Cambridge University Press, 1998); and Martin Butler, *The Stuart Court Masque and Political Culture* (Cambridge: Cambridge University Press, 2008). Butler takes issue with Orgel's claims regarding the "absolute primacy" of the perspectival position of the king in the court masque, proposing a more flexible and heterogeneous account of the politics of the masque that nonetheless remains centered around the staging of monarchical power: "Masques stamped the king's authority onto his court, but the terms of that authority were constantly under negotiation" (5).

6. Orgel, "The Poetics of Spectacle," 370.

7. With the term "public theatre," I refer to commercial theatre that was not commanded by the court, but open to the public, including theatre performed at venues

such as the Globe Theatre and Blackfriars Theatre. These public theatres were closed during the Interregnum, save when D'Avenant debuted a small number of plays, as described below, at public locations. Public theater companies did, on occasion, perform for the court: in this regard see John Astington, *English Court Theatre 1558–1642* (Cambridge: Cambridge University Press, 1999); and Andrew Gurr, *The Shakespearean Stage, 1574–1642*, 4th ed. (Cambridge: Cambridge University Press, 2008). On the public, commercial stage in the early modern period, see Jean E. Howard, *Theater of a City: The Places of London Comedy, 1598–1642* (Philadelphia: University of Pennsylvania Press, 2007); and Steven Mullaney, *The Place of the Stage: License, Play, and Power in Renaissance England* (Chicago: University of Chicago Press, 1988).

8. On D'Avenant's biography, see Arthur Hobart Nethercot, *Sir William D'avenant, Poet Laureate and Playwright-Manager* (Chicago: University of Chicago Press, 1938); Mary Edmond, *Rare Sir William Davenant: Poet Laureate, Playwright, Civil War General, Restoration Theatre Manager* (Manchester, UK: Manchester University Press, 1987); and Alfred Harbage, *Sir William Davenant, Poet Venturer, 1606–1668* (New York: Octagon Books, 1971). For discussion of Milton's intervention on D'Avenant's behalf, see Barbara Kiefer Lewalski, *The Life of John Milton: A Critical Biography* (Malden, MA: Blackwell, 2000), 288, 667–68.

9. See Janet Clare, *Drama of the English Republic, 1649–60* (Manchester, UK: Manchester University Press, 2002), 34–35.

10. William D'Avenant, *Proposition*, in James R. Jacob and Timothy Raylor, "Opera and Obedience: Thomas Hobbes and *A Proposition for Advancement of Moralitie* by Sir William Davenant," *Seventeenth Century* 6, no. 1 (1991): 242–43.

11. See Michel Foucault, *Discipline and Punish: The Birth of the Prison*, trans. Alan Sheridan, 2nd ed. (New York: Vintage Books, 1995). For an analysis of the relation between late eighteenth-century British theatre and the workings of Foucauldian governmentality, see Daniel O'Quinn, *Staging Governance: Theatrical Imperialism in London, 1770–1800* (Baltimore: Johns Hopkins University Press, 2005).

12. Jacob and Raylor, "Opera and Obedience," 222. See also Nigel Smith, *Literature and Revolution in England, 1640–1660* (New Haven, CT: Yale University Press, 1994): "The [*Proposition*] . . . represents the most wholesale and undiluted influence of *Leviathan*" (87).

13. Jacob and Raylor, "Opera and Obedience," 277.

14. As Michel Foucault succinctly states: for Hobbes, "sovereignty is always shaped from below, and by those who are afraid" (*Society Must Be Defended: Lectures at the Collège De France, 1975–76*, ed. Mauro Bertani and Alessandro Fontana, trans. David Macey [New York: Picador, 2003], 96).

15. Christopher Pye, "The Sovereign, the Theater, and the Kingdome of Darknesse: Hobbes and the Spectacle of Power," *Representations* 8 (1984): 86. Pye is here summarizing the claims of Hannah Fenichel Pitkin (*The Concept of Representation* [Berkeley: University of California Press, 1967]) regarding Hobbes.

16. D'Avenant, *Proposition*, 245.

17. D'Avenant, *Proposition*, 249.

18. See Steven C. A. Pincus, *Protestantism and Patriotism: Ideologies and the Making of English Foreign Policy, 1650–1668* (Cambridge: Cambridge University Press, 1996).

19. The letter from D'Avenant to Thurloe is reprinted in C. H. Firth, "Sir William Davenant and the Revival of Drama during the Protectorate," *English Historical Review* 18, no. 70 (1903): 319–21.

20. See Oliver Cromwell, *A Declaration of His Highness, Inviting the People of* England *and* Wales *to a Day of Solemn Fasting and Humiliation*, ed. Council of State England and Wales (London: Henry Hills and John Field, 1655). For discussion of the providential nature of Cromwell's Western Design, see Karen Ordahl Kupperman, "Errand to the Indies: Puritan Colonization from Providence Island through the Western Design," *William and Mary Quarterly* 45, no. 1 (1988): 70–99; David Armitage, "The Cromwellian Protectorate and the Languages of Empire," *Historical Journal* 35, no. 3 (1992): 531–55; and Richard Frohock, "Sir William Davenant's American Operas," *Modern Language Review* 96, no. 2 (2001): 323–33.

21. On the Black Legend, see Margaret Rich Greer, Walter Mignolo, and Maureen Quilligan, eds., *Rereading the Black Legend: The Discourses of Religious and Racial Difference in the Renaissance Empires* (Chicago: University of Chicago Press, 2007).

22. Steven C. A. Pincus, "England and the World in the 1650s," in *Revolution and Restoration: England in the 1650s*, ed. John Morrill (London: Collins and Brown, 1992), 147.

23. My citations are from the 1738 document attributed to Milton: *A Manifesto of the Lord Protector of the Commonwealth of England . . . Written in Latin by John Milton, and First Printed in 1655, Now Translated into English* (London: A. Millar, at Buchanan's Head, over against St. Clement's Church in the Strand, 1738). This manifesto is also included in vol. 13 of *The Works of John Milton*, ed. Frank Allen Patterson and Bruce Rogers (New York: Columbia University Press, 1937): Patterson and Rogers thus attribute the document to Milton. However, the editor of the Yale edition of Milton's work argues that there is no evidence to support this claim: see *Complete Prose Works of John Milton*, ed. Don Marion Wolfe (New Haven, CT: Yale University Press, 1953). For discussion of the publication history of the *Declaration*, see Elizabeth Sauer, "Toleration and Translation: The Case of Las Casas, Phillips, and Milton," *Philological Quarterly* 85, no. 3/4 (2006): 271–91; and John T. Shawcross, "John Milton and His Spanish and Portuguese Presence," *Milton Quarterly* 32, no. 2 (1998): 41–52.

24. Sauer, "Toleration and Translation," 280.

25. The logic of sovereignty based on territorial occupation (Westphalian sovereignty) is not identical to that of popular sovereignty: many a Westphalian territory was ruled by a monarch. It is significant, however, that both Westphalian sovereignty and popular sovereignty are forms of nondivine sovereignty: both authorize sovereignty from below rather than above. This formulation is not dispositive of any causal relation between the two; in other words, Westphalian sovereignty does not necessarily generate popular sovereignty. However, it is the case that shifts in international/global understandings of sovereignty bear directly on the way in which intrastate sovereignty is understood and represented, and this fact has gone largely unrecognized in accounts of nationalism and European imperialism in the eighteenth century.

26. Carl Schmitt, *The* Nomos *of the Earth in the International Law of the* Jus Publicum Europaeum, trans. G. L. Ulmen (New York: Telos Press, 2003), 140.

27. The term "Westphalian sovereignty" has had remarkable staying power and, indeed, has experienced something of a renaissance recently in political theory insofar

as it has become a shorthand for a doctrine of nonintervention across state borders that is a key principle of contemporary United Nations policy and international law. Critics have argued, however, that the actual peace of Westphalia was not as decisive for the implementation of policies of toleration and nonintervention as it has subsequently been credited with. For a historical critique of Westphalian sovereignty, see Andreas Osiander, "Sovereignty, International Relations, and the Westphalian Myth," *International Organization* 55, no. 2 (2001): 251–87; and Edward Keene, *Beyond the Anarchical Society: Grotius, Colonialism and Order in World Politics* (Cambridge: Cambridge University Press, 2002).

28. Schmitt's work, though marked as controversial given his support of the Nazi Party in Germany, has received renewed attention in recent years because of his theorization of global sovereignty. Schmitt's work is useful for the study of the early Atlantic world insofar as it connects questions of sovereignty in Europe with imperial policy in the New World. For critiques of Schmitt's account of a New World that is "beyond the line" of amity, see the articles included in the special issue of *South Atlantic Quarterly* devoted to Schmitt: *SAQ* 104, no. 2 (spring 2005), ed. William Rasch.

29. Armitage, "The Cromwellian Protectorate and the Languages of Empire," 535. Armitage rightly emphasizes that English imperialism has foundational roots in Cromwell's republicanism and that "this republican moment must be recalled from the fit of absence of mind in which historians have lost it; . . . the competitive claims of republics and empires are central to early-modern political discourse" (533).

30. On English justifications for usurping land from Native Americans in the Americas, see Anthony Pagden, *Lords of All the World: Ideologies of Empire in Spain, Britain and France c. 1500–c. 1850* (New Haven, CT: Yale University Press, 1995); and Patricia Seed, *Ceremonies of Possession in Europe's Conquest of the New World, 1492–1640* (New York: Cambridge University Press, 1995).

31. D'Avenant's masque was the third of the four dramas that he staged with state approval between the years 1656 and 1659. However, Janet Clare (*Drama of the English Republic*) suggests that it may have been the first of the four masques D'Avenant wrote: the significance of the New World theme is indicated in D'Avenant's letter to Thurloe, which explicitly states that staging the cruelty of Spaniards to the Indians before an English public is a significant reason for opening a public theatre. Further evidence of the centrality of the Spaniards' treatment of the Indians to D'Avenant's Interregnum theatre appears in a letter written on D'Avenant's behalf by the poet Abraham Cowley: this document reports that D'Avenant had originally planned to include two topics in the staged dialogue, *First Days Entertainment*, that appeared in 1656—a dialogue debating the utility of the theatre for moral instruction of the public, and a dialogue between Spaniards and Native Americans "for and against the right of the Spaniards to the West Indies" (letter from Abraham Cowley to an unnamed addressee, dated April 3, 1656, cited from a private collection by Eric Walter White in *A History of English Opera* [London: Faber and Faber, 1983], 66). Only the first of these two dialogues appeared on stage, but the letter offers intriguing evidence that D'Avenant imagined the two topics to be closely related to one another.

32. On the political import of D'Avenant's *Cruelty of the Spaniards in Peru*, see Clare, *Drama of the English Republic*, 32; Susan Wiseman, "History Digested: Opera

and Colonialism in the 1650s," in *Literature and the English Civil War*, ed. Thomas F. Healy and Jonathan Sawday (Cambridge: Cambridge University Press, 1990), 197, 202; and Frohock, "Sir William Davenant's American Operas." Both Frohock and Clare note that D'Avenant's play eschews the providentialism that has been associated with Cromwell's Western Design. As I argue above, however, Cromwell's *Declaration* makes an argument for English sovereignty in the New World that does not rely on providentialism—namely, an argument justifying territorial sovereignty on the basis of occupation and consent. It is the latter argument that emerges with striking clarity in D'Avenant's masque.

33. See Leslie Hotson, *The Commonwealth and Restoration Stage* (Cambridge, MA: Harvard University Press, 1928), 156; and Wiseman, "History Digested: Opera and Colonialism," 195.

34. Extant drawings of the set design by John Webb have led to a good deal of scholarly commentary on the production and its use of scenery: see Richard Southern, *Changeable Scenery: Its Origin and Development in the British Theatre* (London: Faber and Faber, 1952); Hotson, *The Commonwealth and Restoration Stage*; Peter Holland, *The Ornament of Action: Text and Performance in Restoration Comedy* (Cambridge: Cambridge University Press, 1979); White, *A History of English Opera*; and Clare, *Drama of the English Republic*.

35. William D'Avenant, *The Cruelty of the Spaniards in Peru*, in Clare, *Drama of the English Republic, 1649–60*, 241. All citations are to Janet Clare's edition of the 1658 quarto text (in *Drama of the English Republic*, 241–61), which she has collated with the later folio edition that appeared in D'Avenant's *Collected Works* in 1673. In the latter edition, *The Cruelty of the Spaniards of Peru* appears as the fourth act of a longer work, *A Playhouse to Be Let*.

36. Julie Stone Peters, *Theatre of the Book, 1480–1880: Print, Text, and Performance in Europe* (Oxford: Oxford University Press, 2000), 187.

37. William D'Avenant, *Poem, to the King's Most Sacred Majesty* (London: Henry Herringman, 1663), 26.

38. Lisa Hajjar, "Does Torture Work? A Sociolegal Assessment of the Practice in Historical and Global Perspective," *Annual Review of Law and Social Science* 5, no. 1 (2009): 319.

39. Paul W. Kahn, *Sacred Violence: Torture, Terror, and Sovereignty* (Ann Arbor: University of Michigan Press, 2008), 79.

40. See Talal Asad, "On Torture, or Cruel, Inhuman, and Degrading Treatment," *Social Research* 63, no. 4 (December 1, 1996): 1081–109.

41. *A Memento for Holland or a True and Exact History of the Most Villainous and Barbarous Cruelties Used on the English Merchants Residing at Amboyna in the East-Indies . . .* Thomason Tracts / 189:E.1475[1] (London: Printed by James Moxon, 1653), 9. For discussion of the Amboyna incident in relation to the history of Dutch and English imperialism, see Alison Games, "Anglo-Dutch Connections and Overseas Enterprises: A Global Perspective on Lion Gardiner's World," *Early American Studies* 9, no. 2 (2011): 435–61.

42. The theatrical language is reinforced within the text of the pamphlet as well: "For the better perfecting of this Diabolical Plot, [the Dutch] supplied the Indians

with Arms and Ammunition, which were dispersed in all their habitations, they having a Ship sent them on purpose from Holland, the Fountain of Treacheries, *with all necessary tools for the acting of a second Amboyna Tragedy*" (*The Second Part of the Tragedy of Amboyna: Or, a True Relation of a Most Bloody, Treacherous, and Cruel Design of the Dutch in the New-Netherlands in America. . . .* Thomason Tracts / 109:E.710[7] [London: Thomas Matthews, 1653], 5, emphasis added). My reading of this material has been informed by Kristina Bross's insightful reading of the 1653 pamphlet: her unpublished essay, "A More Horrid Reception," is part of a forthcoming book on violence and empire in the seventeenth century.

43. Carla Gardina Pestana traces the relation between accounts of Amboyna and the Black Legend, concluding that religious discourse remains a significant strain of the argument, and pointing out that the English accuse the Dutch of irreligion rather than popery (as is the case with the Spanish): "the case in favor of [England] seizing the colony of New Netherland relied only lightly on the alleged English ownership of that region and focused instead on flaws in the Dutch character. Their penchant for cruelty, their unscrupulous acts in pursuit of profit, and their religious faults—whether their Calvinism, their wanton permissiveness, or their irreligion—all contributed to the justification for English aggression" ("Cruelty and Religious Justifications for Conquest in the Mid-Seventeenth-Century English Atlantic," in *Empires of God: Religious Encounters in the Early Modern Atlantic*, ed. Linda Gregerson and Susan Juster [Philadelphia: University of Pennsylvania Press, 2011], 54). Pestana is certainly correct that religion does not disappear from accounts of English imperial justification; however, the overarching logic of Protestant against Catholic does not hold against the Dutch (as Pincus points out in "England and the World in the 1650s"). Accordingly, I find it significant that new arguments justifying imperialism that concern cruelty, sympathy, consent, threatened nationalism, and torture gain ground at precisely this moment.

44. Donald Pease's account of the workings of state fantasy are germane here. Following Jacqueline Rose (*States of Fantasy* [Oxford: Clarendon Press, 1995]) Pease argues that the disembodiment of the state in a postmonarchical era renders the state a fantasy. Consent to the state by the citizenry, according to Pease, thereafter takes shape as the alignment of personal desire and state fantasy: "Successfully produced state fantasies effect [the relationship of subject and state] by inducing citizens to want the national order they already have. . . . A state fantasy becomes symbolically effective when it produces a relation with the order it legislates that makes it seem an enactment of the will of the individual national subject rather than an imposition of the state" (*The New American Exceptionalism* [Minneapolis: University of Minnesota Press, 2009], 4–5). The consent of audience members in the Cockpit Theatre partakes of just such a nationalized fantasy structure, insofar as it endows them with the fantasmatic citizenship to which they are already subjected.

45. Jacob and Raylor, "Opera and Obedience," 224.

46. A. Zaitchik, "Hobbes's Reply to the Fool: The Problem of Consent and Obligation," *Political Theory* 10, no. 2 (1982): 256–57.

47. For a related discussion of Hobbes and theatre, see Richard Kroll, "Instituting Empiricism: Hobbes's *Leviathan* and Dryden's *Marriage à la Mode*," in *Cultural Read-*

ings of *Restoration and Eighteenth-Century English Theater*, ed. Douglas J. Canfield and Deborah Payne Fisk (Athens: University of Georgia Press, 1995), 39–66.

48. Paula Backscheider, *Spectacular Politics: Theatrical Power and Mass Culture in Early Modern England* (Baltimore: Johns Hopkins University Press, 1993), 64.

49. Lake and Pincus demonstrate that political appeals by court figures for public approval shifted from being understood as "dangerously seditious appeal[s] to the people inimical to good order" in the Elizabethan period, to becoming "regular features of political communication" in the period of the English Civil War ("Rethinking the Public Sphere in Early Modern England," *Journal of British Studies* 45, no. 2 [2006]: 277, 280). On the evolution of "popularity" as a political force, see also Thomas Cogswell, Richard Cust, and Peter Lake, eds., *Politics, Religion and Popularity in Early Stuart Britain: Essays in Honour of Conrad Russell* (Cambridge: Cambridge University Press, 2002); and Joad Raymond, "Describing Popularity in Early Modern England," *Huntington Library Quarterly* 67, no. 1 (2004): 101–29. On theatre and popular opinion, see Jeffrey S. Doty, "Shakespeare's *Richard II*, 'Popularity,' and the Early Modern Public Sphere," *Shakespeare Quarterly* 61, no. 2 (2010): 183–205.

50. Jeffrey C. Alexander writes, "The ability to understand the most elementary contours of a performance depends on an audience knowing already, without thinking about it, the categories within which actors behave" ("Cultural Pragmatics: Social Performance Between Ritual and Strategy," *Sociological Theory* 22, no. 4 [2004]: 550).

51. Erving Goffman, *Frame Analysis: An Essay on the Organization of Experience* (Cambridge, MA: Harvard University Press, 1974), 130, 131.

52. D'Avenant, *Proposal*, 244.

53. D'Avenant, *Proposal*, 244.

54. As Bronwen Wilson and Paul Edward Yachnin argue, the significance of the public gathered at the early modern theatre had less to do with the nature of debate that occurred there than with the effect of novel forms of association: locations such as the theatre saw "the active creation of new forms of association that allowed people to connect with others in ways not rooted in family, rank, or vocation, but rather founded in voluntary groupings built on the shared interests, tastes, commitments, and desires of individuals" (Introduction to *Making Publics in Early Modern Europe: People, Things, Forms of Knowledge*, ed. Bronwen Wilson and Paul Edward Yachnin [New York: Routledge, 2010], 1). Wilson and Yachnin conclude that some important modes of "public formation [do] not engage with politics at the level of ideology or action but rather achieve [their] sociopolitical effects by way of changing available and normative forms of speech, practice, and association" (7).

55. Paula Backscheider, *Spectacular Politics*, 5.

56. Susan J. Owen, *Restoration Theatre and Crisis* (Oxford: Clarendon Press, 1996), 11–12, 15; emphasis added.

57. Jonathan Sawday, "Re-writing a Revolution: History, Symbol, and Text in the Restoration," *Seventeenth Century* 7, no. 2 (1992): 171–72.

58. Nancy Klein Maguire, *Regicide and Restoration: English Tragicomedy, 1660–1671* (Cambridge: Cambridge University Press, 1992), 7.

59. Jacques Rancière, "Who Is the Subject of the Rights of Man?" *South Atlantic Quarterly* 103, nos. 2–3 (2004): 304.

60. Odai Johnson, *Rehearsing the Revolution: Radical Performance, Radical Politics in the English Restoration* (Newark: University of Delaware Press, 2000), 15.

61. Thomas Babington Macaulay, *The History of England from the Accession of James II*, 5 vols. (New York: Harper, 1856), 1:118.

62. John Ogilvie and Charles Annandale, *The Imperial Dictionary of the English Language: A Complete Encyclopedic Lexicon, Literary, Scientific, and Technological*, new ed., 4 vols. (London: Blackie and Son, 1883), 3:187.

63. For discussion of the significance of public opinion to the Glorious Revolution, see Tim Harris, *London Crowds in the Reign of Charles II: Propaganda and Politics from the Restoration until the Exclusion Crisis* (Cambridge: Cambridge University Press, 1987); Mark Knights, *Politics and Opinion in the Exclusion Crisis, 1678–1681* (Cambridge: Cambridge University Press, 1994); and Steven C. A. Pincus, *1688: The First Modern Revolution* (New Haven, CT: Yale University Press, 2009).

64. See Dougald MacMillan, "The Sources of Dryden's *The Indian Emperour*," *Huntington Library Quarterly* 13 (1950): 355–70.

65. Robert Markley, "Violence and Profits on the Restoration Stage: Trade, Nationalism, and Insecurity in Dryden's *Amboyna*," *Eighteenth-Century Life* 22, no. 1 (1998): 8.

66. Laura Brown, "Dryden and the Imperial Imagination," in *The Cambridge Companion to John Dryden*, ed. Steven N. Zwicker (Cambridge: Cambridge University Press, 2004), 65. For discussion of the imperial politics of *Annus Mirabilis* see also Michael McKeon, *Politics and Poetry in Restoration England: The Case of Dryden's* Annus Mirabilis (Cambridge, MA: Harvard University Press, 1975).

67. Colin Visser, "John Dryden's *Amboyna* at Lincoln's Inn Fields, 1673," *Restoration and 18th-Century Theatre Research* 15, no. 1 (1976): 1–11. Notably, as Ayanna Thompson points out, moveable scenery itself assisted in making possible the mechanism of torture on the Restoration stage: "the stage rack, or strappado, only became possible with the invention of moveable set pieces" (*Performing Race and Torture on the Early Modern Stage* [New York: Routledge, 2008], 29).

68. Blair Hoxby, *Mammon's Music: Literature and Economics in the Age of Milton* (New Haven, CT: Yale University Press, 2002), 187–88.

69. January 1649, *Journal of the House of Commons*, vol. 6: 1648–1651 (1802): 125–26.

CHAPTER 3: TRANSPORTATION

1. On Behn's biography, see Janet M. Todd, *The Secret Life of Aphra Behn* (New Brunswick, NJ: Rutgers University Press, 1997).

2. Aphra Behn, *Oroonoko*, ed. Janet M. Todd (London: Penguin, 2003), 10. According to Todd's annotation of the novel, "The first performance [of Dryden's *The Indian Queen*] (before January 25, 1664) predates Behn's probable return from Surinam, but she may have provided feathers to adorn the play's titular villainess in a revival; one is recorded in 1668. Costumes and scenery from *The Indian Queen* were recycled in its sequel, Dryden's *The Indian Emperor* (1665)" (82).

3. Bridget Orr argues that the torture of Oroonoko in Southerne's play serves to visually cite Dryden's staging of Montezuma's torture on the rack (*Empire on the English Stage, 1660–1714* [Cambridge: Cambridge University Press, 2001], 276).

4. See John Donoghue, "'Out of the Land of Bondage': The English Revolution and the Atlantic Origins of Abolition," *American Historical Review* 115, no. 4 (2010): 958–60. On sugar cultivation in Barbados, see Richard S. Dunn, *Sugar and Slaves: The Rise of the Planter Class in the English West Indies, 1624–1713* (Chapel Hill: University of North Carolina Press for the Institute of Early American History and Culture, 1972); and Richard B. Sheridan, *Sugar and Slavery: An Economic History of the British West Indies, 1623–1775* (Baltimore: Johns Hopkins University Press, 1974).

5. Carla Gardina Pestana, *The English Atlantic in an Age of Revolution, 1640–1661* (Cambridge, MA: Harvard University Press, 2004), 187, 209.

6. Marcellus Rivers, *Englands Slavery, or Barbados Merchandize.* . . . Thomason Tracts / 228:E.1833[3] (London, 1659), 16.

7. See Donoghue, "'Out of the Land of Bondage,'" 950. David Eltis further notes that much labor was coerced, in various ways, in the early seventeenth century: "labour in seventeenth-century England was not 'free' in the sense which it was to become. It is more useful to regard slave and non-slave labour as part of a continuum than as polar opposites" ("Labour and Coercion in the English Atlantic World from the Seventeenth to the Early Twentieth Century," in *The Slavery Reader*, ed. Gad J. Heuman and James Walvin [London: Routledge, 2003], 58).

8. See Hilary McD. Beckles and Andrew Downes, "The Economics of Transition to the Black Labour System in Barbados, 1630–1680," in *Caribbean Slavery in the Atlantic World*, ed. Hilary McD. Beckles and Verene Shepherd (Kingston, Jamaica: Ian Randle, 2000), 239–52.

9. "An act for the better ordering and governing of Negroes," (1661) reprinted in *Slavery*, ed. Stanley L. Engerman, Seymour Drescher, and Robert L. Paquette (Oxford: Oxford University Press, 2001), 105. On the Barbados law and its relation to Jamaican slave law, see David Barry Gaspar, "'Rigid and Inclement': Origins of the Jamaican Slave Laws of the Seventeenth Century," in *The Many Legalities of Early America*, ed. Christopher L. Tomlins and Bruce H. Mann (Chapel Hill: University of North Carolina Press for the Omohundro Institute of Early American History and Culture, 2001), 78–96. On the relation of the Barbados slave code to South Carolina slave law, see Thomas J. Little, "The South Carolina Slave Laws Reconsidered, 1670–1700," *South Carolina Historical Magazine* 94, no. 2 (1993): 86–101.

10. Robin Blackburn, *The Overthrow of Colonial Slavery, 1776–1848* (London: Verso, 1988), 42.

11. In related terms, Immanuel Maurice Wallerstein notes the way in which racism serves as the "magical solution" to the problem of the universality of freedom and the need for conscripted labor that is a structural feature of capitalism: "Whenever we physically eject the other, we gain the 'purity' of environment that we are presumably seeking, but we inevitably lose something at the same time. We lose the labour-power of the person ejected and therefore that person's contribution to the creation of a surplus that we might be able to appropriate on a recurring basis. This represents a loss for any historical system, but it is a particularly serious one in the case of a system whose structure and logic are built around the endless accumulation of capital. . . . Ejection out of the system is pointless. But if one wants to maximize the accumulation of capital, it is necessary simultaneously to minimize the costs of production (hence the costs of

labour-power) and minimize the costs of political disruption (hence minimize—not eliminate, because one cannot eliminate—the protests of the labour force). . . . Racism is the magic formula that reconciles these objectives" ("The Ideological Tensions of Capitalism: Universalism versus Racism and Sexism," in *Race, Nation, Class: Ambiguous Identities*, ed. Étienne Balibar and Immanuel Maurice Wallerstein [London: Verso, 1991], 33).

12. "Thomas Southerne, Oroonoko: A Tragedy," in *Oroonoko: Adaptations and Offshoots*, ed. Susan B. Iwanisziw (Burlington, VT: Ashgate, 2006), 8.

13. Elliott Visconsi, "A Degenerate Race: English Barbarism in Aphra Behn's *Oroonoko* and *The Widow Ranter*," *ELH* 69, no. 3 (2002): 674. See also Laura Rosenthal, "Owning Oroonoko: Behn, Southerne, and the Contingencies of Property," in *Troping Oroonoko from Behn to Bandele*, ed. Susan B. Iwanisziw (Burlington, VT: Ashgate, 2004), 84.

14. The second key emendation of Southerne to Behn's *Oroonoko* (other than the addition of the marriage plot) involves portraying Imoinda as white rather than black: the forbidden interracial sex and reproduction between Imoinda and Oroonoko encodes an impossible futurity. For additional discussion of Imoinda's whiteness in Southerne's *Oroonoko*, see Jennifer B. Elmore, "'The Fair Imoinda': Domestic Ideology and Anti-slavery on the Eighteenth-Century Stage," in *Troping Oroonoko*, 35–58; Susan Z. Andrade, "White Skin, Black Masks: Colonialism and the Sexual Politics of *Oroonoko*," *Cultural Critique* 27 (1994): 189–214; Joyce Green MacDonald, "The Disappearing African Woman: Imoinda in 'Oroonoko' after Behn," *ELH* 66, no. 1 (1999): 71–86; Joseph Roach, *Cities of the Dead: Circum-Atlantic Performance* (New York: Columbia University Press, 1996), 152–61; and Felicity Nussbaum, "Black Women: Why Imoinda Turns White," in *The Limits of the Human: Fictions of Anomaly, Race and Gender in the Long Eighteenth Century* (Cambridge: Cambridge University Press, 2003).

15. On Charles II's colonial policies, see A. P. Thornton, *West-India Policy under the Restoration* (Oxford: Clarendon Press, 1956); and Jack M. Sosin, *English America and the Restoration Monarchy of Charles II: Transatlantic Politics, Commerce, and Kinship* (Lincoln: University of Nebraska Press, 1980).

16. Edward Long, *The History of Jamaica or, General Survey of the Antient and Modern State of the Island. . . .* 3 vols. (London: T. Lowndes, 1774), 1:217–18.

17. The policy of transporting whites to the colonies as a form of punishment did not cease altogether under Charles II but, rather, continued well into the eighteenth century. However, the meaning of whiteness and blackness in the colonies did shift considerably in the late seventeenth century as the demographics of labor were reshaped. An extended debate over the sources of increased racialization and racism in this period has circulated around Bacon's Rebellion in Virginia in 1676. See T. H. Breen, "A Changing Labor Force and Race Relations in Virginia 1660–1710," *Journal of Social History* 7, no. 1 (1973): 3–25; Edmund S. Morgan, *American Slavery, American Freedom: The Ordeal of Colonial Virginia* (New York: Norton, 1975); and Alden T. Vaughan, "The Origins Debate: Slavery and Racism in Seventeenth-Century Virginia," *Virginia Magazine of History and Biography* 97, no. 3 (1989): 311–54. What is a subject of agreement among historians is the fact that racialization (registered in legal and cultural terms) intensified dramatically in this period as the racial demographics of the unfree labor force shifted.

18. Beckles and Downes, "Economics of Transition," 249.

19. For debate over the price of slaves, see Beckles and Downes, "Economics of Transition." For a discussion of the history of metropolitan vs. colonial views concerning the prerogatives of English liberty in the colonies, see Jack P. Greene, "Liberty, Slavery, and the Transformation of British Identity in the Eighteenth-Century West Indies," *Slavery and Abolition* 21, no. 1 (2000): 1–31.

20. For a useful summary of scholarship on *The Enchanted Island*, see Candy B. K. Schille, "'Man Hungry': Reconsidering Threats to Colonial and Patriarchal Order in Dryden and Davenant's *The Tempest*," *Texas Studies in Literature and Language* 48, no. 4 (2006): 273–90.

21. William Shakespeare, *The Tempest*, in *The Norton Shakespeare*, ed. Stephen Greenblatt, Walter Cohen, Jean E. Howard, and Katharine Eisaman Maus (New York: W. W. Norton, 1997).

22. Jodi A. Byrd, *The Transit of Empire: Indigenous Critiques of Colonialism* (Minneapolis: University of Minnesota Press, 2011), 59.

23. John Dryden and William D'Avenant, *The Tempest, or the Enchanted Island. A Comedy: As It Is Now Acted at His Highness the Duke of York's Theatre* (London: J. Macock, for Henry Herringman, 1676), 13–14.

24. Dryden and D'Avenant, *The Tempest, or the Enchanted Island*, 75.

25. Dryden and D'Avenant, *The Tempest, or the Enchanted Island*, 60. Gordon Williams traces the etymology of this phrase to the term "randan" (and the related "rantipole") defined as "whoring or a drunken spree" (*A Dictionary of Sexual Language and Imagery in Shakespearean and Stuart Literature*, 3 vols. [London: Athlone Press, 1994] 1:1140–41).

26. John O'Brien, "Harlequin Britain: Eighteenth-Century Pantomime and the Cultural Location of Entertainment(s)," *Theatre Journal* 50, no. 4 (1998): 503.

27. Michael Dobson, "'Remember/First to Possess His Books': The Appropriation of *The Tempest*, 1700–1800," in *The Tempest: Critical Essays*, ed. Patrick M. Murphy (New York: Routledge, 2001), 247–48. Dobson argues that *The Enchanted Island* is quite literally the founding text of the pantomime tradition in England: "The play, acquiring new musical and visual accretions each season, became a carnivalesque holiday entertainment, a familiar set-piece revived . . . for the socially heterodox audiences attracted to the theatre between New Year's Eve and Twelfth Night. . . . *The Enchanted Island's* assimilation as the standard festive treat of the early eighteenth-century theatre identifies *The Tempest* as the ultimate source of Panto as the London stage still knows it" ("'Remember/First to Possess His Books,'" 248).

28. Dobson, "'Remember/First to Possess His Books,'" 248.

29. Odai Johnson, *Rehearsing the Revolution: Radical Performance, Radical Politics in the English Restoration* (Newark: University of Delaware Press, 2000), 143–44.

30. Herbert McDonald Atherton, *Political Prints in the Age of Hogarth: A Study of the Ideographic Representation of Politics* (Oxford: Clarendon Press, 1974), 160–61; and Paul Langford, *A Polite and Commercial People: England 1727–1783* (Oxford and New York: Clarendon Press and Oxford University Press, 1989), 31.

31. On Walpole's title of "Skreen-Master General," see J. H. Plumb, *Sir Robert Walpole* (London: Cresset Press, 1956), 342; and Colin Nicholson, *Writing and the Rise of Finance: Capital Satires of the Early Eighteenth Century* (Cambridge: Cambridge University Press, 1994), 139.

32. On the development of finance capital, its Atlantic dimensions, and the centrality of slavery therein, see Ian Baucom, *Specters of the Atlantic: Finance Capital, Slavery, and the Philosophy of History* (Durham, NC: Duke University Press, 2005).

33. For the history of the South Sea Bubble, see John Carswell, *The South Sea Bubble* (London: Cresset Press, 1960). The reach of the South Sea Bubble and its collapse in England—in economic, political, and social terms—is difficult to underestimate. For a useful glimpse into the extent and range of cultural production generated around the bubble, see the South Sea Bubble Collection at Baker Library, Harvard University; also available online at http://www.library.hbs.edu/hc/ssb/collection.html, accessed November 26, 2013. The collection comprises 520 items, including pamphlets, playing cards, poetry, musical scores, and prints.

34. On the literary dimensions of the speculative system of eighteenth-century finance capital see Mary Poovey, *Genres of the Credit Economy: Mediating Value in Eighteenth- and Nineteenth-Century Britain* (Chicago: University of Chicago Press, 2008); Catherine Ingrassia, *Authorship, Commerce, and Gender in Early Eighteenth-Century England: A Culture of Paper Credit* (Cambridge: Cambridge University Press, 1998); and James Thompson, *Models of Value: Eighteenth-Century Political Economy and the Novel* (Durham, NC: Duke University Press, 1996).

35. On the Tory opposition to Whig capitalism, see J. G. A. Pocock, *The Machiavellian Moment: Florentine Political Thought and the Atlantic Republican Tradition* (Princeton, NJ: Princeton University Press, 1975); and Isaac Kramnick, *Bolingbroke and His Circle: The Politics of Nostalgia in the Age of Walpole* (Cambridge, MA: Harvard University Press, 1968). On the common cause forged between the laboring poor and the landed gentry, see E. P. Thompson, "Eighteenth-Century English Society: Class Struggle without Class?," *Social History* 3, no. 2 (1978): 100.

36. Vincent Liesenfeld, *The Licensing Act of 1737* (Madison: University of Wisconsin Press, 1984), 61, 149. Notably, members of the house took issue with Walpole's specific concerns about *The Beggar's Opera* and his successful efforts to censor the performance of its sequel, *Polly* (discussed below). The house "declared that the power of the lord chamberlain was already too great, and had been often wantonly exercised, particularly in the prohibition of *Polly*" (Liesenfeld, *The Licensing Act of 1737*, 51).

37. See John Clyde Loftis, *The Politics of Drama in Augustan England* (Oxford: Clarendon Press, 1963). The term "illegitimate" is cited from Jane Moody's work on theatrical performance that fell outside the lines drawn by the Licensing Act. According to Moody, the act helped to create the "decisive emergence of an absolute opposition between authentic and spurious theatrical forms, an opposition which soon begins to be imagined as a nightmarish confrontation between quasi-ethereal textuality and grotesque corporeality" (*Illegitimate Theatre in London, 1770–1840* [Cambridge: Cambridge University Press, 2000], 12).

38. *A Biographical Dictionary of Actors, Actresses, Musicians, Dancers, Managers and Other Stage Personnel in London, 1660–1800*, ed. Philip H. Highfill, Kalman A. Burnim, and Edward A. Langhans, 16 vols. (Carbondale: Southern Illinois University Press, 1973), 5:34.

39. Colin Nicholson notes that Gay himself had invested in South Sea stock, as had other literary figures who were critical of Walpole: for such writers, "personal

circumstance and practice diverge from an espoused political ideology" (*Writing and the Rise of Finance*, 71).

40. Michael Denning, "Beggars and Thieves: The Ideology of the Gang," *Literature and History* 8 (1982): 41–55. For a critical treatment that emphasizes issues of legality over musical form, see William A. McIntosh, "Handel, Walpole, and Gay: The Aims of *The Beggar's Opera*," *Eighteenth-Century Studies* 7, no. 4 (1974): 415–33.

41. On the history and chronology of enclosure in England see J. M. Neeson, *Commoners: Common Right, Enclosure and Social Change in Common-Field England, 1700–1820* (New York: Cambridge University Press, 1993), as well as E. P. Thompson, *Whigs and Hunters: The Origin of the Black Act* (London: Allen Lane, 1975).

42. Thompson, *Whigs and Hunters*, 241.

43. *The History of the Blacks of Waltham in Hampshire; and Those under the Like Denomination in Berkshire* (London: A. Moore, 1723), 7.

44. *The Lives of the Most Remarkable Criminals, who have been Condemn'd and Executed; for Murder, Highway, House-breakers, Street-Robberies, Coining, or other Offences; From the Year 1720, to the Present Time . . . Collected from Original Papers and Authentick Memoirs*, 3 vols. (London: John Osborn, 1735), 1:353.

45. Orlando Patterson, *Slavery and Social Death: A Comparative Study* (Cambridge, MA: Harvard University Press, 1982).

46. Thompson, *Whigs and Hunters*, 63.

47. *The History of the Blacks*, 2.

48. John Gay, *The Beggar's Opera. As It Is Acted at the Theatre Royal in Lincolns-Inn-Fields. Written by Mr. Gay*, 2nd ed. (London: John Watts, 1728), 66.

49. Gay, *The Beggar's Opera*, 70.

50. Gay, *The Beggar's Opera*, 74.

51. For discussion of the suppression of *Polly* on stage as well as the print history of the opera, see Calhoun Winton, *John Gay and the London Theatre* (Lexington: University Press of Kentucky, 1993), 132–44.

52. On the performance history of *Polly*, see Peter P. Reed, "Conquer or Die: Staging Circum-Atlantic Revolt in *Polly* and *Three-Finger'd Jack*," *Theatre Journal* 59, no. 2 (2007): 241.

53. John Gay, *Polly: An Opera. Being the Second Part of the Beggar's Opera. Written by Mr. Gay* (London: Jeffrey Walker, 1729), 30.

54. For a related analysis of Gay's treatment of slavery, see John Richardson, "John Gay and Slavery," *Modern Language Review* 97, no. 1 (2002): 15–25. Richardson writes, "Rather than offering a condemnation of European culture and its impact around the world in [his plays dealing with slavery], Gay creates fictions that both turn upon a slave's liberation and implicitly endorse the institution of slavery. In doing so, he exemplifies and encourages the duplicitous mental habits that allowed liberty to be a central term of British political discourse and slavery to be a central part of British trade" (17). For further (conflicting) assessments of Gay and slavery, see Aparna Dharwadker, "John Gay, Bertolt Brecht and Postcolonial Antinationalisms," *Modern Drama* 38, no. 1 (1995): 4–21; Dianne Dugaw, *Warrior Women and Popular Balladry, 1650–1850* (Cambridge: Cambridge University Press, 1989); and Robert G. Dryden, "John Gay's *Polly*: Unmasking Pirates and Fortune Hunters in the West Indies," *Eighteenth-Century Studies* 34, no. 4 (2001): 539–57.

55. Gay, *Polly*, 29.

56. Gay, *Polly*, 62.

57. According to Robert G. Dryden, Gay does not intend to represent Morano's blackness as a temporary disguise but as a permanent condition: "Morano does not put on and take off blackness according to the convenience of the disguise. From the moment he appears on stage until the moment he is hanged, Morano remains black" ("John Gay's *Polly*," 551). Certainly it seems that Morano is unable to retrieve the identity of Macheath (or whiteness) to exonerate himself from his sentence of death.

58. See John Gay, *L'opera Du Gueux, Avec Les Chansons Sur Les Airs Anglois. Représentée sur le Petit Theatre François dans le Marché au Foin. Traduite de l'anglois de Mr. Gay, par Mr. A. Hallam* (London: Chéz Guillaume Meyer, 1750). For discussion of the banning of the play in France, see Sybil Goulding, "Eighteenth-Century French Taste and 'The Beggar's Opera,'" *Modern Language Review* 24, no. 3 (1929): 276–93.

59. Odai Johnson and William J. Burling, *The Colonial American Stage, 1665–1774* (Madison, NJ: Fairleigh Dickinson University Press, 2001), 64–65. Ahead of *The Beggar's Opera* in popularity are *Romeo and Juliet*, *The Beaux Stratagem*, and *Richard III*.

60. O. G. Sonneck, *Early Opera in America* (New York: G. Schirmer; Boston: Boston Music, 1915), 18.

61. Johnson and Burling, *The Colonial American Stage*, 366.

62. *Boston News Letter*, March 23, 1770; cited in Johnson and Burling, *The Colonial American Stage*, 361–62.

63. *City Gazette and Daily Advertiser*, January 1, 1795. For an unfavorable review of a London production of *Beggar's Opera—Reversed*, see *Public Advertiser* [London], August 28, 1784.

64. For a helpful discussion of civic engagement in colonial clubs that might be said to constitute commons by means of aesthetics see David S. Shields, *Civil Tongues and Polite Letters in British America* (Chapel Hill: University of North Carolina Press for the Institute of Early American History and Culture, 1997).

CHAPTER 4: CHARLESTON

1. *Royal Gazette* [New York], October 18, 1783.

2. The character of Oroonoko was performed by white actors in eighteenth-century England and the colonies. The first performance of Oroonoko by a black actor was most likely that of Ira Aldridge, in London in 1825; see Bernth Lindfors, *Ira Aldridge: The African Roscius* (Rochester, NY: University of Rochester Press, 2007). On the history of blackface performance in England, see Virginia Mason Vaughan, *Performing Blackness on English Stages, 1500–1800* (Cambridge: Cambridge University Press, 2005), and for discussion of black performers and the performance of blackness in the U.S., see Heather Nathans, *Slavery and Sentiment on the American Stage, 1787–1861: Lifting the Veil of Black* (Cambridge: Cambridge University Press, 2009).

3. Following the American Revolution, South Carolina was the eighth state to ratify the U.S. Constitution and thereby became a state in 1788. However, the racial, economic, and juridical structure of the polity remained deeply colonial, as I argue in this chapter. Accordingly, my use of the term "colony" to describe the U.S. state of South Carolina

in the late eighteenth century is intended to signal the colonial nature of culture, power, and performance in the early national period in that location.

4. Giorgio Agamben, *Homo Sacer: Sovereign Power and Bare Life* (Palo Alto, CA: Stanford University Press, 1998), 139.

5. Alan Gallay, *The Indian Slave Trade: The Rise of the English Empire in the American South, 1670–1717* (New Haven, CT: Yale University Press, 2002), 7.

6. William L. Ramsey, "'Something Cloudy in Their Looks': The Origins of the Yamasee War Reconsidered." *Journal of American History* 90, no. 1 (June 1, 2003): 44–75. For additional discussion of the Yamasee War and Native Americans in South Carolina see Gallay, *The Indian Slave Trade*; Thomas M. Hatley, *The Dividing Paths: Cherokees and South Carolinians through the Era of Revolution* (New York: Oxford University Press, 1993); and William L. Ramsey, *The Yamasee War: A Study of Culture, Economy, and Conflict in the Colonial South* (Lincoln: University of Nebraska Press, 2008).

7. Peter H. Wood, *Black Majority: Negroes in Colonial South Carolina from 1670 through the Stono Rebellion* (New York: Knopf, 1974).

8. Henry Melchior Muhlenburg, *The Journals of Henry Melchior Muhlenberg*, 3 vols. (Philadelphia: Evangelical Lutheran Ministerium of Pennsylvania and Adjacent States, 1942–1958), 2:567, cited in Wood, *Black Majority*, 219. For further citations of visitors and residents who mistake the black/white ratio, see Wood, *Black Majority*, 218–21, and Robert Olwell, *Masters, Slaves, and Subjects: The Culture of Power in the South Carolina Low Country, 1740–1790* (Ithaca, NY: Cornell University Press, 1998), 48.

9. On racial demographics in Charleston see George C. Rogers, *Charleston in the Age of the Pinckneys* (Norman: University of Oklahoma Press, 1969), 141; and Bernard Edward Powers, *Black Charlestonians: A Social History, 1822–1885* (Fayetteville: University of Arkansas Press, 1994), 267. The black/white ratios were far higher outside of the city in agricultural/plantation communities: see Olwell, *Masters, Slaves, and Subjects*, 28–31.

10. Josiah Quincy, "Journal of Josiah Quincy, Junior, 1773," *Massachusetts Historical Society Proceedings* 49 (1916): 456.

11. Thomas M. D. Cooper and David James Maccord, eds., *Statutes at Large of South Carolina*, 10 vols. (Columbia, SC: A. S. Johnston, 1836), 7:399–400, 410. In 1800, another law was passed forbidding "the assemblies of slaves, free negroes, mulattoes, or mestizoes, with or without white persons, in a confined or secret place of meeting." See John Belton O'Neall and the State Agricultural Society of South Carolina, *The Negro Law of South Carolina* (Columbia, SC: J. G. Bowman, 1848), 23.

12. Reprinted in Mark M. Smith, *Stono: Documenting and Interpreting a Southern Slave Revolt* (Columbia: University of South Carolina Press, 2005), 14–15.

13. Richard Cullen Rath reports the passage of laws prohibiting drums and horns in Jamaica (1688 and 1717), Barbados (1699), and St. Kitts (1711 and 1722) (*How Early America Sounded* [Ithaca, NY: Cornell University Press, 2003], 79).

14. The larger question of the meaning of music and dance among slaves is quite complex. As Rath demonstrates, drumming in particular was viewed as threatening and was banned by planters in the Caribbean and the Carolina low country. However, as Saidiya V. Hartman's work shows, planters were often interested in having slaves play the violin and dance in ways that demonstrated (to a planter audience) "contentment" and

fitness for slavery. Thus, as Hartman indicates, it was not unusual for planters to provide slaves with fiddles and encourage certain forms of dance. Similarly, Rath argues that fiddles largely replaced drums after 1740 as the instrument of slave music in the low country: "the [fiddle] was not thought of as a threat, as drums were." However, Rath also points out that the ways in which the fiddle was used by slaves were not entirely controlled by white intentions: "While drums were banned, the violin functioned well for quietly representing African drumming traditions that were so feared, but little understood, by planters. The polymeter rhythms of banned drums were stored in the distinctive pulse of the stick knockers and the fiddler's three- or four-note rhythmic pattern" (Rath, "Drums and Power: Ways of Creolizing Music in Coastal South Carolina and Georgia, 1730–90," in *Creolization in the Americas*, ed. David Buisseret and Steven G. Reinhardt [College Station: Texas A&M University Press, 2000], 113, 118). In related terms, Hartman documents the ways in which—in contrast to the efforts of slave owners to generate "simulated jollity" among slaves—musical forms of patting Juba carried countermeanings of New World African autonomy, cultural production, and rebellion against white oppression: "Juba was a coded text of protest. It utilized rhythm and nonsense words as cover for social critique" (Hartman, *Scenes of Subjection: Terror, Slavery, and Self-Making in Nineteenth-Century America* [New York: Oxford University Press, 1997], 70).

15. *South Carolina Gazette*, September 17, 1772.

16. "rout[1] n." *The Concise Oxford English Dictionary*, 12th ed., ed. Angus Stevenson and Maurice Waite (Oxford: Oxford University Press, 2011).

17. The dance described above was not an isolated event. Historian Bernard Powers reports that dances were common in the black community of Charleston in the late eighteenth and early nineteenth centuries (*Black Charlestonians*, 23–25).

18. According to the Merriam-Webster Online Dictionary (www.merriam-webster .com/dictionary. Accessed 29 November 2013) an "aliterate" is a person who can read but chooses not to; for lack of a better term, I am, in effect, shifting the causality here to suggest that the aliterate slave is someone who can read (i.e., has the capability) but has been *forced* not to.

19. For discussion of the public control or "sovereignty" of the stage in Charleston, see chapter 1.

20. I draw on James C. Scott's distinction between "official transcripts" of events that appear in archival records and "hidden transcripts" that often provide a far different account of the meaning and shape of subaltern resistance to domination. See James C. Scott, *Domination and the Arts of Resistance: Hidden Transcripts* (New Haven, CT: Yale University Press, 1990).

21. See the *Columbian Herald*, November 17, 1795.

22. John Lambert, *Travels through Lower Canada and the United States of North America in the Years of 1806, 1807, and 1808* . . . 3 vols. (London: Richard Phillips by T. Gillet, 1810), 2:374.

23. See, for instance, Sean X. Goudie, *Creole America: The West Indies and the Formation of Literature and Culture in the New Republic* (Philadelphia: University of Pennsylvania Press, 2006), 165. Laws regarding slaves in Charleston were routinely flouted in many different regards. Indeed, the fact that laws were often passed repeatedly over a period of decades (regarding curfews, passes, sumptuary laws, alco-

hol consumption, employment in skilled trades, independent commercial activity, housing, etc.) indicates that the laws on the books were not routinely followed: for discussion of the discrepancy between legal codes and lived activities, see Powers, *Black Charlestonians.*

24. *South Carolina Gazette and Timothy and Mason's Daily Advertiser*, May 11, 1796. Additional newspaper articles commenting on theatre attendance by blacks appear in 1795, 1797, 1801, and 1803—evidence indicating the regularity with which black people made up a portion of the theatrical audience during this time period.

25. *South Carolina State Gazette and Timothy's Daily Advertiser*, March 4, 1801.

26. Michael L. Kennedy notes that the society had three names during its short life from 1792 to 1794: "Société patriotique française" in 1792, "Société des amis de la liberté et de l'égalité" in early 1793, and "Société des sans-culottes" in late 1794 ("A French Jacobin Club in Charleston, South Carolina, 1792–1795," *South Carolina Historical Magazine* 91, no. 1 [1990]: 7–8).

27. Kennedy, "A French Jacobin Club," 18.

28. Kennedy, "A French Jacobin Club," 16.

29. *City Gazette and Daily Advertiser*, June 27, 1793, and August 21, 1793.

30. Robert Alderson, "Charleston's Rumored Slave Revolt of 1793," in *The Impact of the Haitian Revolution in the Atlantic World*, ed. David Patrick Geggus (Columbia: University of South Carolina Press, 2001) 93–111.

31. For discussion of public parades and street theatre in Charleston in this period, see David Waldstreicher, *In the Midst of Perpetual Fetes: The Making of American Nationalism, 1776–1820* (Chapel Hill: University of North Carolina Press for the Omohundro Institute of Early American History and Culture, 1997).

32. For discussion of the experiences of refugees from St. Domingue in Charleston, see Winston Babb, "French Refugees from Saint Domingue to the Southern United States: 1791–1810" (PhD diss., University of Virginia, 1954). On the history of Alexander Placide and the Charleston Theatre, see Richard P. Sodders, "The Theatre Management of Alexandre Placide in Charleston, 1794–1812" (PhD diss., Louisiana State University, 1983). For consideration of the influence of musicians from St. Domingue on Charleston's musical community, see Nicholas Michael Butler, *Votaries of Apollo: The St. Cecilia Society and the Patronage of Concert Music in Charleston, South Carolina, 1766–1820* (Columbia: University of South Carolina Press, 2007).

33. *South Carolina Gazette and Timothy and Mason's Daily Advertiser*, April 26, 1797.

34. For discussion of debates over the "freedom of the scenes" in Britain, see Susan Cannon Harris, "Outside the Box: The Female Spectator, *The Fair Penitent*, and the Kelly Riots of 1747," *Theatre Journal* 57, no. 1 (2005): 33–55.

35. *City Gazette and Daily Advertiser*, February 8, 1794.

36. For further discussion of the competition between the French Theatre and the Charleston Theatre, which included wars over performers, see Julia Curtis, "The Early Charleston Stage: 1703–1798" (PhD diss., Indiana University, 1968), 215–77. The pantomime version of Defoe's novel, *Robinson Crusoe or Harlequin Friday*, was written by Richard Sheridan and first performed in London in 1781. However, as discussed below, evidence suggests that considerable variation occurred between Sheridan's version and versions of the harlequinade performed in Charleston.

37. *South-Carolina State Gazette and Timothy's Daily Adviser*, April 21, 1794.

38. *City Gazette and Daily Advertiser*, May 7, 1794.

39. See Olwell, *Masters, Slaves, and Subjects*, 28–31; and Peter A. Coclanis, *The Shadow of a Dream: Economic Life and Death in the South Carolina Low Country, 1670–1920* (New York: Oxford University Press, 1989), 67.

40. Stephen Greenblatt argues that Caliban's curse is an "assertion of inconsolable human pain and bitterness" (*Learning to Curse: Essays in Early Modern Culture* [New York: Routledge, 1990], 26), but I would argue that the curse indicates an ability to assert another scene of meaning, an alternative economy, erected in the space of his own erasure from language. Caliban's language has been the subject of sustained discussion in African diasporic and Caribbean literary and political theory. See, for instance, Anthony Bogues, *Caliban's Freedom: The Early Political Thought of C. L. R. James* (London: Pluto Press, 1997); Shona N. Jackson, *Creole Indigeneity: Between Myth and Nation in the Caribbean* (Minneapolis: University of Minnesota Press, 2012); and George Lamming, *The Pleasures of Exile* (London: M. Joseph, 1960).

41. Fred Moten, *In the Break: The Aesthetics of the Black Radical Tradition* (Minneapolis: University of Minnesota Press, 2003), 6.

42. Quincy, "Journal of Josiah Quincy, Junior, 1773," 463.

43. Richard Brinsley Sheridan, *A Short Account of the Situations and Incidents Exhibited in the Pantomime of Robinson Crusoe, at the Theatre-Royal, Drury-Lane* (London: T. Becket, 1781), 20. For discussion of the London reception of the pantomime, see Mita Choudhury, *Interculturalism and Resistance in the London Theater, 1660–1800: Identity, Performance, Empire* (Lewisburg, PA: Bucknell University Press, 2000), 154.

44. Julian Mates, *The American Musical Stage before 1800* (New Brunswick, NJ: Rutgers University Press, 1962), 159. The degree of the mixture of the Defoe novel and the harlequinade is more evident in advertisements for the pantomime than in the published text that describes the pantomime. In the advertisements, it is clear that Pantaloon—a character in the harlequinade—appears in the first act as well as the second, thus indicating a narrative integration of the first and second scenes.

45. Note that Thelma Niklaus attributes the innovations of the libretto to the comic performer, Carlos Antonio Delpino, who performed in the pantomime of *Crusoe* in London in 1781 (*Harlequin; or The Rise and Fall of a Bergamask Rogue* [New York: G. Braziller, 1956], 159). For a modern edition of the musical score, see Thomas Linley and Richard Brinsley Sheridan, *The Pantomine [sic] of Robinson Crusoe: (1781)*, ed. Richard Hoskins (Wellington, New Zealand: Artaria Editions, 2005).

46. For histories of the harlequinade, see Niklaus, *Harlequin*, and David Mayer, *Harlequin in His Element: The English Pantomime, 1806–1836* (Cambridge, MA: Harvard University Press, 1969).

47. John O'Brien, *Harlequin Britain: Pantomime and Entertainment, 1690–1760* (Baltimore: Johns Hopkins University Press, 2004), xvii–xviii.

48. Daniel Defoe, *The Life and Adventures of Robinson Crusoe* (Harmondsworth, UK: Penguin, 1965), 207.

49. *South-Carolina State Gazette and Timothy's Daily Adviser*, April 21, 1794.

50. A performance of "The Dressing Room; or, the Intriguing Frizeur"—"The whole to conclude with a EPILOGUE, by Mr. M. Sully, Jr., in the character of Harlequin;

to finish with a surprising LEAP, surrounded with FIREWORKS"—is advertised in the *City Gazette and Daily Advertiser*, August 25, 1794. See Thomas Clark Pollock, *The Philadelphia Theatre in the Eighteenth Century, Together with the Day Book of the Same Period* (Philadelphia: University of Pennsylvania Press, 1933), 326, for mention of a play performed by the circus in Philadelphia of "The Dressing Room or the Intriguing Friseur" (described as a comic burletta). See also O'Brien, *Harlequin Britain*, 229, for mention of the character of "Snip" in the harlequinade.

51. On the construction of transatlantic whiteness in relation to settler colonialism and racialization, see David Kazanjian, *The Colonizing Trick: National Culture and Imperial Citizenship in Early America* (Minneapolis: University of Minnesota Press, 2003).

52. In Charleston newspapers of the 1790s, numerous advertisements appear for services offered by non-English-speaking refugees from St. Domingue, including fencing lessons, dancing lessons, music lessons, and French lessons. Clearly the matter of making a living as a non-English speaker in an Anglophone community was a pressing one for these individuals.

53. *Mirza et Lindor* first appeared in France in 1779, choreographed by Maximilien Gardel. For discussion of the French history of the pantomime/ballet, see Susan Leigh Foster, *Choreography & Narrative: Ballet's Staging of Story and Desire* (Bloomington: Indiana University Press, 1996), 128–30; and Joellen A. Meglin, "'Sauvages, Sex Roles, and Semiotics': Representations of Native Americans in the French Ballet, 1736–1837, Part One: The Eighteenth Century," *Dance Chronicle* 23, no. 2 (January 1, 2000): 87–132.

54. *City Gazette and Daily Advertiser*, June 6, 1794.

55. For discussion of the increased number of pantomimes performed at the Charleston Theatre in 1794, see Curtis, "Early Charleston Stage," 228, 269.

56. *South Carolina Gazette and Timothy and Mason's Daily Advertiser*, May 4, 1796.

57. *City Gazette and Daily Advertiser*, December 16, 1803.

58. On the relation between the harlequin figure and Jim Crow, see Henry Louis Gates Jr., *Figures in Black: Words, Signs, and the "Racial" Self* (Oxford: Oxford University Press, 1987), 51–53.

CHAPTER 5: KINGSTON

1. *Postscript to the Royal Gazette*, July 22–29, 1809.

2. See David Eltis's database of African names, "African Origins," http://www.african-origins.org/. Accessed November 29, 2013.

3. For discussion of slave-naming practices in Jamaica, see Trevor G. Burnard, "Slave Naming Patterns: Onomastics and the Taxonomy of Race in Eighteenth-Century Jamaica," *Journal of Interdisciplinary History* 31, no. 3 (2001): 325–46.

4. On the history of theatre in Jamaica, see Richardson Little Wright, *Revels in Jamaica, 1682–1838: Plays and Players of a Century, Tumblers and Conjurors, Musical Refugees and Solitary Showmen, Dinners, Balls and Cockfights, Darky Mummers and Other Memories of High Times and Merry Hearts* (New York: Dodd, Mead, 1937); and Errol Hill, *The Jamaican Stage, 1655–1900: Profile of a Colonial Theatre* (Amherst: University of Massachusetts Press, 1992). On the history of laws governing theatre in the United States, see George B. Bryan, *American Theatrical Regulation, 1607–1900: Conspectus and Texts* (Metuchen, NJ: Scarecrow Press, 1993).

5. In related terms, see David Waldstreicher's discussion of the profits Benjamin Franklin reaped from the advertisement of unfree labor in the pages of his *Pennsylvania Gazette* and, more generally, Waldstreicher's consideration of the centrality of unfree labor to the production of American freedom in *Runaway America: Benjamin Franklin, Slavery, and the American Revolution* (New York: Hill and Wang, 2004).

6. *Postscript to the Royal Gazette*, January 26–February 2, 1793.

7. *Kingston Journal*, August 26, 1789; *Daily Advertiser*, January 2, 1790.

8. See Carole Boyce Davies, ed., *Encyclopedia of the African Diaspora: Origins, Experiences, and Culture, Volume 1* (Santa Barbara, CA: ABC-CLIO, 2008), 335.

9. *Royal Gazette*, June 3–10, 1780; *Supplement to the Royal Gazette*, June 26–July 3, 1779; *Royal Gazette*, April 1–8, 1780.

10. *Supplement to the Royal Gazette*, April 8–15, 1780.

11. *Jamaica Mercury and Kingston Weekly Advertiser*, September 11–18, 1779.

12. *Jamaica Mercury and Kingston Weekly Advertiser*, May 1–8, 1779. According to the *Oxford English Dictionary*, one definition of "pompadour" is a "shade of pink"; a relevant definition of "frog" is "an ornamental fastening originally used on military dress coats or cloaks, consisting of a spindle-shaped button and, on the opposite side of the garment, a loop through which this fits" (*Oxford English Dictionary*, 3rd ed. [Oxford: Oxford University Press, 2010]).

13. *Royal Gazette*, December 30, 1780–January 6, 1781.

14. *The Daily Advertiser*, January 2, 1790.

15. David Waldstreicher, "Reading the Runaways: Self-Fashioning, Print Culture, and Confidence in Slavery in the Eighteenth-Century Mid-Atlantic," *William and Mary Quarterly* 56, no. 2 (April 1999): 244.

16. See Vincent Brown, *The Reaper's Garden: Death and Power in the World of Atlantic Slavery* (Cambridge, MA: Harvard University Press, 2008), for a superb analysis of the way in which new forms of culture (social life) emerged in Jamaica around scenes and practices of death itself.

17. On the economy of Jamaica in relation to the British empire and the Atlantic world, see Richard B. Sheridan, *Sugar and Slavery: An Economic History of the British West Indies, 1623–1775* (Baltimore: Johns Hopkins University Press, 1974); Trevor Burnard, "'Prodigious Riches': The Wealth of Jamaica before the American Revolution," *Economic History Review* 54, no. 3 (August 2001): 506–24; and Barbara L. Solow, "Slavery and Colonization," in *Slavery and the Rise of the Atlantic System*, ed. Barbara L. Solow (Cambridge: Cambridge University Press, 1991), 21–42.

18. Solow, "Slavery and Colonization," 29.

19. See Andrew Jackson O'Shaughnessy, *An Empire Divided: The American Revolution and the British Caribbean* (Philadelphia: University of Pennsylvania Press, 2000), for an account of the British American empire that emphasizes the centrality of the Caribbean colonies.

20. Mary Turner places the percent of whites in the population at "barely ten percent" (*Slaves and Missionaries: The Disintegration of Jamaican Slave Society, 1787–1834* [Urbana: University of Illinois Press, 1982], 8). For additional information on racial demographics in Jamaica, see B. W. Higman, *Slave Populations of the British Caribbean, 1807–1834* (Baltimore: Johns Hopkins University Press, 1984); and Trevor Burnard, "Not

a Place for Whites? Demographic Failure and Settlement in Comparative Context: Jamaica, 1655–1780," in *Jamaica in Slavery and Freedom: History, Heritage and Culture*, ed. Kathleen E. A. Monteith and Glen Richards (Kingston, Jamaica: University of the West Indies Press, 2002), 73–88.

21. Vincent Brown estimates that Jamaica imported as many as 750,000 slaves between the late 17th and early 19th centuries, but in 1838, on the eve of emancipation, the slave population was only 300,000. See Brown, *Reaper's Garden,* 57, as well as Higman, *Slave Populations of the British Caribbean,* 77.

22. The term "garrison society" is used both by Burnard, "Not a Place for Whites?," 82, and O'Shaugnessy, *An Empire Divided,* 9.

23. Turner, *Slaves and Missionaries,* 8. On the nature of slave punishment in Jamaica and its orientation toward terror and dehumanization, see Diana Paton, "Punishment, Crime, and the Bodies of Slaves in Eighteenth-Century Jamaica," *Journal of Social History* 34, no. 4 (July 2001): 923–54.

24. Sidney W. Mintz, "Enduring Substances, Trying Theories: The Caribbean Region as Oikoumene," *Journal of the Royal Anthropological Institute* 2, no. 2 (1996): 295.

25. Patrick Kein, "The Best Method of Cultivating Sugar Canes," *Columbian Magazine,* March 1797, 644.

26. "Domestic Occurrences," *Columbian Magazine,* February 1797, 624.

27. Sibylle Fischer, *Modernity Disavowed: Haiti and the Cultures of Slavery in the Age of Revolution* (Durham, NC: Duke University Press, 2004), 12. See also Hilary McD. Beckles, "Capitalism, Slavery, and Caribbean Modernity," *Callaloo* 20, no. 4 (1997): 777–89. On the concept of conscription in relation to slavery and modernity, see David Scott, *Conscripts of Modernity: The Tragedy of Colonial Enlightenment* (Durham, NC: Duke University Press, 2004).

28. A long-standing historiographical debate about the relation between slavery and capitalism has played out over the past seventy years, much of it following in the wake of Eric Eustace Williams's seminal work *Capitalism and Slavery* (Chapel Hill: University of North Carolina Press, 1944); as the Caribbean historian Hilary McD. Beckles concluded in 2002, "In the Caribbean, . . . the primordial site of the Atlantic slave system, there is virtual consensus among historians that the relationship between the exploitation of enslaved Africans in the plantation colonies was the principal engine that drove the process of sustainable economic development in Europe that became known as the Industrial Revolution. On the other side of the Atlantic there is a substantial rejection of this perspective in academic circles" "Review of *Slavery, Atlantic Trade and the British Economy, 1660–1800,* by Kenneth Morgan," *Albion* 34, no. 4 [December 2002]: 651). Much of this debate (in England, in particular) hinges on how one defines capitalism—as, for instance, a system of economic exchange versus a system involving free wage labor—as well as how one estimates the economic benefit derived by Great Britain from slave colonies such as Jamaica. The book reviewed by Beckles, Morgan's *Slavery, Atlantic Trade and the British Economy, 1660–1800* (Cambridge: Cambridge University Press, 2000), discusses the history of this debate at length, as do Barbara L. Solow and Stanley L. Engerman, eds., *British Capitalism and Caribbean Slavery: The Legacy of Eric Williams* (Cambridge: Cambridge University Press, 1987); and Christopher Leslie Brown, *Moral Capital: Foundations of British Abolitionism* (Chapel Hill:

University of North Carolina Press for the Omohundro Institute of Early American History and Culture, 2006), 15–17. On free wage labor, slavery, and the Industrial Revolution, see Joseph E. Inikori, "Slavery and the Rise of Capitalism," in *Slavery, Freedom and Gender: The Dynamics of Caribbean Society*, ed. Brian L. Moore (Kingston, Jamaica: University of the West Indies Press, 2001), 3–39; on British profits from the slave trade and the Caribbean slave colonies, see Robin Blackburn, *The Making of New World Slavery: From the Baroque to the Modern, 1492–1800* (London: Verso, 1997), 509–80; and Nicholas Draper, *The Price of Emancipation: Slave-Ownership, Compensation and British Society at the End of Slavery* (Cambridge: Cambridge University Press, 2010), 11. Draper concludes, writing in 2010, that "there is now widespread if not universal acceptance of the 'weak' form of [Eric] Williams's argument, that industrialisation and commercial transformation were partly shaped by the slave-economy" (11). Discussion of the geographical separation of production and social reproduction, which I pursue here, has not been addressed in this debate.

29. Leopoldina Fortunati writes, "Under capitalism, reproduction is separated off from production; the former unity that existed between the production of use-values and the reproduction of individuals within precapitalist modes of production has disappeared, and now the general process of commodity production appears as being separated from, and even in direct opposition to, the process of reproduction" (*The Arcane of Reproduction: Housework, Prostitution, Labor and Capital* [Brooklyn, NY: Autonomedia, 1995], 10).

30. Cindi Katz, "Vagabond Capitalism and the Necessity of Social Reproduction," *Antipode* 33, no. 4 (2001): 709.

31. Andrew Jackson O'Shaughnessy reports that roughly three-quarters of Jamaican planters sent their children to Britain for schooling (*An Empire Divided: The American Revolution and the British Caribbean* [Philadelphia: University of Pennsylvania Press, 2000], 19).

32. Vincent Brown, *The Reaper's Garden: Death and Power in the World of Atlantic Slavery* (Cambridge, MA: Harvard University Press, 2008), 56.

33. Edward Long, *History of Jamaica or, General Survey of the Antient and Modern State of the Island. . . .* 3 vols. (London: T. Lowndes, 1774), 2:261–62, 2:265.

34. Michael Craton, "Reluctant Creoles: The Planters' World in the British West Indies," in *Strangers within the Realm: Cultural Margins of the First British Empire*, ed. Bernard Bailyn and Philip D. Morgan (Chapel Hill: University of North Carolina Press for the Institute of Early American History and Culture, 1991), 314–62.

35. Christer Petley, *Slaveholders in Jamaica: Colonial Society and Culture during the Era of Abolition* (London: Pickering and Chatto, 2009), 11.

36. On creole culture and metropolitan views of creoles see also Christer Petley, "Gluttony, Excess, and the Fall of the Planter Class in the British Caribbean," *Atlantic Studies* 9, no. 1 (2012): 85–106; David Lambert, *White Creole Culture, Politics and Identity during the Age of Abolition* (Cambridge: Cambridge University Press, 2005); Trevor G. Burnard, *Mastery, Tyranny, and Desire: Thomas Thistlewood and His Slaves in the Anglo-Jamaican World* (Chapel Hill: University of North Carolina Press, 2004); and Erin Skye Mackie, "Cultural Cross-Dressing: The Colorful Case of the Caribbean Creole," in *The Clothes That Wear Us: Essays on Dressing and Transgressing in Eighteenth-Century Culture*, ed. Jessica Munns and Penny Richards (Newark: University of Delaware Press, 1999), 250–70.

37. Maria Mies and Veronika Bennholdt-Thomsen, "Defending, Reclaiming, and Reinventing the Commons," *Canadian Journal of Development Studies* 22 (2001): 1011.

38. J. B. Moreton, *West India Customs and Manners. . . .* (London: J. Parsons; W. Richardson; H. Gardner; and J. Walter, 1793), 109, 105.

39. For discussion of mixed-race audiences at the theatre in Jamaica, see Hill, *The Jamaican Stage*, 35–37.

40. Hill, *Jamaican Stage*, 23, 29. Additional theatres existed in Spanish Town and Montego Bay.

41. Kathleen Wilson, "Rowe's *Fair Penitent* as Global History: Or, a Diversionary Voyage to New South Wales," *Eighteenth-Century Studies* 41, no. 2 (2008): 232–33.

42. *The Jamaican Mercury and Kingston Weekly Advertiser*, October 1–14, 1780.

43. Michael Scott, *The Cruise of the Midge* (Hartford, CT: Silas Andrus and Son, 1846), 265. Scott was the son of a Glasgow merchant and lived in Jamaica from 1806 to 1822; he managed estates in Jamaica and later worked as a merchant there. The stories in *The Cruise of the Midge* were first published serially in *Blackwood's Magazine* in 1834–35 and were evidently based on Scott's experiences in Jamaica.

44. Nugent, *Lady Nugent's Journal of Her Residence in Jamaica from 1801 to 1805*, ed. Philip Wright and Verene Shepherd (Kingston, Jamaica: University of the West Indies Press, 2002), 147–48.

45. George Raymond and George Cruikshank, *The Life and Enterprises of Robert William Elliston, Comedian* (London: G. Routledge, 1857), 44.

46. Jack Cussans, "Robinson Crusoe," Broadside. U.S. between 1850 and 1870, American Antiquarian Society, American Broadsides and Ephemera.

47. Examples linking Jews and blacks appear with regularity in Kingston's *Columbian Magazine*. A letter to the editor in 1796, for instance, inveighs against the admission of Jews into Free Masonry lodges: "If this mode continues, in a short time I expect to see Free Masonry in this country dwindled into a Meeting of Mulattoes and Negroes, with some of our *worthy Jew Brethren* presiding at their head" (*Columbian Magazine*, December 1796, 468). For further discussion of the Jewish community in Jamaica, see Holly Snyder, "Customs of an Unruly Race: The Political Context of Jamaican Jewry, 1670–1831," in *Art and Emancipation in Jamaica: Isaac Mendes Belisario and His Worlds*, ed. T. J. Barringer, Gillian Forrester, and Barbaro Martinez-Ruiz (New Haven, CT: Yale Center for British Art: Yale University Press, 2007), 151–61 and "A Sense of Place: Jews, Identity and Social Status in Colonial British America, 1654–1831" (PhD diss., Brandeis University, 2000).

48. *The Daily Advertiser*, February 23, 1802.

49. *The Daily Advertiser*, February 11, 1802.

50. Notably, Tessier's advertisement operates in two directions: on the one hand, he advertises the "spacious" and "airy" location of seats for people of color; on the other hand, he makes it clear that these seats are distinct from those for whites and are accessible by a separate entrance. That this form of segregation was a matter of controversy is indicated by the 1815 riot over this issue, discussed below.

51. *Diary and Kingston Daily Advertiser*, March 22, 1802. Note that Wright (*Revels in Jamaica*, 308) mistakenly attributes the opera to Samuel Arnold Sr., but the cast listed in the newspaper is clearly that of Dalyrac's *Azémia*, not Samuel Arnold's *Shipwreck*.

52. Cited by David Charlton, "The Nineteenth Century: France," in *The Oxford Illustrated History of Opera*, ed. Roger Parker (Oxford: Oxford University Press, 2001), 128.

53. Wright, *Revels in Jamaica*, 310.

54. *Diary and Kingston Daily Advertiser*, March 23, 1802.

55. *Postscript to the Royal Gazette*, April 8–15, 1815.

56. *Postscript to the Royal Gazette*, August 21–28, 1813.

57. The church was an important site of abolitionist mobilization in Jamaica—in large part because Methodist and nonconforming churches welcomed blacks into their congregations. Mixed-race congregations were the subject of intense concern for the plantocracy. On the role of the church in abolition in Jamaica, see Turner, *Slaves and Missionaries*.

58. Édouard Glissant, *Caribbean Discourse: Selected Essays*, trans. J. Michael Dash (Charlottesville: University Press of Virginia, 1989), 96.

59. Glissant, *Caribbean Discourse*, 128.

60. Hortense J. Spillers, "The Idea of Black Culture," CR: *New Centennial Review* 6, no. 3 (2006): 25–26.

61. *Royal Gazette*, October 6, 1780.

62. Roderick A. McDonald, *The Economy and Material Culture of Slaves: Goods and Chattels on the Sugar Plantations of Jamaica and Louisiana* (Baton Rouge: Louisiana State University Press, 1993), 112.

63. McDonald, *The Economy and Material Culture of Slaves*, 125–26.

64. On amelioration, see J. R. Ward, *British West Indian Slavery, 1750–1834: The Process of Amelioration* (Oxford: Oxford University Press, 1988).

65. Matthew Gregory Lewis, *Journal of a West-India Proprietor, Kept during a Residence in the Island of Jamaica* (London: J. Murray, 1834), 125.

66. In November 1799 for instance, a letter from the British Parliament is read into the record of the Jamaican Assembly, in which Parliament suggests that slave mothers should not work in the field for two months before and after birth, that raising children be rewarded by "bestowing some marks of distinction or favour, such as a difference of dress, and some pecuniary annual rewards, on such parents as shall have reared a child; those rewards to increase with the number of children" (*Journals of the Assembly of Jamaica*, 1799, 320). For additional accounts of planters who give extra clothing or cloth to slave women bearing children, see McDonald, *The Economy and Material Culture of Slaves*, 120–21.

67. Hilary McD. Beckles and Verene Shepherd, Introduction to *A Historical Study of Women in Jamaica, 1655–1844*, by Lucille Mathurin Mair (Kingston, Jamaica: University of the West Indies Press, 2006), xxiv.

68. Hortense J. Spillers, "Mama's Baby, Papa's Maybe: An American Grammar Book," in *Black, White, and in Color: Essays on American Literature and Culture* (Chicago: University of Chicago Press, 2003), 215.

69. Lucille Mathurin Mair, "Women Field Workers in Jamaica during Slavery," in *Caribbean Slavery in the Atlantic World*, ed. Verene Shepherd and Hilary McD. Beckles (Kingston, Jamaica: Ian Randle, 2000), 392–93.

70. Cecily Forde-Jones, "Mapping Racial Boundaries: Gender, Race, and Poor Relief in Barbadian Plantation Society," *Journal of Women's History* 10, no. 3 (1998): 9.

71. Nugent, *Lady Nugent's Journal*, 126.

72. In 1802, Pauline LeClerc was the first lady of the embattled French colonial regime in St. Domingue: her husband, General LeClerc, had been charged with leading Napoleon's military offensive to reestablish white authority on St. Domingue in the midst of an ongoing anticolonial and antislavery revolution there—a revolution that would soon result in the death of General LeClerc as well as the establishment of the free black republic of Haiti and the vanquishing of the French.

73. Francis Alexander Stanislaus, Baron de Wimpffen, *A Voyage to Saint Domingo in the Years 1788, 1789, and 1790*, trans. J. Wright (London: T. Cadell Jr.; W. Davies; and J. Wright, 1797), 114, cited by Joan Dayan, *Haiti, History, and the Gods* (Berkeley: University of California Press, 1995), 174–75. See also Kay Dian Kriz, *Sugar, Slavery, and the Culture of Refinement: Picturing the British West Indies, 1700–1840* (New Haven, CT: Yale University Press, 2008), 45–46; and Beth Fowkes Tobin, *Picturing Imperial Power: Colonial Subjects in Eighteenth-Century British Paintings* (Durham, NC: Duke University Press, 1999), 162, 164, 169.

74. Spillers, "Mama's Baby, Papa's Maybe," 218–19.

75. Sheridan's *School for Scandal* was the namesake of the first original play produced in Jamaica, *School for Soldiers or, The Deserter* (1781), by the actor John Henry. See Hill, *Jamaican Stage*, 160.

76. Gayle Rubin, "The Traffic of Women: Notes on the 'Political Economy' of Sex," in *Toward an Anthropology of Woman*, ed. Rayna Reiter (New York: Monthly Review Press, 1975), 157–85, 198–200

77. On gender in *School for Scandal*, see Gillian Russell, *Women, Sociability and Theatre in Georgian London* (Cambridge: Cambridge University Press, 2007), 197–225.

78. For a discussion of *School for Scandal* in terms of interior and exterior spaces in the context of England and the American Revolution, see Daniel O'Quinn, *Entertaining Crisis in the Atlantic Imperium, 1770–1790* (Baltimore: Johns Hopkins University Press, 2011), 133–42.

79. Michael Ragussis, *Theatrical Nation: Jews and Other Outlandish Englishmen in Georgian Britain* (Philadelphia: University of Pennsylvania Press, 2010), 2, 11.

80. Richard Brinsley Sheridan, *The New Comic Opera of the Duenna* (Kingston, Jamaica: W. Aikman, 1779), 58.

81. Richard Brinsley Sheridan, *The New Comic Opera of the Duenna*, 29.

82. Kathleen Wilson, "Rowe's *Fair Penitent* as Global History."

83. *Royal Gazette*, September 29, 1781.

84. "Call Again To-morrow: A Tale for the Times," *Gentlemen's Magazine* (Philadelphia), vol. 1, July–December 1837.

85. A. C. Carmichael, *Domestic Manners and Social Condition of the White, Coloured and Negro Population of the West Indies* (London: Whittaker, 1834), 158.

86. Long, *The History of Jamaica*, 2:427. Long mentions, as well, that white creole children have "constant intercourse from their birth with Negro domestics, whose drawling, dissonant gibberish they insensibly adopt and with it no small tincture of their awkward carriage and vulgar manners" (2:278).

87. Nugent, *Lady Nugent's Journal*, 98.

88. For a compelling consideration of the relation of text and textile in the eighteenth-century Atlantic world, see Danielle Skeehan, "Creole Domesticity: Women, Commerce,

and Kinship in Early Atlantic Writing" (PhD diss., Northeastern University, 2013). Skeehan's work has been influential on my understanding of the signifying role of textiles in Jamaica.

89. *Columbian Magazine*, June 1797, 8.

90. Carmichael, *Domestic Manners*, 154, 149, 156.

91. *Columbian Magazine*, August 1796, 237–38.

92. William Beckford, *A Descriptive Account of a Part of the Island of Jamaica with Remarks upon the Cultivation of the Sugar-cane. . . .* 2 vols. (London: T. and J. Egerton, Whitehall, 1790), 1:389.

93. I. M. Belisario, "Creole Negroes," in *Sketches of Character: In Illustration of the Habits, Occupation, and Costume of the Negro Population, in the Island of Jamaica* (Kingston, Jamaica: Published by the artist, 1837), n.p.

94. Carmichael, *Domestic Manners*, 158–59.

95. Henry T. De la Beche, *Notes on the Present Condition of The Negroes in Jamaica* (London: T. Cadell, 1825), 42.

96. Nugent, *Lady Nugent's Journal*, 66.

97. John Stewart, *An Account of Jamaica: And Its Inhabitants* (London: Longman, Hurst, Rees and Orme, 1808), 263.

98. Belisario, "French Set-Girls," in *Sketches of Character*, n.p.; Lewis, *Journal of a West-India Proprietor*, 53; *Columbian Magazine*, October 1797, 288; Michael Scott, *Tom Cringle's Log* (Paris: Casimir, 1854), 243.

99. Ann Rosalind Jones and Peter Stallybrass, *Renaissance Clothing and the Materials of Memory* (Cambridge: Cambridge University Press, 2000), 3.

100. Sara E. Johnson, *The Fear of French Negroes: Transcolonial Collaboration in the Revolutionary Americas* (Berkeley: University of California Press, 2012), 178.

101. *Columbian Magazine*, October 1797, 287.

102. Simon Gikandi, *Slavery and the Culture of Taste* (Princeton, NJ: Princeton University Press, 2011), 273.

103. Peter Marsden, *An Account of the Island of Jamaica; with Reflections on the Treatment, Occupation, and Provisions of the Slaves. . . .* (Newcastle: S. Hodgson, 1788), 33.

104. Cynric R. Williams, *A Tour through the Island of Jamaica from the Western to the Eastern End in the Year 1823* (London: Hunt and Clarke, 1826), 23.

105. Stuart Hall, "Afterword: Legacies of Anglo-Caribbean Culture—A Diasporic Perspective," in *Art and Emancipation in Jamaica*, ed. T. J. Barringer, Gillian Forrester, and Barbaro Martinez-Ruiz (New Haven, CT: Yale Center for British Art and Yale University Press, 2007), 181.

106. Williams, *A Tour through the Island of Jamaica*, 25–26.

107. See Gikandi, *Slavery and the Culture of Taste*, 272–76; Michael Craton, "Decoding Pitchy-patchy: The Roots, Branches and Essence of Junkanoo," Richard D. E. Burton, *Afro-Creole: Power, Opposition, and Play in the Caribbean* (Ithaca, NY: Cornell University Press, 1997), 65–89; and the essays collected in *Art and Emancipation in Jamaica: Isaac Mendes Belisario and His Worlds*, ed. T. J. Barringer, Gillian Forrester, and Barbaro Martinez-Ruiz.

108. Sylvia Wynter, "Jonkonnu in Jamaica: Towards the Interpretation of Folk Dance as a Cultural Process," *Jamaica Journal* 4, no. 2 (June 1970): 35–36.

109. Belisario, "Koo, Koo, or Actor-Boy," in *Sketches of Character*, n.p.

110. Lewis, *Journal of a West-India Proprietor*, 56.

111. Lewis, *Journal of a West-India Proprietor*, 56.

112. Kathleen Wilson, "Rowe's *Fair Penitent* as Global History," 239.

113. Lewis, *Journal of a West-India Proprietor*, 58.

114. Belisario, "Jaw-Bone, or House John-Canoe," in *Sketches of Character*, n.p.

115. Nugent, *Lady Nugent's Journal*, 115, 279, 280, 182.

116. Nugent, *Lady Nugent's Journal*, 288.

117. *Columbian Magazine*, December 1799, 251.

118. Fred Moten, *In the Break: The Aesthetics of the Black Radical Tradition* (Minneapolis: University of Minnesota Press, 2003), 14.

119. Belisario, "Lovey, alias Liverpool," in *Sketches of Character*, n.p.

120. Belisario, "Koo, Koo, or Actor-Boy," in *Sketches of Character*, n.p.

121. Monica L. Miller, *Slaves to Fashion: Black Dandyism and the Styling of Black Diasporic Identity* (Durham, NC: Duke University Press, 2009), 29.

122. Miller, *Slaves to Fashion*, 71.

123. Burton, *Afro-Creole*, 85.

124. See Burton, *Afro-Creole*, 86–89; and Turner, *Slaves and Missionaries*, 148–78.

CHAPTER 6: NEW YORK CITY

1. "Evacuation at the Bowery Theatre," *Traveller and Spirit of the Times* [New York], December 1, 1832, 2.

2. "Evacuation at the Bowery Theatre," *Traveller and Spirit of the Times*, 2.

3. Porter was not well-disposed toward the patrons of the Bowery Theatre: as Dale Cockrell reports, in 1840 Porter wrote, "[the] Bowery, . . . is to be transmogrified into a Circus shortly, the 'Bowery Boys' having lost their taste for the *illegitimate* drama, and they never had any other" (*Demons of Disorder: Early Blackface Minstrels and Their World* [Cambridge: Cambridge University Press, 1997], 33).

4. Richard Butsch, *The Making of American Audiences: From Stage to Television, 1750–1990* (Cambridge: Cambridge University Press, 2000), 3.

5. Frances Anne Butler (Miss Fanny Kemble), *Journal of a Residence in America* (Paris: A. and W. Galignani, 1835), 181.

6. Colley Cibber and William Shakespeare, *The Tragical History of King Richard the Third . . . with Alterations, by Mr. Cibber* (London: W. Mears and J. Browne, 1718), 70.

7. For a superb account of the complexities of popular sovereignty in the early nineteenth-century U.S., and the importance of scenes of spectacle therein, see Jennifer Greiman, *Democracy's Spectacle: Sovereignty and Public Life in Antebellum American Writing* (New York: Fordham University Press, 2010).

8. Montrose Jonas Moses, *The Fabulous Forrest: The Record of an American Actor* (Boston: Little, Brown, 1929), 100.

9. *New York Herald*, May 10, 1849, 4.

10. For a contemporary report of the riot, see *Account of the Terrific and Fatal Riot at the New-York Astor Place Opera House* (New York: H. M. Ranney, 1849). Scholarship on the Astor Place Riot is extensive. For a recent comprehensive account of the riot, see Nigel Cliff, *The Shakespeare Riots: Revenge, Drama, and Death in Nineteenth-century*

America (New York: Random House, 2007). Additional useful works include Peter Buckley, "To the Opera House: Culture and Society in New York City, 1820–1860" (PhD diss., SUNY Stonybrook, 1984); and Richard Moody, *The Astor Place Riot* (Bloomington: Indiana University Press, 1958). On the riot in the context of the history of the working class see Lawrence W. Levine, *Highbrow/Lowbrow: The Emergence of Cultural Hierarchy in America* (Cambridge, MA: Harvard University Press, 1988); Sean Wilentz, *Chants Democratic: New York City and the Rise of the American Working Class, 1788–1850* (New York: Oxford University Press, 1984); and Shelley Streeby, *American Sensations: Class, Empire, and the Production of Popular Culture* (Berkeley: University of California Press, 2002). On the riot in relation to the history of the theatre see David Grimsted, *Melodrama Unveiled: American Theater and Culture, 1800–1850* (Chicago: University of Chicago Press, 1968); Eric Lott, *Love and Theft: Blackface Minstrelsy and the American Working Class* (New York: Oxford University Press, 1993); Bruce A. McConachie, *Melodramatic Formations: American Theatre and Society, 1820–1870* (Iowa City: University of Iowa Press, 1992), and "The 'Theatre of the Mob': Apocalyptic Melodrama and Pre-industrial Riots in Antebellum New York," in *Theatre for Working-Class Audiences in the United States, 1830–1980*, ed. Daniel Friedman and Bruce McConachie (Westport, CT: Greenwood Press, 1985), 17–46.

11. At the Park Theatre, in December 1833, for example, the fourth and fifth acts of *Richard III* were staged, followed by a Mr. Blakeley performing Jim Crow (*American* [New York], December 28, 1833).

12. See Elizabeth Maddock Dillon and Michael Drexler, "Haiti and the U.S., Entwined," *The Haitian Revolution and the Early U.S.: Histories, Geographies, Textualities*, ed. Elizabeth Maddock Dillon and Michael Drexler (Philadelphia: University of Pennsylvania Press, forthcoming).

13. "American Theatre," *New York Daily Mirror*, December 15, 1832, 190. Note that Heather S. Nathans documents a similar public response—increased repugnance and, indeed, race riots, in relation to the performance of miscegenation in *Othello* during this period in Philadelphia (*Slavery and Sentiment on the American Stage, 1787–1861: Lifting the Veil of Black* [Cambridge: Cambridge University Press, 2009]). The reported distaste for mixed-race union seen in these instances is related to the increased binarization of black and white racializations discussed throughout this chapter. For further discussion of the performance of miscegenation in the U.S., see Tavia Amolo Ochieng' Nyongó, *The Amalgamation Waltz: Race, Performance, and the Ruses of Memory* (Minneapolis: University of Minnesota Press, 2009); Diana Rebekkah Paulin, *Imperfect Unions: Staging Miscegenation in U.S. Drama and Fiction* (Minneapolis: University of Minnesota Press, 2012); and Daphne Brooks, *Bodies in Dissent: Spectacular Performances of Race and Freedom, 1850–1910* (Durham, NC: Duke University Press, 2006).

14. See Joseph Norton Ireland, *Records of the New York Stage, from 1750 to 1860*, 2 vols. (New York: T. H. Morrell, 1866–67), 2:56, 2:92. Contra Ireland's claim concerning the original nature of this performance, newspapers report that Oroonoko appeared in New York City for a four-night run in 1783 (*Royal Gazette* [New York], October 18, 1783). Jenna Marie Gibbs notes that *Oroonoko* was performed once in Philadelphia in 1792 and once in New York City in 1793: in both cases the play closed after a single performance, indicating lack of audience interest in the play. Gibbs also reports that *Oroonoko* ap-

peared in New York City in 1838 and in Philadelphia in 1840. See Jenna Marie Gibbs, *Performing the Temple of Liberty: Slavery, Rights, and Revolution in Transatlantic Theatricality (1760s–1830s)* (PhD diss., University of California, Los Angeles, 2008), 181–82.

15. Ireland, *Records of the New York Stage*, 55–56.

16. *The Life of Jim Crow*, in *Jump Jim Crow: Lost Plays, Lyrics, and Street Prose of the First Atlantic Popular Culture*, ed. W. T. Lhamon Jr. (Cambridge, MA: Harvard University Press, 2003), 389.

17. For an insightful discussion of the extent to which commons did exist in colonial North America, see Allan Greer, "Commons and Enclosure in the Colonization of North America," *The American Historical Review* 117, no. 2 (April 1, 2012): 365–86. Greer argues that it is a mistake to see America as a universal commons that was initially and immediately enclosed by way of Lockean property ownership imposed by European colonials; rather, dispossession of native lands (which were held in common according to differing modes of use and custom by different tribes) occurred with the assistance of colonial commons in the form of the grazing of animals in areas surrounding colonial settlements: what Greer describes as "dispossession through colonial commons" occurred when settler livestock encroached on and destroyed indigenous land use practices. Lockean ownership and enclosure followed in the wake of colonial invasion: "A multi-species assault on the native commons really was under way as the colonial commons advanced across the face of the continent, bringing in its wake a colonial enclosure movement that left virtually no room for Indian people" (383). Additional work by scholars including Dana D. Nelson, *Commons Democracy*; Melissah J. Pawlikowski, "The Plight and the Bounty: Squatters, Profiteers and the Transforming Hand of Sovereignty in Indian Country, 1750–1774" (PhD diss., Ohio State University, in progress); and Joanna Brooks, *Why We Left: Untold Stories and Songs of America's First Immigrants* (Minneapolis: University of Minnesota Press, 2013) points to diverse histories of early colonial commoning that scholars are currently exploring in greater depth. Nonetheless, such commoning practices were foreclosed by the horizon of a Lockean regime of exclusive property ownership that assumed particular juridical force in the so-called Marshall trilogy of Supreme Court decisions (1823–32) that codified the legal framework for dispossessing Native peoples of land and sovereignty.

18. Ruth Bogin, "Petitioning and the New Moral Economy of Post-Revolutionary America," *William and Mary Quarterly* 45, no. 3 (July 1988): 394.

19. For discussion of Lockean social contract theory in relation to enclosure, see Michael E. Goodhart, "Origins and Universality in the Human Rights Debates: Cultural Essentialism and the Challenge of Globalization," *Human Rights Quarterly* 25, no. 4 (November 2003): 935–64.

20. Daniel Vickers, "Competency and Competition: Economic Culture in Early America," *William and Mary Quarterly* 47, no. 1 (1990): 3–29.

21. For a useful account of the ongoing colonial and imperial nature of communities in the United States following the formation of the U.S. state, see Ed White, "Early American Nations as Imagined Communities," *American Quarterly* 56, no. 1 (2004): 49–81.

22. *National Advocate*, January 9, 1822; reprinted in George Thompson, *A Documentary History of the African Theatre* (Evanston, IL: Northwestern University Press, 1998), 85. On the history of the African Theatre in New York City see Marvin Edward McAllister,

White People Do Not Know How to Behave at Entertainments Designed for Ladies and Gentlemen of Colour: William Brown's African and American Theater (Chapel Hill: University of North Carolina Press, 2003); Shane White, *Stories of Freedom in Black New York* (Cambridge, MA: Harvard University Press, 2002); Errol Hill, *Shakespeare in Sable: A History of Black Shakespearean Actors* (Amherst: University of Massachusetts Press, 1984); and Michael Warner et al., "A Soliloquy 'Lately Spoken at the African Theatre': Race and the Public Sphere in New York City, 1821," *American Literature* 73, no. 1 (2001): 1–46.

23. Although the script of the play is not extant, its performance is advertised in the *Commercial Advertiser*, January 16, 1822; reprinted in Thompson, *A Documentary History of the African Theatre*, 87–88. For further discussion of "King Shotaway," see Errol Hill, "The Revolutionary Tradition in Black Drama," *Theatre Journal* 38, no. 4 (1986): 409.

24. McAllister, *White People Do Not Know How to Behave*, 50.

25. An account of the riot appears in the *Commercial Advertiser*, August 17, 1822; reprinted in Thompson, *A Documentary History*, 106. The newspaper account reports that the "ruffians" acted "with full intent to break [the theatre] up root and branch."

26. See McAllister, *White People Do Not Know How to Behave*, 143–49. Thompson emphasizes economic rather than racial motives (*A Documentary History*, 107–8); see also Paul A. Gilje, *The Road to Mobocracy: Popular Disorder in New York City, 1765–1854* (Chapel Hill: University of North Carolina Press for the Institute of Early American History and Culture, 1987), 153–59.

27. *National Advocate*, August 3, 1821; reprinted in Thompson, *A Documentary History*, 58–59.

28. McAllister, *White People Do Not Know How to Behave*, 42.

29. See Samuel A. Hay, *African American Theatre: An Historical and Critical Analysis* (Cambridge: Cambridge University Press, 1994); Warner et al., "A Soliloquy 'Lately Spoken at the African Theatre'"; and White, *Stories of Freedom in Black New York*.

30. *Commercial Advertiser*, January 16, 1822; reprinted in Thompson, *A Documentary History*, 87.

31. See David R. Roediger, *The Wages of Whiteness: Race and the Making of the American Working Class*. Rev. ed. (London: Verso, 1999), 102–4.

32. *National Advocate*, September 25, 1821; reprinted in Thompson, *A Documentary History*, 87.

33. Hay, *African American Theatre*, 13. See also McAllister, *White People Do Not Know How to Behave*, 150–66.

34. Noah's own identity as Jewish is significant here as well with regard to efforts to binarize racial identity in this period. For further discussion of Noah's complex relation to race and ethnicity, see Jonathan D. Sarna, *Jacksonian Jew: The Two Worlds of Mordecai Noah* (New York: Holmes and Meier, 1980).

35. *National Advocate*, September 21, 1821; reprinted in Thompson, *A Documentary History*, 61–62.

36. On the erasure of the creole status of whites in the United States, see Sean X. Goudie, *Creole America: The West Indies and the Formation of Literature and Culture in the New Republic* (Philadelphia: University of Pennsylvania Press, 2006). On the politics of white American "Nativism," during the Jacksonian era, see Matthew Frye

Jacobson, *Whiteness of a Different Color: European Immigrants and the Alchemy of Race* (Cambridge, MA: Harvard University Press, 1998); Roediger, *The Wages of Whiteness*; and Wilentz, *Chants Democratic*.

37. Mark Rifkin, "Settler States of Feeling: National Belonging and the Erasure of Native American Presence," in *A Companion to American Literary Studies*, ed. Caroline F. Levander and Robert S. Levine (Wiley-Blackwell, 2011), 353.

38. Aileen Moreton-Robinson, "Writing off Treaties: White Possession in the United States Critical Whiteness Studies Literature," in *Transnational Whiteness Matters*, ed. Aileen Moreton-Robinson, Maryrose Casey, and Fiona Nicoll (Lanham, MD: Lexington Books, 2008), 84.

39. Philip Joseph Deloria, *Playing Indian* (New Haven, CT: Yale University Press, 1998). On the number of plays including Indians written in the nineteenth century, see Richard Moody, ed. *Dramas from the American Theatre, 1762–1909* (Cleveland, OH: World Publishing, 1966); and Don B. Wilmeth, "Tentative Checklist of Indian Plays," *Journal of American Drama and Theatre* 2, no. 1 (fall 1989): 34–54. More generally, on the performance of the Indian chief in this period, see Gordon M. Sayre, *The Indian Chief as Tragic Hero: Native Resistance and the Literatures of America, from Moctezuma to Tecumseh* (Chapel Hill: University of North Carolina Press, 2005).

40. Myron Matlaw, "'This Is Tragedy!!!': The History of *Pizarro*," *Quarterly Journal of Speech* 43, no. 3 (1957): 290. According to Matlaw, Dunlap's version appeared only at the Park Theatre under Dunlap's management; the version that was performed widely in the United States was Sheridan's.

41. For discussion of the Black Legend and seventeenth-century English drama, see chapter 2. Interestingly, Sheridan's version of *Pizarro* also makes reference to a different colonial scene than that of the Americas: namely, English colonialism in East India. Portions of Rolla's most famous speech galvanizing the Inca army to resist the Spanish invaders in *Pizarro* were borrowed directly from Sheridan's own parliamentary speeches delivered at the impeachment trial of the former British governor general of Bengal, Warren Hastings, who had been charged with a variety of crimes, including oppressive treatment of East Indians, personal corruption, and political corruption. Prime Minister William Pitt reportedly remarked, after viewing *Pizarro*, "there is nothing new in it, for I heard it all long ago in his speeches at Hastings' trial" (cited by John Clyde Loftis, "Whig Oratory on Stage: Sheridan's *Pizarro*," *Eighteenth-Century Studies* 8, no. 4 [1975]: 459). Further, Loftis notes that the dynamics of colonialism in the play also resonated with contemporary debates in England concerning the abolition of the slave trade: William Wilberforce, leader of the abolitionist movement in England, reportedly went to the theatre for the first time in twenty years in order to attend and applaud Sheridan's *Pizarro* (Loftis, "Whig Oratory," 461).

42. Richard Brinsley Sheridan, *Pizarro* (act 2, scene 2), in *The Dramatic Works of Richard Brinsley Sheridan*, ed. Cecil John Layton Price. 2 vols. (Oxford: Clarendon Press, 1973), 2:669.

43. Some of the initial enthusiasm for the play in England was evidently due to the fact that Pizarro was construed as the figure of Napoleon Bonaparte, then threatening to invade England. As Julie A. Carlson points out, the play might be understood to refer to English fears of a French invasion as well as the invasion of Peru by Spain, the invasion of East India by England, and the invasion of Ireland by England ("Trying Sheridan's *Pizarro*," *Texas Studies in Literature and Language* 38, no. 3/4 [1996]: 362).

44. "Pizarro," *Massachusetts Mercury*, December 10, 1799.

45. Sheridan, *Pizarro* (act 5, scene 3), 700.

46. On the enduring importance of Metacom to U.S. culture, see Phillip Gould, "Remembering Metacom: Historical Writing and the Cultures of Masculinity in Early Republican America," in *Sentimental Men: Masculinity and the Politics of Affect in American Culture*, ed. Mary Chapman and Glenn Hendler (Berkeley: University of California Press, 1999), 112–23; and Jill Lepore, *The Name of War: King Philip's War and the Origins of American Identity* (New York: Knopf, 1998).

47. John Augustus Stone, *Metamora: or, The Last of the Wampanoags* (1829), reprinted in *Staging the Nation: Plays from the American Theater, 1787–1909*, ed. Don B. Wilmeth (Boston: Bedford Books, 1998).

48. Cited in Richard Moody, *Edwin Forrest, First Star of the American Stage* (New York: Knopf, 1960), 88.

49. For discussion of *Pizarro* as a source for Stone's *Metamora*, see McConachie, *Melodramatic Formations*, 98–99.

50. Deloria, *Playing Indian*, 36–37. In related terms, Dana D. Nelson writes, "The abstracting identity of white/national manhood found one means for stabilizing its internal divisions and individual anxieties via imagined projections into, onto, and against Indian territories, Indian bodies, Indian identities" (*National Manhood: Capitalist Citizenship and the Imagined Fraternity of White Men* [Durham, NC: Duke University Press, 1998], 67). For additional discussions of white U.S. Americans playing Indian, see Carroll Smith-Rosenberg, "Surrogate Americans: Masculinity, Masquerade, and the Formation of a National Identity," *PMLA* 119, no. 5 (2004): 1325–35; Renée L. Bergland, *The National Uncanny: Indian Ghosts and American Subjects* (Hanover, NH: University Press of New England, 2000); as well as Ralph Ellison's classic essay, "Change the Joke and Slip the Yoke," in *Shadow and Act* (New York: Vintage, 1995). For accounts of intercultural performance of and by Native Americans, see Joshua David Bellin and Laura L. Mielke, eds., *Native Acts: Indian Performance, 1603–1832* (Lincoln: University of Nebraska Press, 2011).

51. Gabriel Harrison, *Edwin Forrest, The Actor and the Man. Critical and Reminiscent* (Brooklyn, NY: Brooklyn Eagle Book Printing, 1889), 39.

52. Alan Taylor, "'Stopping the Progress of Rogues and Deceivers': A White Indian Recruiting Notice of 1808," *William and Mary Quarterly*, 42, no. 1 (January 1985): 94.

53. See, among others, Jonathan Elmer's account of this figure in *On Lingering and Being Last: Race and Sovereignty in the New World* (New York: Fordham University Press, 2008); and Brian W. Dippie, *The Vanishing American: White Attitudes and U.S. Indian Policy* (Lawrence: University Press of Kansas, 1991); as well as, more broadly, the work of Gerald Robert Vizenor critiquing the concept of the vanishing Indian and articulating a model of "survivance" to characterize the continued vitality of Native American peoples and culture (*Fugitive Poses: Native American Scenes of Absence and Presence* [Lincoln: University of Nebraska Press, 1998]; *Manifest Manners: Postindian Warriors of Survivance* [Hanover, NH: University Press of New England, 1994]; and *Survivance: Narratives of Native Presence* [Lincoln: University of Nebraska Press, 2008]).

54. Patrick Wolfe, "Settler Colonialism and the Elimination of the Native," *Journal of Genocide Research* 8, no. 4 (2006): 389–90.

55. Newspapers routinely "puffed" Forrest with this term; see *Account of the Terrific and Fatal Riot at the New-York Astor Place Opera House....* (New York: H. M. Ranney, 1849), 7.

56. William Rounseville Alger, *Life of Edwin Forrest, the American Tragedian.* 2 vols. (Philadelphia: J. B. Lippincott, 1877), 1:138–39.

57. "Mr. Placide; Bowery; Indian; Exhibited," *Evening Post* (New York) December 12, 1833, 2.

58. For an excellent account of the war and Black Hawk's tour and imprisonment, see Adam John Waterman, "The Price of the Purchase: Black Hawk's War and the Colonization of the Mississippi River Valley" (PhD diss., New York University, 2008). For further discussion of Black Hawk at the theatre see Rosemarie K. Bank, *Theatre Culture in America, 1825–1860* (Cambridge: Cambridge University Press, 1997), 64–68; Susan Scheckel, *The Insistence of the Indian: Race and Nationalism in Nineteenth-Century American Culture* (Princeton, NJ: Princeton University Press, 1998), 99–111; and Gordon Sayre, *The Indian Chief as Tragic Hero,* 1, 10.

59. "The Indian Hostages," *New York Spectator,* June 13, 1833, 1.

60. James E. Murdoch, *The Stage: Or, Recollections of Actors and Acting from an Experience of Fifty Years* (Philadelphia: J. M. Stoddart, 1880), 298–300.

61. "BLACK-HAWKIANA," *Nantucket Inquirer,* July 6, 1833, 2.

62. "Black Hawk and Party," *Boston Courier,* November 28, 1833, 8.

63. Jodi A. Byrd, *The Transit of Empire: Indigenous Critiques of Colonialism* (Minneapolis: University of Minnesota Press, 2011), xxxix.

64. Byrd, *Transit of Empire,* 63.

65. The Black Caribs of St. Vincent successfully resisted colonization through much of the seventeenth century; by the eighteenth century, however, the French had established a foothold on the island. European claim to the island shifted in battle and treaty negotiations between the English and French over the course of the century: in 1763, St. Vincent was ceded to Britain by treaty at the close of the Seven Years' War; in 1779 the island was restored to French rule; and in 1783, St. Vincent was regained by the British under the Treaty of Versailles. As this history of treaty decisions indicates, the St. Vincent Caribs themselves were not party to these negotiations. Dissatisfied with colonial practices and policies on the island, the Caribs rebelled unsuccessfully against the British in 1795. On the history of the St. Vincent Caribs, see Charles Shephard, *An Historical Account of the Island of Saint Vincent* (1831; repr., London: F. Cass, 1971); William Young, *An Account of the Black Charaibs in the Island of St. Vincent's, with the Charaib Treaty of 1773, and Other Original Documents* (1795; repr., London: F. Cass, 1971); Phillip P. Boucher, *Cannibal Encounters: Europeans and Island Caribs, 1492–1763* (Baltimore: Johns Hopkins University Press, 1992); and Laurent Dubois, *A Colony of Citizens: Revolution and Slave Emancipation in the French Caribbean, 1787–1804* (Chapel Hill: University of North Carolina Press, 2004).

66. Joseph Chatoyer was declared the national hero of St. Vincent in 2002; the descendants of the deported Black Caribs, know as the Garifuna, live primarily in Belize and Honduras today.

67. *Commercial Advertiser,* January 16, 1822; reproduced in George Thompson, *A Documentary History of the African Theatre,* 87.

68. George C. D. Odell, *Annals of the New York Stage,* 15 vols. (New York: Columbia University Press, 1927–49), 3:70–71. According to Thompson, the playbill cited by Odell

"is not now to be found in any of the four libraries where Odell did most of his research" (*Documentary History*, 136).

69. McAllister writes, "As a ship's steward, Brown may have witnessed the 1795 uprising, but I doubt he was born on St. Vincent because when he premiered the play in 1822, he mistakenly placed this insurrection on the island of St. Domingo—or Santo Domingo—not St. Vincent. If Brown was born on St. Vincent, he would surely know the difference between Santo Domingo and his home island" (*White People Do Not Know How to Behave*, 95).

70. Historians have debated whether the conspiracy did, in fact, take place or was largely the fabrication of white plantocratic paranoia. For details of the conspiracy and the historical debate, see Robert L. Paquette, "From Rebellion to Revisionism: The Continuing Debate About the Denmark Vesey Affair," *Journal of The Historical Society* 4, no. 3 (2004): 291–334.

71. Both Earle's novel and Fawcett's libretto are based on an account of the historical figure, Jack Mansong, as reported in *A Treatise on Sugar* by Benjamin Mosley (London: G. G. and J. Robinson, 1799). "Obi" refers to an amulet or charm worn by Jamaican practitioners of Obeah, an African-derived religion, widely practiced among slaves in Jamaica and associated with rebellion against and defiance of European/Christian rule. For accounts of the extensive publication history of versions of *Obi; or Three-Finger'd Jack*, see Robert Hoskins and Eileen Southern, "Introduction," in Samuel Arnold, *Obi; or Three-Finger'd Jack* in *Music for London Entertainment, 1660–1800 Series D Volume 4* (1800, repr. London: Stainer and Bell, 1996) and the editorial introduction by Srinivas Aravamudan to a recent critical edition of Earle's novel, *Obi, or, The History of Three-fingered Jack*, ed. Srinivas Aravamudan (Peterborough, ON: Broadview Press, 2005). A special issue of the online journal *Romantic Circles Praxis Series* (August 2002) edited by Charles Rzepka is devoted to discussions of *Obi* and includes video clips of recent productions of the pantomime and the melodrama versions as well as scholarly articles and reproductions of two scripts of *Obi*: see www.rc.umd.edu/praxis/obi/. Accessed November 29, 2013.

72. See Hoskins and Southern, "Introduction," xiii, xvii; and Peter Buckley, "*Obi* in New York: Aldridge and the African Grove," *Romantic Circles Praxis Series* (August 2002): www.rc.umd.edu/praxis.obi/buckley/buckley.html. Buckley notes that despite remaining in repertoire, "*Obi* cannot, however, be termed a ringing success with Manhattan's public"(1). Buckley suggests that the play had less appeal as a particularly American drama than a British-Atlantic one.

73. Warner et al., "A Soliloquy 'Lately Spoken at the African Theatre,'" 3.

74. William Earle, *Obi, or, The History of Threefingered Jack in a Series of Letters from a Resident in Jamaica to His Friend in England* (Worcester, MA: Isaiah Thomas Jr., 1804), 31.

75. Warner et al., "A Soliloquy 'Lately Spoken at the African Theatre,'" 1–2.

76. For a discussion of Sylvia Wynter's account of indigenization in relation to settler colonialism and creolization in the Caribbean, see Shona N. Jackson, *Creole Indigeneity: Between Myth and Nation in the Caribbean* (Minneapolis: University of Minnesota Press, 2012), 42–44.

77. Charles Haywood, *Negro Minstrelsy and Shakespearean Burlesque* (Hatboro, PA: Folklore Associates, 1966), 80–81.

78. *The Darkey Tragedian. An Ethiopian Sketch, in One Scene* (New York: Happy Hours Company, 1874), 3–4.

79. Henry Llewellyn Williams and J. R. Planché, *The Black Forrest: An Ethiopian Farce, Altered from Planche's "Garrick Fever"* (New York: De Witt, 1882).

80. Ironically, Edwin Forrest is one of the first white actors to "black-up" in 1820, prior to T. D. Rice.

81. *Oh! Hush!* in Lhamon, *Jump Jim Crow*, 150.

82. For my discussion of Jim Crow materials published in England, I rely upon W. T. Lhamon Jr.'s superb collection of these materials, *Jump Jim Crow*.

83. *The Peacock and the Crow*, in Lhamon, *Jump Jim Crow*, 282.

84. Lhamon, *Jump Jim Crow*, 389.

85. Lhamon, *Jump Jim Crow*, 399.

86. Lhamon, *Jump Jim Crow*, 65.

87. Cited in Michael Rogin, *Blackface, White Noise: Jewish Immigrants in the Hollywood Melting Pot* (Berkeley: University of California Press, 1996), 22, who cites Alexander Saxton, *The Rise and Fall of the White Republic: Class Politics and Mass Culture in Nineteenth Century America* (London: Verso, 1990), 166. Note that Lhamon describes the development of blackface performance as a crucial moment in the scenario of proclaiming American independence from British cultural dominance: "Dating from the early to mid-1830s, these texts [of blackface "Jim Crow" plays] constitute some of the first American working-class plays, first distinctly American plays and musicals, and first plays of crossracial identification anywhere in the Atlantic.... These plays supplanted an English farce and melodrama tradition. They stirred a lumpen vernacular with a new Black Stage English that was surely more accurate, certainly more vital and fetishized, than the extant English approximation" (*Jump Jim Crow*, 25).

88. Haywood, *Negro Minstrelsy and Shakespearean Burlesque*, 78.

89. Eric Lott, *Love and Theft: Blackface Minstrelsy and the American Working Class* (New York: Oxford University Press, 1993), 25.

90. Lott, *Love and Theft*, 71.

91. Lhamon writes, "What many commentators in the second half of the twentieth century have assumed worked to derogate blacks, in its own era actually had a more complex effect. Everyone then understood that early incarnations of blackface disrupted and interrogated elite mentalities to their detriment. Blackface confounded the elite capacity to control the mobility" (*Jump Jim Crow*, 27). Similarly, Cockrell observes that with respect to blackface performance, "there is no question that derision is intended; but so too is incorporation of the Other. The power of subsequent laughter, a form of truth, joins rather than divides. Performance suggests time and again that early blackface minstrelsy was as much about healing as about wounding" (*Demons of Disorder*, 60).

92. See, for example, McAllister, *White People Do Not Know How to Behave*; and Saidiya V. Hartman, *Scenes of Subjection: Terror, Slavery, and Self-Making in Nineteenth-Century America* (New York: Oxford University Press, 1997).

93. Useful accounts of the Farren Riot include Bank, *Theatre Culture in America, 1825–1860*, 151–64, and Theodore Junior Shank, "The Bowery Theatre, 1826–1836" (PhD diss., Stanford University, 1956).

94. *New York American*, July 10, 1834.

95. Wilentz, *Chants Democratic*, 264–65.

96. *Commercial Advertiser*, July 10, 1834.

97. *New York Sun*, July 11, 1834.

98. Leonard L. Richards, *"Gentlemen of Property and Standing": Anti-abolition Mobs in Jacksonian America* (New York: Oxford University Press, 1970), 66.

99. Richards (*"Gentlemen of Property and Standing"*) emphasizes anxiety about miscegenation; Wilentz (*Chants Democratic*) emphasizes black and white labor competition; Lott (*Love and Theft*) and Roediger (*The Wages of Whiteness*) emphasize the insecurity of the white working class during this phase of capitalist development; and Gilje (*The Road to Mobocracy*) emphasizes rising white anxiety about black cultural institutions.

100. *Commercial Advertiser*, reprinted in the *New Bedford Mercury*, July 18, 1834.

101. Cockrell, *Demons of Disorder*, 86.

102. Roediger, *The Wages of Whiteness*, 58.

103. Cited by Lhamon, *Raising Cain*, 30.

104. *Commercial Advertiser*, reprinted in the *New Bedford Mercury*, July 18, 1834.

105. On the naming of Haiti see David Patrick Geggus, *Haitian Revolutionary Studies* (Bloomington: Indiana University Press, 2002), 207–20. Geggus reports that General Dessalines adopted the term "indigenes" for his army: "this use of Amerindian symbolism prior to the adoption of the word 'Haïti' appears to show Dessalines's desire to identify with an Amerindian past even in the absence of reliable information about that past" (214).

106. *Weekly Courier and New-York Enquirer*, July 10, 1834.

107. Wilentz, *Chants Democratic*, 265–66.

108. See Roediger, *The Wages of Whiteness*; and Jacobson, *Whiteness of a Different Color*.

109. The petition appeared in the *New York Herald*, May 9, 1849. On Melville's involvement in the affair see Dennis Berthold, "Class Acts: The Astor Place Riots and Melville's 'The Two Temples,'" *American Literature* 71, no. 3 (1999): 429–61.

110. For sources on the Astor Place Riot, see note 10 above. The fatality count of twenty-six deaths is that given by Nigel Cliff in *The Shakespeare Riots*, 241.

111. *New York Herald*, May 8, 1849, 4, cited in Berthold, "Class Acts," 434.

112. Lara Langer Cohen, *The Fabrication of American Literature: Fraudulence and Antebellum Print Culture* (Philadelphia: University of Pennsylvania Press, 2012), 65–100.

113. On the Marshall trilogy and Native American sovereignty, see Joanne Barker, *Native Acts: Law, Recognition, and Cultural Authenticity* (Durham, NC: Duke University Press, 2011), 29–35.

114. Walter Johnson, *River of Dark Dreams*, 5.

115. Cited by Lawrence W. Levine, *Highbrow/Lowbrow: The Emergence of Cultural Hierarchy in America* (Cambridge, MA: Harvard University Press, 1988), 29.

116. On increased physical force used to control audiences, see Peter Buckley, "To the Opera House," and Levine, *Highbrow/Lowbrow*; on the privatization of audiences, see Richard Butsch, *The Making of American Audiences*.

117. *Morning Courier and New York Enquirer*, May 1949, cited in Cliff, *The Shakespeare Riots*, 234.

BIBLIOGRAPHY

ARCHIVES

American Antiquarian Society
Beinecke Library, Yale University
Boston Public Library
British Library
Charleston Library Society
Charleston Public Library, South Carolina Room
Harvard Theatre Collection, Harvard University
Jamaica Archives and Records Department
John Carter Brown Library, Brown University
National Archives of the United Kingdom
National Library of Jamaica
New-York Historical Society
New York Public Library
South Carolina Historical Society
Walpole Library, Yale University
Yale Center for British Art

WORKS CITED

Account of the Terrific and Fatal Riot at the New-York Astor Place Opera House. . . . New York: H. M. Ranney, 1849.

Agamben, Giorgio. *Homo Sacer: Sovereign Power and Bare Life.* Palo Alto, CA: Stanford University Press, 1998.

Alderson, Robert. "Charleston's Rumored Slave Revolt of 1793." In *The Impact of the Haitian Revolution in the Atlantic World.* Edited by David Patrick Geggus, 93–111. Columbia: University of South Carolina Press, 2001.

Alexander, Jeffrey C. "Cultural Pragmatics: Social Performance between Ritual and Strategy." *Sociological Theory* 22, no. 4 (2004): 527–73.

Alger, William Rounseville. *Life of Edwin Forrest, the American Tragedian.* 2 vols. Philadelphia: J. B. Lippincott, 1877.

Amussen, Susan Dwyer. *Caribbean Exchanges: Slavery and the Transformation of English Society, 1640–1700.* Chapel Hill: University of North Carolina Press, 2007.

Anderson, Benedict R. O'G. *Imagined Communities: Reflections on the Origin and Spread of Nationalism.* Rev. ed. London: Verso, 1991.

Andrade, Susan Z. "White Skin, Black Masks: Colonialism and the Sexual Politics of *Oroonoko.*" *Cultural Critique* 27 (1994): 189–214.

Anghie, Antony. *Imperialism, Sovereignty, and the Making of International Law.* Cambridge: Cambridge University Press, 2005.

Aravamudan, Srinivas. Introduction to William Earle, *Obi, or, The History of Three-fingered Jack.* Edited by Srinivas Aravamudan. Peterborough, ON: Broadview Press, 2005.

Aravamudan, Srinivas. *Tropicopolitans: Colonialism and Agency, 1688–1804.* Durham, NC: Duke University Press, 1999.

Armitage, David. "The Cromwellian Protectorate and the Languages of Empire." *Historical Journal* 35, no. 3 (1992): 531–55.

Armitage, David. "Three Concepts of Atlantic History." In *The British Atlantic World, 1500–1800.* Edited by David Armitage and M. J. Braddick, 11–27. New York: Palgrave Macmillan, 2002.

Asad, Talal. "On Torture, or Cruel, Inhuman, and Degrading Treatment." *Social Research* 63, no. 4 (December 1, 1996): 1081–1109.

Astington, John. *English Court Theatre, 1558–1642.* Cambridge: Cambridge University Press, 1999.

Atherton, Herbert McDonald. *Political Prints in the Age of Hogarth: A Study of the Ideographic Representation of Politics.* Oxford: Clarendon Press, 1974.

Avery, Emmett L., ed. *The London Stage, 1660–1800: A Calendar of Plays, Entertainments & Afterpieces. . . . Compiled from the Playbills, Newspapers and Theatrical Diaries, Part 2, 1700–1729.* 2 vols. Carbondale: Southern Illinois University Press, 1960.

Babb, Winston. "French Refugees from Saint Domingue to the Southern United States: 1791–1810." PhD diss., University of Virginia, 1954.

Backscheider, Paula R. *Spectacular Politics: Theatrical Power and Mass Culture in Early Modern England.* Baltimore: Johns Hopkins University Press, 1993.

Bagehot. "Prisoners' Voting Rights: Britain's Mounting Fury over Sovereignty." *Bagehot's Notebook, Economist* (blog), February 10, 2011. Accessed November 30, 2013. www.economist.com/blogs/bagehot/2011/02/prisoners_voting_rights.

Bailyn, Bernard. *The Ideological Origins of the American Revolution.* Cambridge, MA: Harvard University Press, 1967.

Balibar, Étienne. *Masses, Classes, Ideas: Studies on Politics and Philosophy Before and After Marx.* New York: Routledge, 1994.

Bank, Rosemarie K. *Theatre Culture in America, 1825–1860.* Cambridge: Cambridge University Press, 1997.

Bannet, Eve Tavor. "The Marriage Act of 1753: 'A Most Cruel Law for the Fair Sex.'" *Eighteenth-Century Studies* 30, no. 3 (1997): 233–54.

Barker, Joanne. *Native Acts: Law, Recognition, and Cultural Authenticity.* Durham, NC: Duke University Press, 2011.

Barringer, T. J., Gillian Forrester, and Barbara Martinez-Ruiz. *Art and Emancipation in Jamaica: Isaac Mendes Belisario and His Worlds*. New Haven, CT: Yale Center for British Art and Yale University Press, 2007.

Baucom, Ian. *Specters of the Atlantic: Finance Capital, Slavery, and the Philosophy of History*. Durham, NC: Duke University Press, 2005.

Beckford, William. *A Descriptive Account of a Part of the Island of Jamaica with Remarks upon the Cultivation of the Sugar-cane. . . .* 2 vols. London: T. and J. Egerton, Whitehall, 1790.

Beckles, Hilary McD. "Capitalism, Slavery, and Caribbean Modernity." *Callaloo* 20, no. 4 (1997): 777–89.

Beckles, Hilary McD. Review of *Slavery, Atlantic Trade and the British Economy, 1660–1800*, by Kenneth Morgan. *Albion: A Quarterly Journal Concerned with British Studies* 34, no. 4 (December 2002): 650–52.

Beckles, Hilary McD., and Andrew Downes. "The Economics of Transition to the Black Labour System in Barbados, 1630–1680." In *Caribbean Slavery in the Atlantic World*, edited by Hilary McD. Beckles and Verene Shepherd, 239–52. Kingston, Jamaica: Ian Randle, 2000.

Beckles, Hilary McD., and Verene Shepherd. Introduction to *A Historical Study of Women in Jamaica, 1655–1844*, by Lucille Mathurin Mair. Kingston, Jamaica: University of the West Indies Press, 2006.

Behn, Aphra. *Oroonoko*. Edited by Janet M. Todd. London: Penguin, 2003.

Belisario, I. M. *Sketches of Character: In Illustration of the Habits, Occupation, and Costume of the Negro Population, in the Island of Jamaica*. Kingston, Jamaica: Published by the artist, 1837.

Bellin, Joshua David, and Laura L. Mielke, eds. *Native Acts: Indian Performance, 1603–1832*. Lincoln: University of Nebraska Press, 2011.

Bentley, Nancy. "The Fourth Dimension: Kinlessness and African American Narrative." *Critical Inquiry* 35, no. 2 (2009): 270–92.

Benton, Lauren A. *A Search for Sovereignty: Law and Geography in European Empires, 1400–1900*. Cambridge: Cambridge University Press, 2010.

Bergland, Renée L. *The National Uncanny: Indian Ghosts and American Subjects*. Hanover, NH: University Press of New England, 2000.

Berthold, Dennis. "Class Acts: The Astor Place Riots and Melville's 'The Two Temples.'" *American Literature* 71, no. 3 (1999): 429–61.

Bevington, David M., and Peter Holbrook. *The Politics of the Stuart Court Masque*. Cambridge: Cambridge University Press, 1998.

Bickerstaff, Isaac, and Miguel de Cervantes Saavedra. *The Padlock: A Comic Opera: As It Is Perform'd by His Majesty's Servants, at the Theatre-Royal in Drury-Lane*. London: W. Griffin, 1768.

Blackburn, Robin. *The Making of New World Slavery: From the Baroque to the Modern, 1492–1800*. London: Verso, 1997.

Blackburn, Robin. *The Overthrow of Colonial Slavery, 1776–1848*. London: Verso, 1988.

Boggs, Colleen Glenney. *Transnationalism and American Literature: Literary Translation 1773–1892*. New York: Routledge, 2007.

Bogin, Ruth. "Petitioning and the New Moral Economy of Post-Revolutionary America." *William and Mary Quarterly* 45, no. 3 (July 1988): 391–425.

Bogues, Anthony. *Caliban's Freedom: The Early Political Thought of C. L. R. James*. London: Pluto Press, 1997.

Bogues, Anthony. *Empire of Liberty: Power, Desire, and Freedom*. Hanover, NH: University Press of New England, 2010.

Boucher, Phillip P. *Cannibal Encounters: Europeans and Island Caribs, 1492–1763*. Baltimore: Johns Hopkins University Press, 1992.

Breen, T. H. "A Changing Labor Force and Race Relations in Virginia 1660–1710." *Journal of Social History* 7, no. 1 (1973): 3–25.

Brooks, Daphne. *Bodies in Dissent: Spectacular Performances of Race and Freedom, 1850–1910*. Durham, NC: Duke University Press, 2006.

Brooks, Joanna. "The Early American Public Sphere and the Emergence of a Black Print Counterpublic." *William and Mary Quarterly* 62, no. 1 (January 2005): 67–92.

Brooks, Joanna. *Why We Left: Untold Stories and Songs of America's First Immigrants*. Minneapolis: University of Minnesota Press, 2013.

Bross, Kristina. "A More Horrid Reception." Unpublished essay.

Brown, Christopher Leslie. *Moral Capital: Foundations of British Abolitionism*. Chapel Hill: University of North Carolina Press for the Omohundro Institute of Early American History and Culture, 2006.

Brown, Keith. "Thomas Hobbes and the Title-page of 'Leviathan.'" *Philosophy* 55, no. 213 (1980): 410–11.

Brown, Laura. "Dryden and the Imperial Imagination." In *The Cambridge Companion to John Dryden*, edited by Steven N. Zwicker, 59–74. Cambridge: Cambridge University Press, 2004.

Brown, Laura. *Ends of Empire: Women and Ideology in Early Eighteenth-Century English Literature*. Ithaca, NY: Cornell University Press, 1993.

Brown, Vincent. *The Reaper's Garden: Death and Power in the World of Atlantic Slavery*. Cambridge, MA: Harvard University Press, 2008.

Brown, Vincent. "Social Death and Political Life in the Study of Slavery." *American Historical Review* 114, no. 5 (2009): 1231–49.

Bruster, Douglas. *Shakespeare and the Question of Culture: Early Modern Literature and the Cultural Turn*. New York: Palgrave Macmillan, 2003.

Bryan, George B. *American Theatrical Regulation, 1607–1900: Conspectus and Texts*. Metuchen, NJ: Scarecrow Press, 1993.

Buckley, Peter. "To the Opera House: Culture and Society in New York City, 1820–1860." PhD diss., SUNY Stonybrook, 1984.

Bull, Malcolm. "The Limits of Multitude." *New Left Review,* September–October 2005, 19–39.

Burke, Helen M. *Riotous Performances: The Struggle for Hegemony in the Irish Theater, 1712–1784*. Notre Dame, IN: University of Notre Dame Press, 2003.

Burnard, Trevor G. *Mastery, Tyranny, and Desire: Thomas Thistlewood and His Slaves in the Anglo-Jamaican World*. Chapel Hill: University of North Carolina Press, 2004.

Burnard, Trevor G. "Not a Place for Whites? Demographic Failure and Settlement in Comparative Context: Jamaica, 1655–1780." In *Jamaica in Slavery and Freedom: His-*

tory, Heritage and Culture, edited by Kathleen E. A. Monteith and Glen Richards, 73–88. Kingston, Jamaica: University of the West Indies Press, 2002.

Burnard, Trevor G. "'Prodigious Riches': The Wealth of Jamaica before the American Revolution." *Economic History Review* 54, no. 3 (August 2001): 506–24.

Burnard, Trevor G. "Slave Naming Patterns: Onomastics and the Taxonomy of Race in Eighteenth-Century Jamaica." *Journal of Interdisciplinary History* 31, no. 3 (2001): 325–46.

Burton, Richard D. E. *Afro-Creole: Power, Opposition, and Play in the Caribbean.* Ithaca, NY: Cornell University Press, 1997.

Bush, Barbara. "White 'Ladies,' Coloured 'Favourites,' and Black 'Wenches': Some Considerations on Sex, Race and Class Factors in Social Relations in White Creole Society in the British Caribbean." *Slavery and Abolition* 2, no. 3 (1981): 245–62.

Butler, Frances Anne (Miss Fanny Kemble). *Journal of a Residence in America.* Paris: A. and W. Galignani, 1835.

Butler, Martin. *The Stuart Court Masque and Political Culture.* Cambridge: Cambridge University Press, 2008.

Butler, Nicholas Michael. *Votaries of Apollo: The St. Cecilia Society and the Patronage of Concert Music in Charleston, South Carolina, 1766–1820.* Columbia: University of South Carolina Press, 2007.

Butsch, Richard. *The Making of American Audiences: From Stage to Television, 1750–1990.* Cambridge: Cambridge University Press, 2000.

Byrd, Jodi A. *The Transit of Empire: Indigenous Critiques of Colonialism.* Minneapolis: University of Minnesota Press, 2011.

Carlson, Julie A. "New Lows in Eighteenth-Century Theater: The Rise of Mungo." *European Romantic Review* 18, no. 2 (2007): 139–47.

Carlson, Julie A. "Race and Profit in English Theatre." In *The Cambridge Companion to British Theatre, 1730–1830*, edited by Jane Moody and Daniel O'Quinn, 175–88. Cambridge: Cambridge University Press, 2007.

Carlson, Julie A. "Trying Sheridan's *Pizarro*." *Texas Studies in Literature and Language* 38, no. 3/4 (1996): 359–78.

Carmichael, A. C. *Domestic Manners and Social Condition of the White, Coloured and Negro Population of the West Indies.* London: Whittaker, 1834.

Carrington, Selwyn H. H. *The Sugar Industry and the Abolition of the Slave Trade, 1775–1810.* Gainesville: University Press of Florida, 2002.

Carswell, John. *The South Sea Bubble.* London: Cresset Press, 1960.

Casas, Bartolomé de las. *Brevísima relación de la destrucción de las Indias.* Seville: S. Trugillo, 1552.

Cecily, Forde-Jones. "Mapping Racial Boundaries: Gender, Race, and Poor Relief in Barbadian Plantation Society." *Journal of Women's History* 10, no. 3 (1998): 9–31.

Chaplin, Joyce E. *Subject Matter: Technology, the Body, and Science on the Anglo-American Frontier, 1500–1676.* Cambridge, MA: Harvard University Press, 2001.

Charles I. *King Charles His Speech Made upon the Scaffold at Whitehall Gate, Immediately before His Execution, on Tuesday the 30. Of Jan. 1648. With a Relation of the*

Manner of His Going to Execution. Published by Spetiall Authority. London: Peter Cole, 1649.

Charlton, David. "The Nineteenth Century: France." In *The Oxford Illustrated History of Opera,* edited by Roger Parker, 122–68. Oxford: Oxford University Press, 2001.

Choudhury, Mita. *Interculturalism and Resistance in the London Theater, 1660–1800: Identity, Performance, Empire*. Lewisburg, PA: Bucknell University Press, 2000.

Cibber, Colley, and William Shakespeare. *The Tragical History of King Richard the Third. . . . with Alterations, by Mr. Cibber*. London: W. Mears and J. Browne, 1718.

Clare, Janet. *Drama of the English Republic, 1649–60*. Manchester, UK: Manchester University Press, 2002.

Cliff, Nigel. *The Shakespeare Riots: Revenge, Drama, and Death in Nineteenth-century America*. New York: Random House, 2007.

Cockrell, Dale. *Demons of Disorder: Early Blackface Minstrels and Their World*. Cambridge: Cambridge University Press, 1997.

Coclanis, Peter A. *The Shadow of a Dream: Economic Life and Death in the South Carolina Low Country, 1670–1920*. New York: Oxford University Press, 1989.

Cogan, Jacob Katz. "The Look Within: Property, Capacity, and Suffrage in Nineteenth-Century America." *Yale Law Journal* 107, no. 2 (1997): 473–98.

Cogswell, Thomas, Richard Cust, and Peter Lake, eds. *Politics, Religion, and Popularity in Early Stuart Britain: Essays in Honour of Conrad Russell*. Cambridge: Cambridge University Press, 2002.

Cohen, Lara Langer. *The Fabrication of American Literature: Fraudulence and Antebellum Print Culture*. Philadelphia: University of Pennsylvania Press, 2012.

Colbert, Soyica Diggs. *The African American Theatrical Body: Reception, Performance, and the Stage*. Cambridge: Cambridge University Press, 2011.

Colbourn, H. Trevor. *The Lamp of Experience: Whig History and the Intellectual Origins of the American Revolution*. Chapel Hill: University of North Carolina Press for the Institute of Early American History and Culture, 1965.

The Concise Oxford English Dictionary. 12th ed. Edited by Angus Stevenson and Maurice Waite. Oxford: Oxford University Press, 2011.

Cooper, Thomas M. D., and David James Maccord, eds. *The Statutes at Large of South Carolina. . . .* 10 vols. Columbia: A. S. Johnston, 1836.

Cox, Jeffrey N., ed. *Slavery, Abolition, and Emancipation: Writings in the British Romantic Period. Vol. 5 Drama*. London: Pickering and Chatto, 1999.

Craton, Michael. "Decoding Pitchy-patchy: The Roots, Branches and Essence of Junkanoo." *Slavery and Abolition* 16, no. 1 (1995): 14–44.

Craton, Michael. "Reluctant Creoles: The Planters' World in the British West Indies." In *Strangers within the Realm: Cultural Margins of the First British Empire,* edited by Bernard Bailyn and Philip D. Morgan, 314–62. Chapel Hill: University of North Carolina Press for the Institute of Early American History and Culture, 1991.

Cromwell, Oliver. *The Writings and Speeches of Oliver Cromwell*. Edited by Wilbur Cortez Abbott and Catherine D. Crane. 4 vols. Cambridge, MA: Harvard University Press, 1937.

Cromwell, Oliver. *A Declaration of His Highness, Inviting the People of England and* Wales *to a Day of Solemn Fasting and Humiliation.* Edited by the Council of State England and Wales. London: Henry Hills and John Field, 1655.

Cromwell, Oliver, John Milton, and James Thomson. *A Manifesto of the Lord Protector of the Commonwealth of England, Scotland, Ireland, & C.* London: A. Millar, 1738.

Cumberland, Richard. *The West Indian: A Comedy: As It Is Performed at the Theatre Royal in Drury-Lane.* London: W. Griffin, 1771.

Curtis, Julia. "The Architecture and Appearance of the Charleston Theatre: 1793–1833." *Educational Theatre Journal* 23, no. 1 (1971): 1–12.

Curtis, Julia. "The Early Charleston Stage: 1703–1798." PhD diss., Indiana University, 1968.

Cussans, Jack. *Robinson Crusoe.* Broadside. Boston, 1810.

The Darkey Tragedian, An Ethiopian Sketch, in One Scene. New York: Happy Hours Company, 1874.

D'Avenant, Sir William. *Poem, to the King's Most Sacred Majesty.* London: Henry Herringman, 1663.

Davies, Carole Boyce, ed. *Encyclopedia of the African Diaspora: Origins, Experiences, and Culture. Volume 1.* Santa Barbara, CA: ABC-CLIO, 2008.

Davies, K. G. *The Royal African Company.* London: Longmans, 1957.

Davis, David Brion. *The Problem of Slavery in the Age of Revolution, 1770–1823.* Ithaca, NY: Cornell University Press, 1975.

Davis, David Brion. *The Problem of Slavery in Western Culture.* New York: Oxford University Press, 1988.

Dayan, Colin. *The Law Is a White Dog: How Legal Rituals Make and Unmake Persons.* Princeton, NJ: Princeton University Press, 2011.

Dayan, Joan. *Haiti, History, and the Gods.* Berkeley: University of California Press, 1995.

De La Beche, Henry T. *Notes on the Present Condition of the Negroes in Jamaica.* London: T. Cadell, 1825.

Defoe, Daniel. *The Life and Adventures of Robinson Crusoe.* Harmondsworth, UK: Penguin, 1965.

Deloria, Philip Joseph. *Playing Indian.* New Haven, CT: Yale University Press, 1998.

Denning, Michael. "Beggars and Thieves: The Ideology of the Gang." *Literature and History* 8 (1982): 41–55.

Dharwadker, Aparna. "John Gay, Bertolt Brecht, and Postcolonial Antinationalisms." *Modern Drama* 38, no. 1 (1995): 4–21.

Diggs, Dudley. *A Review of the Observations upon Some of His Majesties Late Answers and Expresses.* Oxford: Leonard Lichfield, 1643.

Dillon, Elizabeth Maddock. *The Gender of Freedom: Fictions of Liberalism and the Literary Public Sphere.* Palo Alto, CA: Stanford University Press, 2004.

Dillon, Elizabeth Maddock, and Michael Drexler. "Haiti and the U.S., Entwined." In *The Haitian Revolution and the Early U.S.: Histories, Geographies, Textualities,* edited by Elizabeth Maddock Dillon and Michael Drexler. Philadelphia: University of Pennsylvania Press, forthcoming.

Dippie, Brian W. *The Vanishing American: White Attitudes and U.S. Indian Policy.* Lawrence: University Press of Kansas, 1991.

Dirlik, Arif. "The End of Colonialism? The Colonial Modern in the Making of Global Modernity." *Boundary 2* 32, no. 1 (2005): 1–31.

Dobson, Michael. "'Remember/First to Possess His Books': The Appropriation of *The Tempest*, 1700–1800." In *The Tempest: Critical Essays*, edited by Patrick M. Murphy, 245–56. New York: Routledge, 2001.

Donegan, Kathleen. "'As Dying, yet Behold We Live': Catastrophe and Interiority in Bradford's 'Of Plymouth Plantation.'" *Early American Literature* 37, no. 1 (2002): 9–37.

Donoghue, John. "'Out of the Land of Bondage': The English Revolution and the Atlantic Origins of Abolition." *American Historical Review* 115, no. 4 (2010): 943–74.

Doty, Jeffrey S. "Shakespeare's *Richard II*, 'Popularity,' and the Early Modern Public Sphere." *Shakespeare Quarterly* 61, no. 2 (2010): 183–205.

Doyle, Laura. *Freedom's Empire: Race and the Rise of the Novel in Atlantic Modernity, 1640–1940*. Durham, NC: Duke University Press, 2008.

Draper, Nicholas. *The Price of Emancipation: Slave-Ownership, Compensation and British Society at the End of Slavery*. Cambridge: Cambridge University Press, 2010.

Dryden, John. *Amboyna, a Tragedy as It Is Acted at the Theatre-Royal*. London: T. N. for Henry Herringman, 1673.

Dryden, John, and William D'Avenant. *The Tempest, or the Enchanted Island. A Comedy: As It Is Now Acted at His Highness the Duke of York's Theatre*. London: J. Macock, for Henry Herringman, 1676.

Dryden, John, and Robert Howard. *The Indian Emperour, or, the Conquest of Mexico by the Spaniards Being the Sequel of the Indian Queen*. London: J. M. for H. Herringman, 1667.

Dryden, Robert G. "John Gay's *Polly*: Unmasking Pirates and Fortune Hunters in the West Indies." *Eighteenth-Century Studies* 34, no. 4 (2001): 539–57.

Dubois, Laurent. *A Colony of Citizens: Revolution and Slave Emancipation in the French Caribbean, 1787–1804*. Chapel Hill: University of North Carolina Press, 2004.

Dugaw, Dianne. *Warrior Women and Popular Balladry, 1650–1850*. Cambridge: Cambridge University Press, 1989.

Dunlap, William. *A History of the American Theatre*. New York: J. and J. Harper, 1832.

Dunn, Richard S. *Sugar and Slaves: The Rise of the Planter Class in the English West Indies, 1624–1713*. Chapel Hill: University of North Carolina Press for the Institute of Early American History and Culture, 1972.

Earle, William. *Obi, or, The History of Threefingered Jack in a Series of Letters from a Resident in Jamaica to His Friend in England*. Worcester: Isaiah Thomas, Jr., 1804.

Edmond, Mary. *Rare Sir William Davenant: Poet Laureate, Playwright, Civil War General, Restoration Theatre Manager*. Manchester, UK: Manchester University Press, 1987.

Ellison, Ralph. *Shadow and Act*. New York: Vintage, 1995.

Elmer, Jonathan. *On Lingering and Being Last: Race and Sovereignty in the New World*. New York: Fordham University Press, 2008.

Elmore, Jennifer B. "'The Fair Imoinda': Domestic Ideology and Anti-slavery on the Eighteenth-Century Stage." In *Troping Oroonoko from Behn to Bandele*, edited by Susan B. Iwanisziw, 35–58. Burlington, VT: Ashgate, 2004.

Eltis, David. "Labour and Coercion in the English Atlantic World from the Seventeenth to the Early Twentieth Century." In *The Slavery Reader*, edited by Gad J. Heuman and James Walvin, 58–73. London: Routledge, 2003.

Eltis, David. *The Rise of African Slavery in the Americas.* Cambridge: Cambridge University Press, 2000.

Engerman, Stanley L., Seymour Drescher, and Robert L. Paquette, eds. *Slavery*. Oxford: Oxford University Press, 2001.

Farquhar, George. *The Recruiting Officer. A Comedy. As It Is Acted at the Theatre Royal in Drury-Lane, by Her Majesty's Servants.* London: Bernard Lintott, 1706.

Federici, Silvia. *Caliban and the Witch: Women, the Body and Primitive Accumulation.* Brooklyn, NY: Autonomedia; London: Pluto, 2003.

Federici, Silvia. "Feminism and the Politics of the Commons." In *Uses of a Whirlwind: Movement, Movements, and Contemporary Radical Currents in the United States*, edited by Craig Hughes, Stevie Peace, and Kevin Van Meter for the Team Colors Collective, 283–94. Oakland, CA: AK Press, 2010.

Festa, Lynn M. *Sentimental Figures of Empire in Eighteenth-Century Britain and France.* Baltimore: Johns Hopkins University Press, 2006.

Firth, C. H. "Sir William Davenant and the Revival of the Drama during the Protectorate." *English Historical Review* 18, no. 70 (1903): 319–21.

Fischer, Sibylle. *Modernity Disavowed: Haiti and the Cultures of Slavery in the Age of Revolution.* Durham, NC: Duke University Press, 2004.

Floyd-Wilson, Mary. *English Ethnicity and Race in Early Modern Drama.* Cambridge: Cambridge University Press, 2003.

Forde-Jones, Cecily. "Mapping Racial Boundaries: Gender, Race, and Poor Relief in Barbadian Plantation Society." *Journal of Women's History* 10, no. 3 (1998): 9–31.

Fortunati, Leopoldina. *The Arcane of Reproduction: Housework, Prostitution, Labor and Capital.* Brooklyn, NY: Autonomedia, 1995.

Foster, Susan Leigh. *Choreography & Narrative: Ballet's Staging of Story and Desire.* Bloomington: Indiana University Press, 1996.

Foucault, Michel. *Discipline and Punish: The Birth of the Prison.* Translated by Alan Sheridan. 2nd ed. New York: Vintage Books, 1995.

Foucault, Michel. *Society Must Be Defended: Lectures at the Collège De France, 1975–76.* Edited by Mauro Bertani and Alessandro Fontana. Translated by David Macey. New York: Picador, 2003.

Frank, Jason A. *Constituent Moments: Enacting the People in Postrevolutionary America.* Durham, NC: Duke University Press, 2010.

Frohock, Richard. "Sir William Davenant's American Operas." *Modern Language Review* 96, no. 2 (2001): 323–33.

Gallay, Alan. *The Indian Slave Trade: The Rise of the English Empire in the American South, 1670–1717.* New Haven, CT: Yale University Press, 2002.

Games, Alison. "Anglo-Dutch Connections and Overseas Enterprises: A Global Perspective on Lion Gardiner's World." *Early American Studies* 9, no. 2 (2011): 435–61.

Gaspar, David Barry. "'Rigid and Inclement': Origins of the Jamaican Slave Laws of the Seventeenth Century." In *The Many Legalities of Early America*, edited by Christopher L.

Tomlins and Bruce H. Mann, 78–96. Chapel Hill: University of North Carolina Press for the Omohundro Institute of Early American History and Culture, 2001.

Gates, Henry Louis, Jr. *Figures in Black: Words, Signs, and the "Racial" Self*. Oxford: Oxford University Press, 1987.

Gay, John. *The Beggar's Opera. As It Is Acted at the Theatre Royal in Lincolns-Inn-Fields. Written by Mr. Gay*. 2nd ed. London: John Watts, 1728.

Gay, John. *L'opera Du Gueux, Avec Les Chansons Fur Les Airs Anglois. Représentée sur le Petit Theatre François dans le Marché au Foin. Traduite de l'anglois de Mr. Gay, par Mr. A. Hallam* London: Chéz Guillaume Meyer, 1750.

Gay, John. *Polly: An Opera. Being the Second Part of the Beggar's Opera. Written by Mr. Gay*. London: Jeffrey Walker, 1729.

Geggus, David Patrick. *Haitian Revolutionary Studies*. Bloomington: Indiana University Press, 2002.

Gerzina, Gretchen. *Black London: Life before Emancipation*. New Brunswick, NJ: Rutgers University Press, 1995.

Gibbons, Luke. "Race against Time: Racial Discourse and Irish History." *Oxford Literary Review* 13, no. 1 (July 1991): 95–117.

Gibbs, Jenna Marie. "Performing the Temple of Liberty: Slavery, Rights, and Revolution in Transatlantic Theatricality (1760s–1830s)." PhD diss., University of California, Los Angeles, 2008.

Gikandi, Simon. *Slavery and the Culture of Taste*. Princeton, NJ: Princeton University Press, 2011.

Gilje, Paul A. *The Road to Mobocracy: Popular Disorder in New York City, 1763–1834*. Chapel Hill: University of North Carolina Press for the Institute of Early American History and Culture, 1987.

Gilroy, Paul. *The Black Atlantic: Modernity and Double Consciousness*. Cambridge, MA: Harvard University Press, 1993.

Glissant, Édouard. *Caribbean Discourse: Selected Essays*. Translated by J. Michael Dash. CARAF Books. Charlottesville: University Press of Virginia, 1989.

Goffman, Erving. *Frame Analysis: An Essay on the Organization of Experience*. Cambridge, MA: Harvard University Press, 1974.

Goldsby, Jacqueline Denise. *A Spectacular Secret: Lynching in American Life and Literature*. Chicago: University of Chicago Press, 2006.

Goodhart, Michael E. "Origins and Universality in the Human Rights Debates: Cultural Essentialism and the Challenge of Globalization." *Human Rights Quarterly* 25, no. 4 (November 2003): 935–64.

Goudie, Sean X. *Creole America: The West Indies and the Formation of Literature and Culture in the New Republic*. Philadelphia: University of Pennsylvania Press, 2006.

Gould, Eliga H. "Zones of Law, Zones of Violence: The Legal Geography of the British Atlantic, circa 1772." *William and Mary Quarterly* 60, no. 3 (2003): 471–510.

Gould, Phillip. "Remembering Metacom: Historical Writing and the Cultures of Masculinity in Early Republican America." In *Sentimental Men: Masculinity and the Politics of Affect in American Culture*, edited by Mary Chapman and Glenn Hendler, 112–23. Berkeley: University of California Press, 1999.

Goulding, Sybil. "Eighteenth-Century French Taste and 'The Beggar's Opera.'" *Modern Language Review* 24, no. 3 (1929): 276–93.

Gragg, Larry Dale. *Englishmen Transplanted: The English Colonization of Barbados, 1627–1660.* Oxford: Oxford University Press, 2003.

Greenblatt, Stephen. *Learning to Curse: Essays in Early Modern Culture.* New York: Routledge, 1990.

Greene, Jack P. "Introduction: Empire and Liberty." In *Exclusionary Empire: English Liberty Overseas, 1600–1900,* edited by Jack P. Greene, 1–24. Cambridge: Cambridge University Press, 2010.

Greene, Jack P. "Liberty and Slavery: The Transfer of British Liberty to the West Indies, 1627–1865." In *Exclusionary Empire: English Liberty Overseas, 1600–1900,* edited by Jack P. Greene, 50–76. Cambridge: Cambridge University Press, 2010.

Greene, Jack P. "Liberty, Slavery, and the Transformation of British Identity in the Eighteenth-Century West Indies." *Slavery and Abolition* 21, no. 1 (2000): 1–31.

Greer, Allan. "Commons and Enclosure in the Colonization of North America." *The American Historical Review* 117, no. 2 (April 1, 2012): 365–86.

Greer, Margaret Rich, Walter Mignolo, and Maureen Quilligan, eds. *Rereading the Black Legend: The Discourses of Religious and Racial Difference in the Renaissance Empires.* Chicago: University of Chicago Press, 2007.

Greiman, Jennifer. *Democracy's Spectacle: Sovereignty and Public Life in Antebellum American Writing.* New York: Fordham University Press, 2010.

Grimsted, David. *Melodrama Unveiled: American Theater and Culture, 1800–1850.* Chicago: University of Chicago Press, 1968.

Gurr, Andrew. *The Shakespearean Stage, 1574–1642.* 4th ed. Cambridge: Cambridge University Press, 2008.

Gustafson, Sandra M. "American Literature and the Public Sphere." *American Literary History* 20, no. 3 (2008): 465–78.

Gustafson, Sandra M., and Caroline F. Sloat, eds. *Cultural Narratives: Textuality and Performance in American Culture before 1900.* Notre Dame, IN: University of Notre Dame Press, 2010.

Habermas, Jürgen. *The Structural Transformation of the Public Sphere: An Inquiry into a Category of Bourgeois Society.* Cambridge, MA: MIT Press, 1989.

Hajjar, Lisa. "Does Torture Work? A Sociolegal Assessment of the Practice in Historical and Global Perspective." *Annual Review of Law and Social Science* 5, no. 1 (2009): 311–45.

Hall, Catherine. *Civilising Subjects: Metropole and Colony in the English Imagination, 1830–1867.* Chicago: University of Chicago Press, 2002.

Hall, Stuart. "Afterword: Legacies of Anglo-Caribbean Culture—A Diasporic Perspective." In *Art and Emancipation in Jamaica: Isaac Mendes Belisario and His Worlds,* edited by T. J. Barringer, Gillian Forrester, and Barbaro Martinez-Ruiz, 179–95. New Haven, CT: Yale Center for British Art and Yale University Press, 2007.

Hallward, Peter. "Staging Equality: Rancière's Theatocracy and the Limits of Anarchic Equality." In *Jacques Rancière: History, Politics, Aesthetics,* edited by Gabriel Rockhill and Philip Watts, 140–57. Durham, NC: Duke University Press, 2009.

Handke, Peter. *Kaspar and Other Plays.* New York: Farrar, Straus, 1969.

Harbage, Alfred. *Sir William Davenant, Poet Venturer, 1606–1668*. New York: Octagon Books, 1971.

Hardt, Michael, and Antonio Negri. *Commonwealth*. Cambridge, MA: Harvard University Press, 2009.

Hardt, Michael, and Antonio Negri. *Empire*. Cambridge, MA: Harvard University Press, 2000.

Hardt, Michael, and Antonio Negri. *Multitude: War and Democracy in the Age of Empire*. New York: Penguin, 2004.

Harris, Susan Cannon. "Outside the Box: The Female Spectator, *The Fair Penitent*, and the Kelly Riots of 1747." *Theatre Journal* 57, no. 1 (2005): 33–55.

Harris, Tim. *London Crowds in the Reign of Charles II: Propaganda and Politics from the Restoration until the Exclusion Crisis*. Cambridge: Cambridge University Press, 1987.

Harrison, Gabriel. *Edwin Forrest: The Actor and the Man. Critical and Reminiscent*. Brooklyn, NY: Brooklyn Eagle Book Printing, 1889.

Hartman, Saidiya V. *Scenes of Subjection: Terror, Slavery, and Self-Making in Nineteenth-Century America*. New York: Oxford University Press, 1997.

Harvey, David. *The New Imperialism*. Oxford: Oxford University Press, 2003.

Hatley, Thomas M. *The Dividing Paths: Cherokees and South Carolinians through the Era of Revolution*. New York: Oxford University Press, 1993.

Hay, Samuel A. *African American Theatre: An Historical and Critical Analysis*. Cambridge: Cambridge University Press, 1994.

Haywood, Charles. *Negro Minstrelsy and Shakespearean Burlesque*. Hatboro, PA: Folklore Associates, 1966.

Highfill, Philip H., Kalman A. Burnim, and Edward A. Langhans. *A Biographical Dictionary of Actors, Actresses, Musicians, Dancers, Managers and Other Stage Personnel in London, 1660–1800*. 16 vols. Carbondale: Southern Illinois University Press, 1973.

Higman, B. W. *Slave Populations of the British Caribbean, 1807–1834*. Baltimore: Johns Hopkins University Press, 1984.

Hill, Errol. *The Jamaican Stage, 1655–1900: Profile of a Colonial Theatre*. Amherst: University of Massachusetts Press, 1992.

Hill, Errol. "The Revolutionary Tradition in Black Drama." *Theatre Journal* 38, no. 4 (1986): 408–26.

Hill, Errol. *Shakespeare in Sable: A History of Black Shakespearean Actors*. Amherst: University of Massachusetts Press, 1984.

The History of the Blacks of Waltham in Hampshire; and Those under the Like Denomination in Berkshire. London: A. Moore, 1723.

Hobbes, Thomas. *Leviathan, or, the Matter, Form, and Power of a Common-Wealth Ecclesiastical and Civil*. London: Andrew Crooke, 1651.

Hobbes, Thomas. *Man and Citizen: De Homine et De Cive*. Indianapolis: Hackett, 1991.

Holland, Peter. *The Ornament of Action: Text and Performance in Restoration Comedy*. Cambridge: Cambridge University Press, 1979.

Hoskins, Robert, and Eileen Southern. Introduction to Samuel Arnold, *Obi; or Three-Finger'd Jack* in *Music for London Entertainment, 1660–1800 Series D Volume 4*. London: Stainer and Bell, [1800] 1996.

Hotson, Leslie. *The Commonwealth and Restoration Stage*. Cambridge, MA: Harvard University Press, 1928.

Howard, Jean E. *Theater of a City: The Places of London Comedy, 1598–1642*. Philadelphia: University of Pennsylvania Press, 2007.

Hoxby, Blair. *Mammon's Music: Literature and Economics in the Age of Milton*. New Haven, CT: Yale University Press, 2002.

Hyde, Lewis. *Common as Air: Revolution, Art, and Ownership*. New York: Farrar, Straus and Giroux, 2010.

Ingrassia, Catherine. *Authorship, Commerce, and Gender in Early Eighteenth-Century England: A Culture of Paper Credit*. Cambridge: Cambridge University Press, 1998.

Inikori, Joseph E. "Slavery and the Rise of Capitalism." In *Slavery, Freedom and Gender: The Dynamics of Caribbean Society*, edited by Brian L. Moore, 3–39. Kingston, Jamaica: University of the West Indies Press, 2001.

Ireland, Joseph Norton. *Records of the New York Stage, from 1750 to 1860*. 2 vols. New York: T. H. Morrell, 1866–67.

Irvin, Benjamin H. *Clothed in Robes of Sovereignty: The Continental Congress and the People Out of Doors*. New York: Oxford University Press, 2011.

Iwanisziw, Susan B., ed. *Oroonoko: Adaptations and Offshoots*. Burlington, VT: Ashgate, 2006.

Jackson, Shona N. *Creole Indigeneity: Between Myth and Nation in the Caribbean*. Minneapolis: University of Minnesota Press, 2012.

Jacob, James R., and Timothy Raylor. "Opera and Obedience: Thomas Hobbes and *A Proposition for Advancement of Moralitie* by Sir William Davenant." *Seventeenth Century* 6, no. 2 (1991): 205–50.

Jacobson, Matthew Frye. *Whiteness of a Different Color: European Immigrants and the Alchemy of Race*. Cambridge, MA: Harvard University Press, 1998.

Jamaica Assembly. *Journals of the Assembly of Jamaica, from January the 20th, 1663–4, Etc. (to 22nd December, 1826)*. 14 vols. Jamaica, 1811.

James, C. L. R. *The Black Jacobins: Toussaint L'ouverture and the San Domingo Revolution*. 2nd ed. New York: Vintage Books, 1963.

Johnson, Odai. *Absence and Memory in Colonial American Theatre: Fiorelli's Plaster*. New York: Palgrave Macmillan, 2006.

Johnson, Odai. *Rehearsing the Revolution: Radical Performance, Radical Politics in the English Restoration*. Newark: University of Delaware Press, 2000.

Johnson, Odai, and William J. Burling. *The Colonial American Stage, 1665–1774: A Documentary Calendar*. Madison, NJ: Fairleigh Dickinson University Press, 2001.

Johnson, Sara E. *The Fear of French Negroes: Transcolonial Collaboration in the Revolutionary Americas*. Berkeley: University of California Press, 2012.

Johnson, Walter. *River of Dark Dreams: Slavery and Empire in the Cotton Kingdom*. Cambridge, MA: Harvard University Press, 2013.

Jones, Ann Rosalind, and Peter Stallybrass. *Renaissance Clothing and the Materials of Memory*. Cambridge: Cambridge University Press, 2000.

Kahn, Paul W. *Sacred Violence: Torture, Terror, and Sovereignty*. Ann Arbor: University of Michigan Press, 2008.

Kantorowicz, Ernst Hartwig. *The King's Two Bodies: A Study in Mediaeval Political Theology*. Princeton, NJ: Princeton University Press, 1957.

Katz, Cindi. "Vagabond Capitalism and the Necessity of Social Reproduction." *Antipode* 33, no. 4 (2001): 709–28.

Kazanjian, David. *The Colonizing Trick: National Culture and Imperial Citizenship in Early America*. Minneapolis: University of Minnesota Press, 2003.

Keene, Edward. *Beyond the Anarchical Society: Grotius, Colonialism and Order in World Politics*. Cambridge: Cambridge University Press, 2002.

Kelly, James. "'Era of Liberty': The Politics of Civil and Political Rights in Eighteenth-Century Ireland." In *Exclusionary Empire: English Liberty Overseas, 1600–1900*, edited by Jack P. Greene, 77–111. Cambridge: Cambridge University Press, 2010.

Kennedy, Michael L. "A French Jacobin Club in Charleston, South Carolina, 1792–1795." *South Carolina Historical Magazine* 91, no. 1 (1990): 4–22.

Knights, Mark. *Politics and Opinion in the Exclusion Crisis, 1678–1681*. Cambridge: Cambridge University Press, 1994.

Kramnick, Isaac. *Bolingbroke and His Circle: The Politics of Nostalgia in the Age of Walpole*. Cambridge, MA: Harvard University Press, 1968.

Kriz, Kay Dian. *Sugar, Slavery, and the Culture of Refinement: Picturing the British West Indies, 1700–1840*. New Haven, CT: Yale University Press, 2008.

Kroll, Richard. "Instituting Empiricism: Hobbes's *Leviathan* and Dryden's *Marriage Á La Mode*." In *Cultural Readings of Restoration and Eighteenth-Century English Theater*, edited by Douglas J. Canfield and Deborah Payne Fisk, 39–66. Athens: University of Georgia Press, 1995.

Kruger, Loren. *The National Stage: Theatre and Cultural Legitimation in England, France and America*. Chicago: University of Chicago Press, 1992.

Kruger, Loren. "Our Theater? Stages in an American Cultural History." *American Literary History* 8, no. 4 (1996): 699–714.

Kupperman, Karen Ordahl. "Errand to the Indies: Puritan Colonization from Providence Island through the Western Design." *William and Mary Quarterly* 45, no. 1 (1988): 70–99.

Lake, Peter, and Steven C. A. Pincus. "Rethinking the Public Sphere in Early Modern England." *Journal of British Studies* 45, no. 2 (2006): 270–92.

Lambert, David. *White Creole Culture, Politics and Identity during the Age of Abolition*. Cambridge: Cambridge University Press, 2005.

Lambert, John. *Travels through Lower Canada, and the United States of North America, in the Years 1806, 1807, and 1808. . . .* 3 vols. London: Richard Phillips by T. Gillet, 1810.

Lamming, George. *The Pleasures of Exile*. London: M. Joseph, 1960.

Langford, Paul. *A Polite and Commercial People: England 1727–1783*. Oxford: Oxford University Press, 1989.

Latour, Bruno. *Reassembling the Social: An Introduction to Actor-Network-Theory*. Oxford: Oxford University Press, 2005.

Lawrence, Ken. *Karl Marx on American Slavery*. Tougaloo, MS: Sojourner Truth Organization, 1976.

Lepore, Jill. *The Name of War: King Philip's War and the Origins of American Identity*. New York: Knopf, 1998.

Levine, Lawrence W. *Highbrow/Lowbrow: The Emergence of Cultural Hierarchy in America*. Cambridge, MA: Harvard University Press, 1988.

Lewalski, Barbara Kiefer. *The Life of John Milton: A Critical Biography*. Malden, MA: Blackwell, 2000.

Lewis, Matthew Gregory. *Journal of a West-India Proprietor, Kept during a Residence in the Island of Jamaica*. London: J. Murray, 1834.

Lhamon, W. T. *Jump Jim Crow: Lost Plays, Lyrics, and Street Prose of the First Atlantic Popular Culture*. Cambridge, MA: Harvard University Press, 2003.

Lhamon, W. T. *Raising Cain: Blackface Performance from Jim Crow to Hip Hop*. Cambridge, MA: Harvard University Press, 1998.

Liesenfeld, Vincent J. *The Licensing Act of 1737*. Madison: University of Wisconsin Press, 1984.

Lindfors, Bernth. *Ira Aldridge: The African Roscius*. Rochester, NY: University of Rochester Press, 2007.

Lindley, David, ed. *The Court Masque*. Manchester, UK: Manchester University Press, 1984.

Linebaugh, Peter. *The Magna Carta Manifesto: Liberties and Commons for All*. Berkeley: University of California Press, 2008.

Linebaugh, Peter, and Marcus Buford Rediker. *The Many-Headed Hydra: Sailors, Slaves, Commoners, and the Hidden History of the Revolutionary Atlantic*. Boston: Beacon Press, 2000.

Linley, Thomas, and Richard Brinsley Sheridan. *The Pantomine [sic] of Robinson Crusoe: (1781)*, edited by Richard Hoskins. Wellington, New Zealand: Artaria Editions, 2005.

Little, Thomas J. "The South Carolina Slave Laws Reconsidered, 1670–1700." *South Carolina Historical Magazine* 94, no. 2 (1993): 86–101.

The Lives of the Most Remarkable Criminals, who have been Condemn'd and Executed; for Murder, Highway, House-breakers, Street-Robberies, Coining, or other Offences; From the Year 1720, to the Present Time . . . Collected from Original Papers and Authentick Memoirs. 3 vols. London: John Osborn, 1735.

Loftis, John Clyde. *The Politics of Drama in Augustan England*. Oxford: Clarendon Press, 1963.

Loftis, John Clyde. "Whig Oratory on Stage: Sheridan's *Pizarro*." *Eighteenth-Century Studies* 8, no. 4 (1975): 454–72.

Long, Edward. *The History of Jamaica or, General Survey of the Antient and Modern State of the Island. . . .* 3 vols. London: T. Lowndes, 1774.

Lott, Eric. *Love and Theft: Blackface Minstrelsy and the American Working Class*. New York: Oxford University Press, 1993.

Loughran, Trish. *The Republic in Print: Print Culture in the Age of U.S. Nation Building, 1770–1870*. New York: Columbia University Press, 2007.

Macaulay, Thomas Babington. *The History of England from the Accession of James II*. 5 vols. New York: Harper, 1856.

MacDonald, Joyce Green. "The Disappearing African Woman: Imoinda in 'Oroonoko' after Behn." *ELH* 66, no. 1 (1999): 71–86.

Mackie, Erin Skye. "Cultural Cross-Dressing: The Colorful Case of the Caribbean Creole." In *The Clothes That Wear Us: Essays on Dressing and Transgressing in Eighteenth-Century Culture*, edited by Jessica Munns and Penny Richards, 250–70. Newark: University of Delaware Press, 1999.

MacMillan, Dougald. "The Sources of Dryden's *The Indian Emperour.*" *Huntington Library Quarterly* 13 (1950): 355–70.

Macpherson, C. B. *The Political Theory of Possessive Individualism: Hobbes to Locke.* Oxford: Clarendon Press, 1962.

Maguire, Nancy Klein. *Regicide and Restoration: English Tragicomedy, 1660–1671.* Cambridge: Cambridge University Press, 1992.

Mair, Lucille Mathurin. "Women Field Workers in Jamaica during Slavery." In *Caribbean Slavery in the Atlantic World*, edited by Verene Shepherd and Hilary McD. Beckles, 390–97. Kingston, Jamaica: Ian Randle, 2000.

Mancke, Elizabeth. "The Languages of Liberty in British North America, 1607–1776." In *Exclusionary Empire: English Liberty Overseas, 1600–1900*, edited by Jack P. Greene, 25–49. Cambridge: Cambridge University Press, 2010.

Markley, Robert. "Violence and Profits on the Restoration Stage: Trade, Nationalism, and Insecurity in Dryden's *Amboyna.*" *Eighteenth-Century Life* 22, no. 1 (1998): 2–17.

Marsden, Peter. *An Account of the Island of Jamaica; with Reflections on the Treatment, Occupation, and Provisions of the Slaves. . . .* Newcastle, UK: S. Hodgson, 1788.

Marx, Karl. *Capital: A Critique of Political Economy.* Translated by Ben Fowkes. 2 vols. London: Penguin, 1990.

Maslan, Susan. *Revolutionary Acts: Theater, Democracy, and the French Revolution.* Baltimore: Johns Hopkins University Press, 2005.

Mates, Julian. *The American Musical Stage before 1800.* New Brunswick, NJ: Rutgers University Press, 1962.

Mathews, Charles, and George Cruikshank. *Sketches of Mr. Mathews' Invitations: Comprising a Full Account of This Admirable Lecture on Character, Manners and Peculiarities.* London: J. Limbird, 1826.

Matlaw, Myron. "'This Is Tragedy!!!': The History of *Pizarro.*" *Quarterly Journal of Speech* 43, no. 3 (1957): 288–94.

Mayer, David. *Harlequin in His Element: The English Pantomime, 1806–1836.* Cambridge, MA: Harvard University Press, 1969.

McAllister, Marvin Edward. *White People Do Not Know How to Behave at Entertainments Designed for Ladies and Gentlemen of Colour: William Brown's African and American Theater.* Chapel Hill: University of North Carolina Press, 2003.

McConachie, Bruce A. *Melodramatic Formations: American Theatre and Society, 1820–1870.* Iowa City: University of Iowa Press, 1992.

McConachie, Bruce A. "The 'Theatre of the Mob': Apocalyptic Melodrama and Preindustrial Riots in Antebellum New York." In *Theatre for Working-Class Audiences in the United States, 1830–1980*, edited by Daniel Friedman and Bruce McConachie, 17–46. Westport, CT: Greenwood Press, 1985.

McDonald, Forrest. *Novus Ordo Seclorum: The Intellectual Origins of the Constitution.* Lawrence: University Press of Kansas, 1985.

McDonald, Roderick A. *The Economy and Material Culture of Slaves: Goods and Chattels on the Sugar Plantations of Jamaica and Louisiana.* Baton Rouge: Louisiana State University Press, 1993.

McIntosh, William A. "Handel, Walpole, and Gay: The Aims of *The Beggar's Opera.*" *Eighteenth-Century Studies* 7, no. 4 (1974): 415–33.

McKeon, Michael. *Politics and Poetry in Restoration England: The Case of Dryden's* Annus Mirabilis. Cambridge, MA: Harvard University Press, 1975.

McPherson, Heather. "Theatrical Riots and Cultural Politics in Eighteenth-Century London." *Eighteenth Century* 43, no. 3 (2002): 236–52.

Meglin, Joellen A. "'Sauvages, Sex Roles, and Semiotics': Representations of Native Americans in the French Ballet, 1736–1837, Part One: The Eighteenth Century." *Dance Chronicle* 23, no. 2 (January 1, 2000): 87–132.

Melton, James Van Horn. *The Rise of the Public in Enlightenment Europe.* Cambridge: Cambridge University Press, 2001.

A Memento for Holland or a True and Exact History of the Most Villainous and Barbarous Cruelties Used on the English Merchants Residing at Amboyna in the East-Indies . . . Thomason Tracts / 189:E.1475[1]. London: Printed by James Moxon, 1653.

Mies, Maria, and Veronika Bennholdt-Thomsen. "Defending, Reclaiming, and Reinventing the Commons." *Canadian Journal of Development Studies* 22 (2001): 997–1023.

Mignolo, Walter. *The Darker Side of Western Modernity: Global Futures, Decolonial Options.* Durham, NC: Duke University Press, 2011.

Miller, Monica L. *Slaves to Fashion: Black Dandyism and the Styling of Black Diasporic Identity.* Durham, NC: Duke University Press, 2009.

Miller, Tice L., and Don B. Wilmeth. *The Cambridge Guide to American Theatre.* 2nd ed. Cambridge: Cambridge University Press, 2007.

Milton, John. *Complete Prose Works of John Milton.* Edited by Don Marion Wolfe. 8 vols. New Haven, CT: Yale University Press, 1953.

Milton, John. *The Works of John Milton.* Edited by Frank Allen Patterson and Bruce Rogers. 18 vols. New York: Columbia University Press, 1931.

Mintz, Sidney W. "Enduring Substances, Trying Theories: The Caribbean Region as Oikoumene." *Journal of the Royal Anthropological Institute* 2, no. 2 (1996): 289–311.

Mitchell, Koritha. *Living with Lynching: African American Lynching Plays, Performance, and Citizenship, 1890–1930.* Urbana: University of Illinois Press, 2011.

Molineux, Catherine. *Faces of Perfect Ebony: Encountering Atlantic Slavery in Imperial Britain.* Cambridge, MA: Harvard University Press, 2012.

Montag, Warren. "Who's Afraid of the Multitude? Between the Individual and the State." *South Atlantic Quarterly* 104, no. 4 (2005): 655–73.

Moody, Jane. "Dictating to the Empire: Performance and Theatrical Geography in Eighteenth-Century Britain." In *The Cambridge Companion to British Theatre, 1730–1830,* edited by Jane Moody and Daniel O'Quinn, 21–41. Cambridge: Cambridge University Press, 2007.

Moody, Jane. *Illegitimate Theatre in London, 1770–1840.* Cambridge: Cambridge University Press, 2000.

Moody, Richard. *The Astor Place Riot.* Bloomington: Indiana University Press, 1958.

Moody, Richard, ed. *Dramas from the American Theatre, 1762–1909.* Cleveland, OH: World Publishing, 1966.

Moody, Richard. *Edwin Forrest, First Star of the American Stage.* New York: Knopf, 1960.

Moreton, J. B. *West India Customs and Manners. . . .* London: J. Parsons; W. Richardson; H. Gardner; and J. Walter, 1793.

Moreton-Robinson, Aileen. "Writing off Treaties: White Possession in the United States Critical Whiteness Studies Literature." In *Transnational Whiteness Matters*, edited by Aileen Moreton-Robinson, Maryrose Casey, and Fiona Nicoll, 81–96. Lanham, MD: Lexington Books, 2008.

Morgan, Edmund S. *American Slavery, American Freedom: The Ordeal of Colonial Virginia*. New York: Norton, 1975.

Morgan, Edmund S. *Inventing the People: The Rise of Popular Sovereignty in England and America*. New York: Norton, 1988.

Morgan, Kenneth. *Slavery, Atlantic Trade and the British Economy, 1660–1800*. Cambridge: Cambridge University Press, 2000.

Moseley, Benjamin. *A Treatise on Sugar*. London: G. G. and J. Robinson, 1799.

Moses, Montrose Jonas. *The Fabulous Forrest: The Record of an American Actor*. Boston: Little, Brown, 1929.

Moten, Fred. *In the Break: The Aesthetics of the Black Radical Tradition*. Minneapolis: University of Minnesota Press, 2003.

Muhlenberg, Henry Melchior. *The Journals of Henry Melchior Muhlenberg*. 3 vols. Philadelphia: Evangelical Lutheran Ministerium of Pennsylvania and Adjacent States, 1942–58.

Mullaney, Steven. *The Place of the Stage: License, Play, and Power in Renaissance England*. Chicago: University of Chicago Press, 1988.

Murdoch, James E. *The Stage: Or, Recollections of Actors and Acting from an Experience of Fifty Years*. Philadelphia: J. M. Stoddart, 1880.

Nathans, Heather S. *Early American Theatre from the Revolution to Thomas Jefferson: Into the Hands of the People*. Cambridge: Cambridge University Press, 2003.

Nathans, Heather S. *Slavery and Sentiment on the American Stage, 1787–1861: Lifting the Veil of Black*. Cambridge: Cambridge University Press, 2009.

Neeson, J. M. *Commoners: Common Right, Enclosure and Social Change in Common-Field England, 1700–1820*. New York: Cambridge University Press, 1993.

Negri, Antonio. *The Savage Anomaly: The Power of Spinoza's Metaphysics and Politics*. Minneapolis: University of Minnesota Press, 1991.

Nelson, Dana D. *Commons Democracy*. Forthcoming.

Nelson, Dana D. *National Manhood: Capitalist Citizenship and the Imagined Fraternity of White Men*. Durham, NC: Duke University Press, 1998.

Nethercot, Arthur Hobart. *Sir William D'avenant, Poet Laureate and Playwright-Manager*. Chicago: University of Chicago Press, 1938.

Nicholson, Colin. *Writing and the Rise of Finance: Capital Satires of the Early Eighteenth Century*. Cambridge: Cambridge University Press, 1994.

Niklaus, Thelma. *Harlequin; or, the Rise and Fall of a Bergamask Rogue*. New York: G. Braziller, 1956.

Nugent, Maria. *Lady Nugent's Journal of Her Residence in Jamaica from 1801 to 1805*. Edited by Philip Wright and Verene Shepherd. Kingston, Jamaica: University of the West Indies Press, 2002.

Nussbaum, Felicity. *The Limits of the Human: Fictions of Anomaly, Race, and Gender in the Long Eighteenth Century*. Cambridge: Cambridge University Press, 2003.

Nyongó, Tavia Amolo Ochieng'. *The Amalgamation Waltz: Race, Performance, and the Ruses of Memory*. Minneapolis: University of Minnesota Press, 2009.

O'Brien, John. "Harlequin Britain: Eighteenth-Century Pantomime and the Cultural Location of Entertainment(s)." *Theatre Journal* 50, no. 4 (1998): 489–510.

O'Brien, John. *Harlequin Britain: Pantomime and Entertainment, 1690–1760*. Baltimore: Johns Hopkins University Press, 2004.

Odell, George C. D. *Annals of the New York Stage*. 15 vols. New York: Columbia University Press, 1927–49.

Ogilvie, John, and Charles Annandale. *The Imperial Dictionary of the English Language: A Complete Encyclopedic Lexicon, Literary, Scientific, and Technological*. New ed. 4 vols. London: Blackie and Son, 1883.

Olwell, Robert. *Masters, Slaves, and Subjects: The Culture of Power in the South Carolina Low Country, 1740–1790*. Ithaca, NY: Cornell University Press, 1998.

O'Neall, John Belton, and the State Agricultural Society of South Carolina. *The Negro Law of South Carolina*. Columbia, SC: J. G. Bowman, 1848.

O'Quinn, Daniel. *Entertaining Crisis in the Atlantic Imperium, 1770–1790*. Baltimore: Johns Hopkins University Press, 2011.

O'Quinn, Daniel. *Staging Governance: Theatrical Imperialism in London, 1770–1800*. Baltimore: Johns Hopkins University Press, 2005.

Orgel, Stephen. "The Poetics of Spectacle." *New Literary History* 2, no. 3 (1971): 367–89.

Orr, Bridget. *Empire on the English Stage, 1660–1714*. Cambridge: Cambridge University Press, 2001.

O'Shaughnessy, Andrew Jackson. *An Empire Divided: The American Revolution and the British Caribbean*. Philadelphia: University of Pennsylvania Press, 2000.

Osiander, Andreas. "Sovereignty, International Relations, and the Westphalian Myth." *International Organization* 55, no. 2 (2001): 251–87.

Owen, Susan J. *Restoration Theatre and Crisis*. Oxford: Clarendon Press, 1996.

Pagden, Anthony. *Lords of All the Worlds: Ideologies of Empire in Spain, Britain and France c. 1500–c. 1850*. New Haven, CT: Yale University Press, 1995.

Paquette, Robert L. "From Rebellion to Revisionism: The Continuing Debate About the Denmark Vesey Affair." *Journal of The Historical Society* 4, no. 3 (2004): 291–334.

Paton, Diana. "Punishment, Crime, and the Bodies of Slaves in Eighteenth-Century Jamaica." *Journal of Social History* 34, no. 4 (July 2001): 923–54.

Patterson, Orlando. *Slavery and Social Death: A Comparative Study*. Cambridge, MA: Harvard University Press, 1982.

Paulin, Diana Rebekkah. *Imperfect Unions: Staging Miscegenation in U.S. Drama and Fiction*. Minneapolis: University of Minnesota Press, 2012.

Pawlikowski, Melissah J. "The Plight and the Bounty: Squatters, Profiteers and the Transforming Hand of Sovereignty in Indian Country, 1750–1774." PhD diss., Ohio State University, in progress.

Pease, Donald. *The New American Exceptionalism*. Minneapolis: University of Minnesota Press, 2009.

Pestana, Carla Gardina. "Cruelty and Religious Justifications for Conquest in the Mid-Seventeenth-Century English Atlantic." In *Empires of God: Religious Encounters in the Early Modern Atlantic*, edited by Linda Gregerson and Susan Juster, 37–57. Philadelphia: University of Pennsylvania Press, 2011.

Pestana, Carla Gardina. *The English Atlantic in an Age of Revolution, 1640–1661.* Cambridge, MA: Harvard University Press, 2004.

Peters, Julie Stone. *Theatre of the Book, 1480–1880: Print, Text, and Performance in Europe.* Oxford: Oxford University Press, 2000.

Petley, Christer. "Gluttony, Excess, and the Fall of the Planter Class in the British Caribbean." *Atlantic Studies* 9, no. 1 (2012): 85–106.

Petley, Christer. *Slaveholders in Jamaica: Colonial Society and Culture during the Era of Abolition.* London: Pickering and Chatto, 2009.

Pincus, Steven C. A. *1688: The First Modern Revolution.* New Haven, CT: Yale University Press, 2009.

Pincus, Steven C. A. "England and the World in the 1650s." In *Revolution and Restoration: England in the 1650s*, edited by John Morrill, 129–47. London: Collins and Brown, 1992.

Pincus, Steven C. A. *Protestantism and Patriotism: Ideologies and the Making of English Foreign Policy, 1650–1668.* Cambridge: Cambridge University Press, 1996.

Pitkin, Hanna Fenichel. *The Concept of Representation.* Berkeley: University of California Press, 1967.

Plumb, J. H. *Sir Robert Walpole.* London: Cresset Press, 1956.

Pocock, J. G. A. *The Machiavellian Moment: Florentine Political Thought and the Atlantic Republican Tradition.* Princeton, NJ: Princeton University Press, 1975.

Pollock, Thomas Clark. *The Philadelphia Theatre in the Eighteenth Century, Together with the Day Book of the Same Period.* Philadelphia: University of Pennsylvania Press, 1933.

Poovey, Mary. *Genres of the Credit Economy: Mediating Value in Eighteenth- and Nineteenth-Century Britain.* Chicago: University of Chicago Press, 2008.

Powers, Bernard Edward. *Black Charlestonians: A Social History, 1822–1885.* Fayetteville: University of Arkansas Press, 1994.

Pye, Christopher. "The Sovereign, the Theater, and the Kingdome of Darknesse: Hobbes and the Spectacle of Power." *Representations* 8 (1984): 84–106.

Quijano, Aníbal, and Immanuel Wallerstein. "Americanity as a Concept, or the Americas in the Modern World-System." *International Social Science Journal* 134 (1992): 549–59.

Quincy, Josiah. "Journal of Josiah Quincy, Junior, 1773." *Massachusetts Historical Society Proceedings* 49 (1916): 424–81.

Ragussis, Michael. *Theatrical Nation: Jews and Other Outlandish Englishmen in Georgian Britain.* Philadelphia: University of Pennsylvania Press, 2010.

Rakove, Jack. Review of *Exclusionary Empire: English Liberty Overseas, 1600–1900*, edited by Jack P. Greene. *Journal of Interdisciplinary History* 41, no. 3 (2011): 443–45.

Ramsey, William L. "'Something Cloudy in Their Looks': The Origins of the Yamasee War Reconsidered." *Journal of American History* 90, no. 1 (June 1, 2003): 44–75.

Ramsey, William L. *The Yamasee War: A Study of Culture, Economy, and Conflict in the Colonial South.* Lincoln: University of Nebraska Press, 2008.

Rancière, Jacques. *On the Shores of Politics.* Translated by Liz Heron. London and New York: Phronesis and Verso, 1995.

Rancière, Jacques. *The Politics of Aesthetics: The Distribution of the Sensible.* Translated by Gabriel Rockhill. London: Continuum, 2004.

Rancière, Jacques. "Who Is the Subject of the Rights of Man?" *South Atlantic Quarterly* 103, no. 2–3 (2004): 297–310.

Rasch, William. "Carl Schmitt and the New World Order." *South Atlantic Quarterly* 104, no. 2 (2005): 177–83.

Rasch, William, ed. *World Orders: Confronting Carl Schmitt's* The Nomos of the Earth. Special issue of *South Atlantic Quarterly* 104, no. 2 (2005).

Rath, Richard Cullen. "Drums and Power: Ways of Creolizing Music in Coastal South Carolina and Georgia, 1730–90." In *Creolization in the Americas*, edited by David Buisseret and Steven G. Reinhardt, 99–130. College Station: Texas A&M University Press, 2000.

Rath, Richard Cullen. *How Early America Sounded.* Ithaca, NY: Cornell University Press, 2003.

Ravel, Jeffrey S. "La Reine Boit! Print, Performance, and Theater Publics in France, 1724–1725." *Eighteenth-Century Studies* 29, no. 4 (1996): 391–411.

Rawley, James A. *The Transatlantic Slave Trade: A History.* New York: Norton, 1981.

Raymond, George, and George Cruikshank. *The Life and Enterprises of Robert William Elliston, Comedian.* London: G. Routledge, 1857.

Raymond, Joad. "Describing Popularity in Early Modern England." *Huntington Library Quarterly* 67, no. 1 (2004): 101–29.

Reed, Peter P. "Conquer or Die: Staging Circum-Atlantic Revolt in *Polly* and *Three-Finger'd Jack*." *Theatre Journal* 59, no. 2 (2007): 241–58.

Reed, Peter P. *Rogue Performances: Staging the Underclasses in Early American Theatre Culture.* New York: Palgrave Macmillan, 2009.

Richards, Jeffrey H. *Drama, Theatre, and Identity in the American New Republic.* Cambridge: Cambridge University Press, 2005.

Richards, Jeffrey H. "Politics, Playhouse, and Repertoire in Philadelphia, 1808." *Theatre Survey* 46, no. 2 (2005): 199–224.

Richards, Leonard L. *"Gentlemen of Property and Standing": Anti-abolition Mobs in Jacksonian America.* New York: Oxford University Press, 1970.

Richardson, John. "John Gay and Slavery." *Modern Language Review* 97, no. 1 (2002): 15–25.

Rifkin, Mark. "Settler Common Sense." *Settler Colonial Studies* 3, no. 3–4 (2013): 322–40.

Rifkin, Mark. "Settler States of Feeling: National Belonging and the Erasure of Native American Presence." In *A Companion to American Literary Studies*, edited by Caroline F. Levander and Robert S. Levine, 342–55. New York: Wiley-Blackwell, 2011.

Rivers, Marcellus. *Englands Slavery, or Barbados Merchandize. . . .* Thomason Tracts / 228:E.1833[3]. London, 1659.

Roach, Joseph R. *Cities of the Dead: Circum-Atlantic Performance.* New York: Columbia University Press, 1996.

Roediger, David R. *The Wages of Whiteness: Race and the Making of the American Working Class.* Rev. ed. London: Verso, 1999.

Rogers, George C. *Charleston in the Age of the Pinckneys.* Norman: University of Oklahoma Press, 1969.

Rogin, Michael. *Blackface, White Noise: Jewish Immigrants in the Hollywood Melting Pot.* Berkeley: University of California Press, 1996.

Rose, Jacqueline. *States of Fantasy.* Oxford: Clarendon Press, 1995.

Rosenthal, Laura. "Owning Oroonoko: Behn, Southerne, and the Contingencies of Property." In *Troping Oroonoko from Behn to Bandele*, edited by Susan B. Iwanisziw, 83–107. Burlington, VT: Ashgate, 2004.

Rubin, Gayle. "The Traffic of Women: Notes on the 'Political Economy' of Sex." In *Toward an Anthropology of Woman*, edited by Rayna Reiter, 157–85, 198–200. New York: Monthly Review Press, 1975.

Russell, Gillian. *Women, Sociability and Theatre in Georgian London.* Cambridge: Cambridge University Press, 2007.

Rzepka, Charles, ed. *Obi: A Romantic Praxis Circles Volume.* August 2002. rc.umd.edu/praxis/obi/. Accessed November 29, 2013.

Sarna, Jonathan D. *Jacksonian Jew: The Two Worlds of Mordecai Noah.* New York: Holmes and Meier, 1980.

Sauer, Elizabeth. "Toleration and Translation: The Case of Las Casas, Phillips, and Milton." *Philological Quarterly* 85, no. 3/4 (2006): 271–91.

Sawday, Jonathan. "Re-writing a Revolution: History, Symbol, and Text in the Restoration." *Seventeenth Century* 7, no. 2 (1992): 171–99.

Saxton, Alexander. *The Rise and Fall of the White Republic: Class Politics and Mass Culture in Nineteenth-Century America.* London: Verso, 1990.

Sayre, Gordon M. *The Indian Chief as Tragic Hero: Native Resistance and the Literatures of America, from Moctezuma to Tecumseh.* Chapel Hill: University of North Carolina Press, 2005.

Scheckel, Susan. *The Insistence of the Indian: Race and Nationalism in Nineteenth-Century American Culture.* Princeton, NJ: Princeton University Press, 1998.

Schille, Candy B. K. "'Man Hungry': Reconsidering Threats to Colonial and Patriarchal Order in Dryden and Davenant's *The Tempest*." *Texas Studies in Literature and Language* 48, no. 4 (2006): 273–90.

Schmitt, Carl. *The Nomos of the Earth in the International Law of the Jus Publicum Europeaum.* Translated by G. L. Ulmen. New York: Telos Press, 2003.

Scott, David. *Conscripts of Modernity: The Tragedy of Colonial Enlightenment.* Durham, NC: Duke University Press, 2004.

Scott, James C. *Domination and the Arts of Resistance: Hidden Transcripts.* New Haven, CT: Yale University Press, 1990.

Scott, Michael. *The Cruise of the Midge.* Hartford, CT: Silas Andrus and Son, 1846.

Scott, Michael. *Tom Cringle's Log.* Paris: Casimir, 1854.

Scouten, Arthur H., ed. *The London Stage, 1660–1800: A Calendar of Plays, Entertainments & Afterpieces. . . . Compiled from the Playbills, Newspapers and Theatrical Diaries, Part 3: 1729–1747.* 2 vols. Carbondale: Southern Illinois University Press, 1961.

The Second Part of the Tragedy of Amboyna: Or, a True Relation of a Most Bloody, Treacherous, and Cruel Design of the Dutch in the New-Netherlands in America. . . . Thomason Tracts / 109:E.710[7]. London: Printed for Thomas Matthews, 1653.

Seed, Patricia. *Ceremonies of Possession in Europe's Conquest of the New World, 1492–1640.* New York: Cambridge University Press, 1995.

Seilhamer, George Overcash. *History of the American Theatre.* 3 vols. Philadelphia: Globe Printing House, 1888.

Shaffer, Jason. *Performing Patriotism: National Identity in the Colonial and Revolutionary American Theater.* Philadelphia: University of Pennsylvania Press, 2007.

Shakespeare, William. *The Norton Shakespeare,* edited by Stephen Greenblatt, Walter Cohen, Jean E. Howard, and Katharine Eisaman Maus. New York: W. W. Norton, 1997.

Shammas, Carole. "The Revolutionary Impact of European Demand for Tropical Goods." In *The Early Modern Atlantic Economy,* edited by John J. McCusker and Kenneth Morgan, 163–85. Cambridge: Cambridge University Press, 2000.

Shank, Theodore Junior. "The Bowery Theatre, 1826–1836." PhD diss., Stanford University, 1956.

Sharpe, Christina Elizabeth. *Monstrous Intimacies: Making Post-slavery Subjects.* Durham, NC: Duke University Press, 2010.

Sharples, Jason T. "Hearing Whispers, Casting Shadows: Jail-house Conversation and the Production of Knowledge during the Antigua Slave Conspiracy Investigation of 1736." In *Buried Lives: Incarcerated in Early America,* edited by Michele Lise Tartar and Richard Bell, 35–59. Athens: University of Georgia Press, 2012.

Shawcross, John T. "John Milton and His Spanish and Portuguese Presence." *Milton Quarterly* 32, no. 2 (1998): 41–52.

Shaw-Taylor, Leigh. "Parliamentary Enclosure and the Emergence of an English Agricultural Proletariat." *Journal of Economic History* 61, no. 3 (September 2001): 640–62.

Shephard, Charles. *An Historical Account of the Island of Saint Vincent.* London: F. Cass, [1831] 1971.

Sheridan, Richard B. *Sugar and Slavery: An Economic History of the British West Indies, 1623–1775.* Baltimore: Johns Hopkins University Press, 1974.

Sheridan, Richard Brinsley. *The Dramatic Works of Richard Brinsley Sheridan.* Edited by Cecil John Layton Price. 2 vols. Oxford: Clarendon Press, 1973.

Sheridan, Richard Brinsley. *The New Comic Opera of the Duenna.* Kingston, Jamaica: W. Aikman, 1779.

Sheridan, Richard Brinsley. *Robinson Crusoe; or, Harlequin Friday. A Grand Pantomime, in Two Acts, as Performed at the Theatre-Royal, Newcastle upon Tyne, in 1791.* Newcastle, UK: Hall and Elliot, 1791.

Sheridan, Richard Brinsley. *A Short Account of the Situations and Incidents Exhibited in the Pantomime of Robinson Crusoe, at the Theatre-Royal, Drury-Lane.* London: T. Becket, 1781.

Shields, David S. *Civil Tongues and Polite Letters in British America.* Chapel Hill: University of North Carolina Press for the Institute of Early American History and Culture, 1997.

Sidbury, James, and Jorge Cañizares-Esguerra. "Mapping Ethnogenesis in the Early Modern Atlantic." *William and Mary Quarterly* 68, no. 2 (2011): 181–208.

Skeehan, Danielle. "Creole Domesticity: Women, Commerce, and Kinship in Early Atlantic Writing." PhD diss., Northeastern University, 2013.

Slauter, Eric. "History, Literature, and the Atlantic World." *William and Mary Quarterly* 65, no. 1 (2008): 135–66.

Slauter, Eric. *The State as a Work of Art: The Cultural Origins of the Constitution.* Chicago: University of Chicago Press, 2009.

Smith, Caleb. *The Prison and the American Imagination.* New Haven, CT: Yale University Press, 2009.

Smith, Mark M. *Stono: Documenting and Interpreting a Southern Slave Revolt.* Columbia: University of South Carolina Press, 2005.

Smith, Nigel. *Literature and Revolution in England, 1640–1660.* New Haven, CT: Yale University Press, 1994.

Smith, Susan Harris. *American Drama: The Bastard Art.* New York: Cambridge University Press, 1997.

Smith-Rosenberg, Carroll. "Surrogate Americans: Masculinity, Masquerade, and the Formation of a National Identity." *PMLA* 119, no. 5 (2004): 1325–35.

Snyder, Holly. "Customs of an Unruly Race: The Political Context of Jamaican Jewry, 1670–1831." In *Art and Emancipation in Jamaica: Isaac Mendes Belisario and His Worlds,* edited by T. J. Barringer, Gillian Forrester, and Barbaro Martinez-Ruiz, 151–61. New Haven, CT: Yale Center for British Art and Yale University Press, 2007.

Snyder, Holly. "A Sense of Place: Jews, Identity and Social Status in Colonial British America, 1654–1831." PhD diss., Brandeis University, 2000.

Sodders, Richard P. "The Theatre Management of Alexandre Placide in Charleston, 1794–1812." PhD diss., Louisiana State University, 1983.

Sofer, Andrew. *The Stage Life of Props.* Ann Arbor: University of Michigan Press, 2003.

Solow, Barbara L. "Slavery and Colonization," In *Slavery and the Rise of the Atlantic System,* edited by Barbara L. Solow, 21–42. Cambridge: Cambridge University Press, 1991.

Solow, Barbara L., and Stanley L. Engerman, eds. *British Capitalism and Caribbean Slavery: The Legacy of Eric Williams.* Cambridge: Cambridge University Press, 1987.

Sonneck, O. G. *Early Opera in America.* New York: G. Schirmer; Boston: Boston Music, 1915.

Sosin, Jack M. *English America and the Restoration Monarchy of Charles II: Transatlantic Politics, Commerce, and Kinship.* Lincoln: University of Nebraska Press, 1980.

Southern, Richard. *Changeable Scenery: Its Origin and Development in the British Theatre.* London: Faber and Faber, 1952.

Spillers, Hortense J. "The Idea of Black Culture." *CR: New Centennial Review* 6, no. 3 (2006): 7–28.

Spillers, Hortense J. "Mama's Baby, Papa's Maybe: An American Grammar Book." In *Black, White, and in Color: Essays on American Literature and Culture,* 203–29. Chicago: University of Chicago Press, 2003.

States, Bert O. *Great Reckonings in Little Rooms: On the Phenomenology of Theater.* Berkeley: University of California Press, 1985.

Stewart, John. *An Account of Jamaica: And Its Inhabitants.* London: Longman, Hurst, Rees and Orme, 1808.

Stoler, Ann Laura. *Carnal Knowledge and Imperial Power: Race and the Intimate in Colonial Rule.* Berkeley: University of California Press, 2010.

Stoler, Ann Laura. *Race and the Education of Desire: Foucault's History of Sexuality and the Colonial Order of Things*. Durham, NC: Duke University Press, 1995.

Streeby, Shelley. *American Sensations: Class, Empire, and the Production of Popular Culture*. Berkeley: University of California Press, 2002.

Sypher, Wylie. "The African Prince in London." *Journal of the History of Ideas* 2, no. 2 (1941): 237–47.

Sypher, Wylie. *Guinea's Captive Kings: British Anti-slavery Literature of the XVIIIth Century*. Chapel Hill: University of North Carolina Press, 1942.

Tamarkin, Elisa. *Anglophilia: Deference, Devotion, and Antebellum America*. Chicago: University of Chicago Press, 2008.

Tate, William Edward. *The English Village Community and the Enclosure Movements*. London: Gollancz, 1967.

Taylor, Alan. "'Stopping the Progress of Rogues and Deceivers': A White Indian Recruiting Notice of 1808." *William and Mary Quarterly* 42 no. 1 (January 1985): 90–103.

Taylor, Diana. *The Archive and the Repertoire: Performing Cultural Memory in the Americas*. Durham, NC: Duke University Press, 2003.

Tennenhouse, Leonard. *The Importance of Feeling English: American Literature and the British Diaspora, 1750–1850*. Princeton, NJ: Princeton University Press, 2007.

Thompson, Ayanna. *Performing Race and Torture on the Early Modern Stage*. New York: Routledge, 2008.

Thompson, E. P. "Eighteenth-Century English Society: Class Struggle without Class?" *Social History* 3, no. 2 (1978): 133–65.

Thompson, E. P. "The Moral Economy of the English Crowd in the Eighteenth Century." *Past and Present* 50 (February 1971): 76–136.

Thompson, E. P. *Whigs and Hunters: The Origin of the Black Act*. London: Allen Lane, 1975.

Thompson, George. *A Documentary History of the African Theatre*. Evanston, IL: Northwestern University Press, 1998.

Thompson, James. *Models of Value: Eighteenth-Century Political Economy and the Novel*. Durham, NC: Duke University Press, 1996.

Thornton, A. P. *West-India Policy under the Restoration*. Oxford: Clarendon Press, 1956.

Tobin, Beth Fowkes. *Picturing Imperial Power: Colonial Subjects in Eighteenth-Century British Paintings*. Durham, NC: Duke University Press, 1999.

Todd, Janet M. *The Secret Life of Aphra Behn*. New Brunswick, NJ: Rutgers University Press, 1997.

Turner, Mary. *Slaves and Missionaries: The Disintegration of Jamaican Slave Society, 1787–1834*. Urbana: University of Illinois Press, 1982.

Van Lennep, William, ed. *The London Stage: 1660–1800: A Calendar of Plays, Entertainments & Afterpieces. . . . Compiled from the Playbills, Newspapers and Theatrical Diaries, Part 1, 1660–1700*. Carbondale: Southern Illinois University Press, 1965.

Vaughan, Alden T. "The Origins Debate: Slavery and Racism in Seventeenth-Century Virginia." *Virginia Magazine of History and Biography* 97, no. 3 (1989): 311–54.

Vaughan, Virginia Mason. *Performing Blackness on English Stages, 1500–1800*. Cambridge: Cambridge University Press, 2005.

Vickers, Daniel. "Competency and Competition: Economic Culture in Early America." *William and Mary Quarterly* 47, no. 1 (1990): 3–29.

Virno, Paolo. *A Grammar of the Multitude: For an Analysis of Contemporary Forms of Life.* Cambridge, MA: MIT Press, 2004.

Visconsi, Elliott. "A Degenerate Race: English Barbarism in Aphra Behn's *Oroonoko* and *The Widow Ranter.*" *ELH* 69, no. 3 (2002): 673–701.

Visser, Colin. "John Dryden's *Amboyna* at Lincoln's Inn Fields, 1673." *Restoration and 18th-Century Theatre Research* 15, no. 1 (1976): 1–11.

Vizenor, Gerald Robert. *Fugitive Poses: Native American Indian Scenes of Absence and Presence.* Lincoln: University of Nebraska Press, 1998.

Vizenor, Gerald Robert. *Manifest Manners: Postindian Warriors of Survivance.* Hanover, NH: University Press of New England, 1994.

Vizenor, Gerald Robert, ed. *Survivance: Narratives of Native Presence.* Lincoln: University of Nebraska Press, 2008.

Waldstreicher, David. *In the Midst of Perpetual Fetes: The Making of American Nationalism, 1776–1820.* Chapel Hill: University of North Carolina Press for the Omohundro Institute of Early American History and Culture, 1997.

Waldstreicher, David. "Reading the Runaways: Self-Fashioning, Print Culture, and Confidence in Slavery in the Eighteenth-Century Mid-Atlantic." *William and Mary Quarterly* 56, no. 2 (April 1999): 243–72.

Waldstreicher, David. *Runaway America: Benjamin Franklin, Slavery, and the American Revolution.* New York: Hill and Wang, 2004.

Wallerstein, Immanuel Maurice. "The Ideological Tensions of Capitalism: Universalism versus Racism and Sexism." In *Race, Nation, Class: Ambiguous Identities*, edited by Étienne Balibar and Immanuel Maurice Wallerstein, 29–36. London: Verso, 1991.

Ward, J. R. *British West Indian Slavery, 1750–1834: The Process of Amelioration.* Oxford: Oxford University Press, 1988.

Ward, Kerry. *Networks of Empire: Forced Migration in the Dutch East India Company.* Cambridge: Cambridge University Press, 2009.

Warner, Michael. *The Letters of the Republic: Publication and the Public Sphere in Eighteenth-Century America.* Cambridge, MA: Harvard University Press, 1990.

Warner, Michael, et al. "A Soliloquy 'Lately Spoken at the African Theatre': Race and the Public Sphere in New York City, 1821." *American Literature* 73, no. 1 (2001): 1–46.

Waterman, Adam John. "The Price of the Purchase: Black Hawk's War and the Colonization of the Mississippi River Valley." PhD. diss., New York University, 2008.

Whaley, John. *A Collection of Poems.* London: J. Willis and J. Boddington, 1732.

White, Ed. "Early American Nations as Imagined Communities." *American Quarterly* 56, no. 1 (2004): 49–81.

White, Eric Walter. *A History of English Opera.* London: Faber and Faber, 1983.

White, Shane. *Stories of Freedom in Black New York.* Cambridge, MA: Harvard University Press, 2002.

Wilentz, Sean. *Chants Democratic: New York City and the Rise of the American Working Class, 1788–1850.* New York: Oxford University Press, 1984.

Williams, Cynric R. *A Tour through the Island of Jamaica from the Western to the Eastern End in the Year 1823*. London: Hunt and Clarke, 1826.

Williams, Eric Eustace. *Capitalism and Slavery*. Chapel Hill: University of North Carolina Press, 1944.

Williams, Gordon. *A Dictionary of Sexual Language and Imagery in Shakespearean and Stuart Literature*. 3 vols. London: Athlone Press, 1994.

Williams, Henry Llewellyn, and J. R. Planché. *The Black Forrest: An Ethiopian Farce, Altered from Planche's "Garrick Fever."* New York: De Witt, 1882.

Wilmeth, Don B. *Staging the Nation: Plays from the American Theater, 1787–1909*. Boston: Bedford Books, 1998.

Wilmeth, Don B. "Tentative Checklist of Indian Plays." *Journal of American Theatre* 2, no. 1 (fall 1989): 34–54.

Wilson, Bronwen, and Paul Edward Yachnin. Introduction to *Making Publics in Early Modern Europe: People, Things, Forms of Knowledge*, edited by Bronwen Wilson and Paul Edward Yachnin. New York: Routledge, 2010.

Wilson, Kathleen. "Empire of Virtue: The Imperial Project and Hanoverian Culture." In *An Imperial State at War: Britain from 1689 to 1815*, edited by Lawrence Stone, 128–64. London: Routledge, 1994.

Wilson, Kathleen, ed. *A New Imperial History: Culture, Identity, and Modernity in Britain and the Empire, 1660–1840*. Cambridge: Cambridge University Press, 2004.

Wilson, Kathleen. "Rowe's *Fair Penitent* as Global History: Or, a Diversionary Voyage to New South Wales." *Eighteenth-Century Studies* 41, no. 2 (2008): 231–51.

Wilson, Kathleen. *The Sense of the People: Politics, Culture, and Imperialism in England, 1715–1785*. Cambridge: Cambridge University Press, 1995.

Wimpffen, Baron de, Francis Alexander Stanislaus. *A Voyage to Saint Domingo in the Years 1788, 1789, and 1790*. Translated by J. Wright. London: T. Cadell Jr.; W. Davies; and J. Wright, 1797.

Winton, Calhoun. *John Gay and the London Theatre*. Lexington: University Press of Kentucky, 1993.

Wiseman, Susan. "History Digested: Opera and Colonialism in the 1650s." In *Literature and the English Civil War*, edited by Thomas F. Healy and Jonathan Sawday, 189–204. Cambridge: Cambridge University Press, 1990.

Wolfe, Patrick. "Settler Colonialism and the Elimination of the Native." *Journal of Genocide Research* 8, no. 4 (2006): 387–409.

Wood, Peter H. *Black Majority: Negroes in Colonial South Carolina from 1670 through the Stono Rebellion*. New York: Knopf, 1974.

Worrall, David. *Harlequin Empire: Race, Ethnicity and the Drama of the Popular Enlightenment*. London: Pickering and Chatto, 2007.

Worrall, David. *Theatric Revolution: Drama, Censorship and Romantic Period Subcultures 1773–1832*. Oxford: Oxford University Press, 2006.

Wright, Richardson Little. *Revels in Jamaica, 1682–1838: Plays and Players of a Century, Tumblers and Conjurors, Musical Refugees and Solitary Showmen, Dinners, Balls and Cockfights, Darky Mummers and Other Memories of High Times and Merry Hearts*. New York: Dodd, Mead, 1937.

Wynter, Sylvia. "Jonkonnu in Jamaica: Towards the Interpretation of Folk Dance as a Cultural Process." *Jamaica Journal* 4, no. 2 (June 1970): 37–45.

Yachnin, Paul Edward. "Hamlet and the Social Thing in Early Modern Europe." In *Making Publics in Early Modern Europe: People, Things, Forms of Knowledge*, edited by Bronwen Wilson and Paul Edward Yachnin, 81–95. New York: Routledge, 2010.

Young, William. *An Account of the Black Charaibs in the Island of St. Vincent's, with the Charaib Treaty of 1773, and Other Original Documents*. London: F. Cass, [1795] 1971.

Zaitchik, A. "Hobbes's Reply to the Fool: The Problem of Consent and Obligation." *Political Theory* 10, no. 2 (1982): 245–66.

Zaller, Robert. "Breaking the Vessels: The Desacralization of Monarchy in Early Modern England." *Sixteenth Century Journal* 29, no. 3 (1998): 757–78.

Abolition Act of 1833, 214
Abolition Day, 255
abolitionism, 38, 145, 184–85, 196, 198, 250, 252–55, 258
absolute property, 8, 117–18, 121–23, 125, 223. *See also* property
Actor-Boy, 211–12, 218, 220. *See also* Jonkonnu
actors: African American, 28, 224–25, 227, 229, 240, 246; American, 225; British, 20; casting of, 44; female, 91, 128; Jonkonnu, 207, 211–12; nationality and, 20; St. Domingue refugee, 148–49, 162, 180–81; touring British, 166; white, 28, 229. *See also* Actor-Boy; Aldridge, Ira; Cheer, Margaret; Dibdin, Charles; Dixon, George Washington; Edgar, Hayden; Forrest, Edwin; Macready, William Charles; Rice, Thomas Dartmouth; Savigny, John Horatio
aesthetics, 182, 188–89, 202, 207–10, 214, 254; Atlantic world and, 17, 27; black tradition and, 18, 152, 164, 182–83, 209–11; creole commons and, 199; dandyism and, 199, 210, 218, 256; performative commons and, 18, 20, 22, 26, 29, 33, 129, 201, 205, 213; politics and, 9–10, 21, 27, 49, 91; print public sphere and, 169; sovereignty and, 211; theatre and, 21, 26, 124

Africa, 31, 34, 52, 56, 58, 218, 243, 252; Africanization, 204; slave labor and, 15, 35–36, 99–100, 103–4, 113, 151, 167, 170, 172, 184
African Americans, 55; actors, 28, 224–25, 227, 229, 240, 246; theatre attendance of, 11, 51–52, 140–41
African Grove, 225–27, 229, 246
African Theatre Company, 224, 225, 227, 229–30, 241–47
Agamben, Giorgio, 132
Aikman, William, 191
Alderson, Robert, 145
Aldridge, Ira, 213, 231
Alger, William Rounseville, 237
Alexander, Jeffrey, 89
a-linguistic relations, 155, 158, 159–60
a-literacy, 14, 19, 139
Amboyna (Dryden), 95
Amboyna "Massacre": 67–69, 84–86, 95–96
American Company of Comedians, 25, 116, 176
American Revolution, 2, 20–21, 44, 143, 148, 170, 236
Anderson, Benedict, 14, 89
André (Dunlap), 20
Anglo-Dutch Wars, 68, 71, 95
Annus Mirabilis (Dryden), 95
anti-abolitionism, 225, 250, 252–55. *See also* abolitionism

Arawak, 255
Arendt, Hannah, 17
Armitage, David, 73
Asiento, 36, 113
Astor Place Riot, 1, 23, 28–29, 217, 223, 225, 234, 249, 257–60. *See also* riots
Atlantic modernity, 2, 24, 98, 129, 132, 171. *See also* capitalism, modernity and
Atlantic world: bifurcated subject and, 16; creole public and, 150, 152; culture of, 18–19, 57–58, 129; diaspora, 220; economy and, 24, 31, 53, 57, 100, 117; field imaginary of, 15–16; freedom and, 23, 32, 148; geography of, 31, 143, 171; geopolitics of, 8–9, 15–16, 28, 35–36, 54, 171, 241; history and, 15, 24; performative commons and, 2, 8, 17, 21–22, 28, 33, 36, 49–50, 52, 247, 260; popular sovereignty and, 3, 16, 260; publics and, 10, 14, 17, 20, 51, 54; racial economy of, 98–99, 112, 117, 120, 126, 130, 156; revolutions in, 2, 4, 7, 44; stage figures of, 257; theatre in, 5–6, 11–13, 22–23, 32, 36, 40, 44, 50, 53, 55–56; underclass of, 13; uneven spatial nature of, 15–17, 19, 59
audience: active nature of, 5, 45–46; consent of, 44, 80, 83, 86–89, 91, 93–94, 109, 123, 125, 147–48; Jews and, 177, 181; lighting of, 4; mixed-race nature of, 177, 179–80, 195, 228; Native Americans and, 239; participation of, 118, 123; privatization of, 29; racial composition of, 11, 47, 51–52, 142, 180–81, 224; rights of, 216; segregation of, 181; self-representation of, 5, 45, 141–42, 147; sovereignty of, 29, 42, 45–48, 216, 217; as the "town," 6, 11, 29, 177–78; undisciplined nature of, 111
Audin, Antoine, 144, 149
authorship, 20–21
Azémia (Poisson de La Chabeaussière and Dalayrac), 180

Backscheider, Paula, 88, 92
ballad, 122–23; folk, 118, 124; popular, 117
ballad opera, 25, 116–19, 157, 207

Barbados, 99–100, 103, 133; slave code in, 100, 104
bare labor, 26–27, 35, 134, 138, 152–53, 156, 158, 163, 166–67, 169, 171, 183, 185–86, 210–11, 244; geopolitics of, 199
Bartholomew Fair, 111, 115
Beckford, William, 197
Beckles, Hilary McD., 103, 185–86
Beggar's Opera (Gay), 25, 98, 116–19, 121, 124–25, 127–30, 132, 159, 193, 207; collectivity and, 137, 142, 159; popularity of, 127
Behn, Aphra, 97, 101–2; *Oroonoko*, 97, 101, 165, 243
Belisario, Isaac, 200, 205–8, 210–13
Bellmont, George, 225. *See also* Bellmont Riot
Bellmont Riot, 224. *See also* Bellmont, George; riots
Bennholdt-Thomsen, Veronika, 173
Benton, Lauren, 15–16
Bernard de Mangourit, Michel-Ange, 145
Bickerstaff, Isaac, 52, 211
Biopolitics, 7–8, 174
Black Act, 25, 112, 114, 118–21
Blackburn, Robin, 100
Black Caribs, 241, 244
black commons, 130, 139, 245. *See also* commons
blackface, 127; minstrelsy and, 20, 28, 154, 163–64, 210, 217, 242, 245, 248–49, 256; in theatre, 51, 117, 124–26; Waltham Blacks and, 25, 119
Black Hawk, 239–40
blacking. *See* Waltham Blacks
Black Legend, the, 70–71, 85, 231
blackness, 155; history of, 220; production of, 102
Bogin, Ruth, 222
Bogues, Anthony, 1
Bolster, Jeffrey, 242
Bonaparte, Napoleon, 187
Bone Squash, 246. *See also* Rice, Thomas Dartmouth
Booth, Junius Brutus, 215–16, 218

Coal Black Rose, 246. *See also* Dixon, George Washington; *Oh! Hush!*

Cockpit Theatre, 78–80, 83

Colman, Benjamin, 124–25

colonialism, 156, 169; Atlantic, 183; bodies and, 110; bourgeois wealth and, 55, 192; capitalism and, 15, 98, 100, 190; erasure and, 237; freedom and, 8; second scene of, 133, 155, 162

colonial relation, 31–33, 100–101, 107, 109, 151, 154–55, 160, 162–64, 179, 182, 191, 195, 210, 220; capitalist modernity and, 8, 22–23, 183, 186, 205, 210; creole and, 148; geopolitics and 8, 51, 199; humanness and, 14, 22; intimate distance and, 16, 58–59, 131, 133, 153, 179, 188, 194; performance of, 21, 32, 53, 62, 150, 158; popular sovereignty and, 23, 61; racialization and, 10, 24, 38–39, 131, 260; spatial nature of, 35, 38; theatre and, 50, 78, 160; torture and, 68–69, 78

colonization, 98, 240, 247; societies and, 253–55

commodities: circulation of, 53, 102, 170

commoning practices, 7–8, 10, 214; aesthetics and, 18, 33, 183, 205, 213; theatrical performance as, 99

commons: as assemblage, 4, 6, 98, 112, 213; black, 208, 245; blackface and, 127; as body of people, 2–4, 6, 161; in colonial America, 222; creole, 160, 174–76, 178–82, 195–96; culture of, 123; as embodied, 123, 125, 161, 178; enclosure of, 3, 29, 119, 121, 129, 223, 205; eradication of, 112, 118, 129, 173–74, 210; figurative vs. material nature of, 3, 6, 29, 98–99, 128, 222; as geographical space, 128; history of, 23; as land, 2, 4, 121, 222; as legal, 128; logic of, 121–22; music and, 122–24, 137; New World, 180; as performative, 2, 117, 155, 193; political authority of, 2–4, 61, 112; property and, 119, 222; racial segmentation of, 24, 99; reclaiming of, 126; representation of, 3, 6; segmentation of, 114, 125, 207; at the theatre, 4,

61, 117, 129; in the U.S., 236; virtualization of, 3. *See also* commoning practices; enclosure; performative commons

common sense, 11, 49. *See also* sensus communis

conscription: labor and, 24, 98–99, 112, 120, 132; slavery and, 165, 171

consent: of audience, 44, 80, 83, 86–89, 91, 93–94, 109, 123, 125, 147–48; of the people, 44, 48–49, 61–62, 66–67, 72, 74–78, 80, 83–84, 86–88, 90, 93, 128, 232; torture and, 83–86. *See also* audience; people

Consolidated Slave Acts of Jamaica, 184

Continental Congress, 12, 21

The Contrast (Tyler), 20

Covent Garden, 33, 34, 50, 55

court masque. *See* masque

Craton, Michael, 173

credit economy, 114

Creeks, 259

creole: aesthetics, 152; culture, 20; intimacy, 194; kinship, 196; New World Africans, 17, 255; performative commons, 25, 28, 155; public, 116, 163, 220; rights of, 223; sensorium, 196; U.S., 230; vs. British identity, 187–88, 207; whites, 172–75, 195, 222, 234, 237, 255

creolization, 188

Cromwell, Oliver, 23, 34, 61–62, 64, 68, 99, 102; *A Declaration . . . against Spain*, 70–77, 79, 82; imperialism and, 71–72, 98; nationalism and, 71; providentialism and, 70–71; theatre and, 71; Western Design of, 62, 69–72, 79, 81–82, 99

cross-dressing, 110, 128

crowd, 115; and British commons, 114; moral economy of, 7

cruelty, 67, 70–71, 75–76, 78

Cruelty of the Spaniards in Peru (D'Avenant), 23, 34, 54, 62, 64, 68, 71, 77–82, 95, 231

Crusoe, Robinson, character of, 157–58, 162–63, 180, 190

curse, 20, 151–52
Curtis, Julia, 161
Cussans, J. P., 178–80, 190

Dalayrac, Nicolas, 180
dance, 109, 115–16, 121–23, 128, 174–75, 199,
    203–4, 206–7; African American, 163,
    257; community and, 124; creoles and,
    172; Jonkonnu and, 182, 208; "patting
    Juba" and, 163; performance of, 159, 193;
    Richard III performance of, 215; rope,
    115; T. D. Rice, 217; set girl, 200–202,
    weddings and, 124, 127
dandy, black figure of, 198–99, 210–14,
    246, 256
The Darkey Tragedian, 245–46
D'Avenant, William, 40, 62–63, 109, 111,
    222; biography of, 64–66; court masque
    and, 63–65; republican theatre and,
    64–68, 89; theatrical innovation and,
    71, 78–79; torture and, 67–71. *See also
    individual works*
Defoe, Daniel, 150, 156–57. *See also indi-
    vidual works*
Deloria, Philip Joseph, 230, 234, 236
democracy, 7; Jacksonian, 217, 223. *See also*
    Jacksonian democracy
Denning, Michael, 118–19
dialect, 194–96, 211, 228; use of black
    dialect, 228–29; minstrelized, 245
diasporic Africans: dance and, 204;
    disposable labor and, 132; enslavement
    of, 19, 127; Morano as, 126; as public, 17;
    racialization of, 23. *See also* New World
    Africans
Dibdin, Charles, 178
Die Spanier in Peru, oder Rolla's Tod
    (Kotzebue), 231. *See also* Von Kotzebue,
    August
dissensus, 11, 13, 26–27, 30, 49, 88, 93, 182,
    189, 196, 199, 207, 209, 240, 259–60
Dixon, George Washington, 250–51, 254,
    256–57. See also *Coal Black Rose*; Zip
    Coon
Dobson, Michael, 111

Douglass, David, 46, 116, 166, 191; theatre
    company of, 176
Douglass, Frederick, 258
Downes, Andrew, 103
The Drama of King Shotaway (Brown),
    224, 241
Drury Lane Theatre, 41
Dryden, John, 32, 34, 95, 97, 101, 104–11, 115,
    150, 152, 180. *See also individual works*
Dublin, Ireland, 115, 127
Duenna, The or *The Double Elopement*
    (Sheridan), 189, 191–93, 195, 207
Dunlap, William, 20, 231
Dutch East India Company, 68
Dutch empire, 71, 103

Earle, William, 242
early America: theatre of, 20
East India Company. *See* British East
    India Company; Dutch East India
    Company
Edgar, Hayden, 42–45, 51
electorate: race and gender of, 13
Ellison, Ralph, 163
Eltis, David, 165
emancipation, 210, 253–54
empire: English popular sovereignty
    and, 61; New World and, 72, 204; plays
    concerning, 62; westward progress of,
    19. *See also* Dutch empire; imperialism;
    Spanish empire
The Enchanted Island (D'Avenant and
    Dryden), 25, 104–11, 115–16, 150–52,
    154–55, 180
enclosure, 8, 25, 28–29, 118, 121: Atlantic
    world and, 98; genealogical, 193; own-
    ership and, 127; parliamentary bills and,
    3; privatization and, 98–99; racialized,
    207
England: agrarian workers of, 119, 121;
    identity and, 173, 176; labor in, 121; land
    of, 120; military, 169, 172, 176; slave
    trade closing and, 184
*England's Slavery, or Barbados Merchan-
    dize*, 99

Kingston, Jamaica, 116, 128; French Theatre in, 181; theatre in, 167, 176–77, 180–81, 207

kinship, 166, 168, 188–89, 202; kinlessness and, 188, 189, 202; systems of, 190

Kruger, Loren, 21

labor, 98–101, 104, 119, 170–71, 199; of Africans, 121; in colonies, 103; conscription of, 24, 112, 120; free vs. unfree, 121; kinship and, 167; proletariat vs. slave, 35; property and, 112; racialized segmentation of, 24, 31, 102, 104–5, 148, 151, 160, 170–71, 179, 184, 210; reproduction and, 186; sexual division of, 190; slavery and, 121, 167–68, 258; U.S. structures of, 218. *See also* bare labor; labor force

labor force: in Atlantic world, 130; increase in size of, 103; unfree, 104

Lake, Peter, 88

land, 205; appropriation of, 31; common use of, 2, 4; enclosure of 3; feudal tenure of, 119

Langford, Paul, 112

language instruction, 105, 155, 157–58, 162

LeClerc, Charles, 187–88

LeClerc, Pauline, 187–88

Levine, Lawrence, 28

Lewis, Matthew "Monk," 184–85, 201, 206–7

liberalism, 66

liberty. *See* English liberty

Licensing Act of 1737, 13, 25, 110–12, 114–16, 166

Lincoln's Inn Fields, 34, 79

literacy, print public sphere and, 13–14, 55. *See also* a-literacy.

Locke, John, 40; contract theory and, 222–23; property and, 222

Loftis, John, 115

London: *Oroonoko* performed in, 50–55; patent theatres in, 23, 25, 63, 114–15; performative commons and, 23; public theatre in, 54, 61, 63–64, 111. *See also*

Cockpit Theatre; Covent Garden; Drury Lane Theatre; Lincoln's Inn Fields; New Wells Theatre; patent theatres; Rutland House; Wells Inn Theatre

Long, Edward, 39, 172, 174, 195

Loughran, Trish, 14, 57

Louis XVI (Preston), 43, 45, 51

L'Ouverture, Toussaint, 242, 256

Macbeth (Shakespeare), 217, 241, 257

Macheath, character of, 117, 121–27, 132, 142, 207

Macready, William Charles, 28, 217, 257

Mair, Lucille Mathurin, 186

managers. *See* theatre, managers of

manifest destiny, and U.S. expansionism, 218

Maroons, 241, 244; Maroon Chief, 244, 247

marriage, 32, 121, 191, 193, 207; bourgeoisie and, 124, 126; contracts, 122, 125, 127; cross-racial, 127

Marsden, Peter, 203

Marx, Karl, 2–3, 33–36, 121

masculinity: American, 234, 245; white working class, 248–49, 256

masque, 23, 60–67, 78, 80

Massachusetts, 135

materiality, 182; resistant nature of, 195–96, 209

McAllister, Marvin, 224, 241

McDonald, Roderick, 184

melodrama, 128

A Memento for Holland, 68–69, 85

mercantilism, 102

Merchant of Venice, The (Shakespeare), 184

metacom, 233

Metamora (Stone), 20; character of, 41, 234, 236–39; image of, 235; role of, 217, 222, 223, 245, 250, 256–57

middle passage, 120, 184, 186

Midsummer Night's Dream, A (Shakespeare), 159

Mies, Maria, 173

Miller, Monica, 211, 213
Milton, John, 64, 71
mimesis, 108, 111, 207, 240
Minor Theatre, 227
minstrelsy. *See* blackface, minstrelsy and
Mintz, Sidney, 170
Mirza and Lindor, 160–61
miscegenation, 110, 230, 252
Mitchell, William, 187
mob, 181, 259; control of, 112; demobiliza-
tion of, 114
modernity: Atlantic, 2, 98; capitalist
nature of, 8, 22; colonial nature of, 13,
176; counterculture of, 18; Foucault and,
33–36; map of, 35; Marx and, 34–36;
narratives of, 33–36; political, 78
Montezuma, character of, 97, 101
moral economy, 7, 29, 173, 222, 223, 236–37.
See also Thompson, E. P.
Morano, character of, 117–18, 124–27, 132
Moten, Fred, 152, 209
moveable scenery. *See* scenery, moveable
Muhlenberg, Henry M., 135
multitude, 13, 23, 129; in Atlantic world,
8–9; black, 207; Hobbes and, 48–49, 67;
vs. people, 9–10, 12, 37, 48–49, 56, 67; vs.
"republic of property," 7; at the theatre,
11, 29, 41, 47–48
Mungo, character of, 52, 211, 213
Murdoch, James E., 239
music, 109, 122, 208, 209; dance and,
123–24, 206, 128; folk, 121; noise and, 13;
revolution and, 208; theatre and, 115

narrative, 108; genealogical, 106; masque
and, 78–79; mimetic force of, 157
nation: framing use of, 15–16, 20, 57;
public sphere and, 14–15
nationalism: culture and, 20; imperialism
and, 71; English, 70–71, 77–78, 98; print
and, 19; literature and, 183; as racialized,
248; U.S., 218, 220, 222, 241
Native American(s): creole public and,
148, 160; erasure of, 132; land rights of,
223; multitude and, 13; performance of,

28, 98; public sphere and, 17; racialization of, 22; removal of, 239; representations of, 165, 234; slave trade
and 133–34; sovereignty and, 75–77,
223; Spanish treatment of, 70, 72; theft
of property from, 8, 22, 98, 100, 129;
torture and, 68, 75–77, 100; tortured
royal figure of, 24, 62, 71–72, 78, 81, 86,
98, 101; "vanishing" of, 237–38, 252,
258
nativism. *See* white nativism
Negri, Antonio, 7–9, 48–49
Negro Act of 1740, 134, 136–39
Netherlands, 70
New England Anti-Slavery Society, 250,
252–53, 255
New Wells Theatre, 111
New World: bodies in, 107; conquest of,
126; "discovery" of, 73; settlement of,
102; sovereignty and, 70–77, 97; transportation to, 117
New World Africans, 182; bare labor
of, 189, 205; culture of, 18, 204; staged
performances of, 52–53; theft of labor
from, 8, 22–23, 139. *See also* diasporic
Africans
New World drama, 21, 23–24, 62; forma-
tion of people and, 49, 77–78
New York City, 1, 22, 128, 131; colonial
relation and, 27; stage, 222. *See also* African Theatre Company; Astor Place
Riot; Bowery Theatre; Park Theatre
Noah, Mordecai, 228–29, 245–46
noble savage, 240
noise, 9, 182, 208; multitude and, 48; vs.
music, 13; vs. speech, 18
Nugent, General George, 178
Nugent, George Edmund, 187
Nugent, Lady Maria, 178–79, 187–88, 196,
200, 208

Obeah (Obi), 243
Obi; or Three-Finger'd Jack, 242–44
O'Brien, John, 111, 157
obscenity, 174, 176, 178–79, 191, 208, 210

Odell, George C. D., 241

Oh! Hush!, 246. See also *Coal Black Rose*,
Jim Crow

Olwell, Robert, 135

ontic meaning, 106, 108, 110, 116, 152, 189,
195–96, 202, 207–11, 237–40; cursing
and, 151–54; vs. mimetic meaning, 3, 11,
26, 30, 50, 52, 59, 91, 189, 196, 211, 260;
sound of, 207

opera, 78, 117–18, 128

"O! Poor Robinson Crusoe!" (Cussans),
178–80, 190. See also *Robinson Crusoe*
(Defoe)

Orgel, Stephen, 63

Oroonoko, character of, 31 34, 41, 50, 97,
101–2, 104, 119, 131, 220; African prince,
126, 218; image of, 164, 221; slave name,
165–66

Oroonoko (Behn), 97, 101, 165, 243

Oroonoko (Southerne), 25, 35, 42–43, 52–55,
58, 97, 101–2, 164, 218, 220–22, 165, 166

osnaburg, 218, 184, 188, 196

Othello (Shakespeare), 140, 241

Otway, Thomas, 176

The Padlock (Bickerstaff), 52–53, 211

pantomime, 25, 109–11, 115–16, 128, 149,
156–60, 162

Park Theatre, 224, 230

parliament, 2–3, 60–61, 99, 114, 185; West
Indies lobby and, 173

patent theatres, 23, 25, 63, 114–15. *See also*
restoration, patent theatres and

Patterson, Orlando, 19

The Peacock and the Crow, 247. *See also* Jim
Crow

Penn, Admiral William, 70

Penobscot Indians, 238

people: commons and, 23; as *demos*, 3, 10;
consent of, 44, 48–49, 61–62, 66–67, 72,
74–78, 80, 83–84, 86–88, 90, 93, 128, 232;
embodiment of, 4, 6, 37, 40, 59, 60–62,
66–67, 78, 132; "out of doors," 12–13;
political will of, 3, 66–67; representation of, 4, 6, 8–11, 37, 39–41, 48–49, 52,

60, 67, 181; as sovereign, 3, 9, 67; vs.
multitude, 9, 37, 48–49, 56, 67

performance: cross-racial, 126; community and, 128; excess of, 199, 210;
public citizenship and, 227; labor of,
177; phenomenology of, 19. *See also*
performative commons

performative commons, 182–83; aesthetic
nature of, 20; Atlantic world and, 16–
17, 21, 30, 150, 257; in Charleston, 25, 45,
164; development of, 2–4; embodiment
of, 29–30, 59, 129, 164; erasure and, 17,
147; in Jamaica, 21, 189; in London, 62;
material commons and, 129, 222, 237;
moral economy and, 7; nationalized,
228; theatre and, 131; vs. public sphere,
14–16, 55–58, 220; racialization and, 33,
137; rights to, 237; revolutionary nature
of, 98; song and, 129; as white, 240

Pestana, Carla Gardina, 99

Peters, Julie Stone, 79–80

Petley, Christer, 173

Phillips, John, 71, 231

physicality, 157

Pincus, Steven C. A., 68, 71, 88

pirates, 125–27, 149

Pizarro (Sheridan), 206, 230–32, 240–41

Placide, Alexander, 145, 159, 161

plantation: economy and, 170–74, 196,
244; as machine, 214; model and, 134,
205; slavery and, 18, 186, 204

plantocracy, 184–85, 199; authority of, 132,
142–43, 167, 173, 184, 196, 210; blackening and, 132; racialized divisions and,
173

playing Indian, 28, 223, 230, 234–37, 249,
256. *See also* Native American(s)

poetics, 182

Poisson de La Chabeaussière,
Auguste-Étienne-Xavier, 180

political enfranchisement: of blacks,
227–28

Polly (Gay), 117, 124–25, 129–30, 132, 148,
159, 161

Polverel, Étienne, 145

popular sovereignty: Atlantic world and, 31–32; economy and, 112; imperialism and, 36, 98; history of, 2–4, 24, 36, 54, 60–62; performance of, 6, 42, 51–52, 59; politics of, 2, 23, 25, 29, 44, 48, 112, 132; print public sphere and, 169; race slavery and, 18, 36, 52; triumph of, 216; theories of, 40; torture and, 69; white creole and, 232, 237. *See also* sovereignty, from below; torture, popular sovereignty and

population: race and, 131–32, 134–35, 140, 150

Porter, William T., 216

poverty, 7

primitive accumulation, 34–35, 121

print public sphere, 14–16, 164, 169, 176; blackface minstrelsy and, 229; in Jamaica, 166; literacy and, 13, 55; peoples of color and, 164; vs. performative commons, 16, 55–58

privatization: enclosure and, 118; of material commons, 99; Whig economy and, 98

property: absolute ownership and, 8, 117–18, 121–23, 125, 223; acquisition of, 127; crimes against, 120; expropriation of, 8; and Lockean notion of contract theory, 222–23; privatization of, 8, 222; requirements and, 228; rights and, 121, 223; Whig regime of, 24, 137

A Proposition for Advancement of Moralitie, By a New Way of Entertainment of the People (D'Avenant), 64–69, 71

Prospero, character of, 104–7, 109–10, 152, 157, 162–63

Protestantism, 71, 86

public opinion, 61, 127

publics: Atlantic, 10, 14, 17; embodied at theatre, 21, 40, 44, 51–54, 139; English, 70, 77; mobilization of, 65; pacification of, 66; race of, 181; sovereignty of, 62; unruly, 66

public sphere, 14, 17–19, 55; of Atlantic, 129; bodies in, 162; colonialism and, 36;

common space of, 129. *See also* print public sphere

public theatre, 54, 61, 63–64, 111. *See also* London; patent theatres

Puritanism and theatre, 64

Pye, Christopher, 66–67

Quijano, Aníbal, 15

Quincy, Josiah, 135, 140, 153–54

rabble, 13, 142

racialization, 8, 22–23, 98, 100, 126, 225, 240, 247; binary black and white, 229; in Jamaica, 39; modern sovereignty and, 21; performance and, 102, 223; segmenting nature of, 130

Ragussis, Michael, 192

Rakove, Jack, 38

Ramsey, William L., 134

Rancière, Jacques: aesthetics, 208; distribution of the sensible, 9, 124, 164, 208; theatricality and, 10–11

Rath, Richard Cullen, 137

rational entertainment, 115. *See also* theatre, as rational amusement

Raylor, Timothy, 66

The Recruiting Officer (Farquhar), 52–53

Reed, Peter, 13

reformation, 73–74

regicide, 2, 5–6, 23, 29, 41, 54, 217; of Charles I, 60–61

religion, 54, 64; sovereignty and, 73–74. *See also* Catholicism; Protestanism

representation: ontic vs. mimetic, 3, 17, 30, 50, 151, 154; embodiment and, 4; of the people, 39–41, 48–49, 51–52, 60; political force of, 9; race and, 155

reproduction, 108; of bodies, 110, 186–87, 189; of Englishness, 108, 110; and production, 186; and maternity, 189; sexual, 109–10; of white colonialism, 109; of whiteness, 150–52, 155, 193, 195, 207; of slaves, 184. *See also* social reproduction

republicanism: English, 78; revolution and, 7, 43–44, 143, 148

republican theatre, 45, 64–68, 89. *See also* D'Avenant, William

restoration, 102; drama 63; patent theatres and, 23, 63, 79

Rice, Thomas Dartmouth, 163, 215, 217–18, 220; Jim Crow and, 222, 246–47, 249

Richard III: 184, 206–7; blackface and, 245; character of, 41; 215–16, 218; Cibber version of, 5–6, 20, 217; Jamaican Jonkonnu performances of, 206, 218; performance of, 223, 224, 227–29, 256. See also *The Fall of Tyranny*

Richards, Jeffrey, 20

Rifkin, Mark, 230

rights: and property, 7

Riot Act of 1715, 112, 114

riots, 208–9; at the theatre, 5–6, 11, 28, 49, 181, 195, 217, 223–25, 252–53, 257; of 1834, 253; over food prices, 7, 222; Parliament and, 115. *See also* Astor Place Riot; Bellmont Riot; Farren Riot

Roach, Joseph, 18–19

Robinson Crusoe (Defoe), 149, 154, 157, 178–79

Robinson Crusoe and Harlequin Friday (Sheridan), 149–50, 154–56, 158–60, 161–63, 179–80

Rowe, Nicholas, 184, 193, 206

Royal African Company, 24, 36, 103

royal slave, 98, 100–101

Rubin, Gayle, 189

Rutland House, 79

Sansay, Leonora, 188

Santo Domingo. *See* St. Domingue

satire, 112, 117, 174, 178, 198, 203, 205, 209. *See also* burlesque

Sauer, Elizabeth, 71

Savigny, John Horatio, 221

scenery, 63; innovations in, 67; moveable, 61, 63–64, 78–80, 83; perspectival, 79, 83, 109

Schmitt, Carl, 36, 72–73

School for Scandal (Sheridan), 112, 184, 189–90, 192

Scott, Michael, 177–80, 201

screen: blackface as, 125–26; as decoration, 112; of politics, 112, 129; of racial divisions, 118, 129–30; of scenes, 99, 112, 190–91, 193, 195

screen scenes, 169, 190–91, 194

scripts, 21, 50, 133, 139, 156, 206; censorship of, 25; alteration of, 43

Secret History, The or *The Horrors of St. Domingo*, 188

sensorium, 67, 78, 182, 196, 208–10

sensus communis, 11, 18, 20, 59, 62, 67, 182, 196, 208, 230, 245; performative nature of, 209; racialized nature of, 240

sentimentalism, 35, 70

Sessarakoo, William Unsah, Prince of Annamaboe, 55

settler colonialism, 8, 22, 24, 28, 98, 105–6, 127, 129, 160, 237–38, 240; English, 231; founding of U.S. and, 230; history of, 134, 222–23

Shakespeare, William, 205–6, 209; plays of, 216; plays performed by African Theatre Company, 224, 227, 229, 241, 244; black performance of, 244, 254, 256. *See also individual works*

Sharpe, Christina Elizabeth, 59

Shepherd, Verene, 185–86

Sheridan, Richard Brinsley, 156, 184, 189, 191, 230–31, 233. *See also individual works*

The Siege of Rhodes (D'Avenant), 64, 79

slave labor: economy and, 101; profits from, 121

slavery: Atlantic economy and, 36; Atlantic race, 222; black sociality and, 169, 199; British laws and, 253; English liberty and, 21, 36, 98; imperial geography of, 100, 102; racialization and, 100; rebellion and, 135, 170, 172, 209, 213–14, 242–43; social death and, 19, 120–21, 132, 139, 169, 189, 261; structural violence of, 19, 182, 189; terror and, 136, 170; white, 103, 117

slaves, 99, 172, 174; British trade of, 218; capitalism and, 171; clothing, 184–85, 196–99, 210–11; commodification of, 52;

dancing and, 136–37; drumming and, 136–39; on the English stage, 101; laws and, 250, 254; literacy and, 14; multitude and, 13; naming of, 167; punishment, 170–71; reproduction and, 184–86; as royalty, 222; runaway advertisements for, 166–69; transportation of, 113

social death, 19, 35, 117, 120–21, 126, 154, 160, 166, 169, 195, 202, 211; technologies of, 172, 182, 184, 199, 207, 210

social reproduction, 171–74, 182, 186, 189, 193, 199, 202, 205, 208; commoning and, 27, 205; English, 191, 193, 195; linguistic meaning and, 151; marriage and, 35, 102, 108; vs. production, 27, 171; slavery and, 132

Soliloquy of a Maroon Chief in Jamaica, 243–44

Sollee, John, 145

Solow, Barbara, 170

Sonthonax, Léger-Félicité, 144

South Carolina, 102, 104; slave laws of, 100

Southerne, Thomas, 102. *See also Oroonoko* (Southerne)

South Sea Bubble, 36, 111–14, 120–21

sovereignty: black popular, 246; from below, 16, 62, 66; commons and, 2,4; imperial, 79; internal vs. external, 77; monarchical, 2, 60–61, 64–67, 101–2, 216–17; Native Americans and, 75–77, 132; natural, 240; New World and, 70–77, 79, 97; popular, 2, 24, 225, 232; racialization and, 21; religion and, 73–74, 77; territorial, 16, 54, 62, 72–75, 97, 101; theatre and, 21; Westphalian, 73. *See also* New World, sovereignty and; popular sovereignty; religion, sovereignty and; Native Americans, sovereignty and

Spanish empire: in New World, 62, 69–78; torture allegedly committed by, 68, 72, 75, 80–82

Spanish Town, Jamaica, 178–80

spectacle, 63–64, 67

Spillers, Hortense, 183, 186, 188

Stallybrass, Peter, 202

States, Bert O., 50

St. Domingue, 187, 209, 255–56; actors from, 148–49, 154, 180–81, 162; planters from, 144; refugees from, 143–48, 160, 180; revolution in, 147, 154, 241; white colonials of, 160. *See also* Haitian Revolution

Stone, John Augustus, 233

Stono Rebellion, 134, 136, 150

street theatre, 13

St. Vincent, 241–42; Carib insurrection (1795) in, 224

subaltern knowledge, 154

sugar, 99–100, 170–73, 210, 214; production of, 103, 184, 186, 199

Surinam, 97, 102, 218, 165

Tamarkin, Elisa, 57

taste: 254; of the town, 122–25, 128–29, 259

Taylor, Alan, 236

Taylor, Simon, 187

Tears of the Indians . . . (Las Casas), 71, 75, 221

The Tempest (Shakespeare), 25, 104–10, 150–51, 155, 158, 162, 167, 180, 208

The Tempest, or the Enchanted Island (D'Avenant and Dryden), 150–52, 154

Tennenhouse, Leonard, 57

theatre: as a-linguistic, 111, 116, 145, 158–59, 163; black patrons of, 146–47, 226; censorship of, 111, 114; as civilizing: 65–66; costuming and, 183; as creole commons, 163, 169; defense of, 77; education and, 65; geography of, 6, 80, 160, 177; governmentality and, 176, 195; highbrow vs. lowbrow, 115, history of, 23, 60–61, 182, 217, 223; as illegitimate, 115–16; Jewish representations in, 190, 192; of London, 110, 156; managers of, 43, 46; ontic force of, 157; outlaw of, 110, 166; as performative commons, 142, 217, 260–62; people represented at, 3, 9, 40, 71; politics of, 9, 77; populist sensibility of, 216; prohibition of, 21–22; race and, 11, 145, 176; as rational amusement, 46, 48, 142; riots at, 5–6. *See also* republican theatre